MODERN MILITARY AIRCRAFT IN COMBAT

MODERN MILITARY AIRCRAFT IN COMBAT

GENERAL EDITOR: ROBERT JACKSON

amber
BOOKS

This edition first published in 2008 by
Amber Books Ltd
74–77 White Lion Street
London N1 9PF
United Kingdom
www.amberbooks.co.uk

Copyright © 2008 Summertime Publishing Ltd

ISBN 978-1-904704-87-3

Project Editor: James Bennett
Design: Brian Rust

Previously published in a different format as part of the reference set *World Aircraft
Information Files*

All images courtesy of Aerospace/Art-Tech except:
6, 182–187 © US DoD

Printed in Thailand

Contents

Special Features: Aircraft Profiles

YF-22
N22YF

Introduction

World War II had barely ended before a war of a different kind erupted: a Cold War in which the Western Alliance, soon to become NATO, entered into decades of confrontation with the Soviet Union and its satellites.

The first bloodless confrontation came in 1948–9, with the Berlin Airlift, but in 1950 a shooting war broke out in Korea. This conflict, which lasted three years, saw the first ever jet-versus-jet air battles, with North American F-86 Sabres locked in stratospheric combat with Russian MiG-15s, flown mostly by Soviet pilots.

Another nation in the thick of aerial warfare was Israel, whose constant confrontations with her Arab neighbours formed a deadly testing ground for the combat aircraft of east and west, as French Mystères and Mirages and Russian MiGs fought for the sky over the disputed frontiers of the Middle East.

For a decade, from 1964 to 1974, the eyes of the world were focused on the war in Vietnam, where the United States hurled the full weight of its weapons technology against a guerrilla army that refused to be beaten. It was a war that demonstrated the awesome striking power of the Boeing B-52 Stratofortress, used in the conventional bombing role – and also revealed its vulnerability to surface-to-air missiles when it operated against the heaviest concentration of anti-aircraft weaponry in the world.

Vietnam was a war in which the United States Air Force, Navy and Marine Corps suffered appalling losses in attacks on the heavily-defended north, where F-4 Phantoms battled with MiG-21s and American pilots found themselves locked in combat with highly competent and skilled adversaries.

Far away from Vietnam, in the South Atlantic, the Falklands War of 1982 proved conclusively the value of the V/STOL British Aerospace Harrier, and encouraged further development into the formidable Harrier II, which saw combat in two Gulf wars and in other actions conducted by NATO and the United Nations.

As well as outlining the history of air warfare in the jet age, this book includes features on a range of aircraft that were at the heart of Cold War air combat, and the actions that made them famous.

Above: De Havilland Sea Venoms of Britain's Fleet Air Arm on board the carrier HMS Albion during the Suez campaign of 1965. Note the 'invasion stripes' on the aircraft launching from the catapult.

Left: The F-16 Fighting Falcon has been a key player in the limited wars of the past three decades. Here, two F-16Cs of the 401st Tactical Fighter Wing refuel from a KC-135 Stratotanker during Operation Desert Storm in 1991.

Three Boeing B-29s of the Yokota-based 92nd Bomb Group fly to targets in Korea. B-29s from Guam, forward-deployed to Kadena, actually began bombing operations on 27 June 1950, one day before President Truman formally gave the okay for offensive operations.

Korea

The early months

Up until the end of World War II, Korea had been part of the Japanese empire. Post-war, the question of the government of this small, relatively unknown country led the forces of East and West into the first major conflict of the Cold War.

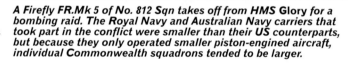

A Firefly FR.Mk 5 of No. 812 Sqn takes off from HMS Glory for a bombing raid. The Royal Navy and Australian Navy carriers that took part in the conflict were smaller than their US counterparts, but because they only operated smaller piston-engined aircraft, individual Commonwealth squadrons tended to be larger.

On 8 August 1945, the day before Nagasaki was bombed, the Soviet Union declared war upon Japan, marched through Manchuria rolling up the remaining occupying forces and eventually reached the Korean peninsula.

During World War II, the US had been content to leave Korea and Manchuria to the Soviets. However, with the war suddenly ending and hostile suspicions between the two nations growing, it re-assessed its position and came to the decision that it would share the occupation of post-war Korea with the USSR. With no natural divisional point, the 38th Parallel was chosen to split the nation, with the US taking the capital city, Seoul. The Soviets quietly agreed to this and, in early September 1945, US forces arrived at Inchon to set up their military occupation of the south, which was gladly received.

Over the next two years, the situation in Korea polarised into two distinctive power-blocs; the north lay under the control of the fiercely communist Kim Il Sung, while the south was under the nominal control of Synmgam Rhee. There were moves made by the inhabitants of both countries for a return to unification, but this became an increasingly remote goal. As in

Europe, post-war reconstruction caused economic chaos and hardship, and there were revolts followed by harsh suppressions by both governments.

In 1948, the United Nations called for free elections in both countries but, due to Soviet rebuttals, elections eventually went ahead only in the south, with the right-wing Rhee being inaugurated president of the new Republic of Korea (RoK). A month later, the Democratic People's Republic of Korea was proclaimed in Pyongyang. During the year, tensions between the two countries grew, with regular incursions being made across the borders while propaganda by both sides whipped up revolts, leading to arrests and imprisonment. In 1948, the Soviet Red Army withdrew most of its forces, as did the US Army in 1949.

By now, the US considered Korea a relatively danger-free zone and this was so much the case that, when Secretary of State Dean Acheson listed the countries for which Americans were willing to "bleed and die" in the defence against communism, he did not think to mention Korea.

This omission spurred the North Koreans who fanatically wanted to unify the country and Kim Il Sung quickly sought, and

gained, approval from Moscow for an assault on the south. The surprise attack was planned, to be spearheaded by T-34 tanks and supported by air power. Documents captured after the war revealed that the north thought that the invasion would take only two months.

Invasion begins

On 25 June 1950, following a dawn artillery barrage, the North

Korean People's Army attacked South Korea. Seven combat-ready divisions of armour and infantry, supported by one air division consisting of Soviet World War II aircraft such as Yak-9s, La-10s and Il-10s, swept the southern forces back into a hopeless retreat.

The UN immediately condemned the action and, within two days, there were calls for military aid for South Korea.

When UN forces retook Seoul's Kimpo airport after the Inchon landings, they found this crashed North Korean Ilyushin Il-10. An Il-10, along with at least one Yak-9P, was later tested in the USA.

KOREAN WAR 1950-1953

After three years of attack and counter-attack, with both sides pushing back the other into its own territory, the result was a settlement on new boundaries which differed little from their pre-war positions.

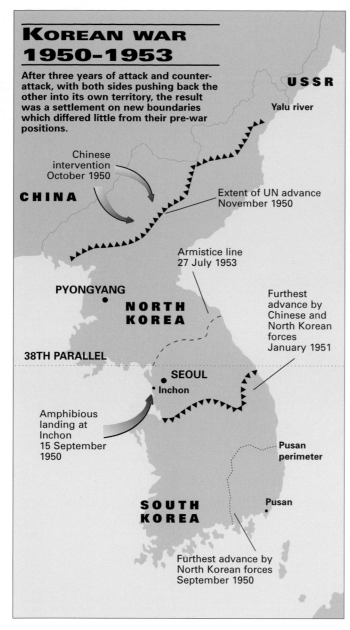

USSR

Yalu river

Chinese intervention October 1950

CHINA

Extent of UN advance November 1950

Armistice line 27 July 1953

PYONGYANG

NORTH KOREA

Furthest advance by Chinese and North Korean forces January 1951

38TH PARALLEL

SEOUL

Inchon

Amphibious landing at Inchon 15 September 1950

Pusan perimeter

SOUTH KOREA

Pusan

Furthest advance by North Korean forces September 1950

The US Navy was heavily involved in the conflict, with several fast escort carriers in-theatre. The F9F-2 Panther (as seen at left) was the staple USN jet fighter during the early months, and the Panther was the first Navy jet to see combat and rack up an aerial victory.

Many in the West believed that this was the first step towards Soviet domination in Asia and, without a thought about the implications of a conflict that could lead to direct confrontation with the Soviets, Congress set America on a course for military involvement in Korea.

Meanwhile, the North Koreans marched relentlessly onwards; on 28 June, the North Koreans entered Seoul and, in an effort to slow them, the bridges leading out of the city were blown up, upon one of which, tragically, were thousands of fleeing refugees.

As soon as the North Koreans attacked the south, the US began to evacuate non-essential personnel from the country and, on 27 June, the first confrontation between the north and the US took place. C-54s from bases in Japan were engaged in flying civilians out of Seoul when five Yak-9s appeared and were attacked by five F-82Gs of the 68th All-Weather Fighter Interceptor Squadron, three Yaks being destroyed. Shortly after, eight Il-10s were spotted and attacked by four F-80Cs, this being the first-ever combat by American jet fighters.

The North Koreans quickly took Seoul and Kimpo airfields and the RoK forces retreated to Suwon, where they were met by General MacArthur, US commander of the region, who had brought the USA and UN to war. With him, came elements of the Far East Air Force (FEAF), including three wings of F-51 Mustangs plus F-80Cs. F-51s were also piloted by South African and Australian volunteers with the UN.

While the air war proceeded in favour of the UN-supported south, with only a single B-29 being lost to NKAF fighters by 12 July and some 110 enemy fighters downed, the ground war was a disaster; the RoK forces, supported by only a small number of UN personnel, were forced further and further back. September 1950 saw all but a small area around Pusan in the extreme south-east being overrun by the invaders.

Allied reversals

However, the southern forces under Rhee were still just managing to resist the north. While Allied troops began to assemble in Pusan, MacArthur conceived a plan to turn the tables on the north which would involve launching an amphibious assault 150 miles (240 km) behind enemy lines. The attack took place on 15 September at Inchon, first with a massive artillery bombardment, and then a Marines assault, all supported by carriers of the US and Royal Navies. Principal support aircraft included F4U-4B Corsairs, AD-4 Skyraiders and F9F-2 Panthers of the US Navy and Marines and Fairey Fireflies and Supermarine Seafires of the Royal Navy.

At the same time as the Inchon landings, UN forces attacked NKA troops out of Pusan, driving them northward. The two attacks were a massive success and, by the end of September, the North Koreans had fallen back to the 38th Parallel.

At this point, the war might have ended, but for Communist China, which declared military support for North Korea, partly due to the fact that General MacArthur was advocating the total military occupation of North Korea.

November, therefore, saw a return to hostilities, with US aircraft engaging North Korean and Chinese aircraft along the border between those two countries. To further increase problems for the allies, the Russian-built MiG-15 jet fighter had now entered the war with the Koreans.

As November continued, the UN advanced far into North Korea, had taken the capital Pyongyang and, due to little opposition from the NKAF, had flown home two of its B-29 groups. However, ground forces were already being attacked by Chinese troops, therefore changing the face of the war. Aircraft from several carriers, including the *Leyte* and *Valley Forge*, were used to attack bridges being used by the Chinese to transport troops and supplies southward.

November was also notable for seeing the world's first all-jet combat between MiG-15s and F-80Cs and, during this month, there were air victories for both sides.

By the end of November, a quarter of a million Chinese troops had crossed the Yalu river. On 26 November, they launched a massive assault that dragged the US into what they wanted to avoid most of all – a full-scale war with China.

Such was the regularity of fighters departing Japan for Korea that the local inhabitants gradually learned to ignore the US aircraft. Pilots of fighters such as this P-80 fought a relatively leisurely conflict, in which their combat sorties were generally restricted to morning missions.

Korea: The final reckoning

Left: The ubiquitous F9F Panther was the stalwart of US Navy jet operations in the theatre. This F9F-2 flew with CAG-19, the Group serving four periods of duty, from USS Princeton and Valley Forge.

Firefly FR.Mk 5s served in both FAA and RAN squadrons. The aircraft wore black and white stripes as a recognition aid for US servicemen.

General MacArthur's ill-founded belief that the Chinese would not commit to the war in Korea was dashed when Chinese forces swarmed against the embattled UN forces.

In spite of efforts made by the UN to prevent China from entering the war, an American F-80C was shot down by Chinese AA guns firing into Korean airspace from across the Yalu river on 1 November 1950. In another incident the pilots of some UN F-51s reported being fired upon by MiG-15s which then made off towards China.

Pyongyang falls

By now American forces had advanced deep into North Korea, their UN sanctioned intention being ostensibly to 'secure peace throughout the Korean peninsula.' The North Korean capital, Pyongyang, had fallen to them on 19 October 1950, and already the USAF had begun to run down its strength in the theatre. At the moment of intervention by the Chinese jets the UN air forces in the Korean theatre comprised three wings of F-51s, two of F-80Cs, two of B-26s and three of B-29s.

No further pretence at non-intervention was made by the Chinese as on 3 November their forces swarmed across the Yalu. An American division was forced to retreat as the powerful US Navy Carrier Task Force 77 sailed north to launch heavy strikes against the Chinese crossing the Yalu. At first the MiG-15 pilots simply flew over Korea in an effort to tempt American aircraft into Chinese airspace, but on 8 November a section of four Communist jets ventured too far and were boxed in by four F-80s in the first all-jet air combat in history. Lieutenant Russel J Brown, USAF shot down a MiG, which crashed 200 yards (185 m) inside Korean territory. On the following day a US Navy F9F Panther pilot also

downed a Chinese MiG. However, it was not totally one-sided and on 10 November 1950 Chinese jets shot down a B-29 heavy bomber.

By the end of the month a quarter million Chinese troops were in the field in Korea. The war had entered a new phase.

The MiG-15 was far superior to all of the fighters then equipping the UN forces, and the decision was made to send a wing of F-86 Sabres, then the latest fighters in USAF service. Early in December the Sabre-equipped 4th Fighter Interceptor Wing arrived at Kimpo airfield. At about the same time the 27th Fighter Escort Wing, with F-84D Thunderjets, also arrived in the war theatre.

Veteran pilots

Although their numbers were not large, many of the newly-arrived American fighter pilots were World War II veterans, whereas US intelligence had determined that the Korean and Chinese pilots were much younger and lacked such experience. It was felt that the new fighters were easily enough to restore UN air supremacy.

The first F-86/MiG clashes were inconclusive, but on 22 December 1950, eight F-86s fought 15 MiG-15s and shot down six. Further combats were not immediately possible because of the advance of the Communist ground forces threatening Kimpo, and the Sabres were moved southwards out of danger.

A 98th BW, 2nd Air Force B-29A unloads bombs against a Communist target. The B-29 required heavy fighter escort if it was to escape the ravages of the MiG-15s.

Now based far from the MiGs patrol areas they were unable to stay long enough to enjoy long patrol sorties. By the same token, however, the Communist advance southwards also moved out of range of the MiGs which remained firmly based around Antung beyond the Yalu.

It was this sequence of events that lent importance to the work of the carrier-borne strike aircraft of the USN and the Royal Navy (the latter contributing the carriers HMS *Theseus*, *Glory* and *Ocean*, which took turns on station with HMAS *Sydney* of the Royal Australian Navy).

Naval air power

Task Force 77 had supported the Inchon landings early in the war with three 'Essex' class carriers, the RN's HMS *Triumph* and two escort carriers, flying aircraft which varied from jet-powered F9F Panthers through to the AD Skyraider and the World War II-veteran F4U Corsair. The two prop-driven machines were to prove exceptionally efficient in the strike role, and the absence of hot jet exhaust meant they could be flown from the wooden flight decks with which many of the American carriers were still

equipped. Indeed a successful attack by torpedo-carrying Skyraiders against the Hwachon dam on 1 May 1951 achieved greater success than previous raids by B-29s and a commando raid by US rangers, so depriving the Communists of the ability to adjust river levels to suit their own troop movements during the build-up for their spring offensive.

The preparation for this offensive included considerable strengthening of the Communist air forces, principally with the established Yak-9s, La-11s, Il-10s and Tu-2s from the Soviet Union, but also with a few MiG-9 fighters. Meanwhile, the 4th Wing's Sabres which had been temporarily moved to Japan while the winter rains flooded their Korean airfields, returned to Korea, and were now based at Suwon. They were not however on hand to prevent an attack on 1 March by nine MiG-15s whose pilots made a single firing pass against a formation of B-29s, three of which crash landed at Taegu.

In a series of moves unknown in the West until comparatively recently, the Soviet Union deployed MiG-15 units to North Korea. The aircraft entered combat in Korean markings, while the pilots wore Chinese uniforms and carried no identification papers.

The tables were turned on 12 April 1951 when some 60 MiGs attacked 48 B-29s, escorted by 36 F-84s and 18 F-86s. Three bombers were shot down, but the Americans destroyed 13 enemy jets. Notwithstanding this success, it was already clear that the F-84 was no match for the MiG-15, which itself was superior in some performance aspects to the early F-86A Sabre. Only the quality of the American pilots was able to redress the balance.

The Communist spring offensive of 1951 failed in its objective to overrun South Korea and had all but petered out by the end of May. Nevertheless, the Chinese intervention had forced the UN to abandon its original aim of unification of North and South. As both sides now attempted to wring the last ounce of propaganda from the military situation, peace talks aimed at securing a truce opened at Kaesong on 10 July 1951 and dragged on for two years.

The UN's military leader, General MacArthur was replaced by the more conciliatory General Matthew Ridgeway, but one of the last operations planned before the change of command was an all-out air offensive against the Communist supply lines which owing to the vulnerability of the railways,

depended almost exclusively on the road network. Launched after the failure of the Communist offensive, it was codenamed Operation Strangle.

All-out grand attacks

All manner of aircraft, from B-26 and B-29 bombers to single-seat F-80s and F-84s, were used. Alongside aircraft of the USN, USMC, the RN, the RAAF and the South African Air Force, they started a prolonged offensive against roads, bridges, supply depots and ports, and quickly provoked reaction from the Communist MiGs, which remained based beyond the Yalu but which were afforded radar warning of the approach of UN aircraft.

Sabre-versus-MiG combats now became commonplace and the Communists quickly became aware that the 4th FW was operating out of Suwon, and this prompted a series of nuisance night raids by antiquated Po-2 biplanes against the base. Extremely difficult to counter, these pinprick attacks, with 25-lb (11-kg) fragmentation bombs, caused little damage but their nuisance value was disproportionately high.

The UN bombing offensive, however, did not come up to expectations because of the Communist ability to repair damage using huge numbers of impressed

labourers. Photo reconnaissance disclosed that the Chinese movement of troops and supplies was almost undiminished. Furthermore, set piece bombing attacks on North Korean cities and major ports met with intense AA fire and the raids were severely restricted by orders to the crews not to overfly neighbouring Chinese territory. Casualties among the big B-29s were fairly high in a force that never exceeded 99 aircraft.

Meanwhile, development of an improved version of the Sabre, the F-86E, had gone on apace in the USA. September 1951 brought deliveries of the F-86Es to the 4th Wing, by now operating from Kimpo. The Communists had also increased their force of MiG-15s by activating a second regiment equipped with the improved MiG-15bis. At once the tempo of air combat increased, and formations of 80 enemy jets were frequently sighted.

One of the war's biggest single combats was fought on 29 October 1951 as eight B-29s escorted by 55 F-84s and 34 F-86s were bombing Namsi: suddenly 100 MiGs appeared and boxed-in the escort as 50 others made for the bombers, shooting down three and severely damaging four others. Six MiGs were shot down for the loss of an F-84.

Concerned at the large number of MiGs available to the Communists, the USAF now began to withdraw some of the old F-80 Shooting Stars, replacing them with F-84Es, and a second F-84 wing, the 116th, was sent to Korea. The night-fighter F-82s of the 347th All Weather Group were also showing their age and 15 Lockheed F-94 Starfires, a two-seat radar-equipped derivative of the F-80, were

dispatched to the war. The Starfire proved a disappointment as it lacked an adequate anti-icing system.

New F-86 wing

By the end of 1951 F-86Es were replacing F-80Cs with the 51st Fighter-Interceptor Wing, and the number of MiGs being destroyed rapidly started to rise. At that time the 4th Wing's combat record showed a total of 144 MiG-15s destroyed for the loss in combat of 14 Sabres. The MiG pilots themselves were becoming more aggressive – indeed some MiGs were being flown by experienced Soviet pilots, and the improved performance of both fighters resulted in numerous combats taking place above 40,000 ft (12,190 m).

Applying further combat experience to the F-86 design, resulted in the F-86F. From June 1952 these aircraft began to be deployed to the 51st Wing. The F-86F was the first Sabre variant which was superior in all respects to the MiG-15bis, although it was used as much in ground attacks as it was in air combat. By the spring of 1953 there were four F-86 wings in Korea, and during the last six months of the war these fighters wholly dominated the skies.

The death of Josef Stalin, on 5 March 1953, instigated a profound change of attitude in the Chinese peace delegation and they finally agreed to a ceasefire on 27 July 1953.

The Korean War was the first major conflict in which large numbers of opposing jet fighters engaged each other and the fleeting nature of those all jet combats graphically demonstrated that the age of gun-only fighter armament was rapidly approaching its conclusion. The era of the air-to-air missile was about to dawn.

Above: The US Air Force Sikorsky H-5 rescued many downed and wounded men and whisked them to safety using an external casualty lifter, as illustrated.

Left: MiG killer Capt. Ralph Parr of the 334th FIS is seen at the controls of this F-86F – which was not his usual assigned aircraft. The 'F' was the first Sabre which could outfly the MiG-15 in all conditions.

Conscious of the threat posed by advancing Communist forces, the UN drew all its land-based air assets back to airfields in the South, giving UN aircraft little time over their targets, since they were operating at the extremities of their range. US Navy jets, such as this rocket-armed Panther, flying from relatively invulnerable carriers, came into their own during this difficult period.

Fighters over Korea

With the arrival of the F-86F, the UN at last had a fighter which was in every way superior to the MiG-15. Air superiority could now be assured.

The Korean air war represented a watershed in aerial warfare. For the first time, the piston-engined, propeller-driven fighter was overshadowed by the prowess of the jet fighter.

The F-84 Thunderjet saw extensive service during the Korean War, although it was to prove little more of a match for the MiG-15 than the F-80. The F-84E/G-equipped 27th Fighter-Escort Group was in theatre from December 1950 to May 1951, and its responsibilities included, in descending order of priority, the destruction of enemy air power, the support of UN ground forces, the performance of armed reconnaissance and offensive strikes, attacks against Communist supply lines, and special missions when required. More than half of the 27th FEG's pilots possessed combat experience from World War II.

The risk of Communist attack saw the Group based far south at Taegu, with its rear echelon at Itazuke in Japan. Despite their 'fighter-escort' designation (having previously been assigned to SAC), the squadrons of the 27th Group (the 522nd, 523rd and 524th) were ordered straight into the air attack role on the Communist supply routes. On 21 January 1951, during a dive-bombing attack on a bridge over the Chongton river, two sections of F-84Es of the 522nd were jumped by 16 MiG-15s, resulting in the F-84's first MiG kill. Two days later, 33 Thunderjets fought 30 MiGs over Sinanju and, by staying low, were able to out-turn the enemy fighters, and destroyed two without loss. By the end of May 1951, the 27th FEG had flown 12,000 combat sorties, but in April, General Curtis E. LeMay, commanding SAC, had ordered the return of the 27th to his command, and its place

at Taegu was taken by the 136th Fighter-Bomber Wing. The 111th, 154th and 182nd Squadrons of the Texas and Arkansas Air National Guards made up the wing and all flew F-84Es.

At the same time as the 136th FBW was arriving in Korea, other F-84Es and F-84Gs were arriving in Japan, to replace the F-80Cs of the 49th FBG. By August 1951, the 136th FBW's 7th and 8th FBS had deployed to Taegu, followed in September by the 9th Squadron.

High Tide

One other F-84 wing deployed to the Far East in 1951. The 116th FBG, also of the ANG, was tasked primarily with the air defence of northern Japan, flying from Misawa and Chitose. However, in December 1951, the 116th embarked on Project High Tide, the training of pilots for inflight

Lt Jacob Kratt Jr flew this F-84E-25-RE with the 523rd FES of the 27th FEG. He was the top-scoring F-84 pilot, downing two MiG-15s and a piston-engined Yak fighter.

In September 1951, FEAF intelligence estimated that China possessed some 500 MiG-15s. Losses soon began to mount, however, with 39 MiGs downed in March 1952 and 44 in April.

From March 1953, No. 2 Sqn, South African Air Force, began flying ground attack missions with borrowed F-86F Sabres. The aircraft flew as part of the USAF's 18th FBW until the end of the war.

On 9 August 1952, Lt Peter 'Hoagy' Carmichael (second from the right) became the only British pilot to score a kill in a British aircraft over Korea. He downed a MiG-15 in this this Sea Fury.

refuelling (IFR) from KB-29P tankers. The first operational missions employing IFR were flown on 28 May 1952, when 16 F-84Gs bombed Sariwon in North Korea. Two further missions were flown, before Project High Tide was successfully concluded.

Daylight operations by USAF Boeing B-29s had been accompanied by growing losses to enemy fighters and flak during 1951, so henceforth they performed the majority of sorties over Korea by night. This growing emphasis upon night operations placed a heavy

burden on the American nightfighters available. From the early months of the war, this force was largely composed of the small number of F-82 Twin Mustangs of the 347th Fighter (All Weather) Group, comprising the 68th and 339th Fighter (AW) Squadrons. Because of their long range the majority of sorties (usually night intruder attacks) were flown from Itazuke in Japan, although pairs were detached for base alert duties at one or two of the airfields in Korea. By 1951 the F-82G was beginning to feel its age and, despite early successes against

North Korean propeller-driven aircraft, it was clearly no match for the MiG-15.

To rectify this, the USAF assigned 15 Lockheed F-94As to the FEAF, followed by some F-94Bs, in March 1951. However, this all-weather, two-seat version of the F-80 initially proved useless as it lacked an adequate anti-icing system, and it was not until December that year that the 68th FIS assigned a pair of F-94Bs to strip alert duties at Suwon.

The following March, the 319th FIS arrived at Suwon from McHord AFB with fully operational F-94Bs, but owing to a fear that the new E-1 radar fire-control system might fall into Communist hands, the USAF forbade F-94B pilots from flying over enemy-held territory. However, concern was being expressed at the mounting losses of B-29s to night interceptions by MiG-15s, which US Marine Corps Grumman F7F-3N Tigercats of VMF(N)-513 were unable to combat, and on 3 November the chief of staff removed the restrictions on the F-94s. Thereafter, the 319th Squadron flew its F-94Bs on 'barrier patrols' between the Chongchon and Yalu rivers to screen the B-29 bomber streams. An La-9 became the first F-94 victim on 30 January 1953.

Sabre supreme

The F-86 was to emerge as a far more adaptable machine than the F-84 Thunderjet. In September 1951 the 4th FIW began receiving its first F-86Es, with 'all-flying' tailplanes. A further 75 F-86s were shipped in

November to replace the F-80Cs of the 51st FIW.

Moreover, it was becoming clear that the Communist pilots were beginning to employ better tactics. One of these, known as the 'upper cut', involved a snap climb to attack the unwary F-86 from below. Pilots from the Soviet Union and other Communist bloc air forces were also flying over Korea, although they seldom, if ever, ventured over UN-held territory.

On 6 November 1951 Colonel Francis S. Gabreski took command of the 51st FIW. The fortunes of the wing soon took a turn for the better, when four MiGs were destroyed on the ground and, later, in a battle which lasted just a few minutes, eight Tu-2s, three La-9s and a MiG-15 were shot down without loss.

By the end of 1951, the 4th FIW had destroyed 130 MiG-15s for the combat loss of 14 Sabres. Early in 1952 the improved manoeuvrability of the F-86E at higher altitude was forcing the enemy to fly still higher and, by February, most jet combats were taking place at 40,000 ft (12190 m) or higher. The MiG pilots were now forced to make diving attacks against UN bomber formations and this new aggressiveness was reflected in a rise in enemy loss rates.

Such losses could not be sustained by the Communists if they were to maintain a strong position at the peace talks and, from then until the war's end, enemy air activity declined. The jet fighter, most notably the USAF's F-86, had won.

Major Edwin L. Heller had reached ace status during World War II with the 8th AF. He flew several F-86Fs, all named HELL-ER BUST, and adopted controversial tactics. He was not averse to trips north of the Yalu River.

Lockheed P-80 Shooting Star

America's first jet fighter

Above: Differing significantly from the prototype, Lulu Belle, the XP-80A's main new feature was the General Electric I-40 engine, based on a Whittle design.

Top: The Acrojets were the first US jet aerial demonstration team, formed in 1948 by the Fighter School at Williams AFB. Their initial purpose was to show the potential of the P-80 to young pilots and those more accustomed to propeller-driven aircraft, but they were soon performing at public air shows.

America's first production jet fighter only just missed combat in World War II, but went on to form the backbone of USAF ground-attack forces in the early part of the Korean War. The Shooting Star was used in many test programmes and then evolved into the T-33 trainer and the F-94 fighter series.

To US combat pilots of the 1940s and 1950s, the Lockheed P-80 Shooting Star was a remarkable engineering achievement and a great aircraft to fling around the sky. To critics, the P-80 took the latest scientific advances and wasted them on a mediocre airframe that retained the shape, size and wings of a propeller-driven fighter (while others were developing jets with a sleeker shape, of a smaller size and with swept-back flight surfaces).

Opinion was almost universal that the P-80 had few, if any faults – well, almost. In a hard-pressed operational setting, pilots and maintainers were furious that doors embraced the nose compartment. One flyer referred to this as a 'bad feature' because the doors had a tendency to pop open in flight when a latch came loose, rendering the P-80 almost uncontrollable. A hinge at the forward edge would have kept the doors closed in flight no matter what happened, but this remedy was never carried out. Pilots also criticised another design fault – the P-80's nose gear bay doors closed as the gear came up.

These were small complaints, however. By the time the first P-80 Shooting Stars became operational, victory was at hand and the Americans were seeing futuristic visions. Thus, in unveilings to the press at Mitchel Field, New York, and in Burbank on 1 August 1945, US Army Air Forces told the world that the Lockheed Shooting Star had the

'out-of-this-world appearance of a Buck Rogers spaceship'. By then, the P-80 was a proven aircraft, with a handful actually reaching Europe before the war ended, although not in time to fight. This was all in marked contrast to the time when the P-80 had been conceived. Then, the war was being lost and the US was in a distant third place, behind the Germans and British, in the race to develop jets.

On 18 June 1943, Clarence L. ('Kelly') Johnson visited Robert Gross, Lockheed's president, at the company's headquarters in Burbank, California. In the office, Johnson found Gross and chief engineer Hal Hibbard. 'Wright Field wants us to submit a proposal for building a plane around a British jet engine,' Johnson told the two corporate leaders. 'I've worked out some figures. I think we can promise them 180-day delivery. What do you think?'

Apart from four aircraft that reached Europe prior to VE-Day, the first overseas P-80s were assigned to the 5th Fighter Group, under Colonel Horace Hanes. The unit received 32 Shooting Stars for its 38th Fighter Squadron at Giebelstadt, Germany, some of which can be seen here being towed through the streets.

Right: In the post-World War II period, the F-80 and the F-47 Thunderbolt, pictured here over the Bavarian Alps, constituted the major part of the USAF's offensive capability. Both aircraft were replaced by the F-84E Thunderjet.

Below: In a show no doubt designed to impress the Soviets, the 36th Fighter Group laid on this display of F-80Bs at Fürstenfeldbruck. At least 72 aircraft can be seen, most with pilots and ground crew in attendance. The 36th FG was based at 'Fursty' from August 1948 to November 1952.

the P-80 before anyone at Lockheed had ever seen any kind of jet engine. The first powerplant, borrowed from Britain, became available only after the initial airframe was nearly completed.

The spinach-green XP-80, nicknamed Lulu Belle, was taken aloft for its first flight on 8 January 1944. By the war's end, two P-80s were in Italy, preparing for combat, two more had reached England, and 16 were flying.

It was the beginning of a revolution. In years to come, the P-80 (to be redesignated F-80 on 11 June 1948) would set numerous records, go to war in Korea, and inspire the F-94 fighter and T-33 trainer. As the first practical, fully operational American jet fighter, however, the Shooting Star had already secured its place in history.

At Johnson's behest, Lockheed established a goal of 180 days to first flight. This was an extraordinary goal. No fighter had ever been designed, developed and flown so quickly, certainly not one which used the revolutionary power of the jet engine.

Ironically, Lockheed could have started sooner. Back in 1939, Johnson's design team – later to be dubbed the 'Skunk Works' – had proposed a jet fighter. Engineers had drawn up plans on the drawing board for several versions, culminating in the model of a futuristic canard design which would have been powered by two company-designed turbojets (which existed only as a vague notion). But pre-war indifference greeted Lockheed's model. Meanwhile, isolationists were arguing that the US should stay out of 'Europe's war', and the USAAF simply had no interest in it – at least, not yet.

But in late 1943, Johnson and his staff put together their new

aircraft sooner than promised – in 143 days. Johnson's team concocted an aircraft that appeared quite conventional, as if it might fly with either a jet or a reciprocating engine. In fact, the design was straightforward, but unorthodox. The XP-80 had straight wings and tail surfaces, and tricycle landing gear. The wing was a low aspect ratio, laminar-flow surface never before tested on a propeller-driven aircraft.

To their credit, factory workers were cutting metal for

An idea of the low-level environment in which the F-80s operated in Korea can be ascertained in this view of a strike south of Pyongyang on 8 May 1952. As it releases its napalm tanks on a supply building and truck park, the F-80 is engaged by a gun position concealed in an embankment. The white blob beneath the aircraft is an AA shell.

Bombers in Korea

The strategic bombers of World War II now became 'medium' bombers in the battle for Korea. The USAF was the only combatant to operate such aircraft and used them to devastating effect against the Communist forces.

Far East Air Force (FEAF) bomber forces in Korea initially comprised one group: the 19th BG(M), utilising the Boeing B-29 Superfortress.

Official records state that, as of 31 May 1950, the Far East inventory for the Boeing bomber was 22 B-29s, six RB-29s, 24 WB-29s and four SB-29s. These figures were well short of the required number and the call went out for assistance. Almost immediately, the 19th BG was rushed to combat and, on 28 June, four B-29s flew combat missions against the invading North Koreans, attacking tanks and troops. Despite not achieving much success in the neutralising of targets, the big bombers did display a show of force to an enemy that was not expecting any opposition.

The first Superfortress to enter into hostile airspace was not from a bomb squadron, but was a WB-29 reconnaissance aircraft on a 'Buzzard Special' mission on 26 June. Over the next three months, reconnaissance aircraft crossed enemy lines daily.

Two more bomber groups, the 22nd and 92nd, were sent to join the 19th BG on 3 July while, on 29 July, the 98th and 307th arrived to provide further support. During that summer and autumn, bomber forces regularly struck North Korean emplacements and troop concentrations across the peninsular. One specialist mission for the B-29s saw the heavy bombers drop large quantities of flares over targets to illuminate them for heavily-armed B-26s. So successful were the bomber missions in neutralising strategic targets that, by 22 October, General Stratemeyer had cut back the number of sorties by B-29s and two groups were returned to SAC bases in the USA.

Only five days after the bombers' departure, the Chinese entered the war. It was decided, however, not to recall the two bomber groups as the remaining three were expected to be capable of thwarting the Chinese.

Top: Invaders of the 731st BS, 452nd BW return to Itazuke, Japan after a low-level sweep over Communist targets in May 1951. Note the replacement fin on the nearest, camouflaged, B-26B.

Above: B-29s of the 19th BG taxi down the ramp, ready for another mission over North Korea. Seen here in 1952, the 19th BG had already spent two years fighting the Communists and had recently celebrated its 500th sortie.

For the remainder of the war, the three in-theatre groups were kept busy. The most profitable targets lay in northwest Korea, but advanced AAA and MiG-15s lay in wait to repulse the bombers. The first six months of 1951 saw an end to most of the major military movement around the front lines. The initial Chinese offensive in November 1950 had pushed the UN forces below the 38th Parallel. In the spring of 1951, however, the lines were stabilised and the Communists were slowly pushed back almost to where they had been when the war started. At this time, the war became a game of chess between the Chinese logistics command and the FEAF. The Chinese would send huge numbers of workers into small areas at night to repair bomb damage, while the bombers would try to find them. However, these aircraft were struggling in the darkness and

The Douglas B-26 Invader stood out as a night intruder which stalked and attacked all kinds of North Korean targets, from front-line soldiers to railway marshalling yards.

A flight of aircraft from the 307th BG taxis along the main runway at Kadena during the late afternoon for a night mission in 1952. Most missions were flown at night, especially during the last two years of the war. The aircraft were protected from night-flying MiG-15s by F-94s and F3Ds.

Below: The most peculiar Invaders in the war were those modified to carry an infra-red detector above the bomb aimer's compartment. The aircraft would hunt trains and, when one was found, flares would be dropped so that other, conventional, B-26s could attack the target more easily.

the decision was made to fit a few B-29s with APN-3 SHORAN radar. Combat tests were successful and two aircraft from each group were equipped with the APN-3. These aircraft could lead the bomber streams and all could drop their ordnance, guided by the lead ships.

Throughout 1951 and 1952, Bomber Command attacked troops, supply dumps, bridges, marshalling yards and runways with successful results. Although the Communists were quickly rebuilding assets, they were failing to build and repair airfields, therefore ensuring that the UN air forces dominated the skies south of the Yalu River.

As 1953 began, the war still seemed without end and the bombers continued to pound Chinese targets, with approximately 16,000 buildings being destroyed. And, on one night, B-29s destroyed 21 enemy fighters on the ground.

When the conflict ended, the B-29's war had been a successful one. Only 16 aircraft had been lost to enemy aircraft, four to AAA and 14 to various operational causes. Impressively, their gunners had shot down 33 enemy fighters. The Korean War had lasted over 1,100 days – and the Superfortresses had flown on all but 26 of these; this equated to 21,000 sorties, delivering 167,000 tons of bombs.

The Invader's war

Douglas B-26 Invaders, many of them veterans of World War II, flew the first and last bombing missions of the Korean War. On 25 June 1950, the first day of the war, two squadrons of B-26s were operating from Japan and, on the night of the 27th, B-26s unsuccessfully attacked a large tank unit approaching Seoul. One of the first missions for the Invaders was escorting *Reinholte*, a ship evacuating civilians out of the port of Inchon. However, poor weather conditions meant

that they found no targets to bomb. The initial targets for the B-26s for the first few weeks were highway and rail bridges. They also used their forward-firing machine guns to strafe the roads, destroying anything that moved.

FEAF soon realised that the role of the B-26 in the Korean conflict would not be diminished, irrespective of the length of the war. The only other light bomber in US service, the new B-45, was not available in quantity and was certainly not suited to low-level missions, flown in darkness over mountainous terrain. More B-26s were therefore requested and a Reserve Group was sent from the United States.

The next big operation for the Invader were the beach landings at Inchon Harbour where B-26s, along with swarms of other fighter-bombers, decimated Communist armour.

The next 90 days saw the B-26s being involved in another arena – the night conflict. It had been quickly noted that the only way to contain an enemy with

enormous manpower was to cut its supply lines. With the North Koreans and, later, the Chinese moving their forces after sunset, the night mission became imperative. By late December, the Chinese were moving south at an alarming rate, even during the daylight hours. B-26s and USMC night-fighters found plenty of targets at night by zeroing in on camp fires.

From 1951 to 1953, B-26s were involved in anti-infantry, anti-rail, anti-armour and reconnaissance missions, all revolving around the premise that Chinese supply lines had to be cut. However, during 1953, the Chinese started to build up forces, in order to prepare for a major spring offensive. There could be no let-up on the pressure on the Communists' logistic network and the Invaders continued to interdict Chinese supplies and also performed close support missions.

The final minutes of the war saw its last bombing mission, flown by a B-26C. Minutes later, an RB-26C surveyed the damage and so the war ended.

Unconventional attackers

Along with the conventionally armed bomber forces, the FEAF used B-29s in the reconnaissance role all over the Korean peninsular. The Communists did not have any 'standard' bombers, but used ageing aircraft such as Po-2s and Yak-18s in nuisance attacks to harass UN forces at night.

RB-29 Superfortress

The 91st Strategic Reconnaissance Squadron played a vital role in the war. Its aircraft flew all over North Korea, unescorted, taking pictures of targets, both potential and post-strike, and dropping propaganda leaflets. When the MiG-15s entered the war in November 1950, the RBs backed off from 'MiG Alley' unless they had fighter protection. The squadron's aircraft had a distinctive 'Circle-X' on their vertical stabilisers.

Yak-18

The Yakovlev aircraft featured in the North Korean inventory as a trainer much like the T-6 Texan. Like its American counterpart, it came to be employed on battlefield surveillance until losses became prohibitive. Thereafter, it joined the Polikarpov Po-2s in the less hazardous, but more 'cost-effective' night nuisance attacks. Nicknamed 'Bedcheck Charlie', these irritating attacks kept everybody awake and dished out more military damage than they were usually credited with.

The Hawker Hunter FGA.Mk 9s of No. 20 Squadron, based at Tengah in Singapore, were the RAF's only in-theatre fighter-bombers. The aircraft were used in the suppression of the initial revolts in Sarawak and Brunei, and against Indonesian armed infiltrators.

Confrontation with Indonesia

The Malayan Emergency had formally ended in 1960. However, it was not long before the UK found itself embroiled in a separate, but operationally similar, flare-up, this time along a frontier disputed with nationalist Indonesia.

Possibly the least known of all post-war RAF operational deployments was that in Borneo between 1962 and 1964. Borneo was the object of territorial ambitions held by neighbouring Indonesia, following the transfer of independence to North Borneo. The campaign had much in common with that in Malaya which had only just ended, not least in the similarity of terrain; Borneo, like the Malayan peninsular, was covered in dense jungle, with few landmarks to aid navigation. Accurate maps were scarce and, on account of frequent tropical rainstorms, flying was impossible except for

about six hours daily between mid-morning and mid-afternoon.

There had been conflict in the region at the end of World War II, when British and Dutch forces clashed with Indonesian nationalists; this ended with the handing over of the United States of Indonesia to President Sukharno in December 1949. Sukharno then fought the Dutch and covert CIA troops over Dutch New Guinea, on the basis that the Dutch colony should belong to Indonesia. After some hostilities, Dutch New Guinea was handed over to Indonesia in May 1963.

In very broad terms, the British conflict can be divided

into three overlapping phases: the suppression of Indonesian-inspired rebellion in Brunei and Sarawak; the subsequent deployment of units of the Far East Air Force (FEAF) to Borneo to counter Indonesian-trained terrorist infiltrators who were crossing the 1,000-mile (1610-km) border with Kalimantan; and wider-ranging operations to counter Indonesian

air sorties across the border and the dispatch of Indonesian parties to Malaya itself.

RAF forces on hand

The FEAF had undergone considerable modernisation since the signing of the SEAC Defence Treaty of 1954. The RAF component comprised a squadron (No. 20) of Hunter FGA.Mk 9s at Tengah, Singapore, together with Javelin FAW.Mk 9s of No. 60 Squadron and Canberra B.Mk 2s of No. 45 Squadron. Also in Malaya were RAF Canberra PR.Mk 7s, Shackleton MR.Mk 2s and a variety of transport aircraft. At the RAAF base at Butterworth were two CAC Sabre squadrons and No. 2 Squadron RAAF with Canberras, and there was also a Canberra squadron (No. 75) of the

The P-51D/K Mustang was the primary Dutch fighter and ground-attack aircraft at the outbreak of hostilities in the Dutch East Indies after World War II. This flight is seen over Medan in Sumatra in October 1948. Following the Dutch withdrawal in 1950, the Mustangs were handed over to the fledgling Indonesian air force, which operated them well into the 1970s.

Labuan became the RAF's operational hub in Borneo, its flight lines accommodating a wide variety of aircraft types. Visible in this photo are Beverley and Twin Pioneer transports, as well as Javelin interceptors and Canberra bombers. Labuan was an offshore island, and was thus easy to protect against infiltration, offering the RAF a secure base for its aircraft.

detachment to the theatre, known as 'Matterhorn', initially of Victors but, from October 1964, composed of Vulcan B.Mk 2s. Although for a time Victors were 'bombed up' and ready to go, the 'Matterhorn' bombers were not used in combat. In February 1964 an air-defence identification zone (ADIZ) was established, after which the Hunters and Javelins, based at Labuan and Kuching, maintained a 24-hour all-weather alert system, their pilots being authorised to engage and destroy any Indonesian aircraft entering the ADIZ.

Indonesian landings

In August of that year, 100 regular Indonesian troops went ashore at three points on the west coast of the Malayan peninsula, and two weeks later an Indonesian Lockheed C-130 Hercules dropped paratroopers on central Jahore. Although these forces had been rounded up by mid-October, there were 40 other landings, and it was against these that the Hunters and Canberras of the RAF, RAAF and the RNZAF were now deployed. Moreover, airborne early warning Gannets from Royal Navy carriers and shore bases were employed to patrol Malayan coastal airspace. However, the most effective way to counter the cross-border raids was the rapid airlifting of troops by helicopter into the area.

Operations in Borneo waned during 1965, and by the middle of 1966, the 'confrontation' was fully over, allowing helicopters to return from their forward-deployed bases in the jungle.

RNZAF at Tengah. In addition, it had become standard RAF training practice to send small detachments of conventionally-armed V-bombers to the Far East for short periods.

Immediately after news of the rebellions in Brunei and Sarawak was received on 8 December 1962, Hastings, Beverleys and Valetta transports began delivering troops to Brunei town, its airfield having been secured from the rebels by Gurkha troops, who were landed first. A single Britannia flew troops to nearby Labuan. Within a fortnight, 3,200 troops had been delivered, together with 113 vehicles and supporting weapons and stores, and the rebellion in Sarawak was put down. Joining the airlift had been an RAAF C-130A

Hercules and an RNZAF Bristol Freighter, as well as RAF Shackletons of No. 205 Squadron. On arrival in Borneo, the troops were moved forward by Beverleys and Pioneers and by Sycamore helicopters; also employed were the big twin-rotor Bristol Belvedere helicopters of No. 66 Squadron.

The rebellion in Brunei was being sustained by neighbouring Indonesia, and to restore the situation in the area British forces were tasked with isolating and mopping up the rebel bands. This involved airlifting troops to the airfields at Seria and the airstrip at Anduki, the former being successfully undertaken by the short-field Twin Pioneers of No. 209 Squadron and the latter by a single Beverley (which was later fired on by the rebels, but

suffered only negligible damage).

The rebellions having failed, Indonesia began infiltrating guerrilla forces across the border, and to counter this the security forces established a number of strongpoints near to the known crossing points. The tiny garrisons were to be sustained wholly from the air, a task which caused a number of new squadrons to be deployed to Borneo, in particular Nos 103, 110 and 230 with the new Westland Whirlwind.

In a general widening of the conflict, Indonesia greatly increased its cross-border incursions, even starting to send F-51 Mustangs into Borneo airspace. The aircraft were particularly difficult to counter as they were able to outmanoeuvre the big Javelins and were virtually immune from the RAF's heat-seeking missiles on account of their piston engines. The RAF V-bomber force supplied a

Above: No. 209 Squadron flew a mix of Pioneers and Twin Pioneers from Seletar and a variety of forward bases. The single-engined Pioneer carried up to five passengers, while the larger Twin Pioneer carried 11 (or nine paratroops). Following their withdrawal from the transport role on 31 December 1968, three Pioneers joined No. 20 Squadron for use on FAC missions, operating alongside the unit's Hunter fighter-bombers.

Canberra B.Mk 2s (pictured) from the RAAF's No. 2 Sqn at Butterworth and Canberra B(I).Mk 12s from the RNZAF at Tengah flew in the light bombing role throughout the conflict.

Malaya 1948-1960

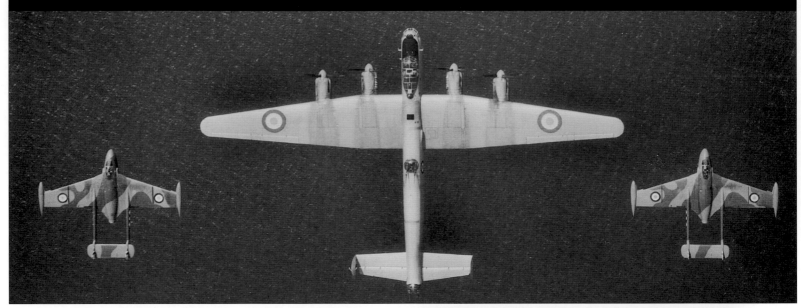

Operation Firedog

When Japan invaded the Malayan peninsular in December 1941, the British supported the Communists in a joint campaign against the Japanese. However, once the war was over, the battle for Malaya restarted and became a costly thorn in the side of Britain for another dozen years.

There had been an anti-British guerrilla movement in Malaya before the Japanese occupation of 1942. However, during the occupation, the British administration supported this Chinese-led organisation as the only element able to harass and spy on the mutual enemy, Japan. Thus, at the end of the war, the British found themselves with a depleted infrastructure of their own, but facing a well-organised and highly-equipped guerrilla force. Under pressure, but otherwise reluctant to grant independence, the British attempted to shepherd the diverse sultanates and states into a federation under the British flag. The Communist-inspired guerrillas now took on the mantle of freedom fighters and unified all independence-seeking groups behind them

against the UK. So started the campaign, generally known as the Malayan Emergency, which lasted until 1960. The military operation in Malaya was known as Operation Firedog.

Forces in-theatre

When the state of emergency was declared in 1948, the RAF deployed a total of eight squadrons of Spitfires, Mosquitoes, Beaufighters and Dakotas at Changi, Seletar and Tengah on Singapore Island, and at Kuala Lumpur in the north. The tropical climate played havoc with the wooden Mosquitoes and these aircraft had to be quickly replaced, along with the Spitfires, the more recently-deployed Tempests which could not carry sufficient stores, and the Beaufighter, which was becoming obsolete.

In came the Bristol Brigand, flown by No. 45 Squadron, and

The war against the terrorists in Malaya provided the helicopter with a unique opportunity to demonstrate its usefulness for supporting jungle warfare. Whirlwinds of No. 848 Squadron, RN, and No. 155 Squadron, RAF, were deployed to Malaya.

although it could put up impressive displays of attacks with guns, bombs and rockets, it was soon discovered that such techniques had little effect on the loose bands of guerrillas operating 'somewhere' under the triple-canopy rainforest below.

Only when Lincolns were deployed from the UK to carry out area bombing did an impression begin to be made. Such deployments were sporadic, since these bombers could not be easily spared from their other duties, but the Royal Australian Air Force contributed Lincolns on

a more permanent basis from 1950 onwards. The Brigands ran into serviceability and safety problems and were supplanted by de Havilland Hornets, which were very manoeuvrable and could attack with precision in conditions of bad weather and tricky terrain.

Jet aircraft arrive

By 1953, jet aircraft began to arrive in the form of Vampires and Meteors and, a little later, Venoms and Canberras. Once again, these were found to be unsuitable, with poor

The nuclear bombs dropped on Hiroshima and Nagasaki ended World War II before the Hornet could enter service, and the jet age rendered it obsolete for home defence. However, the RAF's fastest piston-engined fighter found its niche as a fighter-bomber in the Far East – pictured here are a flight of Hornets from No. 45 Squadron.

Above: The Dragonflies of No. 194 Squadron established jungle operation techniques so, by the time the Bristol Sycamores arrived in-theatre, these lessons could be put to good use. No. 194 Squadron exchanged its Dragonflies for HR.Mk 14 Sycamores in October 1954. One is seen here inserting troops into a jungle clearing.

Below: The Venom proved popular with its pilots and was extensively used in Malaya by both the Royal Air Force and the Royal New Zealand Air Force. Here, a line-up of No. 14 Squadron, RNZAF, prepares for another day's operations from Tengah in 1958.

serviceability, range and payload, plus an inherent inability to operate slowly at low level. The tangible results of all this offensive air support were minimal, although it probably helped the British by keeping the insurgents under pressure and on the move.

Of greater importance was the transport effort. Malaya was devoid of good roads and it was a very slow business for the ground troops to make headway through the jungle and plantations. Resupply from the air was often a necessity, and Dakotas, Valettas and, later, Hastings paradropped essential supplies to the forces in the field, while Yorks ferried material around the peninsula. Paratrooping itself was not often employed, since the dropping zones were seldom hospitable, but Malaya saw the world's first extensive use of helicopters and these soon transformed the tactics of the security forces.

Enter the Dragonfly

Introduced in 1950, the Sikorsky S-51 Dragonfly began to take on casualty evacuation duties, which improved both efficiency and morale. By the mid-1950s, Bristol Sycamores

and Westland Whirlwinds arrived to undertake assault as well as evacuation sorties. Able to insert up to nine troops into remote areas, they introduced mobility into an otherwise tough, debilitating and painfully slow-moving action. Alongside the helicopters, Auster lightplanes were used to support the observation posts and jungle forts which were essential to maintaining local security. The Auster AOP.Mk 6 and the later AOP.Mk 9 were able to land and take off in 492 ft (150 m) and proved to be very useful. Later came the tough Scottish Aviation Pioneer, an aircraft which could carry four passengers instead of the Auster's

one, and could operate out of airstrips only half the length of those required by the Auster.

Perhaps the most essential air task of all fell to a single squadron which performed superbly throughout Operation Firedog. There was little good mapping of Malaya at the start of the operation and it was impossible to fight the war without this and other vital information. No. 81 Squadron was tasked with photographic reconnaissance of the entire peninsula. Flying a variety of aircraft (Spitfire PR.Mk 19, Mosquito PR.Mk 34, Meteor PR.Mk 10, Pembroke C(PR).Mk 1 and Canberra PR.Mk 7), the squadron unstintingly persevered in its

mission and provided vital information for both air strikes and ground operations. It also, incidentally, flew the last operational sorties of the RAF's Spitfire and Mosquito.

The UK eventually moved towards granting independence, fostering the indigenous Malays as the new ruling element. The conflict then took on a racial dimension, with the Chinese isolated against the now unified Malays and British. 'Divide and rule' succeeded and the insurgents fought a losing battle.

Operation Firedog was always a war fought on the ground, but air support in the offensive and transport roles played a valuable and, maybe, vital part in the success of the operation.

Above: Canberras from UK-based Bomber Command squadrons deployed to Butterworth from Binbrook during 1955 and 1956 under Operation Mileage. This Canberra was from No. 101 Squadron. The Far East Air Force (FEAF) gained its own Canberras from 1957.

Left: Bristol Brigands replaced ageing Beaufighters with Nos 45 and 84 Squadrons, but had a short career before they were themselves retired after an alarming spate of structural failures and accidents. Here, a Brigand of No. 84 Squadron attacks a terrorist target. The Brigand gave way to the de Havilland Hornet from 1951.

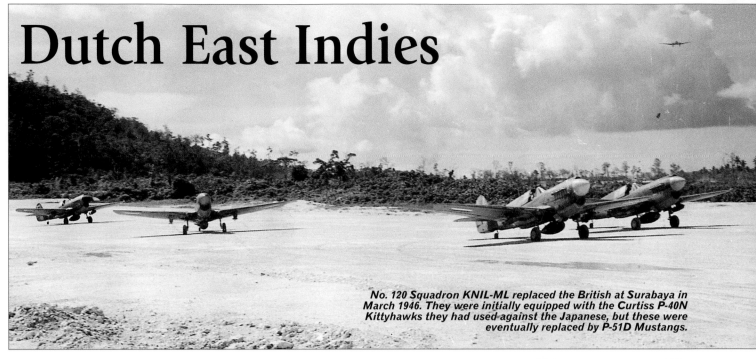

Dutch East Indies

No. 120 Squadron KNIL-ML replaced the British at Surabaya in March 1946. They were initially equipped with the Curtiss P-40N Kittyhawks they had used against the Japanese, but these were eventually replaced by P-51D Mustangs.

World War II marked the start of the struggle for independence, as native peoples sought to throw off colonial rule. One of the first such wars took place in the Netherlands East Indies, where fighting started even before the Japanese surrender.

The Netherlands East Indies were occupied by the Japanese during World War II. On liberation the Dutch expected that power would be restored to them, though the indigenous Indonesians had been promised independence by the Japanese during the closing stages of the war. Sukharno, the nationalist leader, declared independence on 17 August 1945, three days after the Japanese surrender.

The Dutch authorities had their hands full at home, after the German occupation and a brutal famine. They had to rely on British and Commonwealth forces to re-occupy their colony. The Air Headquarters, Netherlands East Indies was established in September, and the British made it clear that they would recognise the new Republic.

Three-cornered war

This did not sit well with either of the factions competing to control the vast island group, and British and Australian forces found themselves opposed both by freed Dutch PoWs and internees, and by the republicans, who naturally suspected that the two European colonial nations would co-operate against their interests. However, it was the Republican forces which most seriously disrupted Britain's PoW repatriation operations, forcing the British into an alliance with the Dutch.

RAF aircraft (principally P-47D Thunderbolts,

Mosquitoes and Spitfire Mk XIVs) began flying sorties against terrorist positions, usually after dropping warning leaflets.

Dutch forces did not begin to replace British units until the beginning of 1946, although Dutch squadrons attached to the Royal Australian Air Force had been active in the theatre since the war. No 18 Squadron flying North American B-25 Mitchells, had been based in Northern Australia in 1942, moving to Biak off New Guinea as the Allies 'Island hopped' towards the Philippines in 1944. P-40N Warhawks of No. 120 Squadron were now based at Surabaya, as were the Catalinas of 321 Squadron of the Dutch Navy.

Dutch take over

Over the next few months a trickle of Dutch units became operational, formally assuming responsibility in September 1946, and by December had largely replaced British units. The B-25s at Tjililitan near Bandoeng and at Palembang on Sumatra had been joined by North American P-51D Mustangs, while the P-40s and Catalinas at Surabaya were reinforced by Fairey Firefly Mk.1s of the Royal Netherlands Navy.

The British had lost over 500 troops in the previous year, primarily fighting to protect road convoys, particularly out of Bandoeng. Air power had been used to attack insurgent positions, to interdict gun-running ships, and to provide vital supplies. Their primary task had been to evacuate

Above: Fairey Fireflys of No. 820 Squadron, Netherlands Naval Air Service, fire rockets at Republican positions in the mountainous heart of Java to the south of Surabaya.

Below: Seen over Java days after the Japanese surrender, the North American B-25 Mitchell provided the Royal Netherlands East Indies Air Force with its strike power.

Allied PoWs and Internees, and that had largely been completed by the end of August.

Local negotiations resulted in an informal agreement that Java and Sumatra would come under the authority of Indonesia, while the Dutch would share the task of bringing the remaining islands into a federation.

There was a ceasefire in early 1947, and an agreement that

Air power was a key element in the Dutch attempt to control the East Indies. Paratroopers were used in the tactically successful 'police action' which took place in December 1947, but the success generated even more guerrilla activity.

Indonesia would be a federal organisation of united states, with some allegiance to the Netherlands, but details were sketchy and ceasefire violations increased. By now the rebels were pressing former Japanese aircraft into service, but reliability was poor.

'Police action'

On 20 July 1947, the Dutch authorities mounted a 'police action' involving three divisions on Java and three brigades on the larger but less-heavily populated Sumatra. They captured most towns, and interned the nationalist leadership, but most insurgents retreated to the hills, from where they continued to mount guerrilla raids. These were subject to air strikes, but more effective was the Dutch blockade of Republican areas: a ceasefire was agreed in August.

The Dutch maintained their blockade, using newly-delivered Spitfire Mk IXs. The Nationalists were split, and a Communist revolt against Sukharno was put down and its leader killed. A second 'police action' which started in December 1947 saw Dutch parachute assaults on republican airfields. Sukharno and most of the Republican government were captured and interned, but this had the effect of inflaming the nationalists, and Guerrilla raids intensified.

Growing international pressure and American threats to withdraw aid forced a formal ceasefire in Sumatra on 11 August 1949, followed by Java four days later. The final transfer of sovereignty to a new United States of Indonesia (under the released Sukharno) took place on 27 December 1949, after four years of conflict. Many of the Netherlands East Indies aircraft were handed over to Indonesia, whose new air force was formed on a core of P-51s, B-25s and C-47s.

The new nation was inherently unstable, encompassing 100 million ethnically and religiously diverse people on 10,000 islands, many of whom had no wish to exchange rule from the Hague for rule from Batavia. Sukharno's expansionist ambition and tolerance of communism led to US hostility to his rule, and the CIA supported his opponents when they staged an abortive rebellion in Sumatra and Celebes in February 1958.

CIA 'dirty tricks'

This support took the form of training, organising and payment of mercenaries, and an air force of ex-USAF aircraft including 15 B-26s, a C-54, various C-46s and C-47s, and, according to some sources, a B-29. These were operated from Manado on the northern tip of Celebes, and one B-26 was shot down during a raid on Ambon on 18 May 1958. An amnesty was offered in 1961, and the rebellion ended.

Sukharno claimed Dutch New Guinea from 1957. By 1960 he was threatening invasion. In response the Dutch deployed No.322 Sqn, with 12 Hawker Hunter F.Mk4s to Biak. There they augmented 12 Neptunes of No. 321 Sqn, a similar number of Firefly AS.Mk 4s of No. 6 Sqn, and a number of C-47s.

New Guinea invasion

An Indonesian invasion fleet arrived on 15 January 1962, covered by F-51D Mustangs and accompanied by a paratroop drop. One landing ship was sunk by a Dutch warship, though negotiations began before the Hunters could intervene. As a result, Dutch New Guinea was handed over to Indonesia as West Irian in May 1963.

NETHERLANDS EAST INDIES – AIRFIELDS & BASES

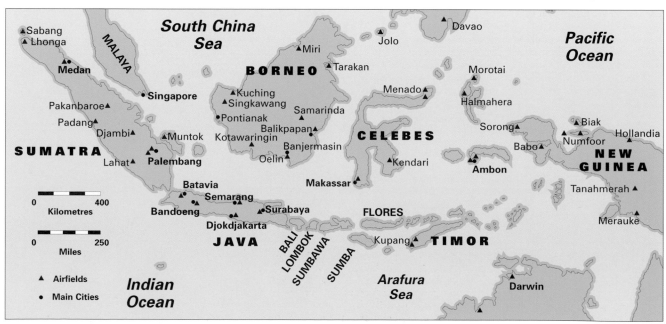

Suez Crisis

Assault preparations

Following President Nasser of Egypt's announcement of 26 July 1956 that the Suez Canal would be nationalised, Anglo-French and Israeli forces began to plan a military response – Operation Musketeer.

President Nasser's nationalisation of the Suez Canal, the trade route between Europe and the Middle East, in July 1956 prompted plans for an immediate military response, called for by Prime Minister Anthony Eden. Britain had previously enjoyed access to the waterway by virtue of an agreement with Egypt for the use and defence of the Canal.

Nasser's Egypt had received financial support from the USSR to fund the Aswan Dam, after the West had withdrawn funds and, furthermore, Egypt had also begun to receive military assistance from the Eastern bloc.

Eden encouraged the Chiefs of Staff to formulate a military response in order to re-establish access to and control of the Canal, with meetings beginning on 27 July. Meanwhile, French Prime Minister Mollet proposed a joint invasion of Egypt, to be led by General Sir Charles Keightley.

Build-up to invasion

On 2 August RAF Bomber Command Canberra Squadrons left the UK for Maltese bases, British reservists were called up, and an invasion force began to assemble at Toulon.

The 16th Parachute Brigade left Portsmouth on 5 August, bound for Cyprus aboard HMS *Theseus*, before returning to the UK in order to receive further training. On 9 August two infantry batallions were dispatched to Malta.

The eventual operation, now codenamed Musketeer Revise, emerged in mid-August, and called for an Anglo-French seaborne and airborne assault on Port Said, with forces pressing on down the Canal towards Ismailia. Airborne interdiction would isolate the war zone, and aerial superiority would have to be gained over the Egyptian air force (EAF).

On 1 September France suggested that Israel take part in Musketeer Revise and, by the end of the month, France had agreed privately with Israel over Israeli fighter and naval support, as well as an Israeli invasion of Sinai. Progress depended on waiting for the invasion fleet

vessels involved to be prepared and loaded. When Israeli forces reached the Suez battle zone, the UK and French governments intended to issue an ultimatum requiring a cessation of fighting between the Egyptians and Israelis, and the withdrawal of their respective forces. This would, no doubt, be rejected by the Egyptians, giving the Allies a justified cause for intervention.

Operation Cordage

Operation Cordage was a measure of the distrust Britain felt for Israel, in that it was intended to disable IDF/AF airfields in the event that Israel were to attack Jordan. British airborne forces were thus prepared to attack Israeli as well as Egyptian targets. Egyptian operations would commence with bombing, to be followed by psychological warfare, with leaflet-dropping and radio broadcasts. For this purpose, a Cyprus-based Pembroke, veteran of the Kenyan psy-war campaign, was made available. Beginning at

Above: A Royal Navy Sea Venom FAW.Mk 21 leaves the catapult bridle behind it as it begins another Suez mission from HMS **Albion.** *Aircraft left the carrier deck every two to three minutes.*

Below: A No. 802 NAS Seahawk aboard the carrier HMS **Albion** *after a sortie over Egypt in December 1956. The aircraft's starboard underwing fuel tank has been badly damaged by AAA.*

Sea Hawk FGA.Mk 6

Wearing black and yellow Suez operation stripes, applied in November 1956, this Hawker Sea Hawk FGA.Mk 6 of No. 804 Sqn, FAA, operated from HMS *Bulwark,* and made attacks on Egyptian airfields, as well as flying ground-support missions. On return from Suez, the squadron embarked aboard HMS *Ark Royal* (O-code) in early 1957, retaining its Suez stripes.

Powerplant
The FGA.Mk 6 was essentially a re-engined FGA.Mk 4, carrying an uprated Rolls-Royce Nene Mk 103 turbojet, providing a static thrust of 5,400 lb (24.3 kN).

Suez losses
One Sea Hawk from HMS *Albion* was shot down during the 40 Commando assault on Navy House – the former headquarters of the Egyptian Navy – on 4 November, but, in all, just two FAA Sea Hawks were lost.

Rocket projectiles
This Sea Hawk carries a typical ground-attack load of six 60-lb (27-kg) unguided rockets (up to eight could normally be carried), mounted on underwing launch rails. Alternatively, 16 25-lb (11.3-kg) rockets could be carried underwing, mounted in two tiers of four on each wing. Cannon were utilised for ground-strafing.

Fuel load
As well as internal fuel tanks providing 395 Imp gal (1796 litres) of fuel, the FGA.Mk 6 could carry two underwing 100-Imp gal (455-litre) drop tanks, an improvement on the 88-Imp gal (400-litre) tanks regularly carried by the FGA.Mk 4. The two main wing hardpoints could also carry 500-lb (227-kg) high-explosive (HE) bombs.

Sea Hawk units
Several Sea Hawk variants were employed by the FAA during the Suez crisis. No. 800 NAS flew the FGA.Mk 4/6 from HMS *Albion*, No. 802 NAS flew the FB.Mk 3 from *Albion*, No. 804 NAS flew the FGA.Mk 6 from HMS *Bulwark*, No. 810 NAS flew the FGA.Mk 4 from *Bulwark*, No. 895 NAS flew the FB.Mk 3 from *Bulwark*, and No. 897 and No. 899 NAS both flew the FGA.Mk 6 from HMS *Eagle*.

Fixed weaponry
The forward fuselage nose section of the Sea Hawk carried four British Hispano 30-mm cannon, each with a total of 200 rounds stored in ammunition tanks behind the cockpit. Spent cartridge ejection chutes can be seen projecting from either side of the lower forward fuselage.

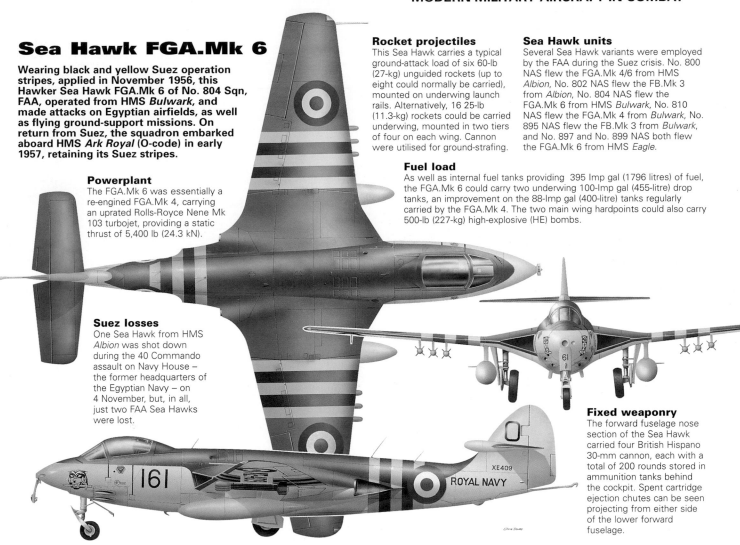

night, RAF bombers would attack Egypt from Cyprus and Malta, with further strikes by FAA carrier-based aircraft, which would also be used to cover the forthcoming invasion.

Following the defeat of the EAF, paradrops would begin the invasion, with landings at Port Said in the west, and Port Fuad in the east, utilising British and French troops, respectively.

Later, seaborne troops would move south down the Canal, with armoured support.

The French invasion convoy left Algeria on 27 October, bound for Suez. The British equivalent left Malta on 30 October. Tragedy had almost struck on 23 October as the RAF Comet flying the Planning Group to Cyprus suffered a total engine failure at 40,000 ft

(12192 m), before the engines re-lit at a lower altitude. As Israeli forces headed towards the Canal, the Allies issued an ultimatum for a cease-fire, set at 16.15 hours on 30 October.

The conditions set by the Allies stipulated that the Egyptian and Israeli forces should retreat 10 miles (16 km) either side of the Canal, as well as permit Allied control and

maintenance of the Canal zone. These conditions were, as expected, rejected by Egypt.

Egyptian strength
The Egyptian air force was believed to be comprised of around 50 MiG-15s, 12 MiG-17s and 40 Il-28 'Beagles' plus 30 Vampire FB.Mk 52s and 16 Meteors. British intelligence regarding the EAF's strength was gleaned from the CIA, whose WRS(P)-2 unit was flying U-2A spyplanes from Incirlik air base in Turkey. During the crisis the US maintained readiness, with SAC's 306 Bomb Wing (B-47s) and 70 Strategic Reconnaissance Wing (RB-47s) on alert in Morocco.

RAF Canberra WH853 of No. 12 Squadron began the bombing campaign on Almaza on the night of 31 October. The initial objective of the RAF was the destruction of the EAF, to be carried out through the systematic aerial bombardment of Egyptian airfields. With five Canberra B.Mk 6 and four Valiant B.Mk 1 squadrons on Malta, and seven more shorter-ranged Canberra B.Mk 2 squadrons on Cyprus, the RAF was ready to begin its Suez offensive in earnest.

Armée de l'Air Noratlas transports dropped both French and British troops (including sappers and the Guards Independent Paratroop Company) on Port Said, and were intended to drop further troops on Ismailia, prior to the cancellation of that operation.

RAF No. 37 Squadron Shackleton MR.Mk 2s were based at Luqa in Malta, and flew both maritime reconnaissance and transport missions. Nos 42 and 206 Sqn aircraft were also impressed into service as makeshift troop transports, flying from the UK to Malta and Cyprus.

Suez Crisis
Allied attack effort

As the aerial campaign for the control of the Suez Canal began, the RAF alone had no fewer than 112 aircraft at Akrotiri, 127 at Nicosia and 46 at Tymbou. Initially attacking key Egyptian air bases, RAF bombing missions began at 19.30 hours on 31 October, as Valiants began to leave bases in Malta.

As Valiants left Luqa, they were, in turn, followed by further aircraft from Cyprus and Malta, the first targets being struck at around 22.30 hours. After the initial wave of Valiant B.Mk 1s had been recalled, the first aircraft to see action were No. 12 Sqn Canberra B.Mk 6s, dropping their bombs over Cairo West airfield. The following day, Egyptian aircraft (including 20 MiG-15s and eight Il-28s), piloted by Soviet aircrew, fled their airfields for Syria. Bomber Command's task therefore became easier still, with clear skies, the absence of

blackout and the Canberras of Nos 18, 109 and 139 Sqns marking targets.

Reconnaissance was provided from dawn on 1 November, with No. 13 Sqn Canberra PR.Mk 7s and EC 1/33 'Belfort' RF-84Fs despatched from Akrotiri. Following the examination of post-strike photography, Canberras were ordered to return to Egypt the same evening, attacking concentrated targets, including Il-28s that had fled south to Luxor. These aircraft were eventually despatched by 20 EC 1 F-84Fs, based at Lydda, equipped with long-range fuel

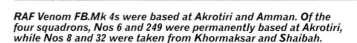

RAF Venom FB.Mk 4s were based at Akrotiri and Amman. Of the four squadrons, Nos 6 and 249 were permanently based at Akrotiri, while Nos 8 and 32 were taken from Khormaksar and Shaibah.

tanks in order to make the flight.

Daytime missions involved Cyprus-based Canberra B.Mk 2s, Nos 1 and 34 Sqn Hunter F.Mk 5s and EC 3 F-84Fs.

The British carrier force arrived off the Egyptian coast, due north of Cairo, on 31 October. With Sea Venom fighter-cover, FAA Sea Hawks attacked airfields, including Cairo West, and other MiG-15 bases. Five hundred sorties were flown on the first day, without loss, and 27

Egyptian aircraft bound for Syria were destroyed on the ground at Abu Sueir.

Photo-reconnaissance

Canberra PR.Mk 7s of No. 13 Sqn confirmed the effectiveness of the attacks, seemingly achieved with a minimum of civilian casualties, as a British-run propaganda radio station broadcast warnings of airstrikes to the Egyptian population. The decision was taken to bomb Cairo radio station, with No. 27 Sqn Canberra B.Mk 2s assigned, and cover provided by F-84Fs.

Above: The Armée de l'Air deployed the Mystère IVAs of 2e Escadre de Chasse from Dijon to Haifa. The unit's 36 aircraft remained at Haifa from October to December 1956, providing fighter cover for Israeli towns.

Right: The Aéronavale's 28F operated the PB4Y-2 Privateer from Karouba in Tunisia during the Suez crisis. Tasked with maritime reconnaissance, the aircraft flew a total of nine operational sorties, supplementing the TBM-3.

Right: Hunter F.Mk 5 fighters were flown by Nos 1 and 34 Squadrons from Nicosia. The aircraft, from the Tangmere wing, operated in the close-support role without loss, and provided defensive cover for Cyprus-based Canberras.

Below: The Arromanches detachment included both TBM-3S and TBM-3W2 (pictured) Avengers. The TBM-3W2 was identified by the APS-20 search radar, and was the 'hunter' complement to the 'killer' TBM-3S Avenger.

The operation, early on 2 November, left the radio station off the air for the following two days.

The second full day of attack, 1 November, saw attacks directed against ground forces, with concentrations at Huckstep being attacked for the following three days. RAF No. 6 Sqn Venoms flew 18 sorties on 1 November, focusing on Dekheila airfield on the Suez delta, supported by No. 830 NAS Wyverns. During the day, the Allies lost a single No. 13 Sqn Canberra PR.Mk 7 to ground fire, and a No. 893 NAS Sea Venom FAW.Mk 21 crash-landed on HMS *Eagle* with an injured observer, after sustaining AAA damage.

French aircraft-carriers joined their Royal Navy counterparts on 2 November, as tactical targets around Port Said, including Damietta road bridge, began to be attacked. One FAA Wyvern was lost as HMS *Albion* withdrew for re-supply. Meanwhile, the remaining RN carriers were still active, with No. 849 NAS Skyraider AEW.Mk 1s particularly busy flying patrols over the task force, together with Aéronavale TBM-3W2s from *La Fayette*.

Malta- and Cyprus-based RAF aircraft remained involved. These included Meteor FR.Mk 9s of No. 208 Sqn on Malta – maintained on readiness, and making a number of intercepts – and No. 39 Sqn Meteor NF.Mk 13s, tasked with the defence of Cyprus. Additionally, Malta-based Shackleton MR.Mk 2s of No. 37 Sqn provided convoy cover, and were briefly flown from Libya. French aircraft flying from Malta

and Cyprus included PB4Y-2s of 28F, and F-84F and RF-84F tactical aircraft at Akrotiri. In Jordan, RAF units flew Venom FB.Mk 4s on close-support missions, as well as a detachment of Hunter F.Mk 5s, and No.13 Sqn Canberra PR.Mk 7s.

Final phase

Activities on behalf of the Allies continued. On 4 November No. 8 Sqn lost a Venom, and HMS *Eagle* left the theatre for refuelling. Action was centred around Port Said, prior to the airborne assault planned for the following day.

The final phase of operations began on the morning of 5 November, as 600 British troops of the 3rd Batallion the Parachute Regiment were para-dropped in a bid to gain control of Egyptian territory.

From their base at Nicosia, the troops had been transported to the Suez zone by Nos 30, 84 and 114 Sqn Valettas, and Nos 70, 99 and 511 Sqn Hastings. The target for 3 Para was Gamil airfield, west of Port Said, marked with flares by a No. 115 Sqn Canberra B.Mk 2. Despite some resistance, the operation was a success.

A second drop by Hastings and Valettas provided the invasion force with reinforcements, and this was followed by over 200 deck landings on HMS *Ocean* by Whirlwinds and Sycamores. Under the protection of FAA 'cab-rank' patrols, the troops made good progress, with over 400 FAA sorties flown in support of the ground forces. Five hundred French troops were dropped to the east of Port Said by ET 61 and ET 63 Noratlases and C-47s, with support from 14F and 15F F4U-7s. The French made progress, with Allied airborne troops effectively surrounding Port Said by nightfall. On this day, following increasing international pressure for an end to the conflict, and intervention from the USSR and the US, a cease-fire was called from 0200 hours on 7 November local time, by which time the leading invasion units were at El Cap, just north of Quantara.

Suez Crisis: ground-attack missions

Hawker Hunter F.Mk 5
The Hunter should, perhaps, have proven the most capable ground-attack asset in the Suez theatre. However, the aircraft's drop tanks had been damaged during firing-practice, limiting their time over the target to just 10 minutes and relegating them to a defensive role. This aircraft flew from Nicosia with No. 34 Squadron, RAF.

Westland Wyvern S.Mk 4
The Wyvern S.Mk 4s of No. 830 NAS were flown from the carrier HMS *Eagle*, on ground-attack missions; these included strikes on the coastal barracks between Gamil and Port Said, and Dekheila airfield. One aircraft was lost to ground fire while attacking the Damietta road bridge, the pilot being rescued by the Whirlwind HAS.Mk 3 planeguard of HMS *Eagle*.

Following Turkey's invasion of northern Cyprus, No. 84 Squadron's Westland Whirlwinds supported UN forces stationed between the Greek and Turkish front lines. The squadron re-equipped with Wessexes in 1981.

Britain in the Middle East

Emerging from World War II as the dominant power in Arabia, Britain was to oversee momentous events during the following 25 years, including the birth of the Arab states, the blocking of Soviet ambitions and the creation of the state of Israel.

During World War II the RAF's Desert Air Force played a crucial role in the defeat of Rommel's Afrika Korps, and then supported the Eighth Army in its drive through Italy. After the war, RAF units returned to the area and resumed the kind of colonial policing roles undertaken between the wars. The first problem faced by the British in the Middle East, following the end of the war, was the deteriorating situation in Palestine, which Britain had administered under a League of Nations Mandate since the 1920s. Massive illegal immigration by displaced Jews, along with terrorism by Jewish extremists, had to be countered until the end of the Mandate in May 1948, when Britain withdrew and the Jews and Arabs went to war, each unhappy with the partition which divided Palestine into separate Jewish and Arab states. The RAF (with massive forces stationed in the Canal Zone in neighbouring Egypt) became involved in this war by accident, when four unarmed Spitfires, flying a tactical reconnaissance mission along Egypt's ill-defined border, were shot down by Israeli Spitfires and ground fire. The following day, a Tempest involved in the search and rescue operation was also shot down. Fortunately, only one pilot was killed.

Britain, which already had links with the Sultanate of Oman going back more than 150 years, signed a new friendship treaty in December 1951. Oman called for help in late 1952, when a group of Saudis occupied an important strategic village at an oasis on the Omani-Abu Dhabi border. The RAF flew intimidatory low-level sorties over the area, then policed a blockade of routes to the oasis, eventually supporting Omani troops who moved in to expel the Saudis in July 1954. Although this problem was solved without a shot being fired, the Saudi-supported Omani Liberation Army (formed by the Imam Ghalib from rebellious tribesmen) proved a tougher nut to crack.

The Imam was captured when British troops attacked his stronghold at Nizwa, but his brother, Talib, escaped and continued the rebellion. In 1957, Venoms from Nos 8 and 249 Squadrons attacked rebel strongholds (after Shackletons had dropped warning leaflets), and in January 1959 supported an SAS assault on the Jebel Akhdar. Unfortunately, Talib escaped, but the rebellion was over.

The Canal Zone initially provided a safe home for British reserves which could be deployed elsewhere in the area as required but, as opposition to the British presence intensified, the position of the Canal Zone bases became steadily more untenable. Units moved to bases in Cyprus, Jordan and Iraq. The MEAF (Middle East Air Force) re-formed in Cyprus in December 1954, and the last flying unit had left Egypt in October 1955. The Arab nationalism which prompted this withdrawal was later to force withdrawals from Iraq and Jordan, and eventually resulted in the Anglo-French invasion in 1956 – the Suez crisis.

Problems in Cyprus

Although Cyprus replaced the Canal Zone as Britain's main base in the area, it proved just as troublesome. A Crown Colony since 1925, Cyprus had a Greek majority who wished for union with Greece (Enosis), against the wishes of the substantial Turkish

Maritime reconnaissance of the region from 1957-67 was the responsibility of No. 37 Squadron, which operated Shackleton MR.Mk 2s from Khormaksar in Aden.

Jet-powered colonial policing

During the British withdrawal from the Middle East, extensive use was made of air power, demonstrating a British presence, controlling insurgent and resistance groups

and retaliating against attacks. Fighter-bombers such as Vampires, Venoms and Hunters provided the firepower, with aircraft such as the Meteor providing reconnaissance.

Venom FB.Mk 4
From 1946, No. 8 Squadron was based at Khormaksar in Aden and operated Venom FB.Mk 4s from 1955-60. The squadron badge, depicting a sheathed Arabian dagger, symbolises the squadron's long service in southwest Arabia.

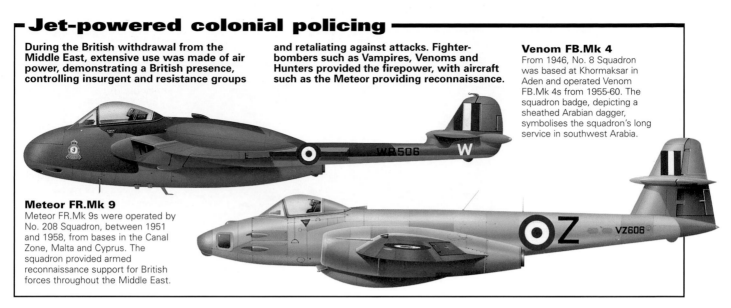

Meteor FR.Mk 9
Meteor FR.Mk 9s were operated by No. 208 Squadron, between 1951 and 1958, from bases in the Canal Zone, Malta and Cyprus. The squadron provided armed reconnaissance support for British forces throughout the Middle East.

minority. From April 1955 to February 1959, Britain was forced to fight a vigorous anti-terrorist campaign against National Organisation of Cypriot Fighters (EOKA) terrorists, using Shackletons to prevent arms shipments from the mainland, Austers, Pioneers and Chipmunks for reconnaissance, and helicopters (principally Sycamores) in search-and-destroy missions.

Growing opposition to the British presence in Iraq led to a 1955 agreement to withdraw and hand over the RAF stations at Habbaniyah and Shaibah, retaining facilities at the former as a staging post. Withdrawal of based aircraft was completed in April 1956, and when RAF aircraft were prevented from using Habbaniyah following the July 1958 coup and assassination of the pro-British king, remaining personnel were withdrawn.

A similar situation arose in Jordan, where the ill-considered Suez operation forced the king to rescind the 1948 treaty with Britain. The single fighter-bomber squadron at Amman withdrew to Cyprus in January 1957. The breakdown in relations with Jordan was short-lived and British forces returned briefly in July 1958, when growing instability in neighbouring Lebanon threatened the stability of the Hashemite kingdom itself.

Relations with Iraq remained strained and, in 1961, matters worsened when Iraq appeared to challenge the independence of Kuwait, with whom Britain had a longstanding (since 1899) treaty. Britain (by now a major customer for Kuwaiti oil) renewed its pledge to defend the country's independence in June 1961, prompting an angry Iraq to move troops to the Kuwaiti border. Kuwait formally requested British assistance on

30 June, and Britain flew No. 45 Commando, Royal Marines, and the Hunters of Nos 8 and 208 Squadrons into Kuwait, where they were later reinforced by a parachute battalion and by Canberras from Cyprus and Germany. An Iraqi invasion was deterred, and Britain was able to withdraw its forces.

With the changing centre of gravity of British forces in the area, the former Middle East Command was renamed Near East Command in March 1961, with its air element becoming the Near East Air Force (NEAF) instead of the Middle East Air Force. Both were headquartered in Cyprus, which steadily gained in importance as forces elsewhere withdrew (most notably in Aden and the Persian Gulf).

Yemeni campaign

A coup and change of regime in the Yemen led to an increase in propaganda and incursions mounted against the British in Aden. This port had gained in importance as the home for a strategic reserve covering East Africa, the Horn of Africa and the western part of Arabia, but Britain had announced its intention to withdraw from Aden by 1968. The Yemeni campaign against Aden was two-pronged, with support for subversion and terrorism in Aden itself, and with

similar support for dissident tribesmen who undertook their traditional activities of raiding caravans in the north of Aden, the Radfan. Successive operations (commencing in January 1964, with 'Nutcracker') by fighter-bombers and heliborne troops and artillery eventually resulted in the capture of the last rebel point, the Jebel Huriyah, on 10 June 1964.

It was less easy to solve the problem of terrorism in the city of Aden, and difficult even to contain it. Helicopters were used to transport troops rapidly to deal with incidents, while Twin Pioneers performed recon-naissance and leaflet-dropping missions. With little reason to remain, and in the face of worsening opposition, the British pulled out in late 1967, with some units relocating to the Gulf.

After the ignominious withdrawal from Aden, the departure of RAF units from the Gulf was altogether more dignified. With the Gulf States able to take over the burden of their own defence (having been trained to do so by the British), the RAF was able to withdraw its two Hunter squadrons from Muharraq, and its Andovers and Wessexes from Sharjah during 1971. The two airfields closed as RAF bases in December.

The Turkish invasion of northern Cyprus brought based

aircraft to a high state of readiness, but Turkish fighters and fighter-bombers avoided threatening the British Sovereign Base areas and the RAF remained on the sidelines. The invasion made training difficult for based units, and a government decision to end the declaration of forces to CENTO led to a mass withdrawal of the remaining units. The NEAF was disbanded and replaced by Air Headquarters (AHQ) Cyprus within RAF Strike Command.

Mid-1976 saw only a single RAF squadron (No. 84) permanently based in the area, whose Whirlwinds performed search and rescue and UN support missions in Cyprus. An Army Air Corps flight with Alouette IIs also flew similar missions after the main withdrawal.

Closer to home, the RAF withdrew from its other Mediterranean base on Malta. No. 203 Squadron disbanded in December 1977, its Nimrods returning to UK-based squadrons. No. 13 Squadron brought its Canberra PR.Mk 7s to RAF Wyton the following year, and the RAF withdrawal was completed in 1979. On Cyprus, the RAF maintained its base at Akrotiri, which was used regularly as a destination for training flights and armament practice.

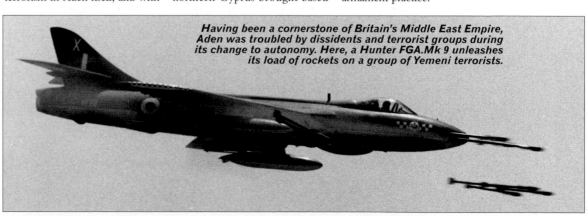

Having been a cornerstone of Britain's Middle East Empire, Aden was troubled by dissidents and terrorist groups during its change to autonomy. Here, a Hunter FGA.Mk 9 unleashes its load of rockets on a group of Yemeni terrorists.

Hawker Hunter

The Hawker Hunter is undoubtedly one of the world's all-time great fighters. Superb handling won it the love of those lucky enough to fly it, while its graceful lines won it a wider circle of admirers.

Above: More than 40 years after entering RAF service, Britain was still operating the Hunter in the form of the T.Mk 7 used by the Empire Test Pilot's School at Boscombe Down. This particular aircraft was lost in an accident in 1998.

Designed by Sidney Camm and his talented team at Hawker – many of whom had previously worked on aircraft such as the Fury, Hurricane, Typhoon, Tempest and Sea Hawk – the Hunter was one of the UK's first swept-wing interceptors. Although the Hunter briefly held the world speed record, it was never at the cutting edge of fighter design, and was actually less advanced, in certain minor respects, than some of the swept-wing fighters from the US which preceded it, including the F-86 Sabre.

Teething problems

On entering service, the first variant of the Hunter was in many ways a disappointment. Limited internal fuel capacity gave the aircraft a tiny radius of action – it was possible to run the tanks dry in 11 minutes at full throttle and very low level. Moreover, the early Rolls-Royce Avon engines powering the Mk 1 suffered from surging problems, especially when the guns were fired at high altitudes.

However, these difficulties proved to be little more than teething problems, and with the advent of the F.Mk 4 (and especially the 'big-bore' F.Mk 6) the Hunter became a highly effective tactical fighter, especially in the air-to-ground role. Development of the Hunter reached its apogee with the RAF's FGA.Mk 9 (and a number of similar export derivatives). These aircraft combined excellent performance with a heavy warload, yet retained the Hunter's traditionally superb handling characteristics.

The Hunter proved extremely popular with export customers, and its modular construction made refurbishing even the oldest aircraft a viable proposition. Aircraft relegated to ground instructional duties were sold back to Hawker Siddeley which rebuilt them for extended service with new operators. Sales of refurbished, 'second-hand' Hunters made the aircraft one of the most successful products of Britain's aircraft industry in the post-war period.

Above: The Hunter F.Mk 6 single-seat fighter became a favourite formation aerobatic mount for a number of Royal Air Force squadrons (such as No. 111 Squadron's Black Arrows) during the 1950s and 1960s. Here the No. 92 Squadron Blue Diamonds display team of 1963 practises its routine.

Left: A total of 47 Hunters was acquired by the Singapore air force in both single-and two-seat variants. These three single-seat F.Mk 74Bs were operated by No. 140 Squadron in the mid-1980s. Both the F.Mk 74s and the two-seat T.Mk 75s continued in service until the early 1990s.

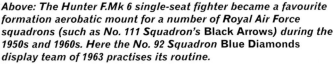

Above: Seen during trial flights in July 1955, this Hunter F.Mk 50 was the first production example for the Swedish air force. Based on the F.Mk 4, this variant lacked the dogtooth wing leading edge.

Right: Among many Middle East customers for the Hunter was Kuwait, which received six single-seat FGA.Mk 57s and five T.Mk 67 two-seat trainers.

But while the Hunter won fame as a superb ground-attack weapon, the aircraft was also a useful air combat trainer, with the powerful Avon engine giving good acceleration and the big wing allowing a surprisingly good rate of turn, especially in conjunction with combat flap. The Hunter also packed an impressive punch with its highly concentrated battery of four 30-mm cannon.

Indian Hunters racked up an impressive combat record (contrary to the claims of the Pakistanis and their apologists), proving superior to the Sabre and F-104 in close-in engagements. In Arab hands Hunters proved to be among the toughest opposition encountered by Israeli pilots. In two Middle Eastern wars Jordanian and Iraqi Hunters scored combat victories against Israeli fighters, including the IDF/AF's much vaunted and Mach 2-capable Mirage III.

Missile capable

Air combat capability was dramatically enhanced by the addition of AIM-9 Sidewinders in Swiss, Singapore, Omani and Chilean service, but missile-armed Hunters never saw combat.

Hunters were finally withdrawn from front-line RAF service in the early 1970s, but then went on to serve with great distinction in the advanced and tactical fighter weapons training roles. Elsewhere, Hunters remained in front-line service into the 1990s, and a handful remained active in Zimbabwe as late as 1997.

A handful of air arms still operated the Hunter in second-line duties into the 21st century. The type long remained a fixture with the Empire Test Pilot's School, being prized for its ability to undertake deliberate inverted spinning, the only swept-wing aircraft cleared to do so.

A growing number of Hunters are being restored to flying condition as civilian-owned 'warbirds', and the distinctive note of the Hunter's Avon engine will remain a common sound for many years to come.

From the second batch of refurbished Hunter F.Mk 58As delivered to Switzerland in 1974-75, this ex-RAF F.Mk 4 (WW590) is seen carrying two AIM-9 Sidewinder missiles for the air-to-air role.

Confronting the Mau Mau

Above: Vampire FB.Mk 9s were detached from No. 8 Sqn, RAF in April 1954; usually based at Khormaksar, Aden, they flew from Eastleigh on ground-attack missions. Tasks included the support of Operation Anvil.

Left: Over Kenya, the Lincoln B.Mk 2 was found to be a suitable platform for bombing terrorist camps and supply dumps. This aircraft was detached from No. 61 Sqn, based at Hemswell.

A thorn in the side of British colonialism in Africa between 1952 and 1959, the Mau Mau terrorist group fought for Kenyan independence. In October 1952 a state of emergency was declared in Kenya.

During World War II, Kenyans had fought for Britain, but returned to their nation still disenfranchised. In colonial Kenya, a British crown colony since 1920, and the jewel in the crown of the British empire in Africa, European settlers lived in prosperity, while their black neighbours remained subjugated, and deprived of the lands they now saw as their own.

Following the war, the Kenya African Union (KAU) was formed, and this in turn spawned the more radical Mau Mau group. A growing population led to job shortages, and meant that the native Africans were working on increasingly less advantageous terms for the European farmers. Since 1948, Britain had faced labour unrest from African workers, fostered by factions within the Kikuyu tribe, which was beginning to gain back the land it had earlier lost to the European settlers. Between 1948 and 1949, the RAF had been involved in leaflet-dropping in order to stem the discontent among the indigenous labour force.

Tribal violence

Long-standing nationalist, British-educated Jomo Kenyatta, President of the KAU (and later Kenya's first president), was arrested by British troops on trumped-up charges of inciting Mau Mau terrorism, but his removal failed to end the rebellion. In October 1952 a state of emergency was declared as violence broke out among the Kikuyu, with attacks on white farmers and the murder of British ally, Chief Waruhiu. In response, troops from the 1st Batallion Lancashire Fusiliers were flown into Nairobi on 21 October aboard No. 511 Sqn Hastings transports, joining four batallions of the King's African Rifles and the Kenya regiment already in the country.

Operation Jock Scot saw the rounding-up and internment of supposed Mau Mau leaders, with the region north of Nairobi designated an operational area, containing two prohibited tracts – security forces could deem anyone found within these areas to be a terrorist. Dense patches of jungle, seen as the haunt of the Mau Mau, were also made exclusion zones, with the result that any black seen in Kenya's forests risked being shot or captured. Army commanders were also known to offer their troops bounty money for dead Mau Mau. Without their leaders, the Mau Mau remained inactive until January 1953, when white farmers again began to be killed. White settlers stormed Government House in Nairobi, demanding action be taken.

RAF strength in the region comprised only two No. 82 Sqn Dakota Mk IIIs and four other types operational with the Eastleigh Communications Flight. In order to improve the British position, ex-Rhodesian Air Training Group Harvard Mk IIBs formed 1340 Flt at Thornhill, before moving to Eastleigh on 23 March 1953, where bombing operations commenced immediately. Armed with 20-lb (9-kg) fragmentation bombs and light machine-guns, the Harvards proved to be reliable ground-attack and counter-insurgency aircraft. They were principally employed in raids upon Mau Mau forces that had been forced to retreat into more isolated areas after pressure from the British Army. Aiding early RAF anti-Mau Mau operations, the Kenya Police Reserve Air Wing (KPRAW), flying a handful of Austers, Cessna 180s, Piper Pacers and Tri-Pacers, was involved in the search for signs of the elusive enemy, as well as missions in support of the local police and army outposts, often dropping supplies to search parties at pre-arranged dropping zones.

Lari massacre

On 26 March 1953, 84 local Kikuyu people were massacred at Lari, outside Nairobi, by the Mau Mau. Although the Mau Mau originated from the Kikuyu, they were as ruthless

Eastleigh-based No. 82 Sqn Lancaster PR.Mk 1s were tasked with photo-reconnaissance duties, as were the Dakota Mk IIIs of the same unit. The aircraft served over Kenya between July and November 1952.

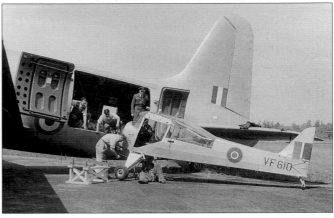

Below: The Auster AOP.Mk 6 (seen here being readied for carriage by a No. 511 Sqn Hastings transport) was fitted with loudspeakers for post-bombing psychological warfare sorties.

Above: Poorly equipped and lightly armed, the secretive Mau Mau, a Kikuyu rebel group, had no power to deal with air attack. The rebels suffered losses of nearly 11,000 during the emergency.

towards their own 'disloyal' tribespeople as they were to Europeans. Chief Luka of Lari was known to the Mau Mau as a British sympathiser.

In reaction, the military commander called for more troops from Britain – a further two batallions were flown in on 7 June, and a separate East Africa Command was established. 1340 Flt and the KPRAW relocated to Nyeri, later Mweiga, in order to co-ordinate bombing in support of ground forces, and security forces stepped up operations in the exclusion zones. The local KPRAW pilots provided vital information on the surrounding terrain for the Harvard pilots; indeed, the KPRAW CO was given tactical command under the RAF Commander of Air Forces.

The Kenyan crisis deepened during the summer of 1953, as the Mau Mau developed an urban infrastructure to support their mountain- and jungle-based rebels. Local opposition and British allegiances were extinguished as the Mau Mau attacked local Kikuyu populations. A further brigade HQ and two more batallions flew out to Kenya on 29 September 1953, on 41 Hastings and civilian charter flights. In the same month, the RAF's Harvards flew 332 sorties, dropping 2,555 bombs, but failing to pinpoint the small Mau Mau groups in isolated mountain hide-outs.

From November, RAF Lincoln B.Mk II heavy bombers were rotated into Eastleigh (from Bomber Command Squadron Nos 13, 21, 49, 61, 100 and 214) in order to wipe out terrorist camps with pattern bombing. Flying early-morning missions in order to avoid low cloud, the Lincolns carried five 1,000-lb (454-kg) bombs and nine 500-lb (227-kg) bombs, or alternatively 350-lb (159-kg) cluster bombs. Directed by the KPRAW, and with fuses set at 25 seconds, the low altitude (around 900 ft/ 274 m) from which the bombs were usually dropped made for hair-raising missions. On 14 August a No. 214 Sqn Lincoln bombing a Mau Mau concentration near Nyeri was struck, after the first device to detonate on the ground sent shock waves up the succeeding stick of bombs, damaging the aircraft and killing the flight engineer. Six Lincolns were maintained at Eastleigh at any one time, and aircraft were rotated from Bomber Command squadrons in turn.

Psy-war operations

In order to promote confusion among the indigenous population, and encourage the surrender of the Mau Mau, two Auster AOP.Mk 6s and a single Pembroke C.Mk 1 were equipped with loud-speakers. A single Sycamore HR.Mk 14 SAR helicopter was also based

at Eastleigh, in order to pick up casualties from the difficult Kenyan terrain. The latter flew a total of 506 hours, evacuating 30 casualties.

In order to sever the links and supply routes between the in-country Mau Mau and their urban support, Operation Anvil between 24 April and 7 May 1954 detained 16,538 suspects in raids around Nairobi, with air support from Vampire FB.Mk 9s of No. 8 Sqn.

Photo-reconnaissance

Addressing the problem of a lack of information on the whereabouts of the Mau Mau, and in order to provide post-strike analysis, two No. 13 Sqn Meteor PR.Mk 10 photo-reconnaissance aircraft were detached from Fayid, Egypt, to Eastleigh. By the end of 1954, the Mau Mau had been seriously weakened, and more than 80,000 Kikuyu had been detained in camps, without charge or trial. Operation Hammer in the Aberdare mountains and Operation First Flute (Mount Kenya) resulted in 161 and 277 Mau Mau dead, in January and February 1955, respectively. Defeated by the cross-country Lincoln sweeps, the Mau Mau continued to be harangued by the Lincoln until July 1955 (when the last such aircraft returned home) and by the Harvards of 1340 Flt, operational in the region until the end of September 1955.

During the Kenyan emergency, 1340 Flt dropped some 21,936 20-lb (9-kg) anti-personnel bombs, losing eight aircraft out of its complement of 19 in the process.

Withdrawal

On 17 November 1956 the British Army withdrew from Kenya, and the operational phase formally ended in December. By that date, according to official estimates, 10,527 Mau Mau had been killed and 2,633 captured. The security forces had lost 602, of whom 534 were Africans. The British government put the cost of the operation at a staggering £55,585,424.

Although the British operations in Kenya had halted terrorism against both the regular Kikuyu and Europeans living in Kenya, the emergency was seen more widely as the beginning of the end of British-style colonialism in Africa. The Mau Mau uprising revealed both the inadequacy of colonial political structures, and the brutality exercised by the British forces within the borders of their own empire. White police were responsible for public hangings and the bloody massacre of political prisoners at the Hola detention camp on 3 March 1959. Eight years after the cessation of violence, Kenya was to become independent from the British Common-wealth, and finally, in 1965, a republic.

Built by Avro in Manchester in late 1945, this Lincoln B.Mk 2 undertook Rolls-Royce engine development at Hucknall and served with No. 7 Sqn in the late 1940s, followed by Nos 49, 148 and 149 Sqns during the early 1950s. It then joined No. 214 Sqn, operating over Kenya.

Algeria 1954–1962

228340

A relic of World War II, the Republic F-47D Thunderbolt was operated in the air defence role before being replaced by the Mistral. It was then tasked with close-support duties, enjoying mixed success against the rebels. This example wears the markings of EC 20 'Lorraine'.

Coming within months of its humiliating defeat by the Viet Minh in Indochina, France was shaken to the core by the rebellion in Algeria. The north African state was considered more a region of France than a fully autonomous nation, and the eight-year fight for independence had far-reaching consequences that are still being felt today.

When the Algerian war of independence broke out in 1954 in the Aurès mountains, it hardly seemed likely that the numerous and technologically advanced French forces would be unable to suppress the ill-organised resistance of the various factions that made up the Front de Libération Nationale (FLN) and its military wing, the Armée de Libération Nationale (ALN). However, the ideology of these insurgents was bedrocked in Algerian nationalism and they were led by the inspirational Ahmed Ben Bella. The spark that lit their revolutionary fire was the refusal by France to grant the same concessions to indigenous nationalism that had been made in Morocco and Tunisia.

As in Indochina, the armed Algerian nationalists possessed no air arm but, having intimate familiarity with local terrain, preferred to conduct guerrilla warfare. Despite the commitment of almost one million troops against them, they proved not only highly proficient but eventually persuaded France that, once again, no military solution was attainable. In 1962, despite everything that sophisticated

Probably the most important transport aircraft flying re-supply missions to French forces in Algeria was the Nord 2501 Noratlas. Some 426 were built, in France and Germany, and the type was widely exported. It equipped two escadres de transports, with three escadrons being based in North Africa.

weaponry could achieve, Algeria won its independence.

At the beginning of the war, in November 1954, the French air force in Algeria comprised a squadron of SE.535 Mistral jet interceptors and a training squadron flying aging F-47 Thunderbolts, as well as a hotchpotch of obsolete second-line aircraft and trainers. None of these aircraft was in any way suitable for operations in the desert against fleet-footed, mobile guerilla forces, whose tactics were based on lightning strike and instant dispersals.

Dedicated COIN

As a matter of expediency, therefore, the local French commanders ordered a host of light aircraft and trainers into operational use, hurriedly modified with machine-guns and light bomb racks. Quite fortuitously, they had hit upon an ideal counter-insurgency weapon and one that was to sire a whole new operational philosophy employing dedicated

Piasecki-Vertol H-21s were used by both the Aéronavale and the Aviation Légère de l'Armée de Terre in Algeria. This H-21C wears the markings of GH-2, which was based at Sétif in early 1962.

COIN aircraft. Such aircraft as the North American T-6 Texan became synonymous with the worldwide problem of mounting anti-guerilla operations.

Thus in 1955, as the regular squadrons of conventional fighters retained their normal air defence tasks, the first escadrilles d'aviation légère d'appui (EALA, or light support squadrons), equipped with Morane-Saulnier MS.500s and 733s, became operational. The following year they were joined by a groupe, GALA 72, of four escadrilles with T-6 Texans, and three of Sipa S.111s and 112s (the latter distributed between Tunisia, Morocco and Algeria).

More significant was the introduction of the Max Holste Broussard, the first aircraft formally customised for the COIN role and capable of lifting small numbers of troops to remote areas of local trouble. Following de Gaulle's resumption of command of the state in 1958, General Maurice Challe was given the task of crushing the Algerian rebellion and undertook a complete overhaul and reorganisation of the air force. One of his first priorities was to replace the excellent, but aged, T-6s which had hitherto flown the majority of operations against rebel forces. An adaptation of the

North American T-6Gs played an important light-attack role during France's involvement in Algeria. Some 700 examples equipped 28 squadrons, with a peak total of 21 squadrons active within Groupe d'Aviation Légère d'Appui 72. The T-6Gs were armed with two 0.3-in (7.5-mm) gun pods, napalm, 22-lb (10-kg) bombs or rockets.

T-28 Trojan, itself a modern derivative of the T-6, was selected (being named Fennec in French service).

Helicopters in support

A major weapon in the COIN arsenal was the helicopter, the Armée de l'Air having formed its first light helicopter squadron in Algeria in 1955 with Bell 47Gs and Sikorsky H-19s (S-55s). Pioneer operations by this escadrille had quickly demonstrated the flexibility of the helicopter, as much for casualty evacuation as for delivery of troops into combat, and by the end of 1956 the 12-man Sikorsky H-34 was in service in the assault role. Within a year, the French forces

in Algeria possessed a total of 250 helicopters, of which the army flew 142, the Armée de l'Air 90 and the Aéronavale 18. In due course the French gave some of their helicopters a 'ground-attack' capability by mounting guns of 0.3-in, 0.5-in and 0.8-in (7.5-mm, 12.7-mm and 20-mm respectively) calibre, as well as rockets. Among the army helicopters were such troop-carrying aircraft as the Vertol-Piasecki H-21.

Increased commitment

As the war dragged on, and the rebel forces (far from acknowledging defeat) stepped up their operations, so the French brought greater pressure to bear in Algeria, not least in the air. Two medium-attack bomber groups were deployed to Algeria, together with a growing number of ex-US Navy AD-4 Skyraiders (of which France had ordered 113 from the USA in 1956).

The latter proved to be highly effective COIN aircraft, capable of delivering a very heavy punch in the ground

attack role and suppressing ground opposition during helicopter assaults.

Effective as Challe's 'steamroller' campaign was – forcing the rebels to revert to isolated guerilla tactics by the end of 1960 – the mounting cost of the war and the depredations imposed on French society by increasing terrorist activities in metropolitan France combined to sap the enthusiasm for an apparently fruitless continuation of the war. In 1962 de Gaulle was forced to accept terms for Algerian independence.

Whatever the war in Algeria demonstrated, in military terms it illustrated the impotence of a conventional air force, equipped and organised for air defence, when it tried to operate in an environment of concerted guerrilla warfare. The lessons were there for the US to digest when, just two years later, it faced a similar threat in Vietnam. Ironically, it took 10 years for the United States to arrive at no less a humiliating political defeat than that suffered by the French in Algeria.

Left: A type almost forgotten today, the Sipa S.12A was the French derivative of the wartime Arado Ar 396. The S.12A, S.121A and variants, with rocket/bomb racks, equipped many GALAs. Note that this example has nosed over on soft sand – a common problem.

Below: A white cabin top and upper centre section were added to the Broussards in Algeria to reduce cabin and fuel-tank temperatures. The type performed liaison and observation duties, supporting aircraft like the MS.500.

The Armée de l'Air used a variety of aircraft types for observation and light reconnaissance duties. Aircraft such as this MS.500 played a vital role in Algeria, helping ground forces to react quickly to incursions and terrorist incidents, and helping to patrol Algeria's least populated areas.

To see Swedish warplanes in action outside Swedish airspace is an extremely rare occurrence, but the Congo emergency of the 1960s saw Saab J 29 fighters flying support missions for UN troops on the ground.

Central Africa

Belgium had for many years adopted a much more exploitative attitude to Africa than other European colonial powers. While many nations quickly acceded to the demands for self-determination in their territories, Belgium at first attempted to hold on to its gains. It later changed its mind, but the Congo was already on the path to civil war.

Flygflottij 22 was a volunteer unit, flying both fighter-bomber and reconnaissance versions of the barrel-like J 29. The photo-ships wore camouflage, while the standard combat aircraft had an overall natural metal finish.

For centuries a handful of European nations had colonised and exploited the raw human and land resources of Africa. Ancient borders and territories were ignored and new countries created. However, the post-war world didn't care for ageing empires and as the 'winds of change' blew through the African continent, resentment against the imperialist forces intensified and the cries for independence grew louder. Nearly 40 colonies were to gain nationhood in two decades, but the process was slow and bloody, resulting in the deaths of thousands and the after-effects are still felt today.

It was to be in the Belgian Congo where one of the first and most serious of the independence movements was to take place. During the 1950s, native peoples in British and French territories had started campaigning for self-determination, but Belgium hoped to prevent such demands spreading to the Congo. It quickly became obvious that such hopes would be in vain, and Belgium reversed its policy overnight and offered immediate political independence in 1960. Civil war of a tribalist nature broke out almost immediately, and continued intermittently for seven years. During this period, numerous acts of atrocity were carried out against Belgian nationals who had chosen to remain in the former colony.

The immediate threat to a peaceful transition to independence was posed when Moise Tshombe led a movement for the separation of the Katanga region from Kinshasa. When the United Nations charter was invoked to provide a peace-keeping force, there were immediate difficulties in selecting forces from member nations that had no colonialist connotations and were thus acceptable in an area seething with violently anti-imperialist hatred.

In due course Sweden, Canada, India and Ethiopia contributed air force elements, of which Sweden's Flygflottij 22 Voluntary Air Component with Saab J 29s proved the most significant part, together with a number of de Havilland Canada Otters and de Havilland Canada Beavers; ground crews were also provided by Norway and Denmark. A particularly remarkable aspect of F22's contribution was the fact that the Swedish air force was not equipped, organised or trained for prolonged operations overseas, yet served with ONUC (Organisation Nations-Unies au Congo) from 1961 until 1963; moreover, when called on to fly operations, the unit maintained a consistent 90 per cent serviceability rate.

The establishment of an armed UN presence in the Congo called for forces from non-aligned countries, calculated to be seen as less likely to be partisan in the vicious civil struggle. India, Ethiopia, Italy and Sweden sent combat aircraft to provide air support for UN forces as they began to take a more active role in the ground fighting, and they soon began flying missions against the Katangan separatists. India's B(I).Mk 58 Canberras were operated in the night intruder role.

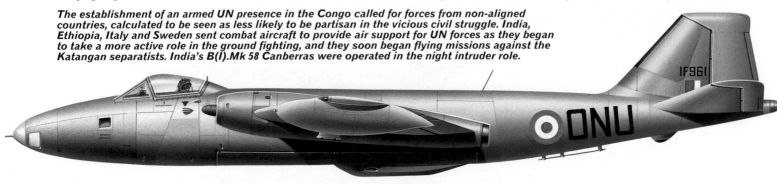

Swedish J 29s in action

Based in turn at Luluabourg and Kamina, the nine J 29Bs and two J 29C reconnaissance versions undertook numerous gun and rocket attacks and reconnaissance sorties, often in company with Indian air force Canberras. The Swedes' most significant operations were the surprise attacks from December 1962-January 1963 against the base at Kolwezi, where almost the entire Katangese air strength was eliminated by the J 29s. The precision of this series of attacks had such a profound psychological effect upon the white mercenaries of the Katangese air force that many promptly defected and escaped to Angola.

Katanga revisited

The Republic of Zaïre, as the former Belgian Congo became, was not to have an easy existence. In March 1977 President Mobutu declared a state of national emergency when foreign mercenaries invaded the southern province of Shaba, with the intention of supporting the establishment of an independent state of Katanga. France and Morocco answered his appeal for military assistance and, in Operation Verveine, 12 Armée de l'Air Transall C.160 transports airlifted 1,500 Moroccan troops to the air base at Kolwezi. With the addition of limited military aid from the

Zaïre's MB.326 trainers should have been of some advantage in the counter-insurgency fighting that has erupted in the last two decades, but poor standards of maintenance and training meant that they never played a major part in the final struggle for the country.

Supporting the Swedish fighters was a contingent of six Indian Canberra bombers. The B(I).Mk 58s were kept busy attacking Katangan targets in the capital Elisabethville on a nightly basis.

United States, and after increased efforts by Mirage IIIs and Aermacchi MB.326s of the Force Aérienne Zaïroise, the initial invasion was repulsed. A second invasion in May 1978 was better supported by air defence weapons, however, and only after about 10 FAZ aircraft had been lost (including six MB.326s) was this attack defeated with the help of French and Belgian paratroops.

Great Lake wars

One area which has seen more than its fair share of warfare in the last two decades has been around the great lakes of central Africa. Idi Amin's Uganda was a brutal dictatorship which was

eventually overthrown by tribal rebels. Although Amin had received a number of MiGs from Warsaw Pact countries, they played little part in the war, which was largely fought out on the ground. Amin's successor, Milton Obote, was in turn overthrown. Further south, Rwanda and Burundi have long been on the brink of (and sometimes plunged into) bitter tribal violence between the majority Hutus and formerly dominant Tutsis. Massacres in the 1970s and 1980s were made to seem as nothing in the 1990s as the tribal communities in each country tore each other apart. Once again, air power played little part in the fighting, although it was the death of the president of Rwanda in an air crash in Burundi which was to spark the worst violence. Air power was, however, vital in transporting relief supplies to the millions of people fleeing the

horrors which had overwhelmed their homes.

Mobutu's fall

The violence in Rwanda and Burundi spilled over into Zaïre, where the ailing President Mobutu's long-time grip on power was starting to slacken. Guerrilla forces under the control of Laurent Desiré Kabila advanced towards the capital, and the collapse of central government led to yet another evacuation by predominantly French and Belgian transport aircraft, with Europeans and Americans being airlifted to safety. European paratroopers were also called in to help keep order on the ground. British forces in the region included a Canberra PR.Mk 9 of 39 (1 PRU) Squadron. Mobutu fled to Morocco, where he died of cancer, while the new government re-named Zaïre – it is now the Democratic Republic of Congo.

A Canberra PR.Mk 9 taxis in at Entebbe after an Operation Purposeful mission over Rwanda. The aim of the RAF deployment was to track down thousands of 'missing' Rwandan refugees believed to be in the jungles of western Zaïre. In the course of 21 missions between 20 November and 19 December 1996, the Canberra found 300,000 refugees. This information saved the UN from mounting a large-scale military peacekeeping effort.

Although Belgium was the major colonial power in central Africa, it is the French, whose imperial possessions tended to be further north, who have been most active in military rescues in the region. French forces have intervened at least 30 times since the 1960s, primarily with troops on the ground, but supported by Armée de l'Air logistics squadrons with aircraft such as this Transall C.160. On occasion, French paratroopers have made combat drops in the course of their duties, almost invariably from the cargo compartment of the C.160 transports.

Bush wars

By the early 1960s, Portugal's surviving colonial possessions in Africa began to reject Portuguese authority. The first armed rebellion emerged in Portuguese Guinea, followed by long-lasting uprisings in Angola and Mozambique.

The rebellion in Guinea broke out in August 1959 with the PAIGC (Partido Africano de Independencia da Guiné de Capo Verde). Only a handful of T-6 Texans of the FAP (Força Aérea Portugesa - Portuguese air force) were available to deal with the emergency, until supplemented by Republic F-84G Thunderjets in 1963.

FAP presence increased to match the rebel activity and in 1967, Esq. 121 'Tigres' with eight G91R-4s was set up at Bissalau. In May 1968 General Antonio de Spinola was appointed governor, and he ordered the deployment of 12 Alouette III helicopters, which were essential for operations in a country that was comprised largely of trackless jungle and swamp.

By 1970 the authorities had taken on a much tougher approach and the FAP was using napalm and defoliants. The PAIGC received limited air support from a number of diverse sources. Conakry-based Nigerian MiG-17s were used for reconnaissance flights, while Soviet-supplied Mi-4s carried out supply flights in the east of the country. Several FAP aircraft were lost to SA-7s and AAA fire: the PAIGC claimed to

have shot down 21 aircraft in seven years.

Guinea withdrawal

The PAIGC declared an independent republic in September 1973. Seven months later, the military seized power in Portugal in a nearly bloodless coup and established a provisional military government which installed Spinola as president. One of its first actions was to grant independence to Guinea-Bissau, on 10 September 1974.

While the situation in Portuguese Guinea was worsening, trouble flared up farther south in Angola. The actions of the Marxist Movimento Popular de Libertação de Angola (MPLA) forced the stationing of FAP C-47s and PV-2 Harpoons at Luanda to support the army. Several major towns soon came under MPLA siege and the small Portuguese army element in Mozambique was stretched to breaking point. A number of civilian aircraft, such as Piper Cubs, were pressed into service as light transports to resupply outlying settlements, while DC-3s and Beech 18s were used as makeshift bombers. These and the other FAP aircraft were joined in June 1961 by F-84Gs. A substantial paratroop-dropping

South Africa's Canberra bombers were used extensively in the post-colonial bush war the SADF fought in Namibia and in the southern reaches of Angola. The Canberra gave the SADF the ability to strike guerrilla bases deep in enemy territory.

effort was sustained, first by the C-47s and later by Noratlases, to relieve several towns under siege. Fighting continued, mostly in the north of the country.

Angola reinforced

Although Portugal was the subject of a US arms embargo due to its African conflicts, seven B-26s were sold to the FAP in 1965 to supplement the PV-2s. These helped to compensate for the F-84G losses, which stood

at five (mostly through accident rather than enemy action) and growing Soviet support for the MPLA.

Yet another guerrilla group materialised in 1966, when a breakaway MPLA group established itself as the Uniao Naçional de Independençia Total de Angola (UNITA), under the leadership of Jonas Savimbi.

FAP aircraft maintained constant attacks against the MPLA, which was advancing

Designed before World War II as a trainer, armed versions of the North American T-6 Texan saw extensive service in the colonial wars of the 1950s and 1960s. The T-6 proved to be a reliable and effective counter-insurgency (COIN) aircraft.

Bush fighters

Aeritalia (Fiat) G.91R/4
During its African combat career the 'Gina' proved to be a reliable and sturdy fighter-bomber and reconnaissance platform even under the most adverse of conditions. The FAP forward deployed its G.91s, refuelling and rearming its aircraft from bases as close to the operational areas as possible. On one occasion during the campaign in Portuguese Guinea, G.91s engaged MiG-17s from Guinea-Bissau, but inconclusively.

HS Buccaneer S.Mk 50
Sixteen Buccaneers were delivered to South Africa from 1966. Operated by No.24 Squadron, they had the range and payload to strike deep into Angola, attacking Guerrilla sites with 1,000-lb (450-kg) bombs and unguided rocket pods.

The Republic F-84G Thunderjet was one of the must numerous types to serve with the FAP. Some 70 of the type were used on ground attack and COIN duties in Angola.

inexorably westward towards the capital. The arrival of G91R-4s in 1972 (some coming from FAP units stationed in Mozambique) boosted the FAPs combat power. Helicopters also became an increasingly important part of operations.

However, the strain of fighting across Africa was proving too much for Portugal. The military coup in Lisbon heralded the end of Portugal's involvement in Angola, which was offered independence on 1 July 1974.

Mozambique
The third chapter of Portugal's African wars concerned Mozambique. Following the other colonies' struggle for independence, Mozambique saw the rise of Eduardo Mondlan's Frente de Libertação de Moçambique (FRELIMO) movement in 1962. Again, only small numbers of FAP C-47s and T-6s were on hand when serious trouble broke out in 1964. In a short space of time, 16,000 troops had arrived in the country and additional T-6s, eight PV-2s, twelve Do 27s and some Alouette IIIs were despatched to support them. FRELIMO operated from bases in Tanzania and later Zambia.

The FAP commitment to Mozambique became larger than that in either Guinea or Angola, though combat operations did not begin in earnest until 1968. Now under the command of Samora Machel (later to become president), FRELIMO began vigorous operations against the Portuguese from 1970.

Once again Portugal found itself fighting a losing battle with a conscript army. The G91s returned to Portugal in 1974 in anticipation of an offer of full independence. Mozambique gained independence on 25 June 1975 and took possession of several T-6s and Noratlases for its own use.

Southwest Africa
Over a period of time, South Africa found itself becoming increasingly involved in a counter-insurgency war in the territory then known as South West Africa. This started in the early 1960s, when the South West Africa People's Organisation (SWAPO), began its infiltration of what it called Namibia.

South African forces had conquered the territory from the Germans during World War I, and South Africa had been awarded a League of Nations mandate to administer the area.

The United Nations did not recognise the mandate, putting South Africa at odds with the international community.

The first SWAPO incursion into Ovamboland in northern South West Africa took place in September 1965. South African police units retaliated by attacking a SWAPO camp at Ongulumbashe, arriving there by Alouette III helicopter. For most of the 1960s and early 1970s, the conflict in Namibia remained at a low intensity, with the Alouettes active in the counterinsurgency role.

Into Angola
A direct result of the 1974 Portuguese revolution and the ensuing withdrawal from Angola was SWAPO's freedom to establish bases, with backing from the de facto rulers of the former colony, the Marxist MPLA. The situation was deemed serious enough for direct military involvement by South Africa.

The resulting Bush War saw South African Defence Force (SADF) units, supported by the SAAF, involved in numerous operations in southern Angola between 1974 and 1987. These saw South African Mirages, Buccaneers, Impalas and Kudus coming up against an increasingly effective Angolan defensive system, with Soviet-supplied and Cuban-manned equipment. Superior South African training gave them the advantage over the MiG-17s, MiG-21s and MiG-23s they encountered, and the use of Alouette III and Puma helicopters gave SADF ground troops exceptional mobility.

By the end of the 1980s, the politicians had succeeded in negotiating a withdrawal of Cuban forces from Angolan soil, in exchange for South African withdrawal from Angola, the granting of independence to Namibia, and the ultimate withdrawal of South African forces from Namibia itself. The last South African forces left Angola during August 1988. Peace had finally arrived – at least in the air. In Angola itself, the civil war continues to be fought out with savage ferocity, several shaky United Nations-brokered peace agreements having been broken in the war-torn former Portuguese colony.

Lieutenant Adriano Bomba of the Mozambique Air Force defected to South Africa in July 1981. His well-maintained MiG-17 was escorted into Hoedspruit air base by SAAF Mirage F1AZs.

Morocco and Chad

From 1978 Morocco received 50 Mirage F1s; they were all based at Sidi Slimane, from where detachments were sent to El Aïoune for combat operations in the Western Sahara. The F1EHs are known to have undertaken attack and reconnaissance missions, during which several were lost to ground fire.

France and Spain's withdrawal from North Africa left the region in turmoil. Several states tried to fill the resultant power vacuum, culminating in two decades of bloodshed.

Chad, which gained independence from France in 1960, was left with a minority Christian government ruling over a majority Muslim population. French forces returned to Chad in 1968 to help fight the Islamic Front de Libération Nationale de Tchad, withdrawing in 1975 after a coup installed an Islamic government.

Libyan leader Colonel Gaddafi was always enthusiastic to support other Islamic movements, and Libyan interest in Chad was further sharpened by the possibility of mineral resources in the disputed Aouzou strip in the extreme north of the region.

Libya occupied the strip in 1973, shortly before the French withdrawal. In 1978 the new Muslim government invited French forces back to eject the Libyans, but the regime proved precarious and in 1980 civil war broke out between the factions of the men who had previously shared power, Habré and Oueddi. Habré was ousted, retiring to the Sudanese border area, where he formed the Forces Armées du Nord (FAN). Oueddi

invited Libyan forces into Chad, which attacked FAN bases in Chad and Sudan (mainly using SIAI-Marchetti SF.260WLs). By 1981, however, Habré controlled most of the east and the centre of the country, including the capital, and his FAN became the Forces Armées Nationales Tchadiennes (FANT). A peacekeeping force from Nigeria, Senegal and Zaïre replaced the Libyans, and Oueddi fled north to raise the Libyan-backed Armée de Liberation Nationale (ALN).

For the next decade the FANT (with support from French and Zaïrean forces) fought off Libyan air attacks and ALN military action. In 1983 French forces established a red line roughly along the 15th Parallel, from Torodum to Oum Chalouba, which became the border between the government and rebel forces. French forces withdrew in autumn 1984, but Libyan forces remained, and built a massive base at Ouadi Doum. The ALN crossed the red line in February 1986, supported by Libyan aircraft from Ouadi Doum. French forces returned to Chad and counter-attacked, putting the

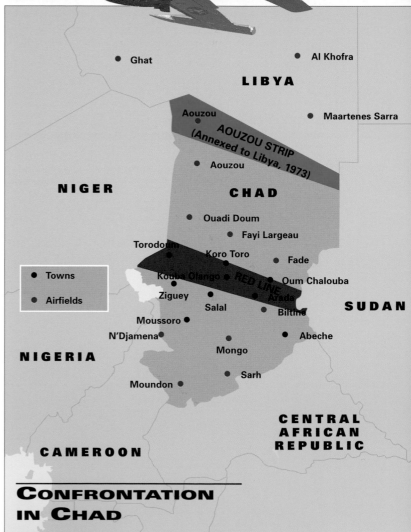

CONFRONTATION IN CHAD

Map labels:
- Ghat
- Al Khofra
- LIBYA
- Aouzou
- Maartenes Sarra
- AOUZOU STRIP (Annexed to Libya, 1973)
- Aouzou
- NIGER
- CHAD
- Ouadi Doum
- Fayi Largeau
- Torodom
- Koro Toro
- Fade
- Kouba Olanga
- RED LINE
- Oum Chalouba
- Ziguey
- Arada
- Towns
- Salal
- Biltine
- Airfields
- SUDAN
- Moussoro
- N'Djamena
- Abeche
- NIGERIA
- Mongo
- Moundon
- Sarh
- CAMEROON
- CENTRAL AFRICAN REPUBLIC

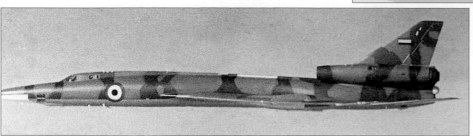

In retaliation for the Ouadi Doum strike, Libyan Tu-22s mounted at least two missions against N'Djamena airport. The first, on 24 February 1986, was successful, putting the airport out of action for two days, while a Crotale SAM system sat idle, unable to engage high-flying targets. On 7 September a Tu-22 was downed over N'Djamena by a Hawk SAM.

Left: BAP-100 anti-runway bombs dropped by Armée de l'Air Jaguar As rain down on the Libyan airfield at Ouadi Doum in illegally-occupied northern Chad. Mounted in February 1986, the strike severely damaged the runway.

Below: France's defence links with its former colony saw aircraft committed to the region. Between 1977 and 1987, French Jaguars undertook a series of missions with mixed results. While the aircraft flew valuable close support, strike and reconnaissance sorties, a number of Jaguars was lost to SAMs, AAA and even to mid-air collisions.

airfield out of action. Libya responded with a high-level bombing raid on N'Djamena by Tu-22s. Fighting broke out again in early 1987, with intensive bombing raids by both sides. French aircraft supported an infantry attack against the north, and Ouadi Doum was captured on 22 March. Aouzou was recaptured on 8 August, and on 5 September Chad invaded Libya, destroying 22 aircraft at Sara airfield before withdrawing. Both sides then accepted a ceasefire, though Libyan overflights have continued sporadically.

Moroccan war

Following the 1974 Spanish withdrawal from Spanish Sahara, Morocco and Mauretania agreed to partition the territory. This was opposed by the Algerian-backed and -based Polisario (Popular Front for the Liberation of Saguiet el-Hamra and Rio de Oro) resistance. Fighting broke out in the spring of 1976 and

Morocco received substantial help from France, including French equipment and deployments of French combat aircraft. Moroccan air force Mirage F1s, Alpha Jets and F-5s (together with Mauretanian BN Defenders) were supported by French Jaguars and Mirage F1s deployed to Dakar. Morocco's F-5A/E force was based at Kenitra and initially bore the brunt of air operations (along with a squadron of Magisters). Mauretania agreed a cease-fire with the Polisario in 1978, following a coup, and the Polisario was then able to operate from bases in the southern part of the Spanish Sahara. However, Morocco's war with the Polisario intensified, and many warplanes fell to Polisario SAMs during subsequent operations. Several F-5s were lost to SA-7s in 1978. Polisario surface-to-air defences were strengthened during the mid-1980s with the supply of SA-6 batteries and these claimed

Moroccan F-5A/Es were heavily committed in the ground attack role against Polisario guerillas and many were downed by SAMs and groundfire. Losses were offset by the delivery of surplus ex-Aggressor F-5Es from the USA in 1980 and 1989, funded by Saudi Arabia.

several Moroccan aircraft, including two F-5Es in 1985 and 1987. An uneasy peace was finally brought to the region in

1991 when a transitional period with UN forces prepared the region for a referendum on its future.

▬ Moroccan COIN air power ▬

Morocco's annexation in November 1975 of the Western Sahara territory vacated by Spain embroiled it in a little-reported war with Algerian- and Libyan-backed Polisario guerillas.

Rockwell OV-10 Bronco
First seeing combat with US forces in Southeast Asia, the Rockwell OV-10 is one of the few aircraft currently in service which was designed from the outset as a counter-insurgency platform. The Moroccan air force received six refurbished former USMC OV-10As in 1981.

Dassault/Dornier Alpha Jet E
The major Moroccan re-equipment programme of the 1980s saw the air force acquire 24 examples of the Franco-German Alpha Jet. Primarily used as an advanced trainer, it can also carry more than 5,512 lb (2500 kg) of ordnance in the light attack role.

Cold War
Introduction

The threat that existed throughout the Cold War years was that of nuclear annihilation. The image of the mushroom cloud became instantly recognisable, and it is no doubt due to the sheer might of these weapons that East and West never went to war.

For nearly 50 years, the immense forces of NATO and the Warsaw Pact faced each other, seemingly ready to go to war at any moment. Ultimately, cool heads prevailed, but the world is still recovering from this tense period of history.

Three months before the defeat of Nazi Germany, Churchill, Roosevelt and Stalin met at Yalta in the Crimea to plan the last stages of the conflict and to discuss the division of the post-war world into 'spheres of influence', each of which would be dominated by one of the Allies. However, cracks were already beginning to appear in the alliance which was set to defeat Hitler's forces.

Stalin mistrusted the West to a great extent, believing that democracy was a disguise for fascism and capitalist oppression. What is more, Russia's fear and hatred of Germany – stemming from three major invasions in 150 years – meant that Stalin felt that some sort of border had to be erected between East and West. This border eventually became a reality due to dithering by the post-war governments of Great Britain and the United States; the 'spheres of influence' granted to the Soviet Union were soon to become 'zones of control'. Within these zones, Stalin was to repress any independent governments or free elections and these nations would become little more than extensions of the Soviet Union. The Yalta Treaty eventually saw the USSR being promised 55 per cent of German reparations payments, as well as a sphere of influence which included all of what would eventually become the countries of the Warsaw Pact.

At the end of the war, the Potsdam Conference split

The Soviets held regular parades to demonstrate their military might to the world. It was in part the huge expense of the constant build-up of weapons, such as these SA-2s and tactical missiles, that led to the demise of the USSR.

Inset: Huge investments were made by both sides in ICBMs (InterContinental Ballistic Missiles) – illustrated is a Titan II.

Germany between the Allies, but previous friendships had now dissolved and arguments about Britain's support for reactionary elements in Greece and Soviet oppression in Eastern Europe further soured relations. However, any disagreements between the UK and the USA were soon papered over when Stalin indicated that he would never abide by the conditions of the Atlantic Charter, which promised freedom of speech, expression and religious worship. Stalin resented any Allied requests for free and democratic elections in the countries falling under his control. In the interests of security, these countries needed to be controlled rigidly and any danger of subversion, counter-revolution or ideological contamination had to be quickly and ruthlessly purged, often by secret police.

Hostile years

With this conflict of interests, hostile feelings between East and West rapidly grew, with each side distrusting the other, and the seeds were sown for almost half a century of mistrust and discord. On 5 March 1946, Churchill made his famous speech in the USA in which he warned of the dangers of communism in Europe, saying "From Stettin in the Baltic to Trieste in the Adriatic, an iron curtain has descended across the continent." The Cold War had begun.

However, what was unusual about the Cold War was that the two sides involved never directly went to war. It soon became apparent that any conflict between the Soviet Union and the forces of the West would be ruinously expensive, both in terms of lives and materials.

In post-war Greece, communist revolutionaries who had once aided the Allies, now had to be crushed as they were opposing the reintroduction of the Greek monarchy. The Berlin Airlift saw Western forces relieving the beleaguered citizens of that city. Communist North Korea, supported by China, invaded its southern neighbour, but was eventually beaten back by a multinational UN force. Anglo-French-Israeli forces fought communist Egyptians over the security of the Suez Canal, while America's CIA constantly battled against the Soviet-supported Fidel Castro in Cuba.

In Vietnam, perhaps the most devastating conflict since the end of World War II, American forces fought in vain against communist insurgence and, later, to try to prevent the North Vietnamese army from capturing the south.

One of the classic examples of Cold War thinking, the MiG-25 (illustrated) was developed in extreme haste to counter the Mach 3-capable North American XB-70 Valkyrie strategic bomber. When the XB-70 was halted, MiG-25 development had proceeded so far that the fighter entered service anyway and was to spawn several variants.

In the Middle East, US-supplied Israeli forces constantly battled against Arab nations. The African continent was a hotbed of activity, with many regimes embracing Russian, Chinese and Cuban aid. Opposing these groups were guerrilla forces, often with CIA backing.

The final major conflict during the Cold War era was in Afghanistan. Here, Soviet forces battled unsuccessfully against the mujaheddin rebels, who were partly supplied with Western equipment such as Stinger surface-to-air missiles.

In the majority of these conflicts, the forces of the West (most importantly those of the USA) and the Soviet Union typically denied any involvement and although actions seemed cold-hearted and cynical, they were preferable to nuclear war.

Military build-up

During the Cold War, there were many on both sides who believed that conflict was inevitable and that therefore their military forces should be built up in terms of numbers and technology. Fear and intelligence reports (often misleading) meant that each nation amassed huge armies, navies and air forces, often to the detriment of other aspects of society. One estimate is that some $8 trillion was spent worldwide between 1945 and 1996 on nuclear and other weapons. At their peak, the world's nuclear stockpiles held 18 billion metric tons of

explosive energy. This can be compared to the 6 megatons of total explosive energy released by all bombs during World War II. It is estimated that as much as 50 per cent of the Soviet national product was spent on defence. In the United States, national defence spending – which had peaked at nearly 40 per cent during World War II – ranged from 5-10 per cent during the Cold War; in 1996 US dollar equivalent terms, it ran at an average of $400 billion annually. However, President Eisenhower warned in 1955 that, "The problem in defence spending is to figure how far you should go without destroying from within what you are trying to defend from without."

The assembled military forces were immense. In America, communism was seen as something akin to evil and successive presidents had little choice but to increase defence spending; to do otherwise would result in them being labelled 'soft' on communism. The enormously powerful Strategic Air Command had nuclear bombers with a worldwide capability. The navy possessed a significant nuclear strength, whether it be delivered by a missile from a submarine or from a carrierborne aircraft. Ground forces were equipped with powerful tanks and nuclear artillery.

In the East, the Soviet forces were even larger, but technologically inferior, the USSR relying instead on

quantity and ease of use over quality. The result was, seemingly, a stalemate and any major conflict between the two sides would no doubt have resulted in a fearsome nuclear exchange, with no definite outcome.

Endings

The Cold War affected the whole of the world, with most nations aligned either to the West or the East – only a few dared to be neutral. Although a nuclear holocaust was avoided, millions died in the conflicts listed above, and in gulags and re-education camps, while covert intelligence groups accounted for many more deaths. More civilians died than uniformed troops, often because they dared to question the abuses of those in power and desired a return to freedom.

However, years of talks and negotiations, not to mention massively expensive spending (although the US spent more), finally resulted in Gorbachev's reforms of the Soviet Union and the introduction of open elections; communism began to be voted out and the Cold War suddenly came to a halt. Although tensions still exist and work remains to be done, the war finally ended without global catastrophe.

In shipboard meetings at Malta in 1989, Gorbachev and Bush agreed that their two nations were finally no longer enemies. The Cold War had lasted from Yalta to Malta.

Right: An RAF English Electric Lightning intercepts a Soviet Tu-95 'Bear' over the North Atlantic. Encounters like this were numerous all around the world, with probing intelligence aircraft attempting to snoop on the enemy. Such incidents often gave each side its first glimpse of new aircraft.

Below: America's SAC (Strategic Air Command) built up a huge force of bombers, like the B-52s pictured below. The B-52 entered service in 1955 and later variants are retained by the USAF, the type still constituting an important part of the US power projection force.

Left: Trucks unload flour from American C-54s at Tempelhof. The citizens of the city worked together to assist the air forces. A new airport was built at Tegel and the Berliners helped unload the aircraft and distribute the aid.

Above: British civilian aircraft played a part in the airlift, one of the more unusual being Avro Lancaster Mk 3 G-AHJW. The aircraft was one of two converted as flying fuel tankers by Flight Refuelling Ltd, and it proved to be a useful carrier of petrol to keep Berlin's essential services running.

The Berlin airlift

When the Soviet Union encircled Berlin, the forces of the West conspired to aid the starving citizens of the city by delivering supplies by air. A mammoth undertaking, the airlift defeated the Soviets and changed people's perceptions of Germany.

As World War II ended, it was decided by the victors to split Germany between the UK, US, USSR and France as means of reparation. However, in the post-war world, previous friendships were fast disappearing and the subject of Germany's future became a contentious issue. The US – and to a lesser extent, the UK – wanted a rebuilt Germany, although France feared the resurgence of its old enemy. The Soviet Union believed that any such plans by the West were proposed merely to antagonise the USSR. Central to all these arguments was the subject of Berlin and who would control it. The city was 100

miles (160 km) inside the Soviet zone but was split between the four victorious nations. Stalin thought that this intrusive presence merely paved the way for the unilateral creation of a virtually independent Germany by the West.

Stalin began to implement stringent controls on surface travel to the three western zones of Berlin, and on 31 March 1948 the Soviets announced that road traffic into Berlin would henceforth be subject to inspection by their guards. The West refused to abide by this decision and cancelled all surface transportation except food and freight trains. At midnight on

18 June, the Soviets formally banned all passenger traffic, and followed this on 24 June by stopping all food trains. They did so on the pretext of 'technical troubles' on the railway line, tearing up some 100 yd (90 m) of track to ensure that no trains could run. The Soviets' purpose was clear: they wanted to force the Western Allies to either change their policies or get out of Berlin altogether.

In London and Washington, the governments remained firm. "We are going to stay, period," said Truman. Britain's equally determined Bevin announced that "the abandonment of Berlin would mean the loss of Eastern Europe."

It soon became clear that action had to be taken; the Soviets had excused themselves from the responsibility of supplying the western sectors of the city, and 2.3 million

Berliners plus the allied garrisons were now cut off. Previously, the western part of the city had relied on the arrival of 12,000 tons of supplies each day. At the time, there was only enough food for 36 days and enough coal for 45.

The airlift begins

The only solution was to proceed with an RAF idea that would involve supplying the beleaguered city by air. It was calculated that 2,000 tons of food and essential supplies would need to be flown in daily to maintain the city. On 26 June 1948, the first American transport aircraft flew into Berlin from their West German bases in an operation codenamed Vittles by the Americans and Plainfare by the British.

In the aftermath of the war, the Allied transport forces had been run down, but everything that was left was immediately mobilised. By 29 June, the whole of RAF Transport Command's 64-strong Douglas Dakota fleet was based in RAF Germany, reinforced by crews from Australia, New Zealand and South Africa. By 1 July, the Dakotas had been joined by the RAF's Yorks and Hastings and two Coastal Command Sunderland flying-boat squadrons. The RAF's entire front-line transport aircraft strength was committed to the operation, supplemented by large numbers of civilian aircraft including Handley Page Haltons, Avro Lancastrians and converted Consolidated Liberator bombers. Aviation businessman Freddie Laker offered his fleet of 12 converted Halifax bombers to the cause.

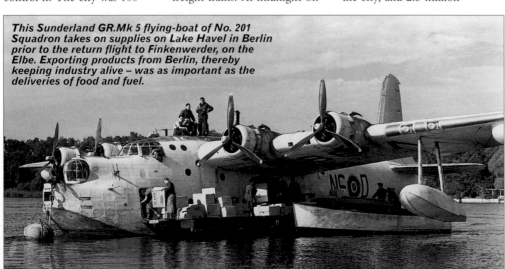

This Sunderland GR.Mk 5 flying-boat of No. 201 Squadron takes on supplies on Lake Havel in Berlin prior to the return flight to Finkenwerder, on the Elbe. Exporting products from Berlin, thereby keeping industry alive – was as important as the deliveries of food and fuel.

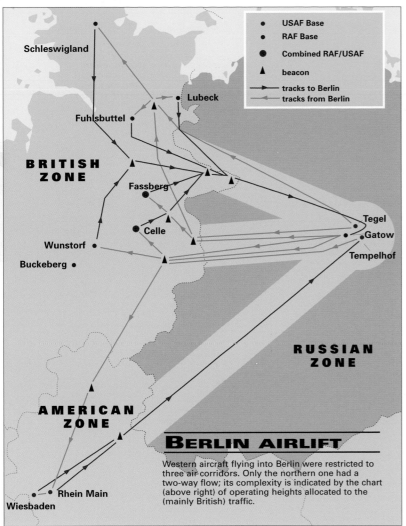

Schleswigland

●	USAF Base
●	RAF Base
⬤	Combined RAF/USAF
▲	beacon
→	tracks to Berlin
→	tracks from Berlin

Lubeck

Fuhlsbuttel

BRITISH ZONE

Fassberg

Celle

Wunstorf

Buckeberg

Tegel
Gatow
Tempelhof

RUSSIAN ZONE

AMERICAN ZONE

Rhein Main
Wiesbaden

BERLIN AIRLIFT

Western aircraft flying into Berlin were restricted to three air corridors. Only the northern one had a two-way flow; its complexity is indicated by the chart (above right) of operating heights allocated to the (mainly British) traffic.

OPERATING HEIGHTS NORTHERN CORRIDOR

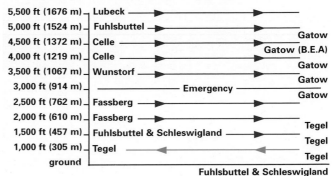

Height	Start	End
5,500 ft (1676 m)	Lubeck →	
5,000 ft (1524 m)	Fuhlsbuttel →	
4,500 ft (1372 m)	Celle →	Gatow
4,000 ft (1219 m)	Celle →	Gatow (B.E.A)
3,500 ft (1067 m)	Wunstorf →	Gatow
3,000 ft (914 m)	— Emergency —	Gatow
2,500 ft (762 m)	Fassberg →	Gatow
2,000 ft (610 m)	Fassberg →	
1,500 ft (457 m)	Fuhlsbuttel & Schleswigland →	Tegel
1,000 ft (305 m)	Tegel ←	Tegel
ground		Tegel

Fuhlsbuttel & Schleswigland

Service of eight squadrons of C-54 Skymasters, each of which could carry 10 US tons (20,000 lb/9072 kg) of freight and required less maintenance than the Dakotas.

New direction

With the C-54s came the leadership of a new commander, Major General William H. Tunner, who set about organising the airlift on a more efficient basis. He was determined to get maximum effectiveness from his resources, preferably using smaller numbers of larger capacity aircraft.

The distance from the US zone bases to Berlin was much greater than from Celle and Fassberg in the British zone, and by mid-August USAF aircraft were using these airfields. The British contribution to the effort diminished as RAF Dakotas and Yorks vacated Celle and Fassberg for the C-54s; they were given less important supplies and passengers, all of which required longer to load and unload. The Dakotas were long past the peak of their efficiency and the Yorks had never been intended for short-haul operations of this nature. Administrative changes and the introduction of the more - capable Handley Page Hastings did somewhat improve the RAF's position.

At the height of the airlift, aircraft took off and landed at Berlin's Gatow and Tempelhof airports every 90 seconds, remaining on the ground at Berlin for an average of 30 minutes.

The Soviet Union finally realised that it could not starve Berlin into submission and the blockade was lifted at 12.01 on 12 May 1949. However, airlifts continued until September to stockpile supplies in case the Soviets interfered again.

The combined efforts had brought almost 1 ton of supplies for each Berliner, in an operation which had gone on around the clock, seven days a week, except for a period in November 1948. Some 1,586,530 tons of coal, 92,282 tons of wet fuel and 538,016 tons of food, plus other materials, had been airlifted for an incredible total of 2,325,809 tons of supplies.

The airlift also made a significant contribution to changing attitudes toward Germany, which was subsequently seen as a valuable ally and a hero of the resistance to Soviet aggression. It prompted the formal establishment of the Federal Republic of Germany (FDR), or West Germany, on 21 September 1949, marking the division of the Germanies until reunification in 1990.

The USAF fleet by then totalled 102 Douglas C-47s, and a fleet of C-54 Skymasters began to assemble in the USA.

It quickly became apparent that the load estimate was far too low: at least 4,000 tons of food and other essentials would have to be flown into Berlin daily to stockpile supplies before the winter weather would make flying conditions impossible. The C-47s/Dakotas could only carry 6,720 lb (3048 kg) of freight, and it was obvious that the force committed was too small to meet the requirements.

Tension increased as lumbering transports were buzzed by Soviet fighters. The USAF responded in July by deploying 50 Boeing B-29 Superfortress bombers to British bases and a wing of Lockheed P-80 fighters to Fürstenfeldbruck, near Munich.

The early achievements of the RAF and the USAF were impressive, as over 2,000 tons were flown into Berlin daily in July, a figure that increased to 3,839 tons and 4,600 tons in September and October, respectively. A key factor in this increase was the deployment by the USAF Military Air Transport

Above: RAF Yorks unload at Gatow, Britain's terminal in Berlin, where operations continued by night as well as day. Derived from the Lancaster, Avro Yorks were the most modern transports the RAF could offer in the early days. These are from the training unit, No. 241 Operational Conversion Squadron.

Right: The last Vittles flight left Rhein Main Air Base on 30 September 1949. In the background, other USAF C-54s of the 61st TCG overfly the base.

Between 1955 and 1991, the **NATO** and Warsaw Pact nations faced each other at a high state of readiness. Hardened aircraft shelters (such as this example containing a Buccaneer) were constructed to protect the aircraft from airfield attack.

NATO & WarPac

Mutual mistrust and misunderstanding between Eastern and Western Europe led to a period of great tension and hostility across the continent. Paranoia led both sides to form alliances, and Europe was divided in two.

The drift towards Europe's division into two armed camps began within months of VE-Day. Retaining only the minimum of troops necessary to police their sectors of defeated Germany, the Western Allies reduced the size of their forces with all possible speed. The USSR, still establishing socialism in the territories from which it had ejected the Nazis, was influenced by the paranoia of its leader, Josef Stalin.

Suspicious of the West's delay in initiating D-Day, fearful of a West German alliance against him, and wary of an ideological 'Trojan Horse' in the generous American offers of reconstruction aid to Europe, Stalin kept the number of troops within the Red Army at five million. The West drew its own conclusions from the Soviet refusal to demobilise. Its first step towards a defence against Stalin's army was taken in March 1948 with the formation of the Western Union, which included Belgium, France, Luxembourg, the Netherlands and the United Kingdom. The alliance was only a few months old when talks commenced on

extending the Union to include the United States and Canada.

When the North Atlantic Treaty was signed on 4 April 1949, Denmark, Iceland, Italy, Norway and Portugal had joined the seven founder members. Greece, Turkey and Spain all joined later on. The member states endorsed a broad declaration of peaceful co-operation and willingness to solve disputes without recourse to arms. But it was the fifth of the Treaty's 14 component articles which contained the most vital assertion:

'The Parties agree that an armed attack against one or more of them in Europe or North America shall be considered an attack against them all.'

It was in June 1950 that NATO began to take the form by which it is now recognised. On 2 April 1951 (two years after the North Atlantic Treaty had been signed), Allied Command Europe became operational under US General Dwight D. Eisenhower. It was only now that NATO began to rearm with US jet aircraft through the Mutual Defense Assistance Program, starting with a handful of Republic F-84E Thunderjets. By mid-1952, the F-84G model was arriving in Europe in its hundreds, and the air forces of Belgium, Denmark, France, Italy, the

Netherlands, Norway and Portugal were soon transformed. The British Air Force of Occupation (BAFO) later changed to the 2nd Tactical Air Force and was equipped with 13 squadrons of de Havilland Vampire FB.Mk 5s and three of reconnaissance Meteors. Later, Greece and Turkey qualified for receipt of the ubiquitous Thunderjet, and more went to southern Europe as the swept-wing F-84F Thunderstreak and its reconnaissance-configured RF-84F Thunderflash compatriot were supplied to Central Europe.

The Soviet Union viewed the creation of NATO with deep misgivings. Although Stalin had died in 1953, his policies were maintained in large measure by the leaders who followed him.

The Republic F-84F was widely used by European NATO countries, serving with the air forces of Belgium, France, Greece, Italy, the Netherlands, Turkey and West Germany. The first of the 180 examples for the Royal Netherlands Air Force arrived in 1955.

P-195

32

The primary goal was to prevent the West from rearming Germany. Numerous attempts were made by Moscow to stall NATO's efforts, and on one remarkable occasion in March 1954, the USSR suggested that it might be prepared to join NATO. This proposal was firmly rejected by the UK, France and the US. West Germany finally became a member of NATO on 5 May 1955. Its efforts having come to nought, the USSR organised its own response to NATO.

Warsaw Pact

The Treaty of Friendship, Mutual Assistance and Co-operation (known as the Warsaw Pact) between Moscow and its client states of Albania, Bulgaria, Czechoslovakia, East Germany, Hungary, Poland and Romania was dedicated to the defence of European territory, and thus excluded the central and eastern Soviet Union. Although NATO loosely referred to the Warsaw Pact as its counterpart, the Eastern alliance merely formalised bilateral treaties already in being and was later modified by status-of-forces agreements with Poland, East Germany, Romania and Hungary in 1956-57 and Czechoslovakia in 1968. The Warsaw Pact had propaganda value in so far as it was formed after NATO and was thus a response to capitalist aggression.

In all practical terms, however, it made no difference to the strategic situation. The Soviet Union continued to dictate the pace of rearmament in its territories, as a concerned NATO looked on. Tension was heightened further when, in 1956, Soviet forces invaded Hungary, in complete contrast to the NATO policy of non-

F-84F-equipped units of Tactical Air Command were important components of the Composite Air Strike Force (CASF) concept, which involved US-based units deploying rapidly into areas of conflict. The unit to which this F-84F belonged, the 405th FBW, demonstrated this ability during Operation Mobile Arch – a deployment exercise to the UK – in September 1955.

interference with the internal affairs of its member states.

The two sides of the Cold War were neatly defined at this time as NATO versus the

Warsaw Pact. In reality, though, both sides were established for reasons of mutual defence. The United States and the Soviet Union came to regard

continental Europe as a convenient 'buffer zone' between the two powers, capable of sustaining a future war fought with conventional weapons.

Luftwaffe Sabres

The first of 75 ex-RCAF Canadair CL-13A Sabre Mk 5s was delivered to the Luftwaffe in January 1957 and the type was declared operational in December of that year. From 1959, a further 226 CL-13B Sabre Mk 6s were acquired, allowing Germany to equip three full wings with the type. These were

joined by two squadrons of Fiat-built F-86Ks, which served until mid-1966. The last Sabre Mk 6 was retired in December 1966, although a number was subsequently converted into target tugs, serving with Condor Flugdienst.

Air-to-air combat
To improve the air-to-air capability of the Sabre Mk 6 over that of the Mk 5, Luftwaffe Mk 6s were modified to enable them to carry the AIM-9 Sidewinder missile in addition to their six machine-guns.

Ground-attack role
In the air-to-ground role, Luftwaffe Sabres could carry various ordnance, including folding-fin and high-velocity aircraft rockets, and napalm tanks.

Under the aegis of Curtis LeMay, SAC reached the peak of its strength in 1956 when its aircraft totalled 3,218 (247 B/RB-36, 97 B-52 (pictured), 254 RB-47, 1,306 B-47, 16 RB-57, 51 C-124, 750 KC-97, 74 KB-29, 366 F-84, 57 RF-84F/K). SAC was never to see such numbers again.

SAC/V-Force alert

For more than four decades, the Communist world trembled at the might of the USAF's SAC. The US bomber command, along with Britain's V-Force, was built up into a formidable bomber power with a global reach.

The concept of being able to deter aggression from a world power by means of the threat of immediate and devastating retaliation became a reality when the two opposing world political blocs acquired nuclear weapons. For over 40 years, the mainstay of the Western world's airborne nuclear deterrent was the USAF's Strategic Air Command (SAC), a force of long-range bombers constantly deployed between bases throughout the world.

Founded on 21 March 1946 under General George C. Kenney, SAC grew to become the world's most powerful long-range bombing force. The Command formed around a mere six companies of World War II-vintage B-29s. They went on to become the only big bombers to operate in the Korean War, a conflict to which the Pentagon gave lower priority than the expected nuclear clash with Moscow.

The Convair B-36 Peacemaker was to be SAC's next bomber and the first examples were delivered to the USAF in the summer of 1948. However, at any given time, SAC never had more than 205 of the giant B-36s (out of 383 built) in service.

However, it was to be the swept-wing, jet-powered Boeing B-47 Stratojet that was to equip SAC through some of the tensest periods of the Cold War, with a peak strength of over 2,000 Stratojets in service during the mid-1950s. The B-47 was fighter-like in appearance, with its swept-back wings and podded turbojet power. It was the most potent bomber of the 1950s and gave the Soviets much cause for concern.

In the 1940s and 1950s, SAC operated fighter escort squadrons, beginning with the F-82 Twin Mustang and culminating in the F-84F Thunderstreak. However, their presence was never really appreciated by SAC's new and most legendary commander, General Curtis LeMay. When RF-84K Thunderflash reconnaissance aircraft went aloft from the bays of B-36 bombers, LeMay dismissed them, due to the fact that "fighters are fun, but bombers are important". The fighter escort force was soon abandoned.

In one way, the most important aircraft in SAC service were the inflight-refuelling tankers: the KC-97 Stratofreighter and the KC-135 Stratotanker. Tankers revolutionised air warfare and gave the bombers worldwide reach.

B-52 supremacy

The Stratojet was later replaced by the B-52 Stratofortress, which was seen as the saviour for the West in the face of the growing Soviet nuclear threat of the 1960s. Though never serving to the extent of the B-47, the B-52 found itself to be the ideal long-range bomber, with at least 12 aircraft remaining aloft 24 hours a day with live hydrogen bombs in their bays. These Chrome Dome missions were seen as an immediate response to any aggression against the US and its allies. Chrome Dome missions were eventually cancelled in 1966 following two accidents which resulted in the temporary loss of a number of hydrogen bombs. By 1971 the dominance of the bomber was being threatened by the introduction of Intercontinental Ballistic Missiles (ICBMs) and submarine-launched missiles.

However, unlike Britain's V-Force, SAC was to remain in existence for another 21 years, serving alongside the ICBMs. By the 1980s, SAC was equipped with Rockwell B-1B Lancers, FB-111As and improved variants of the B-52. The near-invisible B-2 'stealth' bomber, which was designed to be the jewel in SAC's crown, able to attack mobile railway-based ICBMs with deadly precision, would, however, never serve with its intended Command. The collapse of the Soviet empire and the constant reduction in arms spending saw to it that SAC went out of business on 1 June 1992, having fought its final 'war' in 1991 during Operation Desert Storm.

Above: The monstrous B-36 was designed during World War II as an intercontinental bomber, able to hit targets in Germany or Japan from US bases. It went on to become the mainstay of SAC's long-range nuclear bomber force during the service's formative years.

Left: Britain's V-Force trained intensively to be able to be launch aircraft such as this Vulcan and be en route to its targets before hostile bombers or missiles could wipe out its bases.

SAC had helped to maintain the peace between East and West for over 40 years and the command could be justly proud of its motto, 'Peace is our Profession'.

V-Force

By late 1955, with the introduction of the Valiant into service, RAF Bomber Command still utilised conventional bombing techniques, similar to those used in the later stages of World War II. After the mid-1950s, however, the advent of nuclear weapons made greater demands on crews and aircraft and, accordingly, a new set of operational procedures had to be devised. These procedures would see bomber crews maintaining alert duties near to, or within, their fully-armed aircraft.

After the order to scramble, squadron crews would either go straight into training – which involved a cross-country flight with radar bomb scores – or be dispersed to predetermined airfields in clutches of four aircraft. Throughout its career the V-Force relied on dispersal, ultimately to some 36 designated airfields, as security against a surprise attack; unlike SAC, it never maintained an airborne alert force.

As the training and expertise of the V-Force developed, overseas exercises became more frequent. Squadrons would send detachments to Malaya (Exercise Sunflower), and Malta (Exercise Sunspot). There were also single-aircraft Lone Ranger flights mainly to Cyprus and Nairobi; equivalent single-flights to Norway were known as Polar Bears and those to the United States as Western Rangers.

The first nuclear weapon in V-Force service was the Blue Danube, introduced in 1953 and carried by Valiants. A decade later, the formidable hydrogen bomb Yellow Sun Mk 2 was being carried by British bombers. At this time, the highly capable Douglas Skybolt stand-off missile was cancelled, leaving the UK with the less capable Blue Steel. The last nuclear weapon carried by V-Force was the WE 177A free-fall bomb, which was carried by Vulcans and remained in RAF service until 1998.

The V-Force's viability as an effective deterrent was constantly put to the test by war-situation exercises of varying levels. For example, those named Kinsman meant dispersal, while Mickey Finn meant dispersal without notice. In 1962 the readiness of the V-Force was improved further by the inauguration of the Bomber Command's Quick Reaction Alert (QRA) plan, which initially involved one aircraft from each V-Force squadron being on full alert at the

The Boeing B-50 was an interim replacement for the B-29. It was originally designated B-29D, and redesignated in order to win funding at a time when B-29s were delivered straight to storage. These are B-50Ds of the 43rd Bomb Group, 15th AF (identified by the 'circle K' tail marking).

end of the runway. The QRA was maintained for a 10-year period and only once did it seem that the V-Force was to strike for real. This was during the Cuban Missile Crisis in October 1962, when the V-Force was brought up to a high state of readiness and its RAF bases sealed off. The aircraft stood combat-ready for three days before being stood down. In 1964 the V-Force switched to low-level operations, which saw further deployment overseas, in particular Goose Bay in Canada where the large remote areas allowed unrestricted low-flying.

On 30 April 1968, Bomber and Fighter Commands merged to form RAF Strike Command, bringing an end to the V-Force. Fourteen months later, on 30 June 1969, the RAF's QRA strategic nuclear deterrent role was handed over to the Royal Navy's submarine force.

Whether or not the force of V-bombers, of which fewer than 50 were ever combat-capable simultaneously, constituted a credible deterrent (to which the French Force de Frappe might, in certain circumstances, have been added) will forever remain unknown.

BRITAIN'S V-BOMBER BASES

At the height of its capability, in late 1962, the V-Force's strategic nuclear deterrent numbered 15 squadrons, with two wings of three Vulcan B.Mk 2 squadrons, three B.Mk 1A squadrons, two squadrons of Victor B.Mk 1, two of B.Mk 1As and two of B.Mk 2s. These were augmented by three Valiant tactical strike/bomber squadrons and four more Valiant tanker, ECM and recce units.

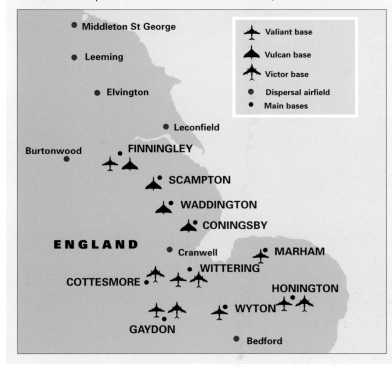

- Middleton St George
- Leeming
- Elvington
- Leconfield
- Burtonwood
- **FINNINGLEY**
- **SCAMPTON**
- **WADDINGTON**
- **CONINGSBY**
- **ENGLAND**
- Cranwell
- **MARHAM**
- **WITTERING**
- **COTTESMORE**
- **HONINGTON**
- **WYTON**
- **GAYDON**
- Bedford

Key:
- ✈ Valiant base
- ▲ Vulcan base
- ✈ Victor base
- ● Dispersal airfield
- ● Main bases

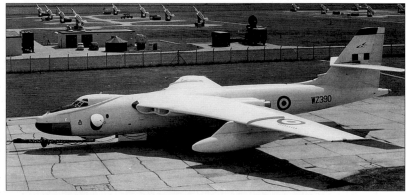

Above: A Valiant of No. 214 Squadron is towed at RAF Marham. No. 214 Squadron adopted the inflight-refuelling tanker role in 1962, but continued to maintain a tactical bombing commitment.

Below: In addition to anti-flash white paint, the V-bombers carried national insignia, toned down to pastel shades to avoid them becoming 'hot spots' on the aircraft skin. This is a Victor B.Mk 2 (BS).

Avro Vulcan

Following their entry into service in 1957, the RAF's Vulcans constituted the sharp end of Britain's nuclear deterrent until 1969, when the responsibility was handed over to the Royal Navy's Polaris ICBM-capable submarines.

The B.Mk 1 entered service with 230 OCU early in 1957, with the first squadron, No. 83, following in July. The second squadron to operate the type was No. 101 (pictured), receiving its aircraft in October.

230 OCU at Waddington was the first Vulcan unit, receiving two B.Mk 1 aircraft in January 1957. This aircraft, the unit's third, was delivered on 3 March, and wears the early silver colour scheme.

The initial weaponry for the V-force was the Blue Danube free-fall atomic bomb. In June 1954, however, the government initiated development of a more powerful hydrogen bomb, and the Violet Club stop-gap weapon was produced from March 1958. In addition to British weapons, the early Vulcan force could be equipped with American Mk 5 nuclear weapons from 1958.

The Yellow Sun Mk 1, the eventual outcome of the government's 1954 H-bomb requirement, became available in 1960, eventually supplanting the US Mk 5 weapons, as well as the Violet Club. The Yellow Sun Mk 1 was, however, only in service until 1963, before being replaced by the Yellow Sun Mk 2, carrying an improved warhead. Waddington received 24 Yellow Sun Mk 2s to equip its B.Mk 1s, while similar numbers were delivered to the B.Mk 2s based at Honington.

In 1963 – by which time the B.Mk 1 fleet had been upgraded under a modification programme to B.Mk 1A status, with the introduction of B.Mk 2 standard ECM equipment – the V-force was assigned to NATO, and given a part to play in the Alliance's nuclear strike plan.

Blue Steel

The run-down of the B.Mk 1A force began in earnest in March 1966, when B.Mk 2s began to arrive at Waddington, replacing the earlier Vulcan equipment. On 10 January 1968, the last front-line B.Mk 1A was finally retired from service.

In order to accommodate the new Blue Steel stand-off weapon, the Scampton-based Vulcan B.Mk 2 fleet was modified to B.Mk 2A standard, with provision for the semi-recessed Blue Steel in special bomb-bay doors. No. 617 Sqn received its first B.Mk 2A in September 1961, and the Scampton wing eventually had a fleet of 26 Blue Steel-configured Vulcans. Following the cancellation of the Skybolt air-launched ballistic missile, the proliferation of Soviet surface-to-air missiles (SAMs) rendered existing high-altitude operations ineffective, at least beyond 1965. Meanwhile, Cottesmore's aircraft were optimised for carriage of the WE177B strategic nuclear bomb. The Waddington wing relinquished its B.Mk 1A/Yellow Sun Mk 2 combination in favour of the WE177B-armed B.Mk 2.

With a speed of Mach 2.3 and a range of 115 miles (185 km), Blue Steel was intended to provide the V-bombers with a high-altitude weapon that did not lead them to expose themselves to the air defences of high-priority enemy targets. Blue Steel operational capability was achieved by No. 617 Sqn on 24 September 1962. By the end of 1964, Nos 27 and 83 Squadrons were similarly equipped, sharing weapons with Wittering-based Victor B.Mk 2s of Nos 100 and 139 Squadrons.

However, Blue Steel had been rendered obsolete as a high-altitude weapon by Soviet SAM advances even before service entry, and was adapted for low-level operations from mid-1964. It remained as a peripheral weapon, and free-fall bombs were the only credible high-altitude nuclear weapons option for the Vulcan fleet. The transition to low-level operations caused serious problems; until the WE177B strategic lay-down bomb could be fielded, the Vulcan had less than ideal weapons. The Yellow Sun and Red Beard weapons required a pop-up to at least 12,000 ft (3660 m) for release, while Blue Steel launched at low level was limited in range. At first, the Yellow Sun force went low-level against primary targets, leaving Blue Steel carriers to attack fringe targets.

On 30 June 1969 the Royal Navy's Polaris submarines took over the nuclear deterrent from

Blue Steel operations

Limited Blue Steel capability was attained by the Vulcan fleet in September 1962. Blue Steel (carried by the specially equipped B.Mk 2A) operations were focused around Scampton (home of Nos 27, 83 and 617 Squadrons in 1962) until 1969/70, when the aircraft reverted to free-fall nuclear bombing with the WE177B. Introduced in January 1962, Quick Reaction Alert (QRA) stated that at least one aircraft from each Blue Steel unit was maintained at Cockpit Readiness (above left), with the crew strapped in, allowing the aircraft to be airborne just 57 seconds after the alert had been sounded (above right). Carrying a Red Snow megaton warhead, the Blue Steel stand-off missile (above centre) had a Bristol Stentor rocket motor, fuelled by a volatile mix of kerosene and High-Test Peroxide, necessitating great care in transport and handling.

Below: The B.Mk 1A, seen here taking on fuel from a No. 90 Squadron Valiant B(K).Mk 1, carried the ECM suite developed for the B.Mk 2, providing defence against high-flying interceptors.

the V-force, and the Scampton wing gave up its Blue Steel QRA role at midnight. No. 617 Squadron flew the last Blue Steel sortie on 21 December 1970.

Other duties

A reduction in nuclear responsibilities freed Vulcan B.Mk 2s for other duties. No. 27 Squadron disbanded at Scampton in March 1972, but re-formed at the same base in November 1973 in the maritime radar reconnaissance (MRR) role. Its aircraft partially replaced the Victor SR.Mk 2s of No. 543 Squadron when they retired the following May. Initially, four were converted to B.Mk 2(MRR)

An obvious change associated with the switch to low-level operations was the use of camouflage, initially applied to Waddington B.Mk 1As in a high-gloss finish. Here, a Cottesmore B.Mk 2 accompanies a white-scheme aircraft from the Finningley OCU.

standard, with the addition of Loran C navigation equipment and removal of TFR from the nose. Standard Vulcans were operated until four more MRR models were added between 1976 and 1978.

The rest of the Vulcan force soldiered on until it was decided to run-down the entire fleet during 1981/82, replacing them with Tornados. However, the Argentine invasion of the Falkland Islands brought a reprieve and a number of long-distance raids were made during April, May and June 1982 under Operation Black Buck.

The conflict in the South Atlantic spurred development of the last Vulcan variant. Concerns about the Victor tanker fleet led

Right: With the shadow of the Jet Provost photo-platform joining that of the Vulcan, the last aircraft built demonstrates its low-level capabilities. The 'pimple' on the nose housed terrain-following radar.

to the hasty modification of six Vulcans to K.Mk 2 standard as inflight-refuelling tankers, with fuel tanks fitted in their bomb

bays and a single hose-drogue unit. They were to be the last operational Vulcans, and were finally retired in March 1984.

Cuban missile crisis

Seen by some as Kennedy's greatest triumph, the Cuban missile crisis brought the world to the edge of nuclear war and only the fact that Khrushchev 'blinked first' prevented a possible conflict.

Fidel Castro seized power in Cuba in 1959 and thereafter, this small Communist country was regarded as a constant thorn in the side of the USA. In response the US carried out a series of actions under the all-encompassing Operation Mongoose, sometimes described as the secret 'Kennedy vendetta'. The aim was to disrupt the Cuban economy and government and to assassinate Castro. Methods ranged from the dropping of propaganda leaflets to bizarre assassination plots, and culminated in the debacle of the Bay of Pigs invasion.

Soviet leader Nikita Khrushchev was well aware of his country's weakness in the 'missile race' and came up with the idea of siting nuclear missiles in Cuba. After all, the United States had Jupiter missiles in Turkey, scarcely seconds in flight time from various Soviet cities. When the matter was first presented to Castro, he was unhappy at the fact that his country would become a Soviet missile base but, believing that the missiles would alter the world-wide strategic balance back in favour of the socialist camp, he agreed.

In July 1962 65 Soviet ships sailed for Cuba, and in early September the installation of missile sites on the island was under way. Each missile could carry a one-megaton warhead and, since America had no missile warning radar covering its southern coasts, this meant that Soviet missiles could be in the air over the USA with little warning. The longer range SS-5s could hit virtually all American cities and all Strategic Air Command (SAC) nuclear bases.

From July Soviet workers and technicians had begun pouring into Cuba and in early August, CIA Director John A. McCone became convinced that the Russians were installing long-range missiles. After failing to gain the attention of the President's advisors, he went directly to Kennedy himself.

On 29 August a U-2 photographed SAM installations under construction. The next U-2 overflight, a week later, provided more evidence of the Soviet build-up. That mission's photographs revealed three more SAM sites and a MiG-21, one of the newest Soviet fighter aircraft, at the Santa Clara airfield. This presence of SAMs reinforced McCone's belief that there were ballistic missiles on the island. He argued that the SAMs were only placed there to deter reconnaissance flights.

Despite this evidence, the Kennedy administration was still not convinced there were nuclear weapons on the island. On 2 September the USSR announced that it was sending

Above: This characteristic star shaped pattern of a SA-2 SAM site, photographed by a high-flying U-2, provided the first evidence that the Soviets had something worth defending on Cuba.

Top: The RF-101 Voodoo was the workhorse of the US low-level reconnaissance missions over Cuba. The Voodoos provided the US leaders with a steady supply of revealing photographs.

'armaments' and technical advisors to Cuba. The US countered this by announcing that it would stop Castro by force if he attempted to try to spread Communism into Central and Southern America.

However, on 11 September, the Soviet ambassador assured the Americans that there were no offensive weapons being exported to Cuba. However, he was lying and there were in fact 40 Soviet medium- and intermediate range ballistic missiles on their way to the island.

All this time, Kennedy was coming under attack from right-wingers who accused him of being soft on the 'reds'.

Soviet forces in Cuba

Meanwhile, the situation in Cuba was developing. Soviet forces based on the island now numbered 42 modern jet fighters,

Throughout the crisis, US Navy patrol aircraft kept a vigil over all vessels in the region. This is the Soviet ship Anosov leaving Cuba with missile transporters on 7 November 1962.

42 unassembled jet bombers, about 350 medium and heavy tanks, 40 ships, 1,300 pieces of field artillery and 700 anti-aircraft guns. Suspicions that the Soviets might be preparing long-range missiles grew stronger until, on 15 October, a U-2 photographed long-range missile launching sites under construction on the island.

Kennedy was shocked that the Soviets had lied to him and he formed an advisory committee, quickly nicknamed ExComm by the press, who plotted against Castro. Their first task was to decide whether or not to bomb the missile sites or try to force the Soviets to dismantle them. Would an air strike take all the missiles out? And would the Soviets retaliate? Kennedy favoured the air strike option and over the next few days methods and tactics were discussed. Air Force General Curtis Le May called for a major air offensive, while others claimed this would merely lead to civilian deaths.

ExComm split into two camps, since called hawks and doves. The hawks wanted to invade Cuba and force Communism out. The doves wanted to pursue diplomatic options and talk with Castro and Khrushchev.

Naval blockade

On Thursday 18 October, the idea of an air strike was rejected in favour of a naval blockade of the island, which would at least slow events down somewhat. On 21 October SAC put its B-52 force on full alert which meant that, at any one time, four squadrons of aircraft armed with nuclear weapons would be airborne and ready to attack the USSR. The following day, Kennedy addressed the nation and declared that if any missile were fired from Cuba, it would be tantamount to an attack from

the USSR and a full retaliatory response would be carried out.

On 23 October American forces were ordered to DEFCON 3, and in the Caribbean 180 US Navy ships were deployed to blockade Cuba; Khrushchev's bold plan had failed. On the 24th U Thant, the Secretary General of the UN, appealed for calm in the face of war. That same day, though, the Soviet ship *Aleksandrovsk* arrived at the Cuban port of La Isabela. Ordered to race on ahead of the Soviet supply fleet, it carried 24 nuclear warheads and had beaten the blockade by a matter of hours. Khrushchev then warned Kennedy that if any attempts were made to stop Soviet ships, Soviet submarines would be forced to fire upon American naval vessels.

At 10.25, however, some of the Soviet ships stopped dead in the water. Dean Rusk (Kennedy's Secretary of State) famously said to McGeorge Bundy (Special Assistant to the President) 'We're eyeball to eyeball, and I think the other fellow just blinked.'

Khrushchev had not yet quite given in. He declared the blockade was an 'act of aggression' and so US forces were raised to DEFCON 2; the only time throughout the whole Cold War they reached this state. The next morning, the first Soviet ship made contact with the blockade. The Soviet tanker *Bucharest* entered the zone, only to be stopped by the USS *Gearing*, but after guaranteeing it was merely carrying oil, the *Bucharest* was allowed to carry on.

As further ships approached the zone, US forces began to mobilise 25,000 Marines in the Caribbean and 100,000 soldiers in Florida. Two aircraft-carriers, the *Enterprise* and the *Independence*, headed at full speed

Taken on 4 November, this picture shows the Mariel port facility, complete with four transporters (top left), four fuel trailers (bottom left) and a series of oxidiser trailers (right). This kind of photography came courtesy of RF-8s or RF-101s flying at low level.

for Cuba. Plans were formulated for an invasion but, when 18,500 US casualties were predicted, Kennedy realised a deal would have to be made. Castro meanwhile, fearful of invasion, suggested that the Soviets prepare a nuclear strike and also ordered his own units to fire on any US aircraft flying over Cuba.

Attorney General Robert Kennedy, brother of the President and one of his closest advisers, then met with the Soviet ambassador who pointed out that the US had nuclear weapons pointed at the USSR from Turkey. On 27 October a letter from Khrushchev was received that said the Soviets would remove their missiles from Cuba if the United States removed theirs from Turkey. This immediately caused dissension within the ExComm ranks with the hawks arguing against the demand. However, Kennedy could not risk global war for the sake of a few missiles in Turkey.

On the brink

There was one final crisis point to pass, however. On Cuba that Saturday 27 October bad weather lashed the island; Soviet technicians tried to cover their missiles to prevent short circuits, while reports that a U-2 had been spotted over the island

spurred anti-aircraft batteries to life. Tension was high and, when the U-2 was seen, it was shot down by a SAM, killing its pilot. US plans called for a reprisal but Kennedy refused to authorise this – a decision that probably avoided an all-out nuclear war.

At 20.00 that evening, Kennedy signed a letter guaranteeing an end to the blockade and no invasion of Cuba if the Soviets withdrew their missiles. The following day, Khrushchev agreed and the weapons began to be dismantled. However, the Jupiter missiles in Turkey would also have to be removed; though this agreement was to be kept secret.

In the United States the settlement was seen as a major Soviet defeat; Kennedy had gone head to head with the Soviets and won. Only the hawks were disappointed, they had wanted war with the Cubans.

In Russia Khrushchev called the event a 'triumph for common sense' with the world's most powerful nations squaring off without war. The fact that the US promised not to invade Cuba was also seen as a major victory for the Soviets.

Castro, however, was outraged that the decision to remove the missiles from Cuba was taken without his consent and he saw the whole thing as a defeat.

Above: The US Navy deployed three attack and four anti-submarine air groups to the Caribbean during the crisis. RF-8A Crusader detachments from VFP-62 operated out of Key West, Florida.

Right: Throughout 1961 and 1962, U-2s spent 459 hours overflying Cuba, providing firm evidence of the Soviet build-up. Although photographic satellites were in use by 1962, they could not provide the highly detailed photography that the U-2s offered.

The Tu-16 was an intermediate range bomber and missile-carrier. Most of its missions passed to the Tu-22 and Tu-22M, but many of the survivors were converted for reconnaissance (illustrated), electronic warfare and tanking purposes.

Soviet bomber threat

The appearance in the mid-1950s of a trio of new bombers sparked the so-called 'bomber gap'. US intelligence experts feared, in the event erroneously, that the Soviets had taken a quantitative and qualitative lead in the strategic bomber field.

So desperate were the Soviets for a true strategic bomber that they reverse-engineered the Boeing B-29 to create the Tu-4 'Bull'. Several USAAF B-29s were acquired intact after landing in Soviet territory while on bombing raids over Japan.

It ought not to have been any shock. The notion that one day the Soviet Union might start building large jet bombers ought to have been taken for granted. Yet on May Day 1954, the appearance of not one but a formation of nine large new swept-wing bombers over Red Square, Moscow, caused shocks and ripples of reaction around the world – and nowhere more so than at the Pentagon. Accompanying the nine was a single example of a much bigger bomber. On Soviet Aviation Day in July 1955, seven gigantic bombers – equipped with swept wings and tail surfaces, as well as turboprop engines – rumbled overhead.

From 1955 to well into the 1960s, the 'bomber gap' was a matter for lively debate. It was based on various suppositions regarding the output of the new crop of Soviet bombers. Actual figures gleaned by the West's combined intelligence sources appear to have been conflicting or non-existent. The only thing known was that the aircraft were flying, and appeared to be impressive.

Everything was ripe for a jittery West to be afraid of the new Soviet bombers, which unquestionably would carry the thermonuclear H-bombs, first exploded only nine months after the first H-bomb of the USA. It also seemed logical to assume that, in due course, the Soviet designers would add cruise missiles (in those days called 'stand-off bombs') to the new bombers.

The most impressive of the new bombers was the four-jet aircraft, the Myasishchev M-4, dubbed 'Bison' by NATO. Few design teams in the West would have dared to build such a large, yet slender, high-aspect-ratio wing and then fit conventional ailerons at the tips – powerfully twisting the wing. Amazingly, the streamlined pods on the tips – whose down-sloping angle indicated the inbuilt twist (washout) of this wing – were variously identified in the West as radomes, mass-balances and combustion heaters. In fact, they were needed to house the retracted outrigger gears that kept the bomber from rolling over when resting or taxiing on its centreline 'bicycle' bogie main gears.

By far the most numerous of the new bombers was the 'Badger', which was actually Tupolev's Tu-88, given the service designation Tu-16. These were the equivalent of the B-47, used for medium-range free-fall missions (although they later acquired missile armament, primarily for the anti-ship mission). The turboprop monster was, of course, the Tu-95 'Bear', which could carry the most massive of the Soviet Union's H-bombs, and even dropped a 50-MT weapon – the largest nuclear weapon ever tested.

Almost certainly the last in the line of Russian strategic bombers, the Tu-160 was a major technical achievement. Sukhoi and Tupolev are currently developing candidates for a sub-strategic Tu-22M replacement.

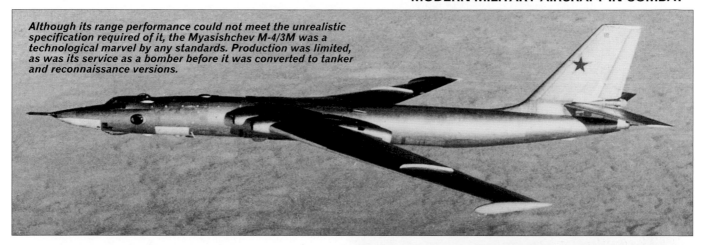

Although its range performance could not meet the unrealistic specification required of it, the Myasishchev M-4/3M was a technological marvel by any standards. Production was limited, as was its service as a bomber before it was converted to tanker and reconnaissance versions.

'Bears', too, adopted stand-off missiles, although they were best known for their reconnaissance and maritime patrol work.

On his June 1956 visit, General Twining was shown an impressive supersonic bomber which NATO at once christened 'Backfin'. The West could hardly be expected to know that the aircraft had already been rejected as a service type. The aircraft that was accepted was not seen until Aviation Day 1961. It was the mighty Tu-105, given service number Tu-22 and the NATO name 'Blinder'.

Dramatically novel in configuration, with its two massive afterburning engines mounted above the rear fuselage on each side of the fin, these aircraft were at first vastly underrated by Western analysts.

Tu-22s were initially used for free-fall bombing, but soon acquired missile armament in the form of the Kh-22 (AS-4 'Kitchen') stand-off weapon. This came in both conventional and nuclear versions, and was especially suited to anti-ship operations. As with other Soviet aircraft, the 'Blinder' spawned reconnaissance versions.

For tactical bombing, Ilyushin produced the Il-28 'Beagle', roughly equivalent to the British Canberra. Large numbers served in Europe, with all Warsaw Pact nations.

Controversial bomber

Far more importantly, the Tu-22 gave rise to the mighty Tu-22M 'Backfire' which, despite its similarity in designation, was a very different aircraft, with its engines located more traditionally in the rear fuselage. Armed with up to three Kh-22s, the Tu-22M represented a major threat to the

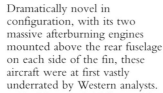

Left: The Tu-22 'Blinder' was the Soviet Union's first supersonic bomber. Despite considerable problems, the type matured as an excellent maritime strike aircraft.

US, especially its carrier battle groups. The aircraft was at the heart of the SALT (Strategic Arms Limitation Treaty) talks.

It did not help that the CIA and Pentagon could not agree on the Tu-22M's true range capability. This governed whether it was classed as a strategic weapon or not. In the event, the Soviets agreed to remove refuelling probes from the Tu-22M, thus restricting its use to non-intercontinental missions. The aircraft nevertheless became one of the most feared by NATO,

especially in the European theatre. Its deployment prompted development of aircraft such as the Tornado F.Mk 3 and raised the importance of long-range maritime air defence, especially over the North Atlantic, from where 'Backfires' were expected to attack western Europe 'through the back door'.

While the Tu-22M was entering service, the US was developing an even more capable form of bomber – the Rockwell B-1A. In answer to this, the Soviet Union began development of a similar aircraft, although larger, known as the Tu-160 'Blackjack'. Like the B-1A, the Tu-160 was to be capable of both low-level and high-level penetration, achieving about Mach 1.9 in the latter. While the B-1 was cancelled and then reborn as a low-level aircraft, Tu-160 development continued as planned, although at a slow rate. By the time the end of the Cold War brought about the termination of 'Blackjack' production, only 22 had entered service and their operations were limited by lack of fuel and funds.

Left: The best-known of the Soviet bombers was the Tu-95 'Bear'. The use of turboprops surprised some, but their immense power combined with the swept wing to make the Tu-95 almost as fast as any contemporary jet bomber.

Cold War reconnaissance

Strategic reconnaissance grew hand-in-hand with the Cold War, the resources devoted to aerial espionage increasing as relations between East and West deteriorated from the end of World War II. The evolving discipline in the West was matched by advances in Communist defences, and the Cold War had reached its height by the time Gary Powers was shot down over the Soviet Union in 1960.

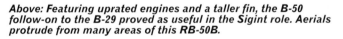

Above: Featuring uprated engines and a taller fin, the B-50 follow-on to the B-29 proved as useful in the Sigint role. Aerials protrude from many areas of this RB-50B.

Top: A unit which regularly intercepted Soviet aircraft was the 57th Fighter Interceptor Squadron, based at Keflavik, Iceland. This self-portrait shows a 57th FIS F-4 pilot flying escort to a snooping 'Bear-D'. Since the ending of the Cold War, incidents such as these have become rare.

Long before World War II drew to a close, the Western Allies were beginning to realise that they had no way of checking on the mighty military machine of the Soviet Union, which was gathering momentum as it swung through Europe. Although an ally, the Soviet Union was viewed with mistrust by both the US and UK governments so that, when the war officially ended in 1945, the chief concern (although unexpressed) was to find some way of monitoring the threat of Communist forces. Traditional human intelligence (Humint) methods would be employed to provide much of the information, but there were large areas of the Soviet Union denied to foreign travellers and locals alike. Aerial reconnaissance was the obvious answer to this dilemma.

Such flights, mainly using photographic intelligence (Photint), gave the West a greater understanding of the Soviet war machine, and throughout the late 1940s the effort was maintained.

MiG threat

Photint missions were being flown sporadically over the Soviet Union between 1945 and 1950, but with the advent of the excellent MiG-15 these had to cease rapidly. The Berlin crisis had worsened East-West relations almost to breaking point, and the appearance of the MiG brought home to the West how far the Soviet Union had advanced in military terms. The need for a huge reconnaissance effort was great, and the Western air forces responded with gusto. At first, Boeing RB-29s answered the call, together with the upgraded

Above: Among the early types employed on covert eavesdropping missions by the US Navy was the Consolidated PB4Y Privateer. This PB4Y-2S served with VP-26, a notorious outfit which was to be the first to lose an aircraft in the espionage war. Note the plethora of 'bumps and bulges' which hid intelligence-gathering antennae.

Left: Avro Lincolns were used for clandestine missions by several RAF squadrons. The belly radome housed special Sigint gear with which the Lincoln B.Mk.2s (illustrated) recorded Soviet emissions.

RB-50 Superfortress. Flying from British, Japanese and Alaskan bases around the peripheries of the Soviet Union, these World War II veterans were later replaced by SAC's newest bomber, the giant Convair RB-36. Stripped of any unwanted equipment the RB-36-III 'featherweight' version reached a height of 55,000 ft (16770 m), safely above the ceiling of the MiG-15.

The USAF was by no means the only Allied air arm involved in such activities. The US Navy was active in both Europe and the Far East, using mainly converted maritime patrol aircraft which, to allay suspicion, often operated in the markings of regular patrol squadrons. Types employed were the Consolidated PB4Y Privateer, Lockheed P2V Neptune and the Martin P4M Mercator. The UK maintained a large clandestine effort using Avro Lincolns and Boeing Washingtons. The latter was a version of the B-29 delivered to the RAF to bridge the gap between the obsolete Lincoln bomber and the arrival of the English Electric Canberra.

Other nations active in the strategic reconnaissance field were Sweden, with Douglas C-47s, and France, which at one point used civil airliners for reconnaissance purposes. Although the Soviet Union had naturally been the focus of much of this attention, the 1949 Communist takeover of mainland China had made that country a target for Western

Sculthorpe Skulduggery

The special relationship between the US and the UK resulted in the formation of one of the RAF's secret Cold War units. Operating from RAF Sculthorpe, Norfolk, USAF-supplied RB-45C Tornados were flown by RAF crews into the heart of the Soviet Union to gain radar imagery that could later by used by SAC navigators and bombardiers. In an effort to conceal their identity, the Tornados wore RAF roundels. Covert RB-45 spy flights were flown throughout 1951 and 1952 until the introduction of the Canberra.

snooping, particularly after the Chinese intervention in Korea.

Secretive Stratojet

By far the most important new type introduced by the USAF during this clandestine war was the Boeing RB-47 Stratojet. The 55th Strategic Reconnaissance Wing, the USAF's premier signals intelligence (Sigint) unit, flew a host of specialised variants around the Soviet border and, on rare (often unauthorised) occasions, across it to photograph missile sites.

Response from the East

Long the victim of overflights and peripheral snooping, the Soviet Union did not feel ready to send out its long-range

bomber trio to perform similar duties around Western navies and coastlines until the 1960s. Tupolev Tu-16 'Badgers', Tu-95 'Bears' and Myasishchev M-4 'Bisons' became regular sights around Western naval formations. The aircraft were equipped for photographic reconnaissance and also for lapping up electromagnetic radiation emitted by the Western ships. The Soviet aircraft began operations from Egyptian bases to monitor Western deployments in the Mediterranean. Such activities rapidly became an accepted part of the overall reconnaissance scene, increasing in regularity until their operations equalled or even overtook those of the West, although no direct overflights of

Western countries were made.

Cold War recce operations were at their height between 1947 and 1977. Some 40 US aircraft were shot down, with over 350 crew on board: 187 people survived and 34 bodies were recovered, but the fate of the remaining 135 souls has never been confirmed. Sweden lost no aircraft, while the UK probably lost a single Lincoln on 12th March 1953.

Above: 'Bears', 'Bisons' and 'Badgers' were constantly monitoring NATO navies and became regular customers for Western interceptors. This Tu-95 'Bear-D' is equipped with Elint blisters and reconnaissance camera ports on each side of the rear fuselage.

RAF spies

Along with those of the USAF the RAF provided a host of dedicated Sigint aircraft during the early 1960s, including the Comet R.Mk 2s (right) and Canberra B.Mk 6 (mod)s (below) of No. 51 Sqn. Both types were in use from 1958, and were seen in a number of configurations. The Comets and Canberras were regular visitors to the RAF's base at Akrotiri, Cyprus. From here, the aircraft probed the southern approaches to the Soviet Union and checked on potential aggressors within the Middle East.

The Phantom was Britain's first line of defence at the height of the 'Bear' flights. Here, an FG.Mk 1 of No. 43 Squadron shadows a Tu-95RT 'Bear-D' which was snooping on NATO manoeuvres. The Soviet patrollers were known to the RAF as 'Zombies' and their activity reached its peak in the late 1970s/early 1980s.

Air defence of the West

The perceived massive build-up of the Soviet nuclear arsenal led the West to spend billions on producing ever-more sophisticated fighters to halt the Soviet bombers before they reached their targets.

To most military personnel, the Cold War was a time of endless training for a war which never came. But there was one group of airmen who went head-to-head with their potential enemies for real. Day in, day out, air defence and interceptor pilots from both East and West took to the air against intruders, weapons live and ready to shoot if called upon.

NATO in its early days had one vital raison d'être: to counter the forcible conversion of western Europe to communism by the might of the Soviet Union. World War II had shown that control of the air was vital to any land campaign, and any move by the thousands of Soviet and Warsaw Pact tanks on the Central Front would have been preceded by an all-out air assault, with the main aim of knocking out NATO air defences.

Germany was on the Iron Curtain's front line. Major

Soviet air bases were only a few minutes' flying time from the country's industrial heartland, and the defence of Germany was a key pillar of NATO strategy. German interceptors served alongside aircraft from Belgium, the Netherlands, Denmark, the United Kingdom, France, the USA and Canada. They were kept on a high state of alert, ready to launch against intruding bombers at a moment's notice.

Britain was the linchpin of NATO's plans for reinforcement across the Atlantic, and its fighters were charged with intercepting bombers far out over the ocean. Soviet long-range maritime aircraft probed the defences regularly, and fighters on quick reaction alert went up to investigate contacts daily. Subsonic Javelins in the 1950s gave way in RAF service to supersonic Lightnings and Phantoms in the 1960s.

Other NATO countries, particularly those on NATO's

flanks bordering directly with the Soviet Union, had problems peculiar to their own geographical locations. The wastes of northern Norway commanded the Arctic, while Turkey was concerned with restricting the progress of the Soviet Black Sea Fleet. Both were key Soviet targets and had to be defended.

And, for the first time, the United States itself was under threat. Although worlds apart politically, the USA's west coast and the Soviet Union's east coast were very close geographically.

In the 1950s, the American military regarded an attack by Soviet nuclear-armed bombers as

a real and imminent prospect. In the Pentagon and in the Canadian Defence Ministry, these officers faced a challenge without precedent – a likely onslaught by air that might wreak the most ghastly destruction, compared to which even the recently-won World War II would pale into insignificance. In 1951, intelligence analysts estimated that Moscow would soon be able to 'deliver a sufficient number of atomic bombs to cause over one hundred detonations in the United States'. This estimate was premature, but within a decade it became real and multiplied. At the height of the Cold War, the

Above: From its inception, the F-106 was intended to carry one Douglas MB-1 Genie, an unguided rocket projectile with a nuclear warhead. The single rocket was expected to decimate an approaching bomber formation.

Left: The Northrop F-89 Scorpion guarded the farthest reaches of the North American continent in the 1950s. Not particularly fast, it was distinguished by long range, a powerful airborne intercept radar, and a sophisticated (for the time) fire-control system.

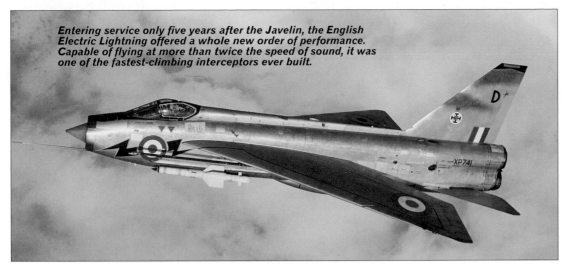

Entering service only five years after the Javelin, the English Electric Lightning offered a whole new order of performance. Capable of flying at more than twice the speed of sound, it was one of the fastest-climbing interceptors ever built.

number of nuclear warheads in the Soviet arsenal amounted to not hundreds, but tens of thousands.

Air Defense Command

The primary defender of the USA was the fledgling Air Defense Command, or ADC, which had been founded on 21 March 1946. In 1947, the year the US Air Force broke away from the US Army to become an independent service, Winston Churchill warned of an 'Iron Curtain' falling over the Communist nations. By 1949, the Soviets had exploded their first atomic device and ADC grew from a 'paper' command to being the operator of a few twin-engined Northrop F-61C Black Widow night-fighters. Expansion with Lockheed F-80 Shooting Stars followed, but by 1951 these relatively slow, straight-winged machines were being superseded by the swept-wing, state-of-the art North American F-86 Sabre.

However, single-seat day fighters could only do part of the job. A number of new all-weather fighters was developed to equip ADC's growing fighter-interceptor squadrons. 'All-weather' was the new term for radar-equipped interceptors that could function by day or by night and in (some) adverse conditions. In the USAF, the new squadrons were called Fighter Interceptor Squadrons, or FISs, pronounced 'fizzes'.

The North American F-86D Sabre, Northrop F-89 Scorpion, and Lockheed F-94 were a trio of 'interim' warplanes tailored to carry airborne radar, guns and rocket projectiles. Crews were trained to scramble against incoming bombers and to intercept them as far as possible from their targets – at best, north of the Arctic circle and far from vulnerable cities.

With the 1957 establishment of the joint US/Canadian North

American Air Defense Command (NORAD), the Canadian Avro Canada CF-100 Canuck joined the fighter interceptor forces arrayed towards the north. They practised radar-guided Ground Controled Intercept (GCI) missions throughout the 1950s, while planners in Washington and Ottawa searched for more advanced interceptors. Their work was characterised in a booklet of the era in which ADC attempted to coin the acronym DIID (Detect, Identify, Intercept and Destroy), but this jargon for the air defence mission never caught on.

Weapon systems

By 1954 the USAF had begun to develop an interceptor using an integrated 'weapons system' approach that would produce the aircraft and its military capability simultaneously. The result was the Convair F-102 Delta Dagger, which overcame early developmental problems to become an effective interceptor. It was joined in ADC squadrons – as well as Air National Guard squadrons, dedicated to the ADC mission – by the McDonnell F-101B Voodoo, a huge, powerful aircraft which was difficult to fly, but which possessed enormous firepower.

In Canada in the mid-1950s, work progressed on the Avro CF-105 Arrow, a giant, delta-winged interceptor which would give NORAD the capability to meet Soviet bombers as far away as the North Pole. Despite test examples flying, the project was doomed by political wranglings and Canada eventually acquired American-built CF-101 Voodoos instead.

The ultimate US interceptor was the Convair F-106 Delta Dart, which eventually reached no fewer than 14 ADC squadrons.

To help the Cold War era's expanding fighter-interceptor force in parrying a bomber strike, NORAD developed a DEW (Distant Early Warning) line of ground radar stations running from Greenland to Alaska, all pointed north. Approaching bombers would be detected by ground-based radar, then ground controllers would track the bombers and direct fighters to the intercept. The fighter pilot would receive short voice instructions intended to get him within sufficient range to be able to use his own radar. Voice-directed Ground GCIs were replaced in the late 1950s with the SAGE (Semi Automatic Ground

Environment) System which 'flew' an interceptor to its target via automatic pilot, the pilot taking over only when it was time to fire. SAGE was used until the late 1970s when improved, secure communication made it possible again to use voice transmissions to vector an interceptor toward its target.

When NORAD came into being during the summer of 1957, the USA and Canada had more than 1,000 aircraft dedicated to air defence. This force level was maintained until well into the 1960s, when it was acknowledged that the manned bomber had been supplanted by the ICBM as the vehicle most likely to be employed as a nuclear weapons delivery system in future. Thereafter, the respective interceptor fleets entered a period of decline, which had a devastating effect on overall force strength. Some idea of this fall from grace can be gleaned from the fact that, by the mid-1970s, the ADC had fallen to just six squadrons (all equipped with the Convair F-106A Delta Dart), ably supported by a rather larger number of second-line Air National Guard units flying the F-101B Voodoo and F-102A Delta Dagger as well as F-106s.

ADC had been renamed Aerospace Defense Command in January 1968, but continued to serve as the combat arm of NORAD. On 1 October 1979, its resources were transferred to Tactical Air Command which took over most of its functions (and which in turn was modified into Air Combat Command in 1992) and, on 31 March 1980, ADC was disbanded. The interceptor force remained at the ready, however. In the 1980s, years of neglect were reversed, prompted in part by Soviet deployment of cruise missile-armed bombers, and the old fighter types were replaced by modern F-15s, F-16s and CF-188s, well able to deal with any threat.

Developed as a long-range interceptor, the Voodoo had a range of more than 1,550 miles (2500 km). Canada's Air Defence Group, which shared responsibility for guarding the polar approaches with the US Air Defense Command, took delivery of 66 Voodoos and operated them into the late 1960s.

The backbone of the Royal Navy's ASW fleet remains the Sea King, the HAS.Mk 6 version in service representing the culmination in a series of rolling upgrades. Equipped with Sea Searcher radar and an integrated passive sonar system, with Sting Ray torpedoes and depth charges, the type provides the fleet with a rugged, autonomous ASW platform.

Anti-submarine warfare

Control of the sea lanes has always been of paramount importance and, during the Cold War, the safeguarding of the world's oceans from marauding submarines was a task conducted rigorously by both East and West. With the advent of the ICBM, sub-hunting became even more important and the art of tracking the underwater menace led to increasingly sophisticated aircraft.

The world was a very different place at the end of the Korean War, with the Cold War suddenly very real. Proxy conflicts (such as Korea) seemed highly likely and the need to keep open the sealanes between Europe and Japan became apparent, as the USSR, which was racing to build a blue-water fleet, was placing emphasis on a powerful submarine fleet.

The US Navy, meanwhile, had commissioned a new class of modern carrier. Displacing 60,000 tonnes, USS *Forrestal* was the first in a series of truly modern carriers, with angled flight decks and steam catapults and the capability of carrying giant air wings. Furthermore, the role of the carrier changed from that of floating airfield to one of power projection, with complements which would include powerful long-range strike aircraft as well as fighters and fighter bombers. Carriers now took on a semi-strategic role and were integrated into SIOP (Single Integrated Operational Plan), the US's ever-changing plan for nuclear war against Russia.

However, these immense new carriers were inviting targets for Soviet submarines, and older carriers were modified to serve as dedicated ASW carriers, equipped with dedicated ASW

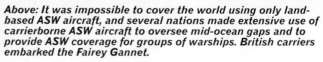

Above: It was impossible to cover the world using only land-based ASW aircraft, and several nations made extensive use of carrierborne ASW aircraft to oversee mid-ocean gaps and to provide ASW coverage for groups of warships. British carriers embarked the Fairey Gannet.

Left: Soviet maritime patrol forces retained flying-boats for longer than most Western nations. The Beriev Be-12 'Mail', photographed here by a Swedish fighter, did not enter service until the mid-1960s and small numbers remain in service in 2000.

Derived from the Il-18 airliner, the Russian (and Indian) navy's Il-38 'May' has a redesigned fuselage which incorporates tandem weapon bays, radar and sonar, and a tail-mounted MAD. At present, the Russian navy is studying plans to replace the Il-38 (and the Be-12) with a maritime variant of the Tu-204 airliner.

helicopters and aircraft. These ships and aircraft would screen the fleet, providing all-round coverage. The fear of the Soviet navy necessitated more constant coverage of the entire oceans than could be achieved by a handful of carrier groups. America, therefore, began to develop land-based, long-range patrol aircraft that were designed to operate both in the maritime patrol role – keeping tabs on Soviet surface roles – and also in the ASW role, monitoring and, if necessary, destroying Soviet submarines.

Meanwhile, there were developments in ASW radar and in active and passive sonar, as well as in new systems, most notably the MAD (Magnetic Anomaly Detector), which could detect changes to the earth's magnetic field caused by the presence of a large steel submarine. Such equipment was fitted to versions of the P-2 Neptune, Avro Shackleton and Canadair Argus.

The introduction of nuclear submarines with 'teardrop' hulls for high underwater speeds presented a challenge to ASW crews and, in the late 1950s, the first ballistic missile-carrying submarines were deployed, driving progressive improvements in ASW aircraft and equipment.

GIUK gap

If World War III had ever broken out, it is likely that the opening shots would have been fired somewhere in the icy waters of the North Atlantic. Soviet naval forces faced a major problem. If they were to interfere with NATO's transatlantic lifeline in a time of war, they had to get out into the Atlantic, but to do so, they had to travel from their bases in the Baltic, Black Sea and the northern Soviet Union, through geographical chokepoints, where NATO would be waiting.

The primary route was via the 'GIUK (Greenland, Iceland, UK) gap' – the 185-mile (300-km) wide Denmark Strait between Greenland and Iceland, and the 500 miles (800 km) of sea between Iceland, the Faroe Islands and Britain.

Even in peacetime, maritime aircraft patrolled the GIUK gap constantly, and the movement of every Soviet vessel passing into or out of the Atlantic was carefully monitored and plotted. ASW crews were among the few NATO personnel who carried out their war roles for real, with live weapons.

The Soviet threat was multi-layered. Missile-armed aircraft like the the long-range Tupolev 'Bear' bomber were one part of the web, along with missile cruisers and destroyers on the surface. But the major threat came from the huge Soviet submarine force. Primitive, noisy and short-ranged in the early post-war years, by the 1980s the

'Red Fleet' was fielding some of the largest and most sophisticated boats ever built.

A submerged submarine presents a unique challenge. In every other military field one can rely on visual, radar or infra-red techniques to detect and home in on targets, but under the sea, except in some special cases, one has to rely on sound. However, it is impossible for an aircraft to detect sound directly through the ocean barrier. An aircraft cannot dip a hydrophone into the water and, without some kind of sound-sensing device, it has to rely on MAD gear.

The solution to the problem is the sonobuoy. Sonobuoys are expendable acoustic systems, ejected from the aircraft into the sea. Floating on the surface, they then relay data via radio wave to the aircraft flying overhead, which can then deploy weapons to attack any target revealed.

It would have been P-3s of the Royal Norwegian Air Force, based at Andøya, which would have been the first to react to any movement of Soviet submarines from the Soviet base on the Kola Peninsula. The first warnings would probably have come from the Sosus (sound surveillance system) line of underwater sensors stretching from Norway to Spitzbergen or from snooping NATO submarines.

Iceland was the hinge upon which NATO's efforts to 'bottle up' the Soviet fleet depended. US Navy P-3s based at Keflavik flew missions over the Denmark Strait and over the gap between Iceland and the Faroes. Even in peacetime, America kept an Orion squadron active on the island, with smaller detachments in Britain and Norway.

Britain's Nimrod maritime patrol aircraft flew out of bases in the far north of Scotland and in the far south-west of England. The Scotland-based aircraft were part of the NATO ASW force assigned to closing the all-important GIUK gap.

Westland's Lynx is one of the most capable light naval helicopters currently in service. It is carried by many NATO and international navy's destroyers and frigates as their principal ASW weapon.

The backbone of the US Navy's ASW force in the early years of the Cold War was the Lockheed P2V (later designated P-2) Neptune. The aircraft was also supplied to a number of export operators and was licence-built by Kawasaki in Japan. The type was gradually superseded by the P-3 Orion with most operators from the early 1960s.

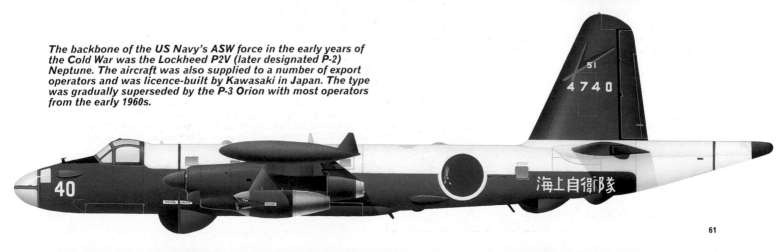

Afghanistan's air war

Soviet interest in the rugged, mountainous country of Afghanistan intensified after World War II. Afghanistan and neighbouring Iran both had long, common borders with the USSR and represented useful buffers against hostile forces.

In 1973 the Afghan monarchy was overthrown. The new republican government under General Mohammad Daud, remained on friendly terms with Moscow. The armed forces acquired large amounts of new Soviet equipment, the air force especially, which by the end of the 1970s had a strength of over 180 combat aircraft, including MiG-17, MiG-19 and MiG-21 fighters, Su-7BM close-support aircraft and Il-28 bombers.

In April 1978 the army and air force led a coup which saw Daud killed and power placed in the hands of the People's Democratic Party of Afghanistan (PDPA) under Mohammad Nur Taraki. He in turn was replaced by Hafizullah Amin.

Herat massacre

Inflamed by a hastily enacted Marxist land-reform programme, there was a popular rebellion, supported by much of the army. In March 1979, the rebels seized the western city of Herat, where they massacred government soldiers and about 50 Soviet advisers and their families.

With over 1,000 Soviet advisers at risk, the USSR began to plan an invasion. Moscow arranged to bolster the regime by

supplying 100 T-62 tanks and 18 Mi-24 'Hind' assault helicopters. Another 18 'Hinds' were sent later, including some potent 'Hind-D' gunships.

The initial Soviet airlift of 6,000 combat soldiers into the air bases at Bagram and Shindand took place over the period 24-26 December 1979. The Russians moved out of their bases and attacked the Kabul regime on 27 December. After deposing Amin, they installed the exiled former Deputy PM, Babrak Karmal, who had 'requested the Soviet assistance' then being fraternally given. Simultaneously, 15,000 troops advanced from the Soviet border, supported by tanks, MiG-21 fighter bombers and Mi-24 'Hind' gunships.

Holy War

The Soviets gained most of their urban objectives very quickly – but the fiercely independent Afghans put up strong resistance in the country areas, declaring a *jihad,* or holy war against the invaders. The Soviet occupation soon degenerated into a stalemate.

The USSR made extensive use of helicopters and air support. The 'Hind-A' and the more heavily armed 'Hind-D'

Muslim guerrillas pose on the wreckage of a government Mil Mi-8 helicopter. The 'Hip' had been shot down in Afghanistan's Zabul province by a missile in October 1990.

were augmented by Mi-8 'Hips', some of them still carrying their civilian Aeroflot markings. Tactics were evolved using mobile ground forces as 'hammers' to drive guerrillas onto heli-landed 'anvils'.

Soviet and Afghan units provided close air support for attacks against guerrilla strongholds. High-performance combat aircraft played a limited part: pitting a Mach 2 Su-24 'Fencer' against ragged hill tribesmen proved ineffective and costly. However, the Su-25 'Frogfoot' made its combat debut and proved much more suitable.

Stalemate

Early 1980 set the pattern for subsequent years as Soviet troops conducted a major spring offensive. During May, Mi-24s were first seen with rearward-facing machine-guns to counter the guerrilla tactic of allowing helicopters to overfly their positions before opening fire.

At first the main guerrilla anti-aircraft weapon had been the twin-barrelled 20-mm cannon,

but further armament was quickly made available through Pakistan from sources as diverse as Saudi Arabia, China, Iran and particularly Egypt. The USA responded to the invasion by covertly arming the resistance.

By 1982, the Soviets were destroying crops and villages, denying their use to returning Mujahideen fighters but further alienating the populace from the Kabul regime. However, rivalry between the resistance groups prevented them from exploiting Soviet weaknesses, and besieged Soviet outposts were generally able to hold out, or even to break out and destroy their attackers.

Despite the growing military success of their offensives, the Soviets were unable to destroy the resistance movement. In 1987 they replaced Karmal with Mohammed Najibullah, former head of the Secret Police.

Soviet withdrawal

The war against the Mujahideen intensified, especially against the forces of Ahmad Shah Massoud, an ethnic Tadjik who had achieved

Above: The Sukhoi Su-25 'Frogfoot' made its combat debut in Afghanistan. A dedicated ground attack aircraft, it is tough, agile, and can carry a heavy and varied range of weaponry.

Right: Even the armoured 'Frogfoot' is vulnerable on the ground, however. The Mujahideen quickly learned that rocket attacks on Soviet airbases like Bagram could pay dividends.

Left: A heavily-armed 'Hip' of the Afghan air force comes in to land. For much of the war the Air Force supported the government, but after the Islamic take-over in 1992, it was purged of unreliable elements like Communists, Uzbeks and Tadjiks.

Below: Trainee Afghan MiG-21 pilots receive instruction before the Muslim take-over. The air force of the Democratic Republic of Afghanistan was Islamicised and purged after 1992, a process which became even harsher under the Taliban regime.

considerable success against the Soviets from the Panjshir Valley in the northeast of the country. At the same time, President Gorbachev announced the start of a Soviet withdrawal. The withdrawal was complete by February 1989. 'Russia's Vietnam' was over.

This did little to halt the fighting, which almost immediately degenerated into a three- or more-sided struggle between former factions of the resistance and the Kabul regime, which amazingly held on to power for three years.

Islam ascendant

President Najibullah was finally overthrown in April 1992, and an Islamic regime was installed. The new President Rabbani's forces, led by Massoud who had been appointed defence minister, went to war with the Pathan Hezb-E-Islam, led by former Prime Minister

Gulbeddin Hekhmatyar. Hekhmatyar's attempt to seize power was opposed by an alliance between Massoud and General Abdul Rashid Dostam, a former communist commander and warlord of the region around Mazar-I-Sharif in the north of the country.

Rise of Taliban

Hekhmatyar's power base had been in the Afghan refugee camps in Pakistan, and it was from those camps that a far more potent force was to emerge in 1994. The Taliban Islamic militia was composed primarily of religious students following the fundamentalist teaching of Mullah Mohammad Umar. Capitalizing on the unpopularity of the various warring factions, the Taliban quickly gained popular support and made rapid gains as they swept through the south of the country, seizing Kabul on 28 September 1996.

But the Taliban alienated many of their former supporters by their insistance on the world's most rigorous interpretation of Islamic law. Massoud and Dostam bounced back, leading resurgent former Mujahideen forces against a common enemy.

Never-ending war

Over the next four years, Dostam's main power base at Mazr-I-Sharif changed hands several times, and the Taliban made inroads into Massoud's territory in the Panjshir valley.

Helicopters had been shot down on both sides, and Taliban aircraft had been used several times to cluster-bomb villages though to be sheltering rebels. In 1998, the USA launched a cruise missile strike against training bases run by wanted terrorist Osama bin Laden.

It would be events on the other side of the world, on September 11, 2001, that would bring the world's attention – and the might of US air power – back to Afghanistan and the Taliban.

Gun armament
The immensely powerful GSh-2-30 twin gun pod, mounted to the right of the cockpit, had the same calibre as the original 'Hind's' grenade launcher, but with twice the range and five times the rate of fire.

Mil Mi-24P 'Hind-F'

The 'Hind-F' was the penultimate production version of the Mi-24, boasting the last word in heavy helicopter armament. Unfortunately, the sheer weight of its guns affected the overall warload. Allied to the 'hot and high' conditions, this meant that Soviet Army Aviation machines in Afghanistan never operated with a full weapons load.

Rockets
Unguided rockets were among the principal weapons of the Afghan War. The B8V20 pod carried 20 folding-fin projectiles, each of 3.15-in (80-mm) calibre armed with a 8.82-lb (4-kg) warhead and with a range of over 2.49 miles (4 km).

IR protection
To defeat the threat from heat-seeking missiles, 'Hinds' were equipped with an infra-red jammer just behind the main rotor head, and with flare dispensers either side of the fuselage beneath.

Armour protection
The Mi-24's vitals were protected by 5-mm steel armour. The windshields were exceptionally strong: none were ever penetrated, even though most of the hits taken in Afganistan by 'Hinds' were head-on as they dived at their targets.

Middle East wars

The F-4 Phantom II entered service with the IDF/AF in 1969 and was acquired in large numbers.

Regarded as one of the most prosperous yet volatile regions in the world, the countries of the Middle East and, in particular, Israel have fought each other for decades.

Following the end of World War II, British forces occupied Palestine, Jordan and Egypt, while the French occupied Lebanon and Syria, countries which they were soon to leave. Palestine Jews opposed to British policy fought the British in Palestine, forcing the withdrawal in 1948. With the creation of the state of Israel, war with its Arab neighbours was inevitable and the West made no effort to intervene. Israel's defence force successfully held out until the ceasefire in 1949, after which began a process of re-equipment.

British withdrawal

Britain withdrew from Egypt in the early 1950s but, following the nationalisation of the Suez Canal in 1956, embarked on the ill-fated Anglo-French parachute drop. The only beneficiary of this operation was Israel, which simultaneously invaded the Sinai peninsula of the Suez Canal, capturing vast amounts of war material before retiring to its original frontier. Two years later, unrest was to spill over into Lebanon and Jordan but, in both cases, the position was stabilised by Western intervention. Israel remained technically at war with its Arab neighbours and, anticipating an Egyptian invasion, in 1967 made pre-emptive air strikes, once again invading Sinai, West Jordan and the Syrian Golan Heights. This time, the captured territory was not conceded.

Jordan was the next to suffer war as Syrian forces invaded in

1970 in support of Palestine irregulars. The Jordanian government had put pressure on the Palestinians to stop using Jordan as a base for attacks on Israel, which offered to intervene against Syria in support of King Hussein.

As Egypt attempted to wear down Israel through a process of attrition, the latter was also planning an invasion across the Suez Canal. The cost of the invasion to the Israelis was high and, recognising the difficulty of holding Sinai, the historic Camp David Peace Agreement was negotiated, through the United States, with Egypt. The peace treaty was the signal for renewed Palestine attacks on Israel, leading to the invasion of Lebanon in 1982 under the guise of a military exercise. Although Israel withdrew its forces following another toughly negotiated peace settlement orchestrated by the United States, the civil war continues today and the IDF/AF makes periodic offensive sorties across the border to attack suspected Palestinian terrorist camps.

The air power of the various Middle Eastern nations can be summarised as follows:

Israel

Despite incurring the wrath of its American backer on several occasions, and being the subject of more than one remarkably brief arms embargo, Israel continues to receive massive US aid, amounting to one quarter of

that supplied by Washington to the entire globe. Israel's agreement not to retaliate during Desert Storm in 1991, following Iraqi 'Scud' missile attacks, resulted in America supplying the IDF/AF with a host of Lockheed Martin F-16 Fighting Falcons and Boeing AH-64 Apaches.

War and constant tensions between Israel and its Arab neighbours has allowed the IDF/AF to be regarded as one of the most effective and efficient air arms in the world. Equipped with the latest generation of American fighters, both long-range interception and ground-attack missions can be undertaken. The success of each aircraft in the dogfight arena can be judged by the number of aces within the ranks of the IDF/AF.

Egypt

Following the severing of ties with the Soviet Union in the mid-1970s and the Camp David Peace Agreement with Israel in 1979, Egypt has become the recipient of mainly Western equipment – among the aircraft supplied are F-16 Fighting Falcons. However, prior to this, and during the periods when tension and air engagements were at their peak, Dassault Mirage 5s and various marks of the ubiquitous Mikoyan-Gurevich MiG-21 'Fishbed' served in the air interception roles. Supplementing the MiG-21s in the ground-attack role were a number of MiG-23 'Floggers', although these were later retired and handed over to the United States and China for evaluation purposes.

Iran

Principal interceptor of the Islamic Republic of Iran Air Force (IRIAF) is the Grumman F-14A Tomcat and its associated AIM-54A Phoenix AAM. However, the fall of the Shah resulted in a fierce embargo by the United States which saw the serviceability of the 80 Tomcats fall to just a handful of operational examples. Serving along side the F-14s were F-4Ds and F-4E Phantom IIs, although their

current operational state remains uncertain and it is thought that only one squadron remains airworthy in spite of offers of covert assistance from Israel.

Iraq

Locked in combat with Iran during the war of attrition begun in 1980, Iraq's air force was filled with Soviet-supplied MiG fighters. Among its ranks were MiG-25 'Foxbat-As' and 20 MiG-23 'Flogger-Es', backed by more than 150 MiG-21 'Fishbeds'. France supplied 30 Mirage F1EQs, along with six trainer F1BQs in January 1981; these were followed in 1983 by a further 23 F1EQ-200s and six F1BQ-200s, both equipped with inflight refuelling probes. Later that year, 24 F1EQ5-200s equipped with Agave radar undertook anti-shipping missions in what became known as the 'tanker war'.

Syria

Having lost many of its aircraft (mostly MiG-21 'Fishbeds' and MiG-23 'Floggers') to Israel during the Lebanon conflict in 1982, financial constraints have resulted in Syria having to 'make do' with three generations of 'Fishbed-D', 'J' and 'L' variants. These are supported by 80 MiG-23 'Flogger-Es' and 30 MiG-25 'Foxbat-As'. Since their shocking defeat at the hands of Israeli pilots, Syrian pilots have shown little taste for a fight when confronted with an opponent.

Jordan

Having replaced ageing Lockheed F-104 Starfighters, Northrop F-5A Freedom Fighters and Hawker Hunters with Dassault Mirage F1s and Northrop F-5E Tiger IIs, Jordan relies on Europe and the US for many of its aircraft and missiles. The Jewish lobby in Washington, however, ensures that Jordan does not receive unilateral support. In October 1997, the first of 16 F-16A/B ADFs were leased to the Royal Jordanian Air Force, to join 25 Squadron, a unit which had previously operated Mirage F1s.

Often confronting the American-built Phantom in the skies over the Middle East was the Russian-built MiG-21 'Fishbed'. Here, an Egyptian MiG-21 rolls in at low level for another strike.

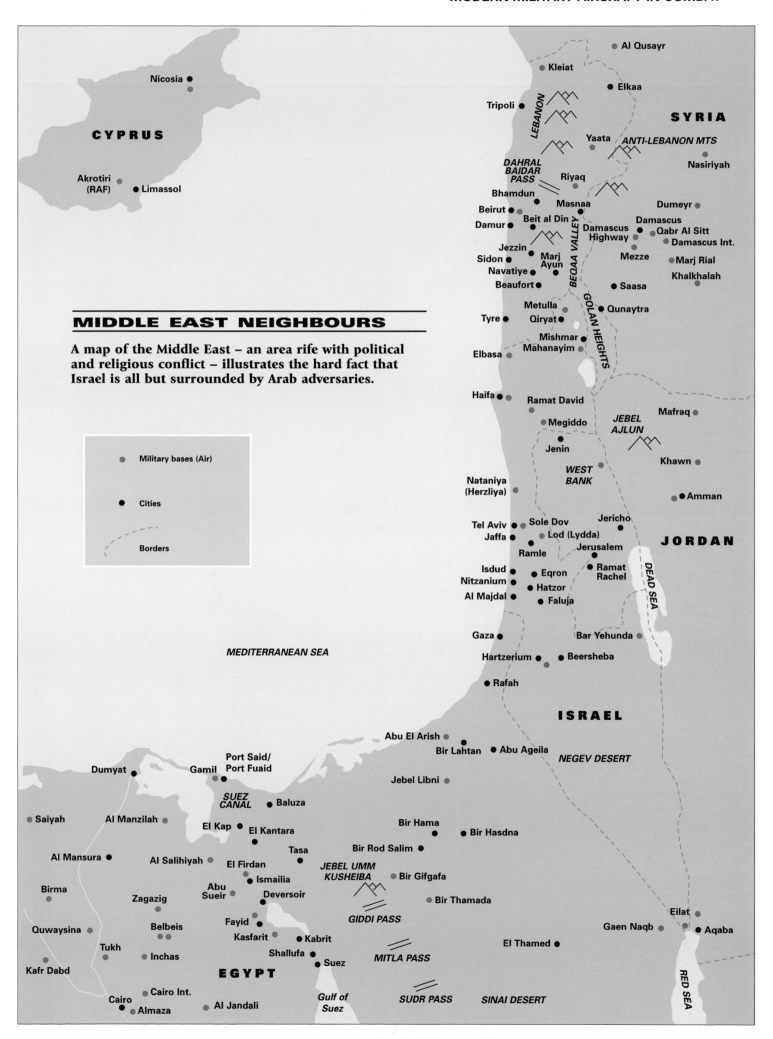

MIDDLE EAST NEIGHBOURS

A map of the Middle East – an area rife with political
and religious conflict – illustrates the hard fact that
Israel is all but surrounded by Arab adversaries.

Military bases (Air)

Cities

Borders

CYPRUS

Nicosia

Akrotiri
(RAF)

Limassol

Al Qusayr

Kleiat

Elkaa

Tripoli

LEBANON

SYRIA

Yaata

ANTI-LEBANON MTS

Nasiriyah

DAHRAL
BAIDAR
PASS

Riyaq

Bhamdun

Masnaa

Dumeyr

Beirut

Beit al Din

Damascus

Damur

Damascus
Highway

Qabr Al Sitt

Damascus Int.

Jezzin

Marj
Ayun

BEQAA VALLEY

Mezze

Marj Rial

Sidon

Khalkhalah

Navatiye

Beaufort

Saasa

GOLAN HEIGHTS

Metulla

Qunaytra

Tyre

Qiryat

Mishmar

Elbasa

Mahanayim

Haifa

Ramat David

JEBEL
AJLUN

Mafraq

Megiddo

Jenin

Khawn

WEST
BANK

Nataniya
(Herzliya)

Amman

Sole Dov

Jericho

Tel Aviv

Lod (Lydda)

Jaffa

Jerusalem

JORDAN

Ramle

Isdud

Eqron

Ramat
Rachel

DEAD SEA

Nitzanium

Hatzor

Al Majdal

Faluja

Gaza

Bar Yehunda

Hartzerium

Beersheba

ISRAEL

Rafah

MEDITERRANEAN SEA

Abu El Arish

Bir Lahtan

Abu Ageila

NEGEV DESERT

Jebel Libni

Port Said/
Port Fuaid

Dumyat

Gamil

SUEZ
CANAL

Baluza

Saiyah

Al Manzilah

El Kap

El Kantara

Bir Hama

Bir Hasdna

Al Mansura

Tasa

Bir Rod Salim

Al Salihiyah

El Firdan

JEBEL UMM
KUSHEIBA

Bir Gifgafa

Birma

Abu
Sueir

Ismailia

Zagazig

Deversoir

Bir Thamada

GIDDI PASS

Eilat

Quwaysina

Belbeis

Fayid

Gaen Naqb

Aqaba

Tukh

Kasfarit

Kabrit

El Thamed

MITLA PASS

Inchas

Shallufa

Suez

Kafr Dabd

EGYPT

SUDR PASS

SINAI DESERT

RED SEA

Cairo Int.

Cairo

Almaza

Al Jandali

Gulf of
Suez

Six-day War

By the 1960s the Arab world of the Middle East had divided roughly in half. The 'revolutionary' states, led by Egypt's Colonel Gamal Abd El-Nasser, comprised Egypt, Syria and Iraq. A more pragmatic group of 'traditionalist' states included Saudi Arabia and Jordan. The two groups found themselves at loggerheads over their approach to Israel. The creation of the Palestine Liberation Organisation in 1964 was an added complication and Palestinian attacks on targets in Israel were met with increasing force. In May 1967 Nasser deployed troops in the Sinai and the Straits of Tiran were closed to Israeli shipping by Egypt. Jordan and Syria also found themselves arrayed against Israel. On 29 May Nasser announced 'we are ready to confront Israel' and, while his actual intentions remained ambiguous, the Israeli High Command decided that they could not afford to give him the benefit of the doubt and prepared to strike.

One of the most numerically important and ultimately effective aircraft in the Israeli air force was the Dassault Mirage IIICJ. Carrying various missile, bomb and rocket combinations, the Mirage was involved throughout the conflict in both ground-attack and interceptor roles.

At dawn on 5 June 1967 40 Israeli air force (IAF) aircraft were spotted on Egyptian coastal radar flying west over the Mediterranean, supposedly on a routine daily training exercise; no action was taken and the Egyptian dawn fighter patrols were stood down. Less than 15 minutes later ten sections, each of four Mirage IIICJs or Super Mystères, struck the Egyptian airfields at Abu Sueir, Beni Sueif, Bir Gifgafa, Bir Thamada, Cairo West, El Arish, Fayid, Inchas, Jebel Libni and Kabrit, bombing and strafing the parked aircraft and cratering the runways. Two more waves followed immediately afterwards while the first returned to base to refuel and rearm before rejoining the attack. In three hours the Israeli pre-emptive strikes destroyed more than 300 Egyptian aircraft, almost all of them Soviet-built MiG-17s, -19s and -21s, Su-7s, Il-28s and Tu-16s. Egypt's two squadrons of Tu-16s (considered to be vital targets because of their ability to carry large stand-off missiles like the AS-5 'Kelt', capable of reaching Israeli cities) were to all intents and purposes wiped out while still on the ground. Israeli sources at the UN revealed that less than 20 Israeli aircraft were lost, including examples of the Mirage IIICJ, Super Mystère B2, Mystère IVA, Vautour and Ouragan. Most of them were lost

to ground-fire encountered during the initial strike.

Arab allies

Within hours Jordan, Syria, Iraq and Lebanon joined the war, Jordan's artillery cratering the vital runways at Ramat David, and its air force (RJAF) launching an attack by 16 Hawker Hunters on Kfar Sirkin and Nataniya. Now the IAF turned its attention to the RJAF with devastating strikes against its bases at Mafraq and Amman, destroying 17 of Jordan's total force of 18 Hunters. With no aircraft for his pilots to fly, King Hussein placed his men at the disposal of the Iraqi air force at its base H3.

It was Syria's turn to be attacked in the afternoon when IAF aircraft struck bases at Damascus, Dumayr, Marj Rial and Seikal. The final attacks of this first day found the IAF hitting Egyptian radar stations in Sinai and along the Suez Canal, followed immediately by airfield strikes on Al Minya, Cairo International Airport and Helwan, as well as Luxor and Ras Banas in the south.

Egyptian defence plans for the Sinai had depended heavily on air support, but with more than three-quarters of the Egyptian air force destroyed on the first day and a successful Israeli Sikorsky S-58 helicopter-mounted commando attack behind the Sinai frontier, Field Marshal Amer decided to pull his forces back from the border on 6 June. Seeing their enemy in retreat, the Israeli army launched two

Three Egyptian air force MiG-17 'Fresco' fighters fly in formation over the Sinai Desert. As with other aircraft types in Arab service, the MiG-17 suffered badly at the hands of the Israeli air force.

The charred remains of four Egyptian MiG-21F 'Fishbed-Cs' of No. 45 Squadron at Abu Sueir provide graphic evidence of the effectiveness of Israeli pre-emptive air strikes. Such scenes were repeated at most Egyptian airfields.

powerful armoured thrusts, which quickly broke through the Egyptian front, to seize the key Giddi and Mitla mountain passes leading to western Sinai. Succeeding in this, the Israeli army trapped large Egyptian forces in the east where they were attacked by Israel's Fouga Magisters (previously held back for home air defence), Mirage IIIs, Super Mystères and Vautour twin-engined bombers.

As desperate efforts were made by the Egyptians to contain the Israelis' advance in the Sinai, their air force strove to make airworthy small numbers of MiG-21 'Fishbeds' with which to attack the IAF when

favourable opportunities occurred. However, significant casualties had been suffered by Egypt's pilots, of whom not more than about 50 of the most experienced now survived, not to mention the badly damaged runways. Pairs of aircraft were sent into action but, almost invariably, they were overwhelmed and shot down.

In the north most of the fighting was in the air at first. An Iraqi Tu-16 'Badger' attacked

the Nataniya industrial area on 6 June, but was shot down. When the IAF then tried to attack Iraqi bases it was heavily engaged by Hunters whose pilots claimed nine of the raiders. A Lebanese reconnaissance Hunter was shot down over Galilee as frequent air battles continued for

the next four days. One of the Jordanian Hunter pilots, Captain Ihsan Shurdom, was credited with destroying one Mirage, two Mystères and a Vautour.

By 8 June the battle in Sinai was nearing its end, with the Egyptian air force powerless to strike effectively. A UN cease-fire came into effect on the 9th, observed by both Israelis and Egyptians in the south. In the north Syria had already accepted a UN cease-fire on 8 June, but the Israelis persisted in land attacks on the Golan heights. The Syrians withdrew the remains of their air force from operations over the front to concentrate on defending Damascus. Hostilities only ended when the Israelis had achieved all their objectives on the ground.

Israel had won the war but failed to impose peace in the area. The Israelis had destroyed 286 Egyptian, 22 Jordanian, 54 Syrian, about 20 Iraqi and one Lebanese aircraft for the loss of between 45 and 60 of their own, as well as some 30 pilots killed or captured. There was to be no reconciliation between Arab and Jew, however; both sides simply set about rebuilding their forces ready to embark on the next, inevitable confrontation.

British-built Hawker Hunters were operated by Jordan and Iraq. This example is an Iraqi F.Mk 59. During the war Jordanian pilots flew under Iraqi command after all their own aircraft were destroyed.

Mystère IVA

The close relationship between France and Israel meant that many French types were operated by Israel during the conflict. This Dassault Mystère IVA depicts the paint scheme, consisting of a light-sand and green camouflage, carried by aircraft assigned to airfield attack. Three squadrons (60 Mystères) were involved,

with only eight lost in total. During these strikes the IAF introduced new weapons, known as 'dibber' bombs, designed to maximise damage to enemy runways. This type of bomb was designed for release at low altitude and at high speed, after which a parachute would open to ensure separation and orientate the weapon

perpendicular to the ground. Two seconds later a booster rocket would fire and drive the hard-nosed bomb deep into the runway, where its explosion would cause a much larger crater than a conventional weapon.

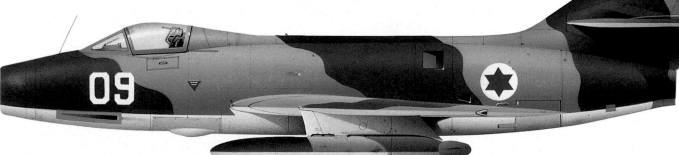

Combat proven
This was not the first time that IAF Mystère IVAs had been in action. In 1956, during the Suez conflict, six Mystères battled an equal number of Egyptian MiG-15 jets over Kabrit, an Egyptian air base near the Suez Canal. One Mystère pilot shot down one of the MiG-15s.

Power plant
A single Hispano Suiza Verdon turbojet provided the Mystère IVA with a thrust of 7,710 lbs (34.2 kN). The aircraft's impressive performance allowed it to perform both fighter interception missions and low-level high speed attacks.

Yom Kippur: part 1

In October 1973, Arab forces seized the initiative for the first time since 1948. Their objectives were more limited than before, however, being primarily to unblock the diplomatic log jam. For the first time, Egypt and Syria also achieved some real military co-ordination, a fact symbolised by new national markings carried by many of their aircraft.

Optimised for the fighter-bomber role with bombs and rocket launchers, a Syrian/Arab air force MiG-17F 'Fresco' hurtles past the fiery remains of an Israeli ground target in the Golan Heights area. The initial Arab air attacks, containing the element of surprise, proved highly effective.

At 14.05 on 6 October 1973, the Suez front erupted with thousands of guns as the Egyptian army prepared to cross the Canal. The Egyptian Air Force (EAF) played a primary role in this initial attack, while air-defence fell largely to a network of radar-controlled anti-aircraft guns and surface-to-air missiles (SAMs). A total of 222 Egyptian aircraft hit El Mulayz, Bir Thamada and El Sur airfields, rear area artillery positions, Hawk SAM batteries, command and communications centres, radar sites, jamming and monitoring stations. Meanwhile, FROG tactical missiles headed towards Israeli bases at Bir Gifgafa and Tasa, to be followed by another wave of aircraft which also hit the Umm Kusheiba command post and communications centres between El Kantara and Abu Aghelia. Tupolev Tu-16s launched about 25 'Kelt' stand-off bombs against targets farther to the east. After an hour of air and gun bombardment, Egyptian troops crossed the canal in dozens of places and began to consolidate their positions.

In the north, Syrian aircraft supported a thrust forward over the Golan plateau. MiG-17 'Frescoes' and Sukhoi Su-7 'Fitters' performed many of the low-level missions, as was the case with Egypt, both countries leaving their MiG-21 'Fishbeds' to provide top cover. Assault troops travelled by Mil Mi-8 'Hip' helicopters to seize objectives, either in Sinai or on the Golan Heights.

Israel's response

The first Israeli aircraft were in the air within 30 minutes, although it would be two hours before the IDF/AF appeared in strength. In the attack role was the McDonnell Douglas A-4 Skyhawk, supported by its more capable stable-mate, the F-4 Phantom. The Dassault Mirage IIICJ, aided by the first few IAI Nesher copies built in Israel, was employed against ground targets, although both it and the Phantom were also useful in the air-defence role. Even a dozen or so ageing Dassault Super Mystère B2s were brought in for attack. Supporting helicopters included the Aérospatiale Super Frelon and smaller Bell UH-1 Huey.

Though the Sinai desert acted as a buffer zone to the south, there was no such luxury for Israel in the north. Thus, the war against Egypt was put on 'hold' and first priority given to defeating the Syrian armies only a few miles from the Israeli towns and villages. The IDF just managed to hold out until reserves could be assembled and brought to bear. However, after three days of fighting, including a fierce tank battle, the Syrians were too weak to exploit their dearly-won gains and were forced to withdraw.

Iraq added a squadron of Hawker Hunters to the Syrian air forces on 7 October, and a unit of MiG-21s soon after this. Jordan's contribution to the air war was restricted to firing SAMs at IDF/AF aircraft coming within range of its territory. With Syrian units now falling back, air defence assumed crucial importance as the IDF/AF ranged almost as far as the Turkish border in its campaign of strategic bombing. By 12 October, the air defence network was in such disarray, with many MiG-21s destroyed or damaged, that the outclassed MiG-17 had to be diverted to interception missions. Although the Syrian air force occasionally got the better of its adversary in dogfights, Israeli forces pressed forward relentlessly in the north.

Meanwhile, on the Egyptian front, matters were not going well for Israel. Within two days of the first attack, the east bank of the Suez Canal was firmly in Egyptian hands, despite 23 Israeli counterattacks. IDF/AF aircraft managed, on 7 October, to disrupt further Mi-8 commando-insertion operations and shoot down 10 helicopters, yet the SAM screen was proving devastatingly effective, as were the anti-tank missiles defending the Egyptian-occupied strip on the ground. The Arabs were now content to let the war of attrition run its course, having implanted 75,000 men and 800 tanks in the corridor along the east of the Canal bank.

SAM scourge

IDF/AF loss returns tell almost the whole story. During the first four days, Israel lost 81 aircraft. This was two-thirds of its total losses during the 19 days of conflict. In 1967, the IDF/AF

The sheer logistics of the conflict put great strain on the transport fleets of both sides, with aircraft flying round the clock to support the forward forces. Illustrated is one of six Iraqi air force Antonov An-12 'Cub-As' used as troop/freight transports.

The Arab world had long been the recipient of military hardware produced by Eastern bloc nations, but some Western types also saw action in support of the Arab cause. Huge numbers of aircraft were committed to the war effort but, by the end of the campaign, losses were very high.

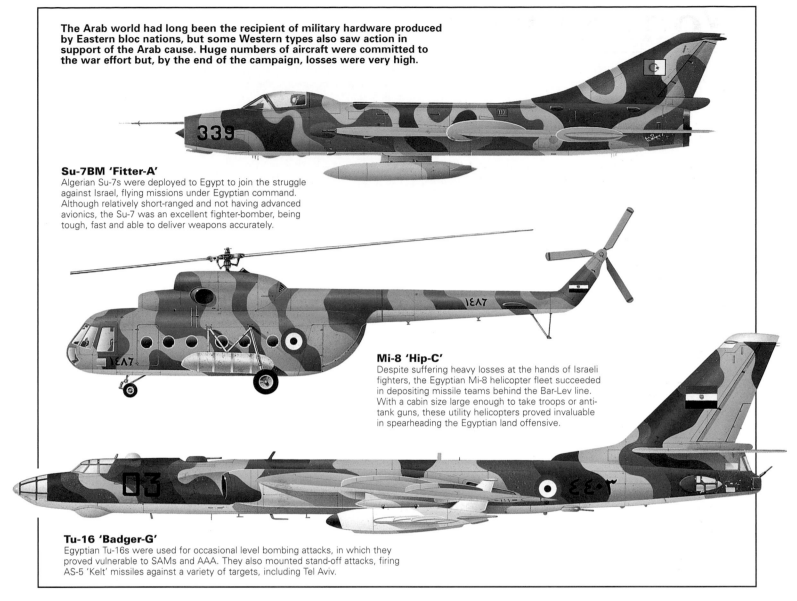

Su-7BM 'Fitter-A'

Algerian Su-7s were deployed to Egypt to join the struggle against Israel, flying missions under Egyptian command. Although relatively short-ranged and not having advanced avionics, the Su-7 was an excellent fighter-bomber, being tough, fast and able to deliver weapons accurately.

Mi-8 'Hip-C'

Despite suffering heavy losses at the hands of Israeli fighters, the Egyptian Mi-8 helicopter fleet succeeded in depositing missile teams behind the Bar-Lev line. With a cabin size large enough to take troops or anti-tank guns, these utility helicopters proved invaluable in spearheading the Egyptian land offensive.

Tu-16 'Badger-G'

Egyptian Tu-16s were used for occasional level bombing attacks, in which they proved vulnerable to SAMs and AAA. They also mounted stand-off attacks, firing AS-5 'Kelt' missiles against a variety of targets, including Tel Aviv.

had contemptuously evaded the SA-2 'Guideline' SAM, and now it suffered for its past over-confidence. Stretching the whole length of the Canal on the Egyptian side were additional new SAMs: the SA-3 'Goa', SA-6 'Gainful', SA-9 'Gaskin' and shoulder-launched SA-7 'Grail' or Strela. The SA-6 was an unknown quantity in the West, and no countermeasures were known for its combined radar and electro-optical guidance system, or for the associated 'Straight Flush' target-acquisition radar.

Attempts to avoid the SA-2s and SA-3s brought IDF/AF fighters into the SA-6 zone. If they then tried the only known countermeasures of diving inside and below the SA-6 before it could reach height and speed, they were exposed to the small SA-7 and SA-9, plus the deadly ZSU-23-4 AAA system. Israeli aircraft losses on both fronts were high as fighter-bombers attempted to press home their attacks. The Arabs took to the wasteful tactic of firing salvoes of missiles, so Israel responded by sending in raids at squadron strength, instead of flights of four. In desperation, the IDF/AF even resorted to using helicopters to spot Egyptian SAMs and allow fighters to take evasive action. The practice was discontinued due to heavy losses.

Missile mishap

The SA-6 proved a mixed blessing, allegedly shooting down 40 Egyptian and four Iraqi aircraft. Before the short war was over, at least six SA-6 fire units had been captured and flown to the USA, where their secrets were probed and appropriate countermeasures devised. Had the Israelis been on the offensive, the IDF/AF would have attacked the SAM sites first. Unfortunately, the plight of ground troops was such that the air force had to provide close support at any cost.

From the brink of defeat, Israel slowly but surely regained the upper hand in what was becoming a war of attrition. Arab positions came under increasing attack from both ground and air forces as strikes were flown throughout the day. Many such missions were flown by A-4 Skyhawks, as illustrated by this example returning from a strike.

Yom Kippur: part 2

After the hectic opening exchanges between Syrian and Israeli forces, both sides exhausted their stocks of materiel to wage war. Seeking military assistance from their respective superpower backers, it was only a matter of time before the second and final round of the war began.

It was now time for both sides to be resupplied with fresh arms from their supporters. Both the USA and USSR had begun airlifting weapons on 9 October 1973, some American aid being flown straight to Sinai airfields. Syria received about 15000 tonnes in 934 transport sorties. USAF C-141 StarLifters and C-5 Galaxies made 566 sorties with 22935 tonnes of equipment (including dismantled CH-53D helicopters) up to 15 November. El Al Boeing 707s and 747s brought a further 5500 tonnes, and there was also a sizeable seaborne effort.

Aircraft losses were restored with the supply of 100 Soviet fighters, mainly MiG-21 'Fishbeds' each to Egypt and Syria, with whose air forces they entered service between 14 and 20 October. Israel had made the exaggerated claim that only four days of war supplies were left by 13 October, resulting in the acceleration of the previously low-key effort. Some 36 USAF McDonnell Douglas F-4E Phantom IIs were transferred from US stocks and delivered to the IAF during Operation Nickel Glass; the USAF units associated with this operation were the 4th and 401st TFW. These aircraft flew 200 combat missions, sometimes in USAF camouflage with only the tailcodes overpainted. During the fighting, the four Phantom units, usually described as Nos 69, 107, 119 and 201 squadrons, had claimed a large number (115) of enemy aircraft destroyed and had carried out devastating attacks on key enemy command centres, airfields and SAM sites.

Along with the F-4s were the first 28 out of a final total of 50 A-4 Skyhawks commandeered from US Navy squadrons. It was not extra fighters which won the war for Israel, however, but the transports. Inside the USAF transports came new technology: airborne ECM kits to confuse SA-2s and SA-3s, Walleye and HOBOS 'smart' bombs, AGM-45 Shrike air-launched anti-radar missiles, AGM-65 Maverick TV-guided missiles, Rockeye cluster bombs and TOW anti-tank missiles for the army. There were also fresh supplies of HAWK SAMs as well as AIM-9 and AIM-7 AAMs.

Turning the tide

Reinvigorated by these new weapons, Israel was well poised to exploit Egypt's tactical error of advancing beyond the protection of its SAM umbrella. On the night of the 15/16 October, Israeli naval units were attacking the Egyptian coast far to the west, and a rift in the Egyptian front line was exploited for the insertion of Israeli troops.

Air operations intensified to the extent that the northern front was sufficiently denuded of cover to allow the Syrians a rare chance to use Mil-17 'Hips' and Su-7 'Fitters' against Israeli bases and an oil refinery. Egypt threw its Aero L-29 Delfin jet trainers into the fray, using them (with little success) in the ground-attack role. Mi-8 helicopters were turned into bombers on 19 October in a futile attempt to disrupt Israeli Suez Canal crossings which were now taking place at a number of points along the bank. With napalm pushed out of the hold at low level, the helicopters met with little success. As the Israeli Army extended its advance, 12 of the 40 SAM sites were captured, leaving Egypt's defensive umbrella in a precarious position.

Above: Israel's F-4s were the backbone of the war, undertaking both air-to-air and air-to-ground missions. This Phantom is from No. 119 'Atalev' (bat) Squadron based at Ramat David in central Israel. Other F-4 squadrons participating in the war were Nos 69, 107, 119 and 201.

Right: An Egyptian MiG-17 plunges towards the ground after a direct hit by an AIM-9 Sidewinder. There was a curious dichotomy in the missile war, with the SAM superiority of the Arab forces being balanced by the Israelis' total dominance in AAM firings.

Pictured at the EAF base Waidi Qina, this MiG-21MF was one of 210 examples of the 'Fishbed' available to the EAF during the early stages of the war. Many later fell victim to Israeli AAMs during frenzied dogfights.

Attrition replacements were critical to both sides, and under Operation Nickel Glass the United States took 32 F-4Es from US Air Force service and transferred them directly to Israel. This F-4E shows how quickly it was pushed into service by sporting Israeli insignia on its USAF camouflage; there simply was not enough time to repaint them.

fell to SAMs and ground fire, respectively, mainly in the opening days, while combined Arab losses were just 17 and 19. Air-to-air, where there were around 400 combats, only 21 IDF losses were admitted, compared with a claimed 335 (two-thirds by cannon, and the rest by AIM-9 Sidewinders or the similar IAI Shafrir AAM at close range) losses from the Arab air forces. 'Own goals' were Israel two, and the Arabs 58.

After the war, analysts looked for the lessons of Yom Kippur. New respect was afforded to Soviet SAM systems, and the importance of ECM equipment was better appreciated. 'Smart' ordnance, which had already been used in Vietnam, gained a wider acceptance in view of its capability during the later stages of the war.

Once again the race was on to obtain better and more sophisticated equipment, so that when war erupted in the Middle East again, which seemed inevitable, both sides would be better prepared.

As the Israeli bridgehead on the western bank of the Suez Canal was consolidated, it became clear that it was going to be Egypt which lost territory, not Israel. In response to its Arab neighbour's plight, Saudi Arabia suspended oil shipments to the West. Egypt simultaneously requested a ceasefire. Under superpower pressure, this was agreed as coming into effect at 18.52 on 22 October. Israel had other ideas, though, and continued its southern drive towards Suez to encircle the Egyptian 3rd Army, until the USA forced it to halt on 24 October. There was jockeying for final positions in the north, too, as Syrian and Israeli helicopters reinforced mountain-top posts under the cover of their

own fighter aircraft. Helicopters and parachute troops assisted in the taking of the observation post atop Mt Hermon in one of Israel's final acts of the conflict.

Conclusions

To this day, each side disputes the other's aircraft loss admissions. What is beyond doubt is that they were staggering. Egypt and Syria suffered the destruction of some 220 machines, to which must be added 21 Iraqi Hunters and MiG-21s, plus 30 Algerian and Libyan fighters. Israel appears to have lost 120, including at least 33 Phantoms, 52 Skyhawks and 11 Mirages. Helicopters are excluded from these lists and account for a further 42 Egyptian, 13 Syrian and six Israeli losses. Some 40 and 31 IDF/AF aircraft

Monitoring the war

In view of the grave situation faced by the Israelis, the US decided to provide aerial intelligence in an effort to assist both the IAF and army. Commencing 12 October, SR-71 Blackbird (64-17979) missions were flown from the US, with 11 KC-135Q tankers as support for the sorties. During its 25 minutes in Egyptian airspace on the first sortie, the SR-71 photographed both Syrian and Egyptian positions; the entire mission lasted 10 hours and 18 minutes. On 25 October, '979 repeated the operation. One final mission was flown after the war by SR-71 64-17964, most of the aerial images gained being passed to Israeli intelligence.

Middle East foes

For the superpowers, Yom Kippur was regarded as a proving ground for their latest fighters but, although the MiG-21 'Fishbed' was a highly capable dogfighter, pilot training was often the deciding factor in an engagement. This being the case, Israeli F-4 pilots often emerged as the victors.

Pilots' report
Although highly trained and motivated, IAF Phantom pilots suffered at the hands of SAMs, AAA and enemy fighters. A total of 37 F-4s was lost during the war.

F-4E Phantom II
First delivered in 1969, Israel's F-4s were already combat veterans by 1973. Sources suggest that – along with the USAF F-4E model – a small number of USN F-4Bs were also transferred, but no photographs were ever released.

Disinformation exercise
The most colourfully-marked F-4s, carrying gaudy shark-mouths on their noses, were described as belonging to No. 113 Squadron. Based at Tel Nov, the unit was formed in 1971 and was supposed to have been heavily involved in the aerial battle, but sources suggest that the unit never existed and was part of an elaborate hoax.

MiG-21MF 'Fishbed-J'
Although most of the 'Fishbeds' active in the war were Egyptian, Syrian MiG-21MFs flew countless offensive strikes against Israeli positions. 'Fishbeds' flew CAPs for ground-attacking MiG-17s and Su-7/20s. Despite the introduction of the AA-2 'Atoll' AAM, most kills were accomplished with the fuselage-mounted GSh-23L 23-mm cannon.

Combat colours
'Fishbeds' wore a host of camouflage schemes, most consisting of green/tan upper surfaces and light blue undersides. This MiG-21 wears the red/white/black roundel with two green stars, adopted after the creation of the Union of Arab Republics with Syria and Yemen in 1958.

In 2004, Pakistan's air force is the last major operator of the Mirage III/5 family, having acquired second-hand examples from various sources including Australia, France and Lebanon.

Dassault Mirage III

Dassault's deltas

Dassault's concept of a lightweight, ultra high-performance fighter resulted in a simpler and cheaper aircraft than its more sophisticated contemporaries. Many advances were incorporated and the aircraft spawned a myriad of variants that achieved considerable export success.

Unquestionably, the aircraft that restored the global reputation of France as a leader in aeronautical design was the Dassault Mirage III. Devastated by World War II, the local aircraft industry strove valiantly in the following decade to catch up with Britain and the United States and was gradually able to satisfy national pride with an increasing proportion of home-designed combat aircraft in the inventory of the Armée de l'Air. Some export successes were gained, but it was with the advent of the Mirage family that the world began to take serious notice of the French arms industry in general, and Générale Aéronautique Marcel Dassault in particular.

'Mirage' has become a generic name for almost all subsequent Dassault fighters and strategic bombers, the initial series being the III, 5 and 50. Adopted by a score of air forces, the remarkably tractable, combat-proven Mirage has enjoyed a production history in excess of three decades, and even now is being refurbished and modified for further service, guaranteeing that it will mark its 50th anniversary while still in harness. Few other aircraft can match the Mirage's diverse history of production, licensed production and pirate production, during which the aircraft has been de-sophisticated and re-sophisticated to meet diverse customer requirements.

Genesis of the Mirage may be traced back to early 1952 when Dassault received a study contract for a variant of its Mystère fighter series, designated M.D.550 Mystère Delta. Some preparatory work had therefore been done when, on 28 January 1953, the Air Staff promulgated a requirement for a light fighter, incorporating what it thought were the lessons being learned in the Korean War. Parameters included a 4-tonne maximum weight, top speed of Mach 1.3, carriage of a single 441-lb (200-kg) air-to-air missile and a landing speed less than 112 mph (180 km/h). Power choice was to be made from – if necessary in combination – the new SNECMA Atar afterburning turbojet, light turbojets, liquid-fuel rocket motors and even solid rockets. Unmanned aircraft were permitted.

Responses included the Breguet 1002, Nord Harpon and Morane-Saulnier 1000, but it was the Sud-Est Durandal, Sud-Ouest Trident and Dassault Mystère Delta that received orders for two prototypes each. First flown on 25 June 1955, the rocket-boosted Mystère Delta – soon to be re-named Mirage I –

was too small to carry radar plus effective armament. Also on the drawing boards were the twin-engined Mirage II; the Mirage III with a single Turboméca Atar turbojet and 'area ruled' fuselage later incorporating simple, but effective variable-geometry air intakes; and the Mirage IV.

Futuristic project

The last-mentioned and most futuristic project impressed upon the Air Staff that the light fighter concept was a *cul de sac* in combat aircraft design and strategic defence. Accordingly, in 1956, the original specification was upgraded to 'Stage II', which called for a multi-role, radar-equipped fighter, which only Dassault was in a position to supply before the end of the decade.

Skipping the Mirage II stage, the firm developed the III to the required standard, while the IV was scaled up into a strategic bomber. With incredible speed, Dassault produced a Mirage III fuselage within the year, permitting the aircraft to take to the air on 17 November 1956.

Turning a research machine into a service fighter was the task

Above: The first production Mirage IIIC was developed from the considerably smaller Mystère Delta research aircraft, via the Mirage III (seen here) and Mirage IIIA. The III was the first of the development airframes to use a SNECMA Atar powerplant.

Below: Powered by an Atar 9 turbojet, Mirage IIIA '05' was the first Mirage completed with a production-standard airframe. Although it had a nose radome, the Cyrano Ibis radar was not fitted.

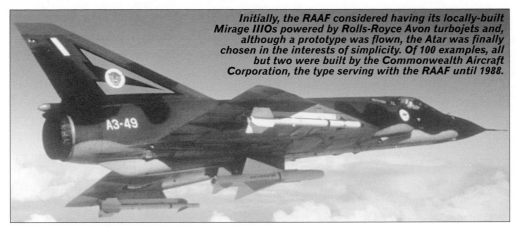

Initially, the RAAF considered having its locally-built Mirage IIIOs powered by Rolls-Royce Avon turbojets and, although a prototype was flown, the Atar was finally chosen in the interests of simplicity. Of 100 examples, all but two were built by the Commonwealth Aircraft Corporation, the type serving with the RAAF until 1988.

of 10 pre-production Mirage IIIAs, which gradually incorporated CSF Cyrano Ibis intercept radar and combat avionics during 1958-59. Considerable time was spent perfecting the SEPR 841 rocket installation in the lower rear fuselage, although it was little used in squadron service and aroused no interest in foreign customers. The rocket was to improve high-altitude performance, and was certainly not necessary lower down where, on 24 October 1958, IIIA No. 01 achieved twice the speed of sound with only the Atar operating. This was the first unassisted turbojet flight at that speed by a European aircraft, for the Mirage III beat the English Electric Lightning to Mach 2 by one month.

Deliveries of the definitive Mirage IIIC interceptor to the first operational squadron began in July 1961. Despite being an advanced aircraft, the Mirage required little in the way of specialised handling and was flown by pilots straight out of training with not much more than 300 hours in their logbooks. Only on the landing approach is special care required because of the narrow delta configuration and correspondingly nose-high attitude. From the outset, training included 'dead-stick' landings – something not attempted in contemporary deltas.

Equipped with Cyrano II air intercept radar, the Armée de l'Air's Mirage IIICs were armed with a large MATRA R.511 (later R.530) radar-homing AAM under the fuselage as a complement to twin internal 30-mm cannon. Ground attack ordnance could also be fitted, and during the 1980s a pair of underwing MATRA Magics was added to replace the optional AIM-9 Sidewinders.

The Mirage became truly multi-role on 5 April 1961 with the maiden flight of the first 'stretched' IIIE. The IIIEs were assigned a battlefield air superiority role as well as surface attack with conventional ordnance or the AN52 tactical nuclear weapon. A related variant, the IIIR, provided all the tactical reconnaissance for the French air force until phased out in 1988.

Export success

Australia adopted the Mirage III as its only single-seat fighter, and Israel made it the top combat machine in the IDF/AF. It was in the Six-Day War that the Mirage III conclusively demonstrated its versatility. On 5 June 1967, wave after wave of Mirages and other IDF aircraft decimated the Egyptian, Jordanian and Syrian air forces on the ground.

Israel was well pleased with the Mirage and ordered a follow-on batch of a simplified variant, lacking radar. A fighter-bomber with fair-weather visual intercept capability, the resultant Mirage 5 opened new markets for Dassault by offering a low purchase price and reduced maintenance requirements.

Abu Dhabi, Egypt, Libya and Pakistan all received aircraft with 'Mirage 5' painted on the side, but which were IIIEs in all essential respects, including Cyrano radar. Perhaps this ploy was to obviate political and press criticism of high-technology exports, although it certainly has confused aviation historians since.

Other derivatives

Meanwhile, the Mirage 5 launch customer had been denied its aircraft when France correctly divined that there was more money to be made by selling arms to the neighbouring Arab nations. After its Mirage 5s were embargoed, Israel built its own copy, the IAI Nesher, from 1971. A redesigned derivative with an American engine and Israeli avionics, the IAI Kfir, followed and was first delivered to squadrons from April 1975 onwards.

Chile and Venezuela purchased the Mirage 50, a Mirage 5 variant with an uprated Atar 9K50 engine of the type fitted to the Mirage F1. Several Mirages underwent mid-life improvement programmes featuring upgraded avionics and other changes. Chile and South Africa utilised Israeli technology to produce their own upgraded aircraft, namely the Pantera and Cheetah, respectively. In all (including licensed production), 1,422 Mirage IIIs, 5s and 50s were built.

The key to the Mirage's ubiquity and longevity was found in the careful blending of simplicity with adapted technology. It was a 'minimum risk' programme, relying on constructional materials and manufacturing techniques readily available in Europe during the mid-1950s. Likewise, the Atar turbojet lagged behind equivalent British and US engines in efficiency even when installed in the prototype Mirage III, yet has stood the test of time. One must be clever to make things look simple, and the genius of Dassault was to make an aircraft that was more than the sum of its component parts.

Above: As with most new single-seat fighters of the period, there was a two-seat trainer variant – the Mirage IIIB. Examples were purchased by the Armée de l'Air and the air forces of Israel (IIIBJ), Switzerland (IIIBS) and South Africa (IIIBZ).

Left: Spain's Mirage IIIEEs were known locally as C.11s. Like many Mirage operators, the Ejército del Aire planned to upgrade its Mirages, but budget cuts saw their premature retirement in 1992.

In the aftermath of the Iranian revolution, serviceability of the equipment of the county's once-strong armed forces deteriorated markedly due to lack of maintenance and spares supply. Six Lockheed P-3F Orions were acquired for ASW patrol, but only two were reported operational by the mid-1980s.

Iran-Iraq War

Iraq and Iran share a 910-mile (1448-km) border and skirmishes were common, particularly along the southern frontier at the Shatt el-Arab waterway; this vital link to the Persian Gulf allows Iraq to export its oil to the West and ensures economic growth for the country. Following the revolution in Iran in the early 1980s, Iraqi leaders became concerned about their nation's position. In an attempt to secure a more stabilised future for the region, Iraq commenced a pre-emptive strike in what they believed would be the beginning of a brief and victorious war.

War between Iran and Iraq became inevitable following the Islamic revolution in Iran. The Mullahs loudly declared their intent to export their fundamentalist revolution to neighbouring nations which had turned away from Islam. Iraq feared that the new regime would renounce the 1975 agreement which placed the border of the two nations along the Shatt al Arab, and feared for the future of the tiny strip of land which gave it access to the Persian Gulf.

Political pressure on Iran to withdraw from a number of islands in the Shatt drew little response, apart from desultory artillery shelling of frontier positions on 4 September 1980. Iraq pre-empted further action by launching an attack on Iran. On 22 September Iraqi aircraft attacked 10 Iranian airfields, and on the next day Iraqi troops invaded on several fronts. Iraqi aircraft mounted additional raids, and Iranian F-4 Phantoms and F-5E Tiger IIs attacked Baghdad, Kirkuk and a number of airfields. Eight Iraqi Tu-22 'Blinders' bombed Tehran on 28 September, flying on to sanctuary in Riyadh. Both sides had large air forces but air activity was limited, although inflated kill claims suggested otherwise: Iraq claimed 140 enemy aircraft, and Iran 68.

Nature of the war

Iraq hoped that its attack would prompt a new revolution in Iran, expecting that the Iranian armed forces would have little loyalty to the new regime. When they met fierce resistance, it became clear that the war would become a grinding battle of attrition. For its part, Iran bombed targets in Kurdestan, hoping to provoke a Kurdish uprising against the Ba'ath party regime in Baghdad.

After the initial weeks of the war, further sporadic air activity was largely restricted to the battle zone by a mutual undeclared agreement. It brought attacks on enemy troops and oil installations by aircraft and surface-to-surface missiles, with some strategic raids against power stations and command facilities.

There was intermittent air activity in support of the regular offensives and counter-offensives. Helicopter gunships were used more than fixed-wing close-support aircraft, even when Iran mounted a major armoured counter-attack at Susangerd in January 1981.

Fighter combat

Some fighter combat occurred in early 1981 during the fighting around Qsar-e-Shirin, in which Iraqi MiG-21 'Fishbeds' scored some kills with French Magic AAMs, and Iranian F-14 Tomcats countered Iraqi raids – but this was exceptional. Ground-attack aircraft occasionally flew intensive close-support operations, with the Iraqi air force generating 400-500 sorties per day at peak times. In mid-1983 Iraq admitted to the loss of 85 aircraft (including about 35 MiG-19 'Farmers' and MiG-21s, and six Mirage F1s) since the beginning of hostilities, two years earlier.

Bombing raids on cities (notably by high-flying Tu-22 'Blinders') had been restricted to 'nuisance raids' by one or two pairs of aircraft.

The Imperial Iranian Air Force (IIAF) became the second-largest foreign operator of Phantoms, with an eventual total of 32 F-4Ds (illustrated), 177 F-4Es and 16 RF-4Es.

Left: Iran's Boeing 747s were capable of refuelling in flight from the IIAF's fleet of 14 Boeing 707-3J9C tankers. Iran's fleet of US-supplied aircraft was handicapped by the shortage of spares caused by sanctions.

The war soon assumed a predictable pattern. Iran used its Revolutionary Guards (or Pasdaran) to launch impressive but ultimately futile human wave assaults on Iraq's defensive positions, often in a massive spring offensive intended to finally finish the war. In March 1982 the push was from Dezful, and in February 1983 across the marshes towards Al Amarah. In May 1982 the Iranians recaptured Khorramshahr, but a massive offensive in July was unable to take Basra. In March 1984, Iran pushed across the Hawizah marsh, intending to drive a wedge between the defenders of Al Amarah and Basra.

Iranian offensives

In February 1986 Iran successfully captured Al Faw after crossing the Shatt. Encouraged by this success, it launched another major offensive against Sulamaniyah. Tanks massing at Dezful were prevented from launching a third push only by a massive Iraqi

fighter-bomber operation, involving more than 50 MiG-23BN 'Floggers' alone. The January 1987 Karbala 5 offensive against Basra (with a second front against Sumar) threatened to break Iraq, and both Jordan and Saudi Arabia offered to send F-5s and pilots to help stem the Iranian push, which was halted for the loss of at least 50 Iraqi aircraft. Further offensives were launched against Kurdestan in March, and Basra in April.

There was no Iranian offensive in 1988, with Iraq attacking and retaking the Faw peninsula, pushing on until both sides were left where they had been in 1980. There was little more fighting on the ground.

From late 1983 it had become clear the Iraq enjoyed a measure of superiority in the air, but could not make a serious impact on the ground. Merely halting Iranian attacks required extreme measures, and Iraq began using napalm and chemical weapons. On the other side, the Iranian air force was hampered by the poor serviceability of its aircraft and

lack of experienced pilots. Serviceability improved as Israel began covert support, but the release of imprisoned aircrew to fight had mixed effects, many taking the opportunity to defect in their F-4s to Turkey and Saudi Arabia. With stalemate at the front, both sides looked to continue the war elsewhere, launching strategic attacks on each other's cities and also against oil targets and shipping in the Gulf.

The Iraqi air force began attacking Iranian population centres during late 1983, in an effort to undermine civilian morale and perhaps provoke revolt. Iran responded with similar attacks on Iraqi cities. The offensive petered out but was resumed in December 1986 when Iran launched 'Scud' missiles against Baghdad, to which Iraq retaliated with air strikes. Iraq mounted 200 sorties against Iranian cities from January 1987, losing two Tu-16 'Badgers' in the process. In February 1988 there was another round of city attacks, with Iraq

firing 40 SS-12s at Tehran and the holy city of Qom.

Tanker war

The oil industry was of such vital economic importance to both nations that it was always a key strategic target. Iraq attacked the oil production plant at Abadan within a month of the war starting, while Iran attacked Kuwaiti oil facilities (on the basis that they were handling Iraqi oil) during 1981. Iraqi aircraft using Exocet missiles attacked Iran's main oil terminal at Kharg Island from 1983, sinking a Greek tanker there on 22 November 1983 and a British tanker in February 1984. Iran began to retaliate by attacking tankers leaving Kuwaiti and Saudi ports, since they were believed to be exporting Iraqi oil. F-4Es firing AGM-65 Maverick missiles were Iran's weapon of choice for its tanker attacks. Two F-4Es were shot down by Saudi F-15s on 5 June. The pace of attacks increased steadily and it was only a matter of time before the West became involved.

Iranian air power

Under the Shah, Iran was one of the best customers for American weapons and systems; he was determined to build a truly modern air force and was able to pay cash. When the Shah was toppled, the revolutionary Islamic regime which took over had to operate a host of American weapons systems without US support, and in the face of strict sanctions.

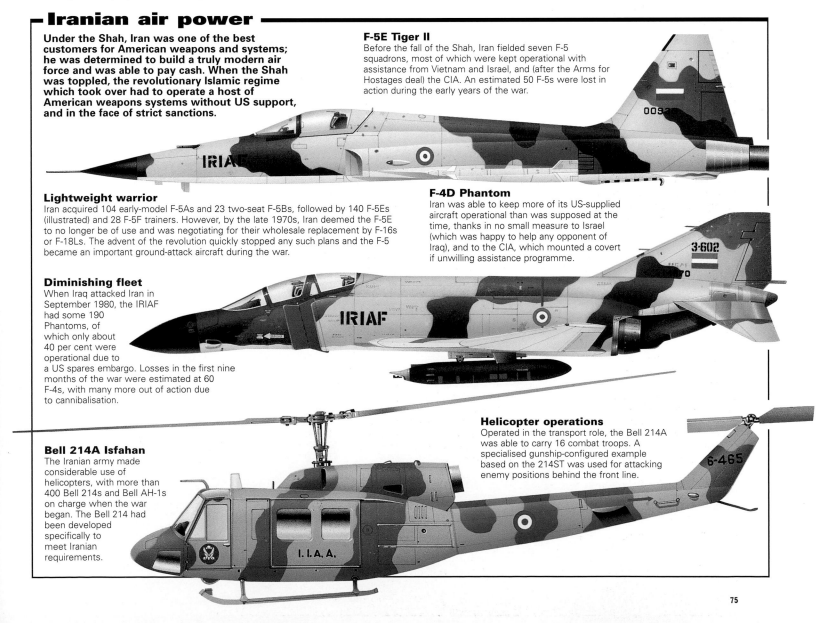

F-5E Tiger II
Before the fall of the Shah, Iran fielded seven F-5 squadrons, most of which were kept operational with assistance from Vietnam and Israel, and (after the Arms for Hostages deal) the CIA. An estimated 50 F-5s were lost in action during the early years of the war.

Lightweight warrior
Iran acquired 104 early-model F-5As and 23 two-seat F-5Bs, followed by 140 F-5Es (illustrated) and 28 F-5F trainers. However, by the late 1970s, Iran deemed the F-5E to no longer be of use and was negotiating for their wholesale replacement by F-16s or F-18Ls. The advent of the revolution quickly stopped any such plans and the F-5 became an important ground-attack aircraft during the war.

F-4D Phantom
Iran was able to keep more of its US-supplied aircraft operational than was supposed at the time, thanks in no small measure to Israel (which was happy to help any opponent of Iraq), and to the CIA, which mounted a covert if unwilling assistance programme.

Diminishing fleet
When Iraq attacked Iran in September 1980, the IRIAF had some 190 Phantoms, of which only about 40 per cent were operational due to a US spares embargo. Losses in the first nine months of the war were estimated at 60 F-4s, with many more out of action due to cannibalisation.

Bell 214A Isfahan
The Iranian army made considerable use of helicopters, with more than 400 Bell 214s and Bell AH-1s on charge when the war began. The Bell 214 had been developed specifically to meet Iranian requirements.

Helicopter operations
Operated in the transport role, the Bell 214A was able to carry 16 combat troops. A specialised gunship-configured example based on the 214ST was used for attacking enemy positions behind the front line.

War in the Gulf

Iraq took delivery of 109 Mirage F1s, of 128 ordered. Delivery of the remainder was halted because Iraq was having difficulty in paying for them; they were then embargoed following the 1990 invasion of Kuwait. Thirty-eight of the Mirages were F1EQ-5s and 6s, with Agave radar for compatibility with the Exocet anti-ship missile.

Throughout the 1980s, Iran and Iraq fought a desperate war at sea, on land and in the air. Air power was used mainly in support of costly ground offensives, but also played a large part in the tanker war which eventually dragged the Western powers into the conflict.

As their war spilled out into the Gulf, Iran and Iraq scoured the world, looking to purchase further arms in an effort to bring the conflict to a swift and decisive end.

Post-revolutionary Iran has few true friends, but it succeeded in finding enough allies to keep it in armament. Early in the war Iran infuriated the USSR by publicly rejecting a secret offer of weapons, and then turned to Libya and Korea for supplies of virtually the same equipment. Israel delivered military equipment, including F-4 Phantom spares, to sworn enemy Iran and it is alleged even to have provided support for F-14A Tomcats and Hawk SAMs. This help was provided on the logical assumption that, as Iraq was also an enemy, prolonging the war would keep the two countries too busy to hatch plots against the Jewish nation. Israel not only provided logistical assistance, but launched an attack on Iraq's nuclear reactor on 7 June 1981. One year earlier, a similar bombing raid by Iranian Phantoms had proved unsuccessful. Such was the accuracy of the Israeli attack that the nuclear reactor was completely destroyed, removing the possibility of Iraq developing material for a nuclear weapon.

Iraqi options

To offset the losses incurred early on in the air war, Chinese Shenyang F-6s (MiG-19 'Farmers') and Xian F-7s (MiG-21 'Fishbeds') were assembled in Egypt and Jordan to swell the ranks of the Iraqi air force. The USSR supplied MiG-25 'Foxbats' and 40 Czech-built Aero L-39ZO armed jet trainers. The eight MiG-25RBs supplied to Iraq saw limited service on highly successful bombing raids on Iranian oil rigs and Tehran. One 'Foxbat' was shot down by a Hawk SAM and another was lost when an engine tossed a turbine blade, forcing the pilot to eject. However, no Iraqi MiG-25Ps were lost in air combat. When Soviet military experts visited Iraq, they noted that Iraqi pilots were very pleased with the aircraft. Saudi Arabia, Kuwait and other Arab countries, fearful of Iranian expansionism, provided immense war loans to Iraq, allowing the procurement of Italian-built naval helicopters, Spanish-assembled MBB BO 105s (armed with HOT anti-tank missiles) and Hughes 300Cs and 500Ds from the United States.

France also became a major supplier of arms to Iraq, having delivered no fewer than 89 Mirage F1s in 1981-84 as a matter of priority. Such was the urgency that Armée de l'Air squadrons were forced to wait an additional seven months prior to receiving their examples. Along with the F1s, Iraq also took a large slice of AM39 Exocet production as well as buying Aérospatiale AS30L ASMs to provide a precision air attack capability, and Euromissile Roland SAMs. During the war France maintained a staff of 1,000 advisers in Iraq, alongside 6,000 provided by the USSR to assist with the operation of its weaponry.

Included in the Mirage order was a batch of 20 Mirage F1EQ-5s, equipped with Agave radar for overwater operations, and armed with Exocets. When these could not be delivered as quickly as required, France

Left: There was little in the way of air combat during the war, with many aircraft being destroyed on the ground. This Iranian Phantom lies chopped in half, the victim of an Iraqi raid on Mehrabad Airport, Tehran.

Below: As an interim solution to acquiring its own fixed-wing maritime strike capability in the form of Exocet-capable Mirage F1EQs, Iraq leased five Dassault Super Etendards, along with a large number of AM39 Exocet missiles.

loaned five Super Etendards for a two-year period commencing in October 1983. One Super Etendard was lost in a landing accident, although the Iraqi pilot managed to eject. Iraq made much play on the potential of the Super Etendard for anti-shipping attacks in the Gulf, even though Exocet-equipped SA 321H Super Frelons had already been used on anti-ship missile attacks. The first admitted use of the aircraft/ Exocet combination came on 27 March 1984, and subsequently gradually increased.

By 1984, the total number of sinkings came to 51 confirmed – the result of Iraqi retaliation against tankers entering Iranian, Kuwaiti or Saudi ports. Many more hits were claimed than objective reports substantiated because of the great range at which the Exocets were launched and the use by Iran of simple radar-reflective decoys in the water. Those that did strike home had their momentum absorbed by the victims' cargoes of thick crude oil, so that the effect was far short of what may have been expected. However, with the West's oil tankers now targeted, a swift and decisive response by the navies of America, Britain and France was imminent.

The first decisive action occurred on 21 September 1987 when two US Army AH/MH-6 helicopters attacked an Iranian naval vessel laying mines in the international shipping lanes. Following this engagement, US Navy RH-53Ds of Helicopter Minesweeping Squadron 14

Operation Prime Chance saw US Army OH-58Ds operating against Iranian patrol boats attacking tankers transitting the Persian Gulf. On one occasion, a rig used by Iranian Revolutionary Guard speedboats was destroyed after an attack by US Navy SEALs, supported by US Army Special Forces helicopters and naval gunfire.

(HM-14) aboard USS *Guadalcanal* swept the dangerous Straits of Hormuz, while French and US carrier aircraft provided air cover. Further clashes followed on 18 April 1988. Under the codename Praying Mantis, A-6E Intruders of VA-95 launched from the decks of USS *Enterprise* to attack the Iranian 'Saam'-class frigate, *Sablan*. After the aircraft had dropped two GBU-10 Paveway LGBs, the frigate immediately erupted into a ball of flames. Other minor clashes were to follow, which would see the US Navy engage with aircraft from the USS *Enterprise* and with USMC attack helicopters from the deck of USS *Guadalcanal*.

For striking at Iranian oil installations, Iraq unveiled the Soviet SS-12 'Scaleboard' surface-to-surface missile (SSM) in January 1984. However, the missile's impact was overshadowed by the eventual delivery of the Mirage F1EQ-5s in October 1984, which brought more warnings of an escalation in February 1985 when the aircraft became operational.

By the late 1980s, both countries were exhausted. Although Saddam Hussein and the Ayatollah each refused to admit defeat, neither had the supplies

to conduct a sustained campaign. Western observers were baffled by what they saw as Iraq's clear advantage on paper, contrasted with its inability to translate this into battle with clever strategic manoeuvres. On 19 July 1988 two Iranian F-14As were shot down over the Gulf by Iraqi fighters. On the same day, Iran accepted UN Resolution 598 calling for a ceasefire. What remained of the Iraqi war machine following the signing of an uneasy peace settlement in July 1988 was mostly destroyed in Operation Desert Storm in 1991.

Below: France was the major supplier to the Iraqi war machine, with the Mirage F1 featuring heavily in the fighting. In 1984 it was claimed that Iraq was looking to purchase up to 60 Mirage 2000s, possibly with Saudi financing. Ultimately, this deal fell through, but if the purchase had gone ahead, the Iraqi air force might have been able to put in a more credible performance during Desert Storm.

Above: Iran managed (with Israeli aid) to keep a high proportion of its F-4D and F-4E Phantom fleet serviceable. Though initially denied, covert CIA assistance, under the leadership of Colonel Oliver North, was also supplied in return for the release of hostages in the infamous Iran-Contra affair.

Below: The Aero L-39ZO is a dedicated weapons trainer, with four underwing hardpoints and a simple bombsight. The Iraqi air force operated two squadrons of these aircraft, based at Mosul and Kirku, in the light ground-attack role.

Excursion into Lebanon

Left: Modern-day warriors over ancient ruins at Massada – this quartet of Israeli F-15 Eagles typifies the formidable air power available to this small nation. Visible under each wing are the double-launch rails for short-range missiles such as the Shafrir 2 and Python 3.

Inset: Time and again the IDF/AF has proved itself far superior to the Arab air opposition in the region, with F-15s blasting large numbers of MiGs out of the sky with relative impunity. This Eagle has four Syrian 'kills' and its name translates as 'Scourge of the skies'.

Israel's adventures in Lebanon were supported by its massive air arsenal, which enjoyed great success. The fighting over the Bekaa Valley was the fiercest of all, with the Israelis scoring a resounding aerial victory over the disorganised and tactically weak Syrians.

The event which provoked the furious air battles of June 1982 was Syria's movement of its troops into neighbouring Lebanon in a gesture to halt the Lebanese civil war. During this period Israel continued to be the victim of terrorist attacks by the Palestine Liberation Organisation (PLO), based in southern Lebanon.

It is almost certain that, for some time, Israel had been planning an armoured thrust into Lebanon to remove the PLO. In order to lessen international reprobation, the onslaught was to be presented initially as revenge for a PLO atrocity, and the trigger point became the wounding of the Israeli ambassador in London on 3 June.

The attack begins

At 15.15 on the following afternoon, F-4s and A-4s of the Israeli Defence Force/Air Force (IDF/AF) streaked over Beirut, the Lebanese capital, attacking the refugee camps in which the PLO guerrillas lived, and destroying an ammunition dump in a football stadium. For 90 minutes, the aircraft ranged free over the city, treating enemy AAA and SAMs with little respect. However, during the ensuing attack on the Beirut coast road, an A-4 Skyhawk, flown by IDF/AF reserve pilot Aharon Ahiaz, was downed by at least three PLO shoulder-launched SA-7s – this was to be the first casualty of the war.

Syria responds

The Syrian air force (SAF) first appeared on 7 June in a limited attempt to intercept Israeli F-16s over Beirut, losing two MiGs for its trouble. To protect its flanks, Israel used CH-53 heavy-lift helicopters to airlift troops into the mountains (southeast of Beirut) on the following day. These positions threatened the Syrians in the Bekaa Valley, and their response was to launch a helicopter attack on the Israelis with Gazelles. By now, it was clear to the Israelis that the Syrians would have to be prevented

The new Rafael Python 3 air-to-air missile made its combat debut over Lebanon, with the IDF/AF slowly releasing further details. These Kfirs each carry two Pythons on their wing pylons.

from interfering with any anti-PLO operations.

Syrian SAM sites along the Bekaa Valley had increased to 19 and, in time, would threaten IDF/AF aircraft over the entire region. In four closely-spaced raids on 9 June, at least 17 of these sites were put out of action by a combined force of more than 90 aircraft. The raids were led by Phantoms armed with AGM-65 Maverick and anti-radar missiles. With their sites almost completely blind, the Syrians could do little as a flight of over 40 Phantoms, Skyhawks and Kfirs ripped apart the remaining batteries with cluster bombs. Two further waves of attacks were launched, which resulted in the remaining SAM sites and Syrian positions being destroyed.

Higher above, the top-cover component of IDF/AF F-16s and F-15s kept the SAF at bay. Forces of MiG-21 'Fishbeds'

and MiG-23 'Floggers' were severely mauled, resulting in IDF/AF claims of 22 shot down plus seven damaged, for no loss.

Dogfights

Israeli supremacy over the SAF was absolute and, as with all aerial victories, it owed as much to the support elements as to the fighter pilots who fired the guns and AAMs. It should be remembered that, at the time, Syria had little or no warning of the raids and possessed no AEW platforms. Still, the Israeli pilots did not have everything their own way. During one hectic dogfight, a quartet of IDF/AF F-15s was ambushed by two MiG-21s; although the MiGs were downed, one F-15 pilot lost an engine to AAA, and was forced to fight for control of his Eagle for over 20 minutes until he landed.

In all, 40 SAF aircraft (equally divided between MiG-21s and MiG-23s) were claimed by the 37 F-15s then in IDF/AF service. The remaining 44 SAF aircraft losses were claimed by 72 F-16s. Overall, Israel claimed a total of 92 SAF aircraft/helicopters destroyed. Although this final figure is still the subject of much debate, one thing is clear – IDF/AF F-15s and F-16s reigned supreme over the battlefield.

'Wild Weasel' versus SAM

Central to the Israeli victory in the air was the destruction of Syrian SAM defences. Operating under the strict control of E-2 Hawkeye AEW&C aircraft, specially-equipped Phantoms gradually knocked out the offending radars, leaving the helpless missiles and support vehicles to the mercy of heavily-armed Kfirs. The diagram below shows how a typical SAM strike was carried out, from the insertion of remotely-piloted vehicles (RPVs) to the site's eventual destruction by Kfirs.

Specially-modified Boeing 707s provide stand-off electronic countermeasures for the Israeli air operations. As well as carrying out jamming and spoof signal transmission, the 707s also carried an extensive ELINT suite.

F-15 Eagles provide fighter escort for the entire strike. Their priority is to protect the E-2 Hawkeye, however. The Hawkeye is the linchpin of the operation, providing airborne radar coverage and keeping in contact with all facets of the strike.

1a Mastiff RPVs are sent towards the SAM sites to trick the Syrians into turning on their SAM tracking radars. These RPVs are remotely flown from the Hawkeye and have radar signatures similar to those of an attacking aircraft.

1b The RPV is detected by Syrian search radar. Thinking the RPV is an attacking aircraft, the Syrians turn on their SAM tracking radars, which are located next to the missiles.

2b Once in the vicinity of the SAM site, the F-4E 'Wild Weasel' flies a racetrack pattern at low level, using the cover of the hills to shield it from the Syrian radars.

2a The F-4E Phantoms are armed with Shrike or Standard anti-radiation missiles (or both). When the RPV approaches the suspected SAM site, the Hawkeye calls the F-4Es into the area.

2c During each circuit of the racetrack, the F-4E 'pops-up' above the hills to allow the EWO to use the aircraft's highly sophisticated radar detection equipment. If the SAM tracking radar is detected, the F-4 moves in to the attack. If no radar is detected, the racetrack is resumed.

2d When the tracking radar is detected, the F-4 breaks cover quickly by climbing steeply from behind the hills. Following a half-roll, the anti-radiation missile is launched in an 'over-the-shoulder' manoeuvre which gives it a high trajectory. The missile is programmed to home onto the tracking radar emissions.

2e Following missile release, the F-4E is free to escape. The half-loop brings it out on a heading for home at tree-top height. A weaving egress is made to deter any attacks from the rear until the aircraft once again reaches the safety of the hills.

3 After the SAM radar has been knocked out, Kfir fighter-bombers are called in by the Hawkeye to strike the SAM site with conventional bombs and cluster munitions in an effort to destroy the missiles themselves.

RPVs were used widely throughout the Bekaa fighting, for both decoy and reconnaissance work. This is an IAI Scout, complete with a glass cover and other reconnaissance gear. The cedar tree symbols on the side denote 14 successful combat missions over Lebanon.

Struggle for Vietnam

The air war in South Vietnam was characterised by the counter-insurgency campaign against the Viet Cong. For these 'mud-moving' missions against an elusive enemy hiding under the jungle canopy, it was found that obsolete propeller-driven aircraft like the A-1 Skyraider were more effective than high-tech fast jets.

It was America's longest war. The military might of the world's greatest power was thrown against a wily and elusive enemy. In spite of using the latest technology, with air power being the main difference between the sides, the American military never got to grips with Communist Vietnamese forces.

Vietnam became a quagmire for America; the more the US struggled, the more deeply engulfed it became. The USA began that war by forgetting – or choosing to ignore – all the lessons the French had learned during their eight-year war with the Communist Viet Minh.

Under President Kennedy, the US military presence in Vietnam escalated rapidly. For the professional soldiers, sailors and airmen called upon to manage the war, it was to be a continuing frustration. There was no defined objective for the US involvement. Rules of engagement severely restricted operations. Orders came directly from political leaders in Washington, taking precedence over the usual prerogative of a field commander to run the war from the scene of the action.

With no goal, and with no way of measuring the progress toward a goal, the war degenerated into a conflict whose purpose seemed to be the production of favourable, cost-effective statistics: so many trucks and bridges destroyed, so many Communist guerillas killed.

The experiences gained by US airmen fighting the air war in Vietnam have been retained as some of the basic tenets of air warfare doctrine today. Vietnam saw the first widescale use of precision-guided munitions to attack targets at stand-off ranges. The fundamental tactics of defence suppression – using both electronic warfare and anti-radar missiles – were developed in Vietnam. The poor kill-to-loss ratio achieved by US fighters in air combat against North Vietnamese MiGs led to improvements in missile technology, and the formation of dedicated units, such as 'Top Gun' and 'aggressor' squadrons, to teach the basic principles of air combat manoeuvring.

But the air war in Vietnam was characterised mainly by widespread and frequently indiscriminate bombing. More than 6.3 million tons of bombs fell on Vietnam, and on neighbouring Laos and Cambodia, during the war years from 1964 to early 1973. Just over one-third of this number helped to defeat both the Third Reich and the Japanese Empire during World War II.

And yet, for all the massive air strikes and continued bomber offensives, the air war was never run in the way that was wanted by the airmen. One senior US air officer said later, "The way the strikes were flown, they were of no importance. They accomplished virtually nothing. It was not worth the effort." A basic truth about the war in Vietnam that was never broadly recognised or understood was that an ideology cannot be destroyed by killing its adherents.

Vietnam was perceived as a war of attrition, but the USA achieved only a stalemate. By any measurable terms, the United States came out of the war in far worse shape than when it had entered it, and that is one of the definitions of a defeat. America's involvement in Vietnam was a cruel lesson in fighting the wrong war in the wrong place at the wrong time.

The full potential of the helicopter was realised by the US military in Vietnam. Key roles were air assault – rapid insertion of troops under protective fire support – transport and medical evacuation.

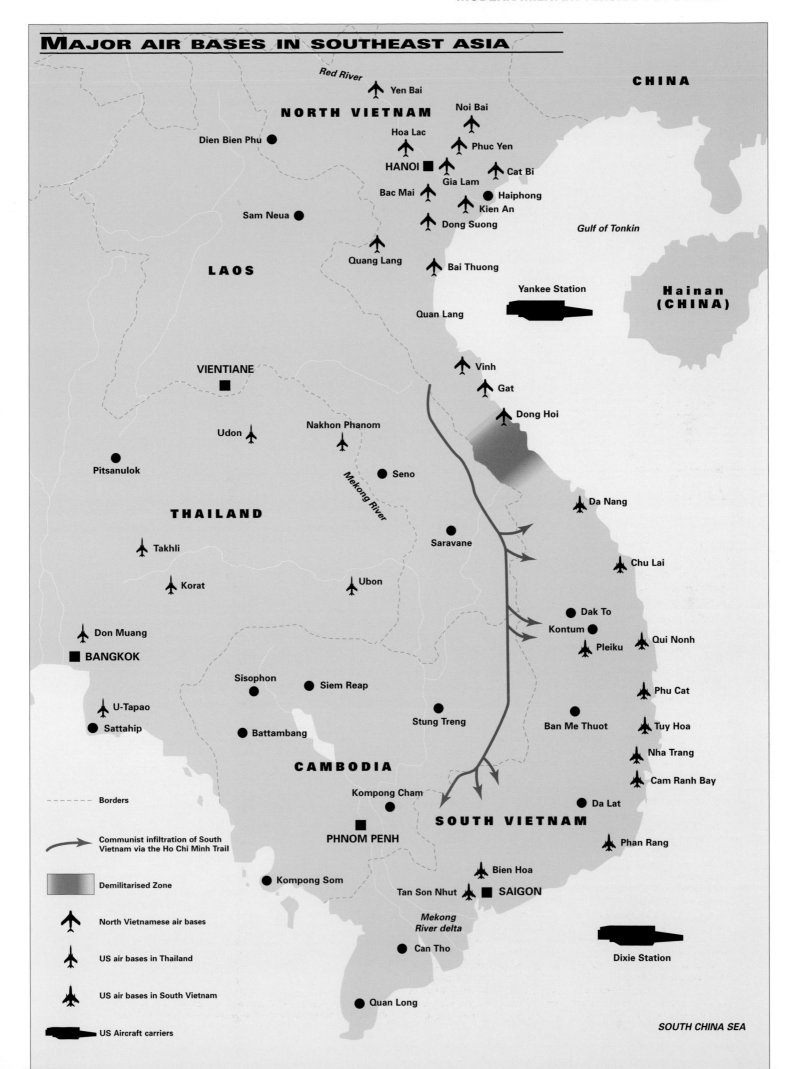

MAJOR AIR BASES IN SOUTHEAST ASIA

CHINA

Red River

NORTH VIETNAM

Yen Bai

Noi Bai

Dien Bien Phu ●

Hoa Lac

Phuc Yen

HANOI ■

Cat Bi

Gia Lam

Bac Mai

Haiphong ●

Kien An

Sam Neua ●

Dong Suong

Gulf of Tonkin

LAOS

Quang Lang

Bai Thuong

Yankee Station

Hainan (CHINA)

Quan Lang

VIENTIANE ■

Vinh

Gat

Nakhon Phanom

Dong Hoi

Udon

Pitsanulok ●

Seno ●

Da Nang

THAILAND

Saravane ●

Chu Lai

Takhli

Korat

Ubon

Dak To ●

Kontum ●

Qui Nonh

Pleiku

Don Muang

Phu Cat

BANGKOK ■

Sisophon ●

Siem Reap ●

Stung Treng ●

Ban Me Thuot ●

Tuy Hoa

U-Tapao

Nha Trang

Sattahip ●

Battambang ●

Cam Ranh Bay

CAMBODIA

Kompong Cham ●

Da Lat ●

PHNOM PENH ■

SOUTH VIETNAM

Phan Rang

Kompong Som ●

Bien Hoa

Tan Son Nhut ■ SAIGON

Mekong River delta

Can Tho ●

Dixie Station

Quan Long ●

SOUTH CHINA SEA

Mekong River

---- Borders

→ Communist infiltration of South Vietnam via the Ho Chi Minh Trail

Demilitarised Zone

✈ North Vietnamese air bases

✈ US air bases in Thailand

✈ US air bases in South Vietnam

US Aircraft carriers

French involvement

The Japanese surrender at the end of World War II left France eager to strengthen its influence and maintain a renewed state of stability in the area.

France had studied various plans to commit units of the Armée de l'Air to Indochina following the surrender of Japanese forces at the end of World War II. The French Government had announced a vague plan for the incorporation of Annam, Cambodia, Cochinchina, Laos and Tonkin – the five nations of Indochina – into a French-style commonwealth. However, as neither the Vietnamese nor the French governments could come to an agreement, the '30-Year Air War' was about to start.

Independence announced

French troops, initially invited by the British to assist in the disarming process, were greeted with little enthusiasm by the Vietnamese population. On 2 September, 10 days after the arrival of the first of these forces, the independence of Vietnam

was unilaterally proclaimed. Soon, Viet Minh bands began murdering or incarcerating French settlers and officials and, accordingly, France decided to take a more aggressive stance to protect its interests.

To equip its units in Indochina with their first genuine combat aircraft, the Armée de l'Air sent British-built Supermarine Spitfires. Transport was provided by ex-American and ex-RAF C-47s and Ju 52/3ms, which had the additional duty of acting as light bombers. The bombing mission was accomplished through the dropping of drums filled with jellied gasoline from the cargo door.

Harsh conditions

It soon became apparent that the Spitfires operating with the Armée de l'Air were not only restricted in operational range, but were also hindered by the

*A Grumman F6F-5 Hellcat straddles the catapult on the starboard side of the flight deck of the carrier **Arromanches**. Although dating from World War II, such aircraft were highly effective.*

lack of suitable airfields. De Havilland Mosquitos were therefore shipped to the expanding war zone. Built entirely of wood, the few examples that arrived offered little in the way of increasing the Armée de l'Air's strike

capabilities. New aircraft, more suited to the difficult conditions of the theatre, were urgently required if the French forces were to oppose the increasing strength of the Vietnamese guerrillas.

American assistance

The growing threat of an expansion of communism in South East Asia led to the American government having a change of heart about supplying aircraft for the Indochina campaign. Soon, a steady flow of advanced US-built aircraft was

Left: The French navy's first aircraft in Indochina was this Catalina, which arrived on 27 October 1945. Standing round the aircraft are former Japanese P.O.W.s, who were then still present in large numbers all over Indochina.

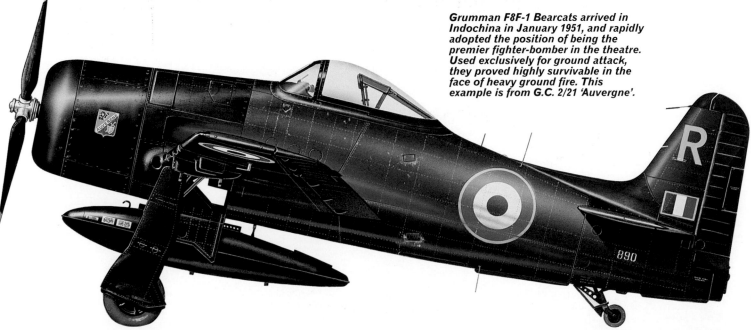

Grumman F8F-1 Bearcats arrived in Indochina in January 1951, and rapidly adopted the position of being the premier fighter-bomber in the theatre. Used exclusively for ground attack, they proved highly survivable in the face of heavy ground fire. This example is from G.C. 2/21 'Auvergne'.

entering French service, countering the communist threat, while at the same time avoiding the commitment of US ground forces to the combat zone.

Reliable aircraft at last

With the huge American supply operation gaining momentum, some 25 Douglas B-26 bombers, 25 Chance Vought AU-1 and 12 Grumman F8F-1 fighter-bombers, and 18 Douglas C-47 transports arrived, as well as small numbers of Cessna L-19 observation aircraft, Beech C-45 and de Havilland Canada L-20 light transports, and Sikorsky H-19 helicopters. Although appearing too late to influence the final outcome of the war, the aircraft proved to be decisive during particular battles.

Invader returns

Perhaps one of the most important aircraft supplied to the Armée de l'Air was the Douglas A-26 Invader. Having proved itself a highly capable attack platform during World War II, it was still operational in huge numbers within the USAF. Following a French request, four

Above: A vintage Supermarine Sea Otter of Escadrille 9S receives attention aboard the sea plane tender-ship, Robert Giaurd, *somewhere off the coast of Tonkin. Such amphibians were regularly employed in the search for Viet Minh smugglers along the sea border with China.*

Below: Playing a key role in Vietnam were the French-built Ju 52/3ms, known as Toucans, which not only operated in the transport role, but were also utilised as light bombers. Numerous examples were lost in landing accidents at remote airfields.

Below: The conflict in Vietnam introduced the French navy to helicopter combat operations. Piasecki HUPs replaced Sikorsky S-51s with Escadrille 58S on plane-guard duties. The French did much to further helicopter warfare during their use in Indochina.

Invaders arrived at Tan Son Nhut on 4 November 1950. Taken on charge by Groupe de Bombardment 1/19 'Gascogne' at Tourane (later known as Da Nang), combat operations commenced on 1 February 1951.

Fighter operations

A complete absence of fighter opposition resulted in the Armée de l'Air's Bearcats, Hellcats and Corsairs being adapted for ground attack duties. Operated under rudimentary conditions throughout the war, the aircraft quickly weathered to give a battered appearance. Although a lack of opposing fighters reduced the risk of interception, the role of ground attack was still highly dangerous.

The progressive strengthening of the Vietnamese army due to Chinese and Soviet intervention, saw to it that French aircraft and pilot losses steadily increased, the first occurring on 19 January 1950.

Despite the enormous assistance supplied to the French by the American government, the conclusion of the war could already be foreseen. The combination of a shortage of suitable airfields near the battle fronts, confusing signals from Paris on how the war should be fought, and the unbreakable resolve of the Vietnamese people to resist the French occupation, meant that France would require more than sophisticated air power to achieve success.

France operated both the gun-nosed B-26B alongside the glazed nosed RB-deliver a bomb-load of 6,000 lb (2722 kg), and provide heavy forward-firing power through its sixteen 0.5-in (12.7-mm) machine-guns. Although initially highly successful, the Invader was later adapted for night interdiction duties, for which it received an overall black camouflage scheme. Ten years later, the Invader would fly the same skies again with the USAF.

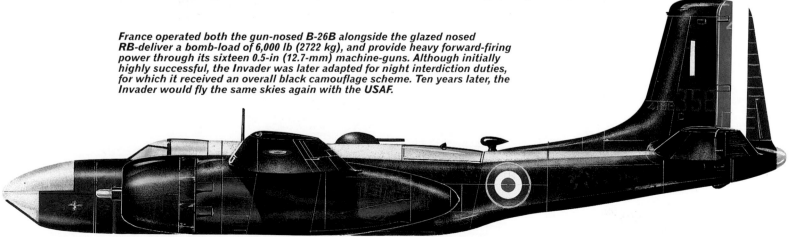

Last stand at Dien Bien Phu

France's final catastrophe

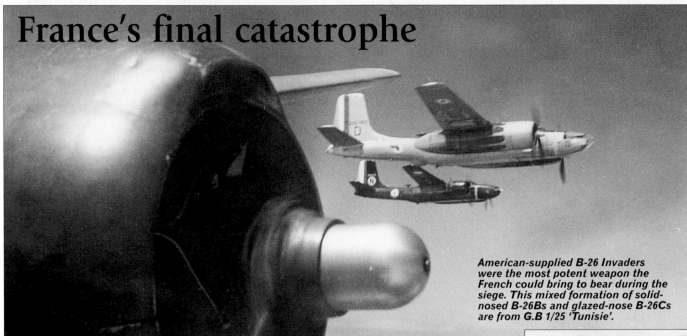

American-supplied B-26 Invaders were the most potent weapon the French could bring to bear during the siege. This mixed formation of solid-nosed B-26Bs and glazed-nose B-26Cs are from G.B 1/25 'Tunisie'.

Originally devised as a plan to inflict a decisive blow against the Viet Minh guerrillas, the battle at Dien Bien Phu resulted in catastrophic failure for the French, who lost more than 2,000 troops, as well as 48 aircraft, during 1,019 sorties. French military leaders had failed to appreciate the strength and determination of the Vietnamese opposition.

France and the Viet Minh had waged an indecisive war in Vietnam from 1947. With complete mastery of the skies against non-existent Viet Minh opposition, French forces were still unable to stop the flow of supplies reaching the Vietnamese guerrillas. Many of the Vietnamese people viewed their struggle as a war of independence against French oppressors, and were effectively united in their fight against the French.

Year of change

By 1953, the war had reached a critical stage. With huge numbers of aircraft and troops committed, the French population now appealed for a decisive end to the conflict. Many were unaware of the fighting conditions in the country, and generals and political figures in Paris were still basking in the successful outcome of World War II. The determination of the Viet Minh saw to it that 1953 would be a year to remember for the newly-appointed French ground commander, General Henri Navarre.

With most of the fighting now taking place in Western Tonkin

and north-eastern Laos, the new French commander devised a tactical concept to defeat the Viet Minh. Isolated garrisons would be established in enemy territory and supplied from the air. The theory behind these positions was that the garrisons would prove too tempting a target for the Viet Minh, so leading to a decisive battle in which superior French equipment and firepower would prevail. Early successes proved the tactic and paved the way for a major garrison to be established near the village of Dien Bien Phu, close to the border between North Vietnam and Laos.

Support from the air

With the decision taken in May 1953, the village of Dien Bien Phu first had to be

successfully occupied and established as an 'airhead'. Against strong opposition from within the French army, General Navarre appointed General de division Rene Cogny to assume overall control of the operation. Over a period of four days beginning on 20 November 1953, five parachute battalions, dropped from Douglas C-47 Skytrains, began digging field defences in the face of strong enemy opposition. At this stage it looked as though Operation

Right: On 20 November 1953, five battalions of French, Vietnamese and Algerian paratroops were dropped from 64 C-47 transports to establish the garrison at Dien Bien Phu. Upon landing, many were immediately engaged in ferocious fire-fights.

Below: Flown by American and French civilian pilots, the C-119 Boxcar was crucial in the supply operation to the besieged garrison. Most of the C-119s leased to the French Air Force came from the USAF 314th and 304th Troop Carrier Groups based in South Korea and Japan.

Left: Enemy attacks on Dien Bien Phu meant that the Grumman F8F Bearcat would play only a restricted role in the battle for the base. The aircraft carried a useful weapon load and possessed high speed which increased the pilot's chances of survival during low level attacks, but its radius of action was limited.

Below: PB4Y-2 Privateers operated by the French navy were able to strike Viet Minh targets anywhere in Vietnam. Based at Saigon and Tan Son Nhut, they could deliver up to 12,000 lb (5443 kg) of bombs. During the course of the war, four Privateers were destroyed.

Castor, as it was now called, would be a resounding success.

With orders to hold Dien Bien Phu and turn it into a fortress 'without any thought of withdrawal', Colonel Christian de la Croix de Castries parachuted into the village to assume command of the ground forces. Once the base was established, offensive patrols were to be mounted with a view to linking up with other French forces in Laos. During the following weeks, 10,814 soldiers were parachuted into the growing garrison. Units consisted of Thai infantry, and Algerian and Moroccan tirailleurs, along with four highly experienced Foreign Legion battalions.

Surprise attack

To the complete surprise of Colonel Castries, the vital landing strip near the village immediately came under fire from Vietnamese 105-mm guns, and the barrage increased as the weeks passed.

Unknown to the French forces at the time, the brilliant Vietnamese tactician General Vo Nguyen Giap, who would later develop similar tactics against the Americans, was already assembling a far larger force than the French thought possible. By March 1954, three Viet Minh infantry divisions comprising 28 battalions (50,000 men) were in position, supported by 105-mm artillery, heavy mortars and recoilless rifles – none of which the French knew the Viet Minh to possess at Dien Bien Phu.

Anti-aircraft weapons of every calibre were arriving with each day that passed and, by mid-April, the American and French civilian pilots flying the Fairchild C-119s dropping supplies to the garrison were refusing to fly over what they now dubbed 'the chamber-pot'.

On 13 March, the French

troops came under accurate and heavy fire which blew in shelters, smashed trenches and set alight every aircraft on the ground, except for three F8F Bearcats. These aircraft were immediately scrambled and forced to divert to Hanoi because of the almost total destruction of the runway. After the artillery barrage came a succession of 'human wave' infantry assaults against the eight small outposts at the perimeter of Dien Bien Phu. These attacks were delivered with complete disregard for Vietnamese casualties. Although they were therefore costly to both armies, Giap accomplished his first objective. During the next weeks, the Viet Minh grip on Dien Bien Phu tightened mercilessly. The only way to support the isolated French garrison was from the air.

Naval support

With French air force fighters lacking range, the Aéronavale, France's naval air arm, was charged with supporting its beleaguered countrymen. Consolidated PB4Y-2 Privateers were withdrawn from their maritime reconnaissance patrols and assigned to long-range bombing missions. American-supplied AU-1 Corsairs, a specially designed attack variant of the World War II fighter, were operated by Flottille 14F. Under the direction of ground forces, the AU-1s flew countless strikes against Viet Minh artillery positions.

The French surrender

The end of the battle came on 7 May 1953, when Giap unleashed a rocket attack and artillery barrage. With only 1,000 of his troops remaining fit for action, Castries told Giap that his men would cease firing at 17.30.

Giap allowed 900 of the most seriously wounded French troops to be flown out, but the rest,

some 9,000 men, were marched into captivity, an ordeal which only 3,000 would survive.

Dien Bien Phu proved a turning point for France's involvement in Indochina. French forces had sustained 2,293 dead

and 5,134 wounded, but what was most humiliating to France was the fact that 11,000 soldiers had been captured. Unable to support these losses, France negotiated a peace treaty that would see its troops withdrawn in 1954.

Bandaged and bloodstained, a Foreign Legion lieutenant emerges from his dugout. Although reinforced from the air, French forces were unable to defeat the massed attacks by the Viet Minh.

American escalation

In 1960, President Kennedy began to promote the concept of counter insurgency warfare. Not long after this, Americans found themselves in Vietnam.

By the dawn of the 1960s, the US was at loggerheads with the Soviet Union, a situation exacerbated by the shooting down of a U-2 reconnaissance aircraft. Meanwhile, a new US President, John Fitzgerald Kennedy, took his seat at the White House. Kennedy was an ardent advocate of new combat tactics, particularly that of counter insurgency warfare. His choice of Secretary of Defense was one Robert S. MacNamara, now regarded as the architect of the US build-up in Vietnam.

The US was still gripped by anti-communist hysteria and affirmed its support for nations facing the communist threat, often overlooking the calibre of their leaders. South Vietnam and the government of President Ngo Dinh Diem were no exceptions.

US involvement

American presence in Indochina dated back to World War II and, since 1954, the US had been sending military equipment to the area for use by the beleaguered French. Under the Kennedy administration, the decision was taken to further increase US presence in south-east Asia.

In April 1960, a single US Navy aviator, Lt Ken Moranville, was sent to Vietnam, along with six reworked ex-US Navy AD-6 Skyraider attack aircraft. The aim was to reinforce the fledgling VNAF (South Vietnamese Air Force) who, at that time, depended largely on World War II vintage aircraft, many of

which had been left behind by the fleeing French. The enemy insurgents in the south, by now known as the National Liberation Front (NLF), were gaining in strength, as were the frequency and seriousness of their attacks against government forces. Even at this early stage, the backing of the corrupt and ruthless Diem regime by the Americans and MacNamara's insistence that the communist threat originated from Hanoi, sealed the US's fate and ensured its unpopularity among large sections of the rural South Vietnamese population.

Advisory role

At first, the role of the Americans was to advise and instruct the VNAF and the ARVN (South Vietnamese Army) on how to operate their new equipment and how best to use it against the enemy. With the NLF representing an increasing threat, Diem requested further US support, and MacNamara duly responded by supplying more

equipment. This included Sikorsky H-34 Choctaw helicopters for the ARVN, as well as extra 'advisory' Americans.

Political instability

Lt Moranville recalled that, during his time in South Vietnam, there were several coup attempts against the Diem government. Involved in some of these attempts were VNAF Skyraider pilots, whom Moranville had been sent to advise, who were flying close support for the rebels.

In addition, a detachment of McDonnell Douglas RF-101C Voodoo reconnaissance aircraft (belonging to the 15th Tactical Reconnaissance Squadron) was deployed to Tan Son Nhut air base, near Saigon, in September 1961. These were the first USAF jets sent to Vietnam, under the codename of Pipe Stem, and they soon began flying photo sorties over the Mekong Delta in search of Viet Cong (as the NLF were now popularly known) activity. Under the command of Major Russell Crutchlow, the 15th TRS had difficulty in locating any trace of the insurgents, despite rumours that the Soviets were assisting

B-26s were the most capable aircraft available in the early years of the Vietnam conflict. Flown by US pilots, they carried Vietnamese markings for political reasons.

them by dropping supplies by air which would, presumably, have brought them out of hiding and into the open.

Covert operations

On 14 April 1961, the USAF's Chief of Staff, General Curtis LeMay, established the 4400th Combat Crew Training Squadron (CCTS) at Eglin AFB in Florida (codenamed Jungle Jim). The purpose of this was to train aircrew for guerilla warfare, using obsolete, prop-driven aircraft. Vice President Lyndon Johnson visited Vietnam the following month, meeting with President Diem. An agreement was made to increase the number of advisers to 1,000 and to bolster the VNAF by supplying more aircraft. A further 25 Skyraiders were sent, along with T-28B Trojans (for a second VNAF fighter squadron

Above: Ex-US Navy T-28B Trojans were sent to Vietnam in 1961, initially equipping just one VNAF squadron at Nha Trang. The aircraft were used primarily to attack Viet Cong insurgents.

the 6091st Tactical Reconnaissance Squadron deploying its RB-57E Canberras to Tan Son Nhut. This was as part of operation Patricia Lynn, in which flights were made over Vietnam in an attempt to photograph Viet Cong activity.

No turning back

With more equipment arriving by the day, the Americans became targets for Viet Cong sappers, who managed to inflict considerable damage upon aircraft and installations at a very low cost to themselves. Meanwhile, an incident involving an attack by North Vietnamese patrol boats on an American destroyer, the USS *Maddox*, resulted in President Johnson initiating a sustained bombing campaign against North Vietnam. Furthermore, Defense Secretary MacNamara began to instigate a major build-up of American forces in Vietnam, appointing General William Westmoreland as commander-in-chief at MACV. More aircraft arrived in the area, including F-100 Super Sabres which were sent to Da Nang and Bien Hoa. At the same time, large numbers of F-105 Thunderchiefs took up residence at bases in Thailand in preparation for bombing strikes.

While US Air Force and Army personnel arrived in theatre, the US Navy was also deployed in Vietnamese waters. Two carriers, the USS *Constellation* and USS *Ticonderoga,* arrived in the Gulf of Tonkin. Navy aircraft were soon in action, attacking North Vietnamese patrol boats in the Gulf. By this stage, it was clear that the US was deeply committed to Vietnam and, as 1965 dawned, the forecast was for yet more reinforcements. Sustained strikes against North Vietnam began in earnest, under operations Flaming Arrow and Rolling Thunder. In the south, meanwhile, instead of merely advising, Americans were now in actual combat.

at Bien Hoa air base), plus additional L-19 Bird Dogs for the VNAF liaison squadrons. Unlike the Skyraiders, the smaller T-28s of the 2nd Fighter Squadron were to be flown by the Jungle Jim pilots, and thus began the direct involvement of US military personnel in Vietnam. The aircraft were soon joined by a contingent of Douglas C-47 Skytrains and eight Douglas B-26 Invaders. Air support for the ARVN also arrived in the form of Piasecki H-21 Workhorse helicopters.

Into action

By November 1961, the 4400th CCTS (soon renamed the 1st Air Commando Squadron) began combat sorties under the codename Farm Gate. All the aircraft carried VNAF markings and a Vietnamese 'observer' was mandatory on combat missions, although in reality it was the Americans who were doing the fighting, the VNAF being unable or reluctant to get involved

themselves. With the presence of the B-26s and T-28s over the countryside, the Viet Cong insurgents soon reduced the number of attacks on trains and truck convoys. The Farm Gate pilots were primarily tasked with hitting such targets as sampan boats, truck parks, military structures and personnel. However, the lack of open space in the Vietnamese countryside prevented them from achieving much success. The T-28Bs were also used to escort helicopters to their landing zones (a favourite target for Viet Cong attack).

Widening conflict

By 1962, US involvement in Vietnam was increasing. A new combat field command was set up in Saigon, under the name of Military Assistance Command Vietnam (MACV). A squadron of F-102A Delta Daggers arrived at Tan Son Nhut amid rumours of possible strikes by Chinese bombers (which never happened),

together with further men and equipment. This included a detachment of US Marines, who began operating in the Mekong Delta along with the ARVN. Considerable numbers of the Bell UH-1 Iroquois helicopter also began to appear, initially being used primarily in the gunship role, operating out of an increasingly crowded Tan Son Nhut. In the meantime, however, the insurgents had not been dormant. They now had in their possession Chinese- and Soviet-built heavy machine-guns, which were taking their toll on the air commando pilots.

Build-up gathers speed

By the end of 1963, the political situation in South Vietnam was becoming increasingly unstable and the month of November proved a crucial turning point. President Diem was overthrown and murdered, while in the US President Kennedy was assassinated during a tour of Dallas. Despite these events, the war continued and, although a new regime was established in Saigon, it did not prove any more popular. In the US, Lyndon Johnson took up the presidency and, with it, US involvement in Vietnam.

Operations continued as before, the air commandos still flying their ageing aircraft out of Bien Hoa, although Farm Gate exchanged its T-28s and B-26s for A-1E Skyraiders, which proved more suitable for the counter insurgency role. More USAF jets had also begun to arrive in theatre, with

Above: Big, slow and lumbering, the A-1 Skyraider proved the ideal weapon with which to hit the Viet Cong and was utilised by the VNAF, USAF and USN.

Right: US Army CH-21s and UH-1Bs. The CH-21, already old, served for just two years in Vietnam, while the UH-1 became one of the most enduring symbols of the war.

Rolling Thunder

Above: As the key aircraft in Rolling Thunder, the Republic F-105D Thunderchief was designed as a nuclear bomber. However, the 'Thud' found fame as a bomb-truck over Vietnam.

Rolling Thunder began on 2 March 1965 and ended on 1 November 1968. It was the first sustained US bombing campaign against North Vietnam.

The Rolling Thunder campaign of 1965–68 was the first of four distinct phases in the air war against North Vietnam. It was immediately followed by the 'bombing halt' (1968-72), the Linebacker Campaign (May-

October 1972) and the final 'eleven-day war' known as Linebacker II (17–29 December 1972).

Rolling Thunder, as conceived and begun, had three objectives: to reduce infiltration; to boost South Vietnamese morale; and to

make it clear to Hanoi that continuation of the insurgency in the South would become increasingly expensive.

In Hanoi, however, Rolling Thunder was seen as one more obstacle to overcome in a long struggle to remove foreign influence and unify a divided Vietnam under Vietnamese rule. Ho Chi Minh's followers had removed the Japanese and the French. Now, they would search for a way to withstand the American air assault. They would seek to make the war too expensive for the US to maintain.

On 2 March 1965 the USAF participated in Rolling Thunder for the first time, with B-57s, F-100Ds, and F-105Ds. Of the 150 aircraft available at Thai bases,

Armed with 500-lb (227-kg) Mk 82 'slick' bombs, a USAF F-100D heads for a target. The F-100 was heavily used in the initial stage of Rolling Thunder, but was later restricted to missions over South Vietnam.

Above: A stalwart of the early part of the Vietnam War was the Martin B-57. In addition to the wing pylons (from which M117 bombs are dropping) the B-57 had a rotating bomb bay.

25 F-105Ds from the 12th TFS and 67th TFS (both part of the 18th TFW) accompanied B-57s to an ammunition depot at Xom Bong, about 35-miles (56-km) above the DMZ (demilitarised zone) and inflicted heavy damage.

USAF losses

On this first raid, two F-100D Super Sabres and three F-105D Thunderchiefs were destroyed, the latter type achieving the dubious honour of suffering more losses over Vietnam than any other USAF type. In addition, Captain Hayden J. Lockhart became the first USAF pilot to be taken prisoner. Already, early illusions that sustained bombing would quickly subdue North Vietnam required further and careful examination.

From the beginning, critics of the sustained campaign against North Vietnam would argue that it didn't really roll and wasn't particularly thunderous. The planning of air strikes was a complex and unwieldy business that began in the Situation Room at the White House where President Johnson retained firm control over what could and could not be attacked. Decisions as routine as the choice of ordnance for a particular sortie were made at this level, thousands of miles from the fighting.

The USAF headquarters in Saigon, the 2nd Air Division, made recommendations but could not choose targets. Lt Gen. Joseph Moore, who commanded 2nd Air Division, was an accomplished old fighter hand who kept making

The USAF principally used the Douglas EB-66 in the electronic warfare role, but it was also employed as a bomb-leader, using its superior navigation equipment to provide through-cloud bombing cues.

suggestions for an effective campaign against the North Vietnamese road and rail transportation network, only to find targets approved on what seemed a random basis.

North Vietnamese threat

A complicating factor was the expansion of the North Vietnamese air force. Radar-directed AAA guns were a serious enough challenge to the US strike aircraft but they would soon be joined by MiGs and by SAMs. The first electronic countermeasures (ECM) capability to be mounted in the conflict was employed on 29 March 1965, when three RF-101C Voodoos, each carrying QRC-160 pods, flew ECM support missions accompanying a Rolling Thunder strike force to a target. The QRC-160 proved unsatisfactory and was quickly withdrawn from the combat theatre, but invaluable work had been done towards some means of jamming or deceiving the enemy's radar defences.

F-105D Thunderchief

Republic's tough Thunderchief flew from Thai bases during the Rolling Thunder campaign. Between 1965 and 1970 it was the USAF's prime attack aircraft for raids over North Vietnam, before being superseded by the more versatile McDonnell Douglas F-4 Phantom II.

Bombload
This F-105D carries a typical bombload of six 500-lb (227-kg) Mk 82 bombs on a centreline MER (Multiple Ejector Rack) and two 250-lb (114-kg) Mk 81 bombs on the wing pylons. The latter are fitted with 'daisy-cutter' fuse extenders for maximum above-ground blast effect.

Area ruling
The F-105 was a prime example of area-ruling, its pinched-in waist helping to preserve a smooth cross-sectional area curve from nose to tail.

Combat losses
Despite the aircraft's sturdiness, large numbers of 'Thuds' were lost during Rolling Thunder. A total of 334 F-105s were lost in combat, with another 63 operational losses; 23 fell to MiGs, 32 to SAMs and 279 to AAA.

Camouflage
F-105s went to war wearing their peacetime natural-metal finish, but from late-1965 began to adopt the classic three-tone Southeast Asia camouflage. This was known as T.O. 114 after the technical order which specified it.

Cannon
The F-105D carried an internal 20-mm M61 Vulcan cannon. This weapon was useful for strafing, but was also employed to gain the F-105 several victories over MiGs.

Wild Weasel 'Thuds'
In addition to standard single-seat F-105D bombers, the USAF also used two-seat F-105F and F-105G Thunderchiefs. These were equipped with radar receivers and anti-radiation missiles for knocking out air defence radars.

Powerplant
The F-105D was powered by the Pratt & Whitney J75. This powerplant was barely sufficient for take-off at high weight and in the hot climate, but proved to be enormously tough.

Night interdiction
The unseen enemy

With air superiority accomplished early in the war, the US was able to unleash its massive air armada on strike and interdiction duties. To crews flying these missions, this meant a nightly routine of low-level flying to avoid anti-aircraft artillery, and the dropping of bombs on elusive targets obscured by the jungle canopy.

Halting the stream of war supplies from North Vietnam into South Vietnam became of prime concern to the USAF. It was impossible to observe and attack targets located beneath the thick jungle canopy, but those that were caught in the open were quickly dealt with by orbiting strike aircraft from either the USAF, USMC or USN. Having learned some painful lessons early in the conflict, the North Vietnamese high command quickly restricted almost all major troop movements to the cover of darkness.

Meanwhile, following pressure from within the White House over the aircraft losses

and civilian casualties arising from the sustained USAF bombing campaign against the North Vietnamese, this campaign ('Rolling Thunder') had been temporarily suspended in May 1965.

New tactics

During the bombing halt, which followed, Professor Roger Fisher, of the Harvard Law School, proposed an alternative to the costly aerial bombing campaign. Fisher's plan advocated the creation of an anti-infiltration barrier extending from the South Vietnamese coast to Tchepone in Laos. This 'air-supported

Above: The F-4 Phantom II had already acquired an excellent reputation during daytime Rolling Thunder raids. Now, fitted with sensors, flares and Loran bombing equipment, the Phantom would prove to be equally successful at night.

Above: This B-57G underwent testing at Eglin AFB, Florida, equipped with a gimbal-mounted downward-firing M61A1 20-mm cannon under the PAVE GAT programme. The B-57G went on to serve in Vietnam alongside the RB–57E (codenamed 'Patricia Lynn'), but without the 20-mm cannon installation.

barrier' would stop ground infiltration and halt truck convoys down the Ho Chi Minh Trail. To interdict the columns of traffic, the scientists proposed scattering miniature anti-personnel mines, along with acoustic sensors that would report movement to a central headquarters. Here, an electronic display, showing the location of all sensors, would indicate those that had been activated. Aircraft would then bomb the trails where activity had been detected. In the case of motor vehicles, engine noise or the explosion of anti-vehicular mines would trigger the sensors, so sending a response to the American intelligence specialists. Scientists estimated the cost of such a barrier at about $800 million

per year, far less than a second proposal, the Linebacker bombing campaign.

Changing roles

Operating under the 'Commando Hunt' programme, the then USAF Director of Operations, Major General Maurice Talbott, declared the McDonnell Douglas F-4 Phantom II fighter-bomber to be the "backbone of the interdiction force".

When attacking the night convoys, some specially-equipped Phantoms operated under radio guidance from the infiltration surveillance centre. The strings of sensors placed along stretches of road alerted the analysts at Nakhon Phanom to the location and general size of the convoy. The computer

As North Vietnamese AAA defences improved, the lumbering C-123s which had been used for sensor dropping, were replaced by F-4Ds flying high-speed sensor drops. This F-4D of the 25th TFS is seen on 30 January 1969, carrying SAO-1 sensors.

Phantom interdiction

Operating from Ubon RTAB, this F-4D was part of the 497th TFS 'Night Owls' belonging to the 8th TFW. Often the Phantoms carried a large cartoon illustration of an owl and moon on the intake. This particular example carried the name *Sweet Vicki* on the nose, a reference to the pilot's wife. The demanding nature of the missions resulted in Phantoms adopting an extremely battered and weathered appearance. As well as Snakeyes, the aircraft carried SUU-42 flare dispensers and an ALQ-87 ECM pod positioned in the forward fuselage missile bay. Upon returning from a strike, pilots often allowed the back-seater to fly the aircraft back to base.

No lights
Every light on the Phantom was blacked out in an effort to reduce the aircraft's conspicuousness. In addition, the cockpit lights were turned down in an attempt to improve the crew's night-vision.

Underwing load
For interdiction work, the most successful weapons proved to be Mk 82 Snakeye bombs, fitted with fuse-extenders. Fuel tanks were mounted on each of the outer wing pylons.

Camouflage colours
Night interdiction Phantoms wore standard SEA (South East Asia) camouflage, over gloss black.

With a load of 18 Mk 82 500-lb (227-kg) Snakeye bombs, an A-6A Intruder of VA-85 'Black Falcons' takes off from USS Kittyhawk. The Intruder was operated by both the USMC and USN, and was able to undertake attack missions in all weathers, by night or day.

Other missions flown by the 'Night Owls' included those of gunship escort, night strike and Forward Air Control, as well as a number of daylight raids. The most dangerous of these tasks was held to be that of AC-130 gunship escort. The 'Night Owls' particularly hated the thought of diving against ground targets through the AC-130's orbit, with the ever-present risk of a collision with the gunship.

The night interdiction operations continued until the end of the war. Despite the bravery of the crews and the technology available to them, however, these operations were ultimately without success.

continuously recorded the convoy's movement, displaying the exact co-ordinates, and so enabled the Phantom to achieve maximum damage. Aircraft operating alongside the F-4 Phantoms were specially-modified B-57 bombers known as B-57Gs, and carrier-based USN and land-based USMC Grumman A-6 Intruders.

Night Owls

Flying alone, the crews of the night interdiction aircraft were considered to be the elite of their squadrons. Entry to this exclusive 'club' required pilots and navigators to be selected by their commanding officer, after having proved themselves in daytime attack missions. Some 15 check-out rides were then flown, during which these flight crews had to learn night refuelling, gunship escort and flare techniques, together with

visual and blind bombing using Loran radar equipment – this involved utilising various onboard systems linked to ground sensors to provide long-range navigation to the weapons release point.

Operating from Ubon, Thailand, the 497th TFS of the 8th TFW was the only dedicated night attack squadron in South-East Asia. Other squadrons operated at night, but none flew regularly in the dark, month after month, as did the aptly-named 'Night Owls'. The 497th's brief ran from 1800 to 0600, the period between dusk and dawn, widely regarded as the worst time for close-attack work. With missions lasting anything from four to four and a half hours in length, and including up to five aerial refuellings, night interdiction was seen as one of the most demanding and complex missions flown in the entire air campaign.

The pilot of an F-4 Phantom prepares for another night attack mission. Night after night, crews faced hundreds of lethal AAA and SAM batteries. These constant threats, combined with the complexities of night flying led to extreme levels of fatigue.

Air assault
Riding into battle

The war in Vietnam will be remembered for its massive use of helicopters. Images of soldiers being delivered to landing zones under fire were broadcast to homes around the world.

Helicopters had seen action in Korea, Malaya and Algeria, but it was Vietnam which was to become the first true helicopter war. Helicopters flying into 'hot' landing zones became one of the most enduring images of the war. To soldiers on the ground, the sound of thrashing rotors was sometimes welcomed, but often feared. It could mean that the helicopters were there to rescue them from a firefight deep in the jungle, or to carry them from the comparative safety of their bases into battle. By the end of the war, the US Army had become the world's third largest air force, after those of the Soviet Union and the USAF, using its helicopters for a host of transport, attack and rescue missions.

The first complete US Army units in action in Vietnam were the 8th and 57th Transportation Companies, which arrived in December 1961, flying in 32 twin-rotor Piasecki H-21s from the USS *Card*. Less than two weeks later, they were in action, airlifting 1,000 Vietnamese paratroops in a surprise attack on a suspected Viet Cong headquarters. This mission was the first major use of US combat power in the war, and is seen as the start of the air mobility era.

Early in 1962 the H-21s were joined in-country by Marine Corps Piasecki HUS-1 Seahorses which operated in the Mekong Delta. But the most notable arrival of the year was the US Army's 57th Medical Detachment. Its medical evacuation mission, soon to be nicknamed 'Dust Off', introduced one of the great symbols of the war, the Bell UH-1 Iroquois. Known universally as the *Huey*, the UH-1 also equipped the Utility Tactical Transport Helicopter Company (UTTHC), based at Tan Son Nhut.

Experience gained by the UTTHC quickly saw the vulnerable helicopters armed with rockets and door-mounted machine-guns. As the US Army adapted its doctrines and equipment to the jungle conditions in Vietnam, numerous helicopter units were activated in the USA for deployment to the theatre. When American ground troops were committed to action in 1965, they came accompanied by large numbers of helicopters.

Leading the field in airmobile operations, as far as experience was concerned, were the units from the 11th Air Assault Division from Fort Benning. Later renamed the 1st Cavalry Division (Airmobile), this division proved to be one of the most effective combat formations to serve in Vietnam.

Apart from assault missions, other helicopters, such as the agile Hughes OH-6A Cayuse (known as the *Loach*) performed reconnaissance duties, seeking out enemy forces and calling fire support to neutralise the threat. Once an area was clear, the big twin-rotor Boeing Vertol CH-47 Chinook was able to deliver further troops, complete with 105-mm howitzers to allow the area to be secured in American hands. The Chinook acted as a recovery helicopter, too, retrieving thousands of downed aircraft, worth a reported $2.9

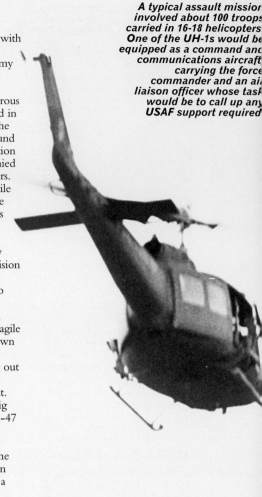

A typical assault mission involved about 100 troops carried in 16-18 helicopters. One of the UH-1s would be equipped as a command and communications aircraft, carrying the force commander and an air liaison officer whose task would be to call up any USAF support required

Right: One man and his dog... when the army moved camp, the Hueys shifted absolutely anything that could be carried.

billion. The Sikorsky CH–54 Tarhe crane helicopter was also used in this role and was capable of transporting items like bulldozers to engineers for the establishment of remote mountain-top artillery fire-bases.

The most potent of all helicopters in the war in terms of fire power were the AH-1 HueyCobras. Equipped with an armament mix of Miniguns, 20-mm cannon, automatic grenade-launchers and high-explosive rockets, they entered service in Vietnam in 1967. By 1968, a total of about 50 assault helicopter companies had been deployed, equipped with between 600 and 700 HueyCobras. They were based at such locations as Ban Me Thuot, Bien Hoa, Nha Trang, Phuoc Vinh, Pleiku and Tuy Hoa.

By the early 1970s, when America began to disengage from Vietnam, the process of Vietnamisation saw a large number of UH-1 and CH–47 helicopters supplied to the VNAF.

The aim was to make the Vietnamese self-sufficient by the time the Americans left. However, American financial aid did not match the massive inventory of equipment left behind. By the time North Vietnam overran the

south in 1975, most of the once powerful South Vietnamese helicopter force was grounded and in storage due to lack of spares and operating funds.

But the helicopter still had one major role to play. When

the North Vietnamese army finally took Saigon in April 1975, American and Vietnamese helicopters lifted thousands of refugees to safety during the last days of Operation Frequent Wind.

AH-1G HueyCobra

As the specialised gunship version of the famous Huey, the AH-1G built up an impressive combat record and helped to reduce transport helicopter losses by providing effective fire suppression during airmobile operations.

Combat-tested Cobra
One of the few aircraft actually to reach the war zone after real combat experience gained in Vietnam was used in its design, the AH-1G was developed as the AAFSS (Advanced Aerial Fire Support System) following a design competition which began in August 1965.

Battlefield response
The HueyCobra was equipped with VHF and UHF radios and associated electronics gear to enhance communications between helicopters, and between the air and the ground.

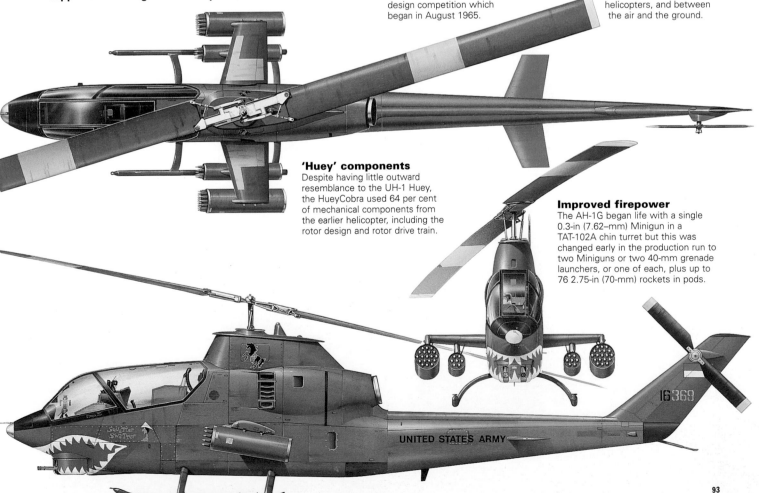

'Huey' components
Despite having little outward resemblance to the UH-1 Huey, the HueyCobra used 64 per cent of mechanical components from the earlier helicopter, including the rotor design and rotor drive train.

Improved firepower
The AH-1G began life with a single 0.3-in (7.62–mm) Minigun in a TAT-102A chin turret but this was changed early in the production run to two Miniguns or two 40-mm grenade launchers, or one of each, plus up to 76 2.75-in (70-mm) rockets in pods.

UNITED STATES ARMY

16369

Riverine
The Brown Water war

A rocket-armed UH-1B escorts a light patrol boat up one of the numerous creeks of southern Vietnam. Under Operation Game Warden, the Navy was responsible for cutting enemy supply routes through the Mekong Delta.

Although less glamorous than naval carrier operations, the maritime surveillance of Vietnam's network of waterways was crucial if the movement of supplies by the Viet Cong was to be halted.

The war in Vietnam was often a study in contrasts. No better illustration of this can be found than in the role played by the United States Navy. In the Tonkin Gulf, naval aviators, flying supersonic jets off the decks of huge super carriers, participated in the aerial campaign against North Vietnam, while cruisers and the battleship *New Jersey* bombarded enemy coastal areas. Further south, a vast array of small craft, few of which were ocean-going, carried out a variety of tasks along the coast, and up the various rivers and canals which dissected this war-torn land.

The kind of warfare that was waged on the inland and coastal waters had last been practised by the United States Navy during the Civil War, almost one hundred years earlier. Mistakes were made, as was to be expected but, in the end, the resourceful individuals of these land, sea and air forces learned their lessons well and became a formidable fighting force which deprived the enemy of the use of these internal waterways.

Combined operations

Each component had its own distinct function but also worked in conjunction with the other two when the situation dictated. Task Force 115 (Market Time), had responsibility for coastal patrol, surveillance, and the interception of enemy gun runners on the high seas. Using equipment that ranged from patrol aircraft such as the Lockheed P-2 Neptune and P-3 Orion, to small 'Swift'-class boats, and even US Coast Guard cutters, Market Time carried out the usually monotonous duty of interdicting communist supplies along the coast of Vietnam.

Task Force 116 (Game Warden) carried the war as far up the rivers and canals of Vietnam as its shallow draft boats would allow it to go. Using various modified landing craft, armoured

Above: The US Marine Corps and, later, the Navy (the latter with its squadron VAL-4 'Black Ponies') operated the OV-10 Bronco for spotting, convoy escort, and other combat duties. To Bronco crews, the enemy was up close and the war was very personal.

power boats, helicopters and even the fixed-wing Broncos, it eventually swept the Viet Cong from the Mekong Delta.

The final component of the riverine navy, Task Force 117 (Mobile Riverine Force), was equipped with gunboats, armoured troop carriers, refuellers, and a brigade of the 9th Infantry. These combined to provide a self-contained strike force that could operate through the roadless Mekong Delta in order to engage the enemy forces. Collectively, these riverine units made up the Brown Water navy.

Aerial support

As a result of recommendations made by naval authorities in 1965, eight UH-1Bs were armed with door-mounted M60 machine-guns and rockets. These formed the Light Attack Helicopter Squadron Three (HAL-3), nicknamed 'Seawolves', which was activated on 1 April 1967.

A 'Seawolves' UH-1B from HAL-3 skims over the Delta. The UH-1s watched ahead for Viet Cong ambushes, and then used their guns and rockets to attack the enemy forces.

Enter the Bronco

VAL-4 'Black Ponies' flew the North American OV-10A Bronco on missions over the Mekong Delta. Light attack duties could be undertaken, as well as FAC missions for the carrier wings sailing at 'Dixie Station'.

Weapon load
Ordnance was mixed to achieve optimum results during a sortie. In addition to the sponson machine-guns, this OV-10 carries two sets of 5-in (127-mm) Zuni rockets mounted on the fuselage sponson hard points and two 2.75-in grenade launchers underwing.

Camouflage colours
Once in combat, the overall light-grey colour scheme of OV-10As was quickly replaced by a more war-like drab green upper surface in order to reduce their visibility at low altitude.

Combat proven
The OV-10 Bronco proved easy to maintain and VAL-4 was able to achieve a high sortie rate. The squadron left Vietnam in early 1972 after almost three years of flying support for US and Vietnamese Brown Water units.

These helicopters were initially located at primitive shore bases, but later also flew from heavily-armoured support vessels known as Landing Ship Drydocks (LSDs) which were anchored among the network of canals and riverways.

Primarily operating over the Mekong Delta, HAL-3's mission was to provide air support and convoy escort to the naval patrol boats intercepting river traffic. Other missions flown by the squadron included supporting the invasion of Cambodia in 1970. So effective did these armed naval helicopters become that operations were expanded to include the provision of Special Forces Sea, Air, Land (SEAL) commandos, casualty evacuation and general transport services for shore-based naval units. What was surprising, in view of HAL-3's highly dangerous missions, was that only one helicopter was lost in 64 months of combat operations.

Nocturnal Neptunes
The Navy soon discovered that the Viet Cong were masters at taking advantage of the night to move troops and equipment across the rivers. An urgent request for

an aircraft capable of detecting this activity meant that four SP-2H Neptune patrol aircraft were suitably modified. Designated AP-2Hs, these sensor-equipped aircraft carried Mk 82 GP bombs, Mk 77 incendiary bombs, and SUU-11A/A Minigun pods. They utilised a FLIR turret to seek out and attack road and river traffic in the Mekong Delta and Ho Chi Minh Trail.

Battling Broncos
Also deployed to Vietnam, VAL-4, nicknamed the 'Black Ponies', employed 16 OV-10A Broncos in the Counter-Insurgency (COIN) role. Divided into two flights, one based at Binh Thuy and the other at Vung Tau, VAL-4 began flying combat sorties in March 1969. The Broncos quickly proved themselves highly suitable in the roles of close air support, convoy escort, and armed reconnaissance. Operating on pre-planned sorties in support of convoys or offensive operations, or flying combat air patrols for quick reaction when riverine forces were ambushed, the OV-10As were armed with four sponson-mounted M60C 0.3-in (7.62-mm) machine-guns and

Above: An armed UH-1B of HAL-3 is about to touch down on the deck of the USS Harnet County during Game Warden riverine operations in the Mekong Delta. The UH-1B on the forward section of the amidships deck carrys Navy titles, but in fact belongs to the US Army's 197th Aviation Helicopter Company, the unit which provided combat training for HAL-3.

carried up to 3,600 lb (1633 kg) of external stores. A typical external weapon load included one SUU-11A/A Minigun pod, two LAU-3A/A pods each containing four 5-in (127-mm) Zuni rockets, and one LAU-10A pod with seven 2.75-in (70-mm) rockets.

VAL-4 Broncos remained true to their light attack classification. Usually flying in two-ship formations, the OV-10As performed countless reconnaissance missions at comparatively high altitudes, before diving to tree-top height to unleash an arsenal of weapons at a Viet Cong encampment. The versatility and manoeuvrability of the Bronco was well appreciated by navy

crews when high speed was required to evade enemy fire.

Combat losses
During its three years in Vietnam, VAL-4 lost seven Broncos through combat and operational accidents; six crew members were killed, and the other eight were rescued. Despite these losses, VAL-4 maintained an average of more than one sortie per day until the unit ceased combat operations at the end of March 1972. Surprisingly, the unit's withdrawal from Vietnam coincided with the launching by the Viet Cong of their 1972 spring invasion. VAL-4 was disestablished on 10 April 1972, ten days after flying its last combat sortie.

Above: Photographed at NAF Cam Ranh Bay on 7 September 1968 are AP-2Hs of VAH-21, a US Navy unit which flew night interdiction sorties over the Mekong Delta and portions of the Ho Chi Minh Trail in Cambodia. These gunship Neptunes were equipped with engine exhaust silencers to reduce their detectability during low-altitude missions.

Right: After their combat test during Operation Quai Vat, US Navy hovercraft took the call sign 'Monster' and their crews painted sharks' mouths on the crafts' bows. The sight of these machines frightened more than a few Vietnamese peasants into co-operating with the US Navy crews.

The 'in-country' war

While the high-tech jets heading north to bomb industrial targets, communications facilities and airfields stole most of the glory during the war in Southeast Asia, a large number of aircraft were concerned with fighting the Viet Cong, guerrillas within South Vietnam itself. This campaign lasted for 12 years.

When American airmen first arrived in Vietnam during 1961-2 under the guise of 'advisors' to the South Vietnamese, their task quickly involved flying combat missions over the jungles of South Vietnam, attacking Viet Cong (VC) guerrilla installations and supply depots. Known to many as the 'in-country' war, whereby air operations were restricted to the southern side of the demilitarised zone, the missions were seen as an extension of the ground war, with many aircraft providing aerial support to the US and Vietnamese troops engaged in the fighting.

During these early years, the principal aircraft operated by the USAF were veteran World War II Douglas B-26 Invaders and North American T–28 Trojans, the latter then serving as a US-based training aircraft for the USAF and US Navy. President Kennedy's enthusiasm for Special

Forces-style units allowed these early USAF squadrons to operate in an autonomous fashion, planning their own missions and selecting targets of opportunity. Their renegade behaviour, both in the air and on the ground, soon saw these units dubbed the 'air commandos'.

The air commandos found the B-26 Invader to be ideally suited to its role, although sufficient numbers of the bomber were lacking. The aircraft were painted in South Vietnamese markings, but were flown by American crews with a Vietnamese observer present – very often, the extra crewman would fall asleep, his presence being akin to a political agreement rather than to any real tactical role. The veteran aircraft soon presented problems. Wing fatigue led to

Top: Attacks against guerrilla installations were usually made from low level, employing 'dumb' ordnance. Napalm was a favourite, illustrated here by a North American F-100D in the Bac Lieu region.

Above: The Northrop F-5C underwent a full combat evaluation under the 'Skoshi Tiger' programme, at first over North and then later over South Vietnam. Found by the USAF to be too short-legged, most were later handed over to the VNAF.

the loss of one B-26 (44-33507) and its crew, bringing a temporary halt to Invader operations. The B-26 would later return to the war zone, however, as the much modified and improved B-26K variant.

Fighting increases

The expansion of the aerial campaign against North Vietnam was reflected in the south in early 1965. New aircraft, such as

the Martin B-57, Douglas A-1 Skyraider and North American F-100 Super Sabre, quickly arrived in the theatre – the latter was to bear the brunt of the air war in the south.

On a typical mission against the VC, the B-57 would carry nine 500-lb (227-kg) bombs in a fixed position under the fuselage where a rotary bomb bay had initially been installed, as well as four 750-lb (340-kg) bombs on wing

Carrying rocket pods and napalm canisters, this Douglas B-26 Invader is being readied for a mission from Bien Hoa, with VNAF Skyraiders in the background. After the grounding of the B-26 in February 1964, the air commandos began to receive the Douglas A-1 Skyraider to enable them to continue their covert attack operations.

The 'screaming bird'

Deployment of the B-57B in Southeast Asia commenced in August 1964, with a total of 36 aircraft. Initially, they were unpainted but, in time, tactical camouflage was adopted. This 13th Bomb Squadron aircraft was based at Phan Rang AFB, and illustrates the black undersurface adopted following requests from air crews for better

concealment during night operations. B-57Bs were the first US jets to drop bombs in the Vietnam War, and specialised versions continued to perform combat missions until 1972.

Bombload
The B-57 was able to deliver up to 6,000 lb (2722 kg) of bombs carried within the bomb bay and underwing hard points.

Night attack
B-57s often operated with FAC O-2As, the small aircraft directing the bomber to its target with the aid of flares and rockets.

racks. Mounted in the nose were four M39 20-mm cannon, each containing 200 rounds. The aircraft initially fought in their peacetime silver finish, but combat soon saw the adoption of the standard SEA colours of two greens and a tan and, later, black undersides were to be given to the aircraft. The sight of these bombers diving down from medium altitude to attack VC positions resulted in the B-57 being dubbed the 'screaming bird' by the unfortunate Viet Cong.

Enter the 'Hun'

With little or no air threat from enemy fighters when operating over South Vietnam, American fighters soon adopted the close air support role. Withdrawn from use 'up north' following its poor performance, the North American F-100D Super Sabre proved remarkably effective in the south, where toughness, brute strength and 'survivability' were all-important. Armed with four 20-mm M39 cannon and able to deliver eight 750-lb (340-kg) bombs, the F-100 soon established itself an enviable combat record.

An indication of the contribution of the F-100 can be seen by the number of combat missions flown. By 1969, the four tactical fighter wings (the 3rd, 31st, 35th and 37th) flying the

aircraft had flown more combat sorties than the 15,000-plus North American P-51 Mustangs built during World War II. The F-100D continued to fly close air support 'in-country' until July 1971, when the 35th TFW was finally withdrawn. By this time, the multi-role F-4 Phantom II had taken over.

Skoshi Tiger

Frustrated at being unable to stem the flood of supplies reaching the VC after years of bombing, the USAF tested numerous aircraft in the theatre. A late arrival was the Northrop F-5C Freedom Fighter, under the programme evaluation name 'Skoshi Tiger'. The aircraft was tested first over North Vietnam, where it was found to lack the necessary range for bombing missions. It was operated initially over South Vietnam by the 10th Fighter Commando Squadron, based at Bien Hoa. However, with other more capable aircraft in their inventory that offered longer endurance over the combat zone, the F-5Cs were passed to the South Vietnamese air force (VNAF) who operated the type on interdiction duties.

Other missions

A host of other missions were performed by US airmen while

fighting inside South Vietnam. Fairchild C-123 Provider cargo aircraft are best remembered for the 'Ranch Hand' programme, under which defoliant was sprayed on the forest canopy, but these stubby transports were also employed to drop South Vietnamese paratroops and to run supplies into distant outposts.

The Bell UH-1P Huey helicopter carried out psychological warfare and other

special missions for the 20th Helicopter Squadron, which began life as an air commando unit, and then continued as a special operations outfit involved in transporting American SEALS and Green Berets.

Like their brethren who fought the war on carrier decks, and from bases outside South Vietnam, the men of the 'in-country' war were finally withdrawn with the truce of 27 January 1973.

No aircraft symbolised the in-country war more potently than the North American F-100D Super Sabre. The 'Hun' flew over 300,000 sorties throughout the conflict.

Fast-moving 'Hun'

Operating with the 308th TFS, 35th TFW at Tuy Hoa, this F-100D Super Sabre carried the name *Jeanne Kay* on its nose. Tuy Hoa had the largest number of assigned Super Sabres during the war in Vietnam. It operated five full squadrons – three were regular units of the 31st TFW, and two were Air National Guard squadrons gained by the 31st.

Combat colours
Arriving in the theatre wearing their peacetime natural metal finish, the Super Sabres quickly received the standard Vietnam camouflage. The rear fuselage was often left unpainted, as heat from the engine exhaust had a tendency to burn the paint off.

Warload
With hardpoints able to carry bombs, napalm and unguided rockets, the Super Sabre was also equipped with four 20-mm M39 cannon mounted under the nose.

MiG killers
Air combat over Vietnam

Originally trained to defeat large fleets of Russian bombers, American pilots had to adapt to their new air combat role. Later in the war, specialised instruction and missile technology would enable USAF and USN pilots to achieve victory in the air.

As the air war over Vietnam expanded and American bombers struck north in an effort to destroy the enemy's ability to wage war, the beleaguered North Vietnamese soon realised that, if they were to survive, they would require a response to the American aerial onslaught. During the early campaigns of the war, American pilots were lulled into a false sense of security, to such an extent that escorting F-4 Phantom IIs, which were meant to provide aerial protection to the F-105 Thunderchief bombers, were also loaded with bombs, negating their use as an effective fighter escort.

The North Vietnamese realised that the bombers were the real threat and, with Soviet assistance, implemented an upgrade of their air defences. Along with huge quantities of SAMs came

Russian-built MiG-17s, -19s and the then highly capable MiG-21. Vietnamese pilots were despatched to Russia and China for conversion training on the new aircraft. They also received instruction in the art of aerial combat from veteran Soviet pilots. Upon their return, the stage was set for what was to be one of the most dramatic and brutal periods of jet combat the world had ever seen.

Opening rounds

The first MiG kill of the war was accomplished by Lt(jg) Terrence M. Murphy and Ens Ronald J Fegan from VF-96 (the world-famous 'Fighting Falcons') of the US Navy. Flying their F-4B Phantom II on 9 April 1965, they engaged in a high-altitude chase with an enemy MiG-17. After a few minutes, Murphy launched an

Colonel Robin Olds, Commander of the 8th TFW 'Wolfpack', was an extremely popular commander. A World War II ace, Olds brought the experience and leadership necessary to make the 8th the most successful MiG-killing wing in Vietnam. Olds was personally responsible for four of the 24 kills achieved by the 8th TFW while under his command.

AIM-7 Sparrow at the rapidly-fleeing MiG, which fireballed and was seen to tumble towards the ground. Mystery surrounds what then happened to the victorious Phantom crew, as both aircraft and crew disappeared without trace. Sources within the Vietnamese government indicate that the F-4 was brought down by another American fighter in the immediate vicinity, but this has never been confirmed.

Following these opening clashes, the US Navy – with its heavy carrier presence in the Gulf of Tonkin – soon began to encounter MiGs on a regular basis. The second US Navy kill of the war was a MiG-17, which was struck with an AIM-7

launched from an F-4B belonging to VF-21 on 17 June 1965. During this early period, the inexperience of the North Vietnamese pilots was obvious. In one highly unusual engagement on 20 June, two A-1H Skyraiders belonging to VA-25 downed a MiG-17 with 20-mm cannon fire, the MiG having apparently ventured too close to the propeller-driven attackers. The Skyraider pilots, Lt Charlie Hartman and Lt Clinton B. Johnson, each received a half kill credit for their unorthodox dogfight victory.

The pilots of the USAF proved to be equally adept at downing the small, tight-turning, MiG fighters. The first USAF kill

Above: Captain Steve Ritchie, of the 555th TFS/432nd TFW, was the USAF's only fighter pilot ace of the Southeast Asia war. Flying with Captain Charles B. DeBellevue as his WSO, he shot down one MiG-21 on 10 May 1972, two on 8 July, and one on 28 August. His other victory, also against a MiG-21, was obtained on 31 May, with Captain Lawrence H. Pettit as his WSO.

Right: The end of the game – a NVAF MiG erupts into a fireball following an aerial engagement with F-4 Phantoms. The inexperience of North Vietnamese pilots was at its most evident during the early period of the air war over Vietnam.

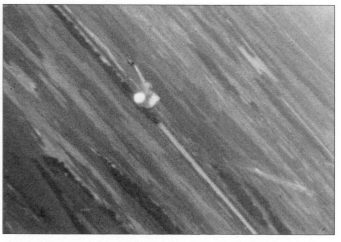

was claimed by Captains Kenneth E. Holcombe and Arthur C. Clark, who manoeuvred their F-4C Phantom into a missile-firing position on 10 July 1965, and successfully downed one MiG-17.

It was not only the F-4 Phantom IIs that established themselves as MiG killers. In the early years of the air war, the four 20-mm cannon of Vought's F-8 Crusader proved equally capable of downing MiGs, and many F-8 pilots used a combination of cannon fire and AAMs to bring down the enemy fighters. On 12 June 1966, Cdr Harold L. Marr of VF-211 achieved one of the first double kills of the war, bringing down two MiG-17s after a hectic low-altitude chase across the North Vietnamese countryside.

Achieving an equally respectable reputation as a 'gun fighter' was the Republic F-105 Thunderchief, particularly those of the 355th TFW. On one single day in May 1967, F-105s from this wing downed four enemy fighters, most falling prey to the Thunderchief's deadly 20-mm M61 internally-mounted cannon.

American aces

Throughout the history of aerial warfare, there are always individuals who possess an innate ability to shoot down enemy fighters; the Vietnam War proved to be no exception. The leading US Navy ace was Lt Randall H. Cunningham, who was often referred to by his callsign 'Duke'. Of the five kills he achieved during his tour in Vietnam, the final of the three successful engagements on 10 May 1972 is widely regarded as one of the most demanding and complex dogfights in history. His foe was an experienced North Vietnamese ace, who was ultimately downed with an AIM-9 Sidewinder after a series of vertical 'scissors' manoeuvres. Cunningham's Phantom was then hit by an SA-2 SAM, forcing Cunningham and his WSO to eject from their aircraft, to be rescued by approaching US Navy helicopters.

Leading US Navy ace, with a total of five kills to his credit, 'Duke' Cunningham relives his dogfight to an eager press audience. Cunningham was a graduate of the US Navy's Top Gun programme.

Mirroring his naval counterpart, Phantom pilot Captain Steve Ritchie of the 555th TFW achieved his five kills between May and August of 1972. With none of his dogfights lasting more than two minutes, Ritchie displayed the exceptional qualities that allowed him to become the only USAF pilot ace of the war. Beating both Cunningham and Ritchie in terms of MiG kills was Captain Charles B. DeBellevue. Present on six MiG-killing flights, DeBellevue served as a WSO with the 555th TFW.

MiG-killing F-4J Phantom

SHOWTIME 100 (its radio callsign) was the F-4J Phantom (Bureau No. 155800) flown on 10 May 1972 by VF-96 pilots Lts Randall 'Duke' Cunningham and William P. 'Willie' Driscoll. In standard US Navy gull-grey and white, with typical squadron markings for the time, this F-4J achieved glory, then fell to a SAM missile, all in a single action.

Flying powerhouse
The F-4J shipboard fighter was powered by two J79-GE-19 turbojets rated at 17,000-lb (8119-kg) thrust with afterburning. As with previous Phantoms, in order to control airflow into the air intakes, a movable splitter plate separated the undisturbed airflow from the sluggish boundary layer close to the skin of the aircraft. The distinctive 'burner cans' at the exhaust of the F-4J were forged to contain the enormous heat kicked back by the engines.

Air-to-air load
On its 10 May mission, the F-4J carried a full complement of AIM-9 Sidewinder heat-seeking missiles, but only two radar-guided AIM-7 Sparrows. Cunningham and Driscoll required just three Sidewinders to down the three MiGs they claimed that day.

Versatile F-4J
The US Navy initially classed the Phantom as a 'fleet defence interceptor', able to defend the carrier battle group from air attack. But in Vietnam, this defensive role became secondary as the Phantom went on the offensive, hunting MiGs deep inside enemy airspace. It also carried large loads of bombs and rockets, becoming a truly 'multi-role' combat aircraft.

F-4J characteristics
Outwardly almost indistinguishable from the F-4B, the F-4J took advantage of an improved AN/ASW-21 datalink system, originally designed for the little-known US Navy F-4G. This provided an automated carrier-landing capability which included automatic approach power compensation.

Flying controls
To operate at optimum performance, the F-4J used an air data computer to monitor control input by the pilot, thus ensuring that the airframe was not overstressed. Three independent hydraulic systems activated the primary flight controls, and electric power was supplied by an AC generator. The F-4J had an AN/APQ-13 radar and an AN/AJB-7 bombing system.

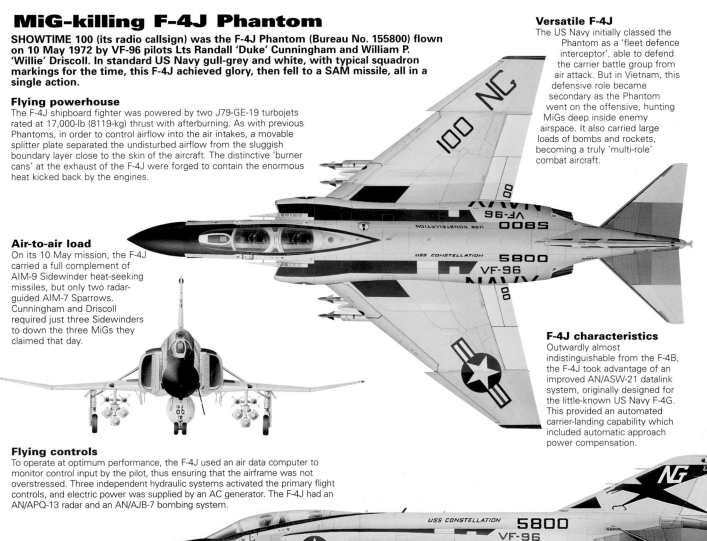

Mikoyan-Gurevich MiG-15 'Fagot'

Soviet fighter pioneer

Designed and produced in great haste, the MiG-15 came to be built in enormous numbers in four countries, and formed the basis of the Soviet air force's wholesale entry into the jet age.

Above: The square-cropped jetpipe, subsequently shortened and faired, identifies this as one of the I-310 prototypes. Production aircraft were surprisingly similar.

Top: Poland was a major MiG-15 user, building the type as the Lim-1/2. The first Polish-built aircraft flew on 17 July 1952.

While the Mikoyan-Gurevich design bureau was struggling in the race to get its MiG-9 'Fargo' first-generation jet fighter into service, design teams were also working flat-out on a successor. In March 1946 the Soviet bureaux had been called to the Kremlin and issued with a requirement for a jet fighter capable of transonic speeds. MiG realised that the required performance could only be met using swept wings. Research into swept wings was well advanced in the Soviet Union before the war but, as in the US, it was the influx of German aerodynamic data and personnel which allowed it to proceed to the point of hardware.

While aerodynamic and structural design work continued apace, alongside other important work such as the provision of a high-speed ejection seat, the development of a powerplant proved troublesome. Soviet engineers had only the BMW 003 and Jumo 004 jets to work from, and neither could be developed sufficiently to provide anything

like the power needed by the new fighter. Soviet powerplant engineers were dispatched to the UK to study at first-hand the excellent Rolls-Royce Nene and Derwent jets. Shortly after, in September 1946, 10 Nenes were sold to the Soviet Union, another 15 following in March 1947.

Reverse-engineered, the Nene soon began pouring from the lines of state aircraft factory (GAZ) no. 45, under the designation RD-45.

MiG, meanwhile, had been working on a variety of studies for the new aircraft. These had evaluated a number of configurations, but settled on a simple fuselage with the engine buried in the rear fuselage, aspirated via a bifurcated intake in the extreme nose. This design was known in-house as the I-310, or simply the S.

Initial flight

Production of three prototypes was conducted through 1947, two powered by the Nene 1 and one powered by the Nene 2 (RD-45). On 30 December 1947, the first S took to the air.

With testing only just started, the Kremlin ordered the aircraft, as the MiG-15, into full-scale production in mid-March 1948. Flight tests of the first three aircraft led to numerous changes being incorporated into the design, the most obvious being the shortening of the jetpipe to offset a loss of thrust. The MiG showed generally good performance and handling, although the rival Lavochkin La-15 also showed promise, and was also ordered into production.

On 30 December 1948, exactly a year after the first prototype, the first production MiG-15 took to the air. Production quickly ramped up, the first aircraft entering service in January 1949 following clearance in October 1948.

Development of the basic MiG-15 continued as rapidly as construction. The early RD-45 aircraft was replaced by the RD-45F, with improved reliability. Production line anomalies, which resulted in some asymmetry in

flight, were rectified. More importantly, engine designer Vladimir Klimov had refined the RD-45 to produce considerably more thrust. As the VK-1, this engine was fitted to a MiG-15 prototype known as the SD. Flight trials resulted in the SD going into service as the MiG-15bis, which became the most numerous variant.

Armament was also improved: the first MiG-15s featured one NS-37 37-mm cannon and two NS-23 23-mm cannon, mounted on a removable pack under the nose. The SV variant replaced the NS-23s with newer NR-23s, and later replaced the NS-37 with the better N-37. These changes, and others, were introduced gradually on the production lines.

In January 1949 the first MiG-15s reached operational units of the PVO (Troops of Air Defence), and deliveries to the VVS (air force) began shortly after. The more powerful MiG-15bis version reached the front line in early 1950.

During late 1948 the NII confirmed its interest in a two-seat trainer version. MiG was already well advanced with the ST, or I-312T. A prototype flew in January 1949, and the first production MiG-15UTIs were delivered during the spring.

As a simple and inherently good aircraft, the MiG-15UTI enjoyed a long career as an advanced/ conversion trainer, proving admirable for conversion to the MiG-17 and MiG-19.

Single-seat development

For the escort role, long-range versions of both basic fighter variants were developed as the MiG-15S and MiG-15bisS. These had oversized underwing tanks and were employed as escorts for heavy bombers. The SR, or MiG-15bisR, was a tactical reconnaissance version with cameras mounted in an underfuselage fairing.

The MiG-15 also played its part in the nascent fighter radar industry, although the only radar-equipped version to reach (limited) production, was the MiG-15P (SP-5), which sported Izumrud radar and two NR-23 cannon.

Other Soviet versions worthy of mention are the MiG-15T/bisT, which was used for target-towing, the MiG-15bisF with cameras in a faired pod under the forward fuselage, and the MiG-15SB fighter-bomber with wing racks for bombs and rockets.

Although Soviet factories churned out MiG-15s by the hundred, additional sources were sought. WSK-Mielec in Poland built the MiG-15 as the Lim-1, MiG-15UTI as the SBLim-1, and the MiG-15bis as the Lim-2. In Czechoslovakia Letov and, later, Aero built the type as the S.102 (MiG-15), S.103 (MiG-15bis) and CS.102 (MiG-15UTI). Chinese unlicensed production was handled by Shenyang, which built the J-2 (MiG-15bis) and JJ-2 (MiG-15UTI). In total, at least 7,500 MiG-15s were built.

On 1 November 1950 MiG-15s entered the fray in the Korean War, operated by Soviet, Chinese and North Korean forces. In addition, virtually all of the Soviet Union's client states received the type, many taking aircraft from Czech or Polish production.

On 21 September 1953, this North Korean MiG-15 defected to Kimpo. The aircraft was shipped to Kadena for trials (flown by, among others, Major 'Chuck' Yeager), and then to the United States. It now resides in the USAF Museum at Wright-Patterson AFB.

The MiG-15UTI (NATO/ASCC codename 'Midget') outlived the single-seat versions by a considerable margin. The installation of the second cockpit reduced internal fuel capacity and armament.

Below: In Czechoslovakia the MiG-15 was built in some numbers for local use. Agreement for production was signed in April 1951, leading to a first flight by a Czechoslovak aircraft on 6 November. One hundred and sixty were built at Letnany before production transferred to Aero Vodochody in 1953, which provided another 821 S.102s and 620 S.103s by the time production ended in 1957. Two-seater CS.102 (MiG-15UTI) production reached a staggering 2,013 machines by 1961, many for overseas customers. This aircraft is one of the roughly 1,000 in Czechoslovak service in the type's peak period in 1957, painted in a special scheme as part of a three-ship aerobatic team.

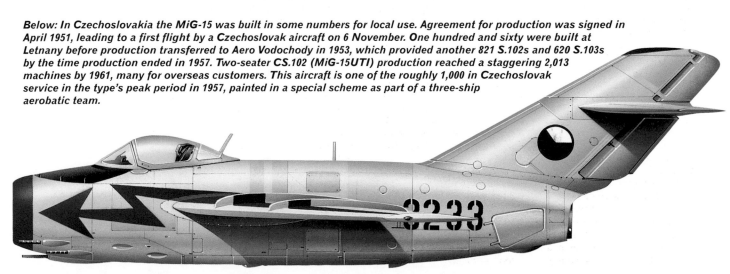

Ho Chi Minh Trail

America's inability to stop the flow of supplies along the Ho Chi Minh Trail was a source of great frustration to the US during the Vietnam War.

In any war, whether it be large or small in scale, the support and supply infrastructure has a particularly important part to play for, without a constant flow of equipment and other supplies, the fighting forces soon become powerless to continue. This was certainly true in Southeast Asia during the late 1960s and early 1970s, when US military might was ultimately matched and surpassed by North Vietnam's determination to succeed in its aims.

Perhaps the most vital factor in the eventual communist victory lay in the Ho Chi Minh Trail, actually a collection of roads and paths extending through Laos and parts of Cambodia. Starting from modest beginnings, by 1967 the trail had progressed to a complex network of tracks and roads, many of which were suitable for trucks. Maintenance depots, staging posts, radio and telephone links were added along the trail. The more vital the route became to the communist war effort, the greater the number of AAA emplacements that were added along its length.

As the enemy's principal means of supply, it was hardly surprising that American warplanes flew countless sorties against the trail, often with little effect in the early years. The thick jungle canopy and the ingenuity of the Vietnamese in the concealment of the truck convoys frequently resulted in ineffective air strikes.

Air intelligence

American planners were soon to realise that, with more accurate intelligence of the enemy's progress along the trail, air strikes could be timed to interdict the convoys at precise map co-ordinates, at times when the enemy was most vulnerable. With this in mind, a host of exotic programmes was implemented and tested under actual combat conditions.

One of the first, codenamed Igloo White, involved the dropping of ground sensors either side of the trail. Buried deep in the ground and camouflaged as small trees, the sensors would remain active for 30-45 days, detecting heavy

Top: The immense bombload of the Boeing B-52s could wreak havoc on a Viet Cong truck convoy, although their slow reaction time often allowed the quarry to escape before the aircraft were over the target area.

Below: High-tech strike aircraft such as the General Dynamics F-111, whose avionics allowed it to operate autonomously in appalling weather, also undertook low level interdiction missions against the trail, late in the war.

THE ROAD TO WAR

At the start of the Vietnam War, the Ho Chi Minh Trail was no more than a single track, with insurgents moving on foot between staging posts one day's march apart. Guides were responsible for specific sections of the trail, shepherding transient groups of up to 50 men through their own 'patch' before handing over to the next guide. Between 1966 and 1971, the trail expanded into a network of paths, with many being surfaced to facilitate the use of trucks in all weathers. With small bridges concealed just below the surfaces of rivers and the thick jungle canopy providing the ideal concealment, the monitoring of the enemy's movement along the trail became a constant thorn in the side of USAF planners.

Left: The first task in effective interdiction was the location of targets on the trail. Camouflage often made this impossible by conventional means but, in open spots such as this section of the Mu Gia pass, aerial cameras could sometimes find the prey – here, intelligence officers spotted 26 trucks on 9 February 1967. Supplying the photographs were RF-101 Voodoos, RF-4 Phantoms and the high-flying SR-71A Blackbirds.

Below: Replacing the Lockheed Constellation EC-121Rs on radio relay duties were the USAF Beech YQU-22A (illustrated) and QU-22B drones.

Above: Highly sophisticated AC-130s succeeded the elderly AC-47 and more advanced AC-119 on truck-hunting missions over the trail. Based on standard C-130s, these gunships orbited for hours on the worst of nights, knocking out hundreds of sensor-located trucks.

Centre at Nakhon Phanom. Initially, the signals were relayed in the air via Lockheed Constellation EC-121Rs, but the increase in enemy AAA and the cost of operating the lumbering Constellations saw the adoption in 1971 of unmanned drone aircraft. Purchased from the civilian market, the single-engined Beech Debonairs were suitably modified and designated QU-22Bs. They flew unescorted along the trail, relaying signals to USAF intelligence planners. Immediately any movement was detected, the progress of the convoy would be monitored while US jets were scrambled to intercept the trucks further down the trail.

A more conventional method of interdicting supplies was the use of Forward Air Controllers (FACs), usually flying Cessna O-2s. The FAC's job was an unenviable one, as it involved flying as close as possible to likely targets. When enemy movement was detected (often in the form of AAA against the FAC aircraft),

the pilot would pinpoint the exact position, call up friendly attack aircraft and then mark the target with pyrotechnic rockets or other markers. The enemy soon came to fear the small orbiting FAC aircraft, and Vietnamese gunners would often single them out for special attention. In one instance, the pilot of a downed FAC aircraft was discovered by US Navy SEALs in a former enemy camp – he had been skinned alive.

Although countless missions were flown by USAF F-4 Phantom IIs, F-105 Thunderchiefs and F-111s, as well as by the huge waves of B-52s from U-Tapao in Thailand, two specialised aircraft proved to be highly effective in the interdiction of enemy traffic along the trail.

The gunships

Having already proved itself in countless other wars, the Douglas C-47 found a new role in Vietnam. Equipped with side-firing Miniguns, the transport

was designated AC-47 although, to troops on the ground, the aircraft came to be known as 'Puff the Magic Dragon'. Flying slow circular orbits over the trail, the AC-47s were able to deliver a stream of fire into an area the size of a football field – for convoys caught in the open, the effects were devastating.

Despite their early success, the AC-47s proved to be only an interim design while the highly sophisticated AC-130 Spectres were developed. Fitted with infra-red to spot the hot truck engines, and equipment which detected ignition sparks, the AC-130s were constructed in a number of different variants, each with progressively heavier armament. Later variants of the AC-130A, even carried two 40-mm Bofors cannon and a single 105-mm Howitzer cannon for destroying trucks. Deep from within the aircraft's fuselage, sensor operators would scan the jungle canopy for signs of the advancing convoy and, once it was detected, the Spectre would go to work, unleashing a volley of fire into the area. The crew would then call up

orbiting F-4 Phantoms to complete the task, so leaving the convoy a smouldering heap of twisted metal.

Flying alone in the worst of weathers, like the gunships, were the Grumman A-6 Intruders of the US Navy. Launched from carriers stationed in the Gulf of Tonkin, the sophisticated avionics of the A-6 Intruder provided the crew with the ability to attack targets in the dead of night, to the complete surprise of the enemy. Despite the dangerous nature of these missions, enemy supplies at best were only temporarily halted. The will and resolve of the North Vietnamese would continue to find a way through for the supplies, even to the extent of carrying ammunition on bicycles.

In spite of all the sophistication employed by the American forces against the trail, the hopeless situation could only best be described thus by one American fighter pilot after an interdiction mission: "At times the trail was like the Long Island Expressway in rush hour".

Flying alongside their USAF counterparts were the strike aircraft of the US Navy. Seen rolling in on the target for its final pass is this F-4B Phantom II from VF-96 'Fighting Falcons'. The aircraft is armed with Zuni 5-in (130-mm) unguided rockets and AIM-7 Sparrow AAMs for self-defence. The Phantom proved itself to be a highly capable aircraft for interdiction missions along the trail. With intelligence supplied via ground sensors, the USAF was able to operate its Phantoms on night-attack missions, relying on flares and AC-130 gunships to illuminate the North Vietnamese trucks.

Close air support

As well as flying bombing missions against North Vietnam, American fighter-bombers flew countless strikes in support of troops on the ground.

At the peak of American involvement in the war in Southeast Asia, a daily average of 800 sorties was flown by fighter-bomber aircraft operating in support of ground forces. Three out of every four sorties launched from airfields in South Vietnam were of direct assistance to the troops in the field – the great majority of the missions being for close air support (CAS) and tactical airlift. About half of the CAS sorties were flown by the USAF, with one third of the effort coming from aircraft of the US Marine Corps, and the remainder from

the Vietnamese air force. Additional CAS was available from the attack aircraft of the US Sixth Fleet operating from carriers in the Gulf of Tonkin, although they chiefly flew against targets in North Vietnam or the Ho Chi Minh Trail.

Over half of the close air support sorties flown in a day were pre-planned, so that the pilots could be briefed in advance and the aircraft armed with ordnance suitable for the target. For example, 500-lb (227-kg) or 750-lb (340-kg) bombs were most effective against troops sheltering in fortified bunkers or beneath the

Top: A USAF F-4 Phantom II screams over the heads of huddled American troops to deliver its bombs on an enemy stronghold. Co-ordination between pilots and ground troops was vital during such missions.

Above: A Douglas A-1 Skyraider sets out on a support mission for US ground forces. Such missions were ably fulfilled by the A-1, with its useful loiter endurance, low speed and heavy weaponload.

As night falls over Ia Drang valley, dead and wounded American soldiers lie in a jungle clearing not far from the Viet Cong. Exhausted and surrounded, the US troops relied on close air support to assist them in their escape.

dense jungle canopy, whereas cluster bombs or napalm were better suited to troops in the open.

However, not all CAS demands could be anticipated and, for this reason, a number of fighter-bombers were held on alert. They were armed with a variety of ordnance, so as to be able to deal with any target. Once a request for air support was received, an alert flight of two or four aircraft was scrambled and arrived over its target within 40 minutes. If the need for aerial firepower was so urgent that a quicker reaction time was needed, then aircraft already in the air could be diverted from their original targets. On the rare occasions

when ground forces were so vulnerable that their requests for close air support had to be met immediately, then the distress radio call 'Broken Arrow' was broadcast, followed by an airborne alert being flown over the area. This was wasteful of fuel and resources, however, and so was not often practised. But when the emergency call went out from troops surrounded on the ground, pilots of all services responded without hesitation.

Ia Drang valley

By mid–October 1965, the North Vietnamese Army had received enough supplies to begin a major offensive against the south. Starting in the Central Highlands, three North

Below: This 345th TAS, 314th TAW C-130E explodes in flames having received a direct hit from communist mortars. This sight would become all too familiar to US Marines at Khe Sanh, although the C-130 crews would later develop specialised delivery tactics to avoid the enemy guns.

Vietnamese Army regiments were assembled near the Cambodian border in Ia Drang valley with, the intention of mounting an assault that would cut South Vietnam in two. Commander of US Military Assistance Command Vietnam, General Westmoreland, directed the 1st Air Cavalry Division to seek out and destroy this enemy force.

Facing three North Vietnamese Army regiments, the initial helicopter assault proved to be surprisingly easy, with the 1st Air Cavalry suffering few casualties. But, by mid-afternoon, the North Vietnamese had mounted a ferocious artillery barrage on the landing zone, which was quickly followed by a human wave assault. To the American troops on the ground the fire-fights were being fought on three sides, and replacement troops arriving in Huey helicopters were met with a stream of enemy fire.

As the battle raged, American soldiers on the ground realised their precarious position and the distress call of 'Broken Arrow' was made. Within minutes, tactical jets such as F-100s, F-4s, F-105s and a US Navy carrier air wing were orbiting the area. There were so many jets in the

Right: Aswell as providing their own Marines on the ground with close air support, the F-4 Phantoms from VMFA-542 often flew missions in support of other troops in battle. Operating over South Vietnam the F-4s often flew without any air-to-air missiles so allowing a larger bomb load to be carried.

sky that air controllers stacked the aircraft from 3,000 ft (914 m) to 30,000 ft (9144 m). Each flight would descend on the valley in turn to deliver its deadly load under the direction of an observer on the ground. This continued until the North Vietnamese withdrew. This was one of many occasions when CAS saved the lives of troops on the ground.

Siege of Khe Sanh

Three years later, the small base of Khe Sanh was to be brought to the attention of the whole world. Situated in the northwestern area of South Vietnam, it was 10 miles (16 km) from Laos and 15 miles (25 km) from the Demilitarised Zone – well within striking distance of North Vietnamese troops. With a single 3,900-ft (1188-m) runway, the base was able to accommodate the large C-130 transport aircraft.

For the US Marines based there, the siege began on 21 January 1968 with a barrage of mortar and artillery fire. One of the enemy shells hit the ammunition dump, which blew up, destroying 98 per cent of the ammunition on the base. The North Vietnamese also managed to crater 1,500 ft (457 m) of the runway badly enough to prevent its use. Yet USAF C-123s managed to keep the base supplied, while heavy air strikes by F-105s and F-4s took place around the base.

The only method of resupplying Khe Sanh was by air, but this was fast becoming one of the most dangerous and demanding flying jobs in the world. Because the base was surrounded by enemy troops, there were no safe approaches. Landing aircraft were subjected to a hail of 30- and 50-calibre machine-gun fire. And, once on the ground, the resupply aircraft became what the Marines described as 'mortar magnets'. The enemy registered the spots where the aircraft unloaded, and tried hard to destroy as many C-123s and C-130s as possible (the North Vietnamese were later to use PT-76 light tanks for the first time in the war). February proved to be the toughest month

of the siege, some days seeing more than 1,000 enemy shells descend on the base. American air power was again unleashed to help the troops at the base, who were in dire need of assistance.

This time, the Seventh Air Force flew 9,961 sorties, dropping over 14,223 tons of bombs. B-52 Stratofortresses of the 3rd Air Division flew 2,548 sorties, dropping 59,542 tons of bombs, while the Marines and Navy flew 7,078 and 5,337 sorties, respectively. B-52s dropped bombs closer to friendly lines than at any other time in the war, using the reliable Sky Spot bombing system. A flight of bombers was over Khe Sanh every three minutes, around the clock – the landscape around the base soon came to resemble that of the moon. Having sustained an estimated 10,000 casualties, the North Vietnamese finally withdrew from the battle, unable to counter the aerial bombardment.

CAS had once again proved its worth to American commanders. Its efficacy was best described thus by one US Marines captain: "Good close air support allowed us never to have to send a man where we could send either a bomb or bullet."

The North American F-100 Super Sabre performed more close air support missions than any other aircraft in the war. Here an F-100 drops a bomb on a suspected enemy stronghold.

Strategic reconnaissance

For most of the war in Southeast Asia, the skies over the combat zone were filled with aircraft involved in all manner of operations. High above them flew Lockheed's U-2s and SR-71s, watching with impunity events on the ground from their perch way above the clouds. Flying below these two aircraft were the lumbering RC-135s.

Above: The most capable reconnaissance 'snooper' in Vietnam was the Boeing RC-135U. Although only deployed to the war zone temporarily, it possessed vast intelligence-gathering capabilities.

Following the downing of Gary Powers in his Lockheed U-2 over Russia in 1960, President Eisenhower promised that no further manned reconnaissance overflights would be undertaken. The implications of this statement left the USAF reconnaissance crews without any 'real' missions to perform. With no war to fight, and relegated to flying air-sampling missions following Soviet missile tests, the crews of the U-2s and RB-47 Stratojets waited impatiently for the call to battle.

In March 1964, the call arrived and, as the war in Southeast Asia escalated, America soon found itself committing increasing numbers of ground troops to the war zone. The U-2 (dubbed the 'Dragon Lady') was stripped of sampling equipment and, instead, re-configured with Photographic Intelligence (Photint) and Signals Intelligence (Sigint) collection receivers. Deploying from Davis-Monthan AFB, the 4080th SRW was based at Bien Hoa (later U-Tapao) under the deployment codename of Lucky Dragon. Here, the U-2Cs immediately commenced their primary (Photint) mission.

Flying alongside the U-2s on the early missions were Ryan AQM-34 pilotless drones, launched from specially configured Hercules DC-130s. The increase in North Vietnamese SA-2 'Guideline' SAMs meant that the drones flew over the areas with the highest risk, which often resulted in their complete destruction.

As the air threat increased, the role of the U-2Cs was changed

to that of collecting both enemy radio communication and Sigint. Later, the U-2's name would be changed to 'Trojan Horse' and, later still, to 'Olympic Torch'.

The greatest impact on U-2 operations in Vietnam came with the introduction of the U-2R variant and, along with this, came the change in unit designation from the 4080th to the 100th SRW. The improved U-2R offered increased payload capability, range and safety. Most pleasing to the pilots were the improved flight controls which allowed the pilot a greater margin of safety during landings, particularly important after a fatiguing six-hour mission that would see the aircraft fly close to the Chinese border and around North Vietnam.

Later, with other reconnaissance aircraft arriving in the theatre, the U-2s would spend most of their airborne hours monitoring signals within China rather than in Vietnam. So vital did these missions become that the U-2s were some of the last USAF aircraft to leave the theatre, finally leaving Thailand in March 1976, with the 100th SRW having acquired the distinction of being the first U-2 unit to complete 500 combat hours in a single month (accomplished in January 1973).

America's other strategic reconnaissance asset, the SR-71 Blackbird, deployed to Kadena AFB, Okinawa, in 1967. Known as Detachment 1, the unit operated from a far corner of the air base under tight security. Despite constant denials from USAF officials that the

A Lockheed SR-71 slides away from its KC-135Q tanker high over the South China Sea during a Vietnam reconnaissance mission. The SR-71s operated from Kadena under the codename Giant Scale.

Blackbird had been deployed there, whenever an SR-71 took off, a huge crowd gathered outside the base to watch the awesome spectacle.

Each mission would last about three and a half hours, with an inflight refuelling halfway through. Cruising at 80,000 ft (24385 m) at a speed of Mach 3, the aircraft had a turning radius of 160-180 miles

(260-290 km) at best. As a result, all missions were flown in a gentle arc across the area of interest. The first pass might take the SR-71 across Thailand, Laos, North Vietnam and out over the Gulf of Tonkin for a refuelling rendezvous with a KC-135Q. The route might then be reversed, with a refuelling taking place over Thailand. After refuelling, the Blackbird would make a second loop to cover different areas, which could be Chinese targets on the aircraft's return trip to Kadena. Despite numerous North Vietnamese SAM launches, the Blackbirds performed their missions with impunity.

A U-2R from the 99th SRS floats across the threshold at U-Tapao in Thailand, from where most U-2 operations were conducted. The aircraft carries Comint (communications intelligence) antennas.

COMBAT APPLE OVER SOUTHEAST ASIA

For over four years, RC-135M aircraft (occasionally RC-135Ds) were on station 24 hours a day on Combat Apple duties, 'listening' to North Vietnamese signals. All missions started from Kadena AFB on the Japanese island of Okinawa, where a large tanker force was also based. A flight of less than four hours' duration took Combat Apple to the war zone, where a 12-hour orbit was set up over the Gulf of Tonkin. Refuelling was usually accomplished at the southern end of the orbit, near the DMZ. If the aircraft found something of interest, a small orbit could be set up in the vicinity to analyse it further, before the aircraft returned to the larger orbit. After 12 hours, the aircraft was relieved and it could return to Kadena, its total flight time in the region of 19 hours.

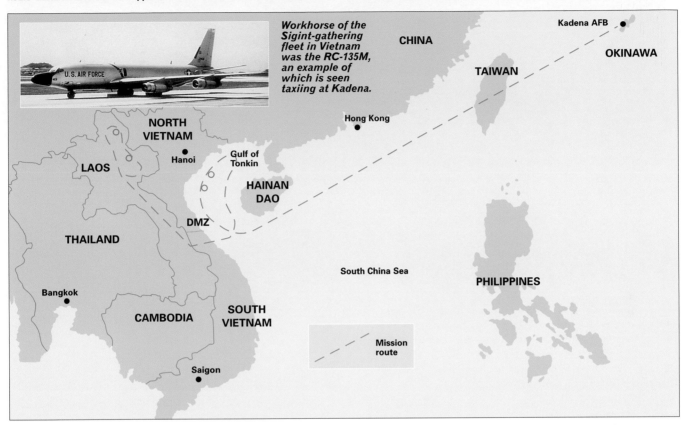

Workhorse of the Sigint-gathering fleet in Vietnam was the RC-135M, an example of which is seen taxiing at Kadena.

Mission route

Combat Apple

Operating alongside the SR-71s at Kadena AFB were the RC-135Ms of the 82nd SRW. With the RB-47 Stratojets having been retired from covert operations around the Soviet borders, the unit arrived in the theatre on 25 August 1967. At first, missions were limited to 30 a month, but the escalating air war saw the RC-135s being used increasingly, to the point where 24-hour coverage was required. The impact made by these aircraft under the Combat Apple programme proved to be extremely beneficial to USAF commanders.

Combat Apple involved the aircraft flying 12-hour orbits over the Gulf of Tonkin, and later Laos too, collecting electronic intelligence. Special attention was devoted to the picking-up of

RC-135Ds were only operated on Combat Apple missions when the RC-135Ms were returned to the United States for maintenance.

signal indications from the North Vietnamese 'Fan Song' radar associated with the SA-2 'Guideline' SAM. These signals enabled US experts to pinpoint the location of SAM sites, which could then be relayed to strike aircraft. Those areas where the RC-135s searched most intensively included North Vietnam, Hainan Island and along the DMZ.

When the RC-135s went 'up north', out came the MiGs. On several occasions, MiG-21 'Fishbeds' would streak out over the Gulf at supersonic speeds and challenge the RC-135. After a few close interceptions, an escort was provided in the form of F-4 Phantoms and F-8 Crusaders. During these escort missions, the fighter crews would tuck themselves tight underneath the wings of the RC-135, without being detected by enemy radar. When MiG-21s appeared again, they were ambushed by the escorting fighters, and several were downed before the North Vietnamese decided to abandon this tactic.

Weather conditions over Vietnam played havoc with the complex intelligence-gathering systems on board the RC-135s, however, and rain found its way into the aircraft's fuselage, shorting out engines and systems. When the time came for the RC-135Ms to undergo maintenance, they were replaced by the less capable RC-135Ds.

As intelligence-gathering technology increased, newer and more capable variants of the RC-135s were developed. Designated RC-135U and operated in Vietnam under Combat Sent, the 'U' was the most elaborate and capable special-mission aircraft ever to be built. There were only two examples which, between them, had to cover the world and, accordingly, a deployment to Kadena would last only three months. Even with this tight

schedule, the Combat Sent aircraft were able to detect changes in the fusing and guidance of North Vietnamese SAMs. This information would later be passed to B-52 Stratofortress crews during the Linebacker bombing campaign.

As the war drew to a close, RC-135 activity increased. Crews monitored the North Vietnamese build-up in South Vietnam as American forces retreated. Reconnaissance and intelligence-gathering missions continued to be flown around the area, with SR-71s and RC-135s remaining at Kadena AFB long after the final shot had been fired. Vietnam proved to be the ideal testing ground for the USAF's reconnaissance assets. Not only was new technology designed and tested here, but a variety of tactics were put into practice, tactics that are still in use today.

During the latter stages of the Vietnam war, the RC-135Us underwent numerous modifications in an effort to locate North Vietnamese radar installations.

Operating in concert with his more glamorous jet counterparts, the FAC pilot's contribution to the war was inestimable. Here Captain McClellan, an OV-10 pilot, searches for signs of enemy movement during a mission in September 1972.

Forward Air Control

Few jobs in the Vietnam air war came tougher than flying the Forward Air Control mission. Piloting lightplanes into heavily-defended areas at low level demanded extreme skill and bravery, illustrated by the awarding of 12 Medals of Honor to USAF FAC fliers during the conflict.

An important complement to air support operations in Vietnam was the Forward Air Control (FAC) system. Flying a relatively slow observation aircraft – initially the Korean War-vintage Cessna O-1 Bird Dog and, later, the more powerful, twin-engined Cessna O-2 or North American OV-10 Bronco – the FAC pilot was the link between the often high- and fast-flying attack aircraft and friendly forces on the ground. The pilot sought out targets that a fast jet pilot would never have seen and then marked them for attack, firing smoke rockets. In contrast to World War II and Korea, when FAC was necessary only for close air support missions in the vicinity of friendly troops, the Vietnam War required FAC personnel to carry out visual reconnaissance over South Vietnam to detect traces of an elusive enemy. Two types of FAC operation evolved during

the conflict in Vietnam. One was in support of friendly troop movements, with FACs assigned to all major ground combat units. The other was concerned with daily reconnaissance over a single Vietnamese province, so that an experienced FAC pilot, familiar with his territory, could immediately spot any unusual ground activity that might betray the presence of an enemy unit. He could then call in a ground patrol to investigate.

The elderly Cessna O-1 Bird Dog carried the burden of FAC duties for much of the war. A two-seat, high-wing observation aircraft, it had first entered service with the US Army in 1950. The Bird Dog was powered by a single 213-hp (159-kW) Continental 0-470-11 air-cooled piston engine, which gave it a maximum speed of 115 mph (185 km/h), and a range of 530 miles (850 km). The aircraft was unarmed apart

from its marker rockets and the crew's sidearms. One enterprising FAC pilot, Captain Roger Krell, flew an O-1G Bird Dog nicknamed *Little Puff*, one of two modified aircraft that were fitted with a sideways-firing 0.30-calibre (7.62-mm) M60A1 machine-gun mounted in the rear seat. This modification proved ineffective, however, and was soon abandoned. The Bird Dog's most serious faults were its lack of endurance and power reserves, plus the total absence of protection for the crew and fuel tanks. With the purchase of more capable aircraft, many Bird Dogs were passed over to the VNAF to continue their hazardous observation missions.

The Bird Dog's successor, the Cessna O-2, was a conversion of the civilian Cessna 337 Super Skymaster. Its performance was a considerable improvement over the O-1, as its twin 210-hp (157-kW) Continental IO-360-C/D air-cooled piston engines (mounted in an unusual arrangement, with one as a tractor and the other a pusher) provided considerably more power. Its maximum speed was nearly 200 mph (332 km/h) and its range was increased to 1,060 miles (1705 km). Furthermore, the underwing marker rockets could be supplemented by a 7.62-mm minigun pod, giving the FAC pilot a chance to fight back against ground fire. Yet, with all these positive virtues, the O-2 still lacked armour protection for the crew and vital aircraft systems. A total of 510 O-2s was delivered to the USAF,

designated O-2As, later replaced on some missions by O-2Bs. The latter were specially developed for psychological warfare operations, the 51 examples delivered forming part of the 9th Special Operations Squadron based at Nha Trang. The O-2Bs were equipped to drop propaganda leaflets from a hand-operated dispenser, or to relay messages to enemy troops via three 600-watt loudspeakers mounted on the fuselage. The O-2s quickly proved themselves to be capable of performing a wider range of duties than FAC missions, and it has been rumoured that the nimble aircraft performed covert operations over North Vietnam on behalf of the CIA during the final stages of the war.

However, the most effective FAC aircraft in Southeast Asia proved to be the twin-engined, twin-boom North American OV-10 Bronco. The Bronco itself was never intended for the FAC role and was delivered to the USAF as a low-maintenance aircraft for anti-guerrilla operations. Pilots initially considered the aircraft, equipped with two 600-shp (447-kW) engines, to be underpowered. Although improved powerplants became

Preceding the O-2 as the principal FAC aircraft was the Cessna O-1 Bird Dog, which was already a veteran of the Korean War. A phosphorus rocket-armed example is seen here rolling towards the thick jungle canopy to mark a target in November 1966.

Based on the civilian Cessna Model 337, the O-2A featured military communications equipment and hardpoints for weaponry. The large whip aerial above the centre-section transmitted calls from the FAC officer to strike aircraft.

Tiger Pause *was the name painted on the nose of this O-2A, seen tied down and well-protected in its revetment. The extensively-glazed doors on the starboard side afforded the pilot improved visibility.*

available later, the Bronco was noted for its long take-off run in hot weather which, when operating close to the front line within the confines of a semi-prepared airstrip, resulted in several examples being lost. Despite the powerplant restriction, the OV-10 was bigger and far more formidable than any other aircraft assigned to the FAC role. It had a maximum speed of 228 mph (463 km/h) and a perch for a second-seat FAN (forward air navigator), a seat occupied more frequently on OV-10 missions than on those carried out by the O-2.

A typical OV-10 combat sortie in Southeast Asia lasted around five hours. The normal configuration included a 230-US gal (870-litre) fuel tank on the centreline, two LAU-59/A rocket pods with 2.75-in (70-mm) marking rockets on the weapon sponsons and, if armed, 2,000 rounds for its four M60 machine-guns.

The OV-10 pilot had at his disposal a complete radio kit including HF (HF-103), VHF (FM-622A), and UHF (AN/ARC-51) sets. Both pilot and observer were protected by 268 lb (121 kg) of armour. The Bronco typically carried about 2,000 lb (907 kg) of ordnance, including numerous combinations of flares, smoke rockets, machine-guns, rockets, and light bombs. The OV-10 replaced the O-2A in Tactical Air Support Squadrons (TASS) and also served with the US Navy's VAL-4

'Black Ponies', and the Marine Corps' VMO-1 and -2, who also undertook FAC missions.

The contribution made by FAC pilots in Vietnam was enormous, especially in the early days, before the OV-10 was in existence, when the Bird Dog was the only way to confront the Viet Cong. One way to gauge the importance of the FAC effort is to look at the price: 338 USAF FAC pilots lost their lives in the conflict. A total of 161 Bird Dogs were lost in combat and 150 in 'operational' mishaps, the latter being strongly influenced by the gruelling conditions. About 45 per cent of the top awards for valour given to pilots in Vietnam went to FAC personnel.

The North American OV-10 Bronco supplanted the O-2 on FAC duties. Although louder and larger, it had armour, self-sealing tanks and four integral 0.3-in (7.62-mm) machine-guns. This OV-10A from the 19th TASS at Bien Hoa is seen on a mission near Lai Khe in South Vietnam.

O-2A 'Super Skymaster'

The O-2A 'Super Skymaster' was a development of the 1966 version of Cessna's Model 337 light business aircraft. Cessna was willing to develop a narrow-cabin variant for the FAC role, but the USAF accepted a limited adaption of the standard civilian aircraft fitted with hardpoints and extra radio equipment. The 'black FACs' of the

20th and 23rd TASS were based at Nakhon Phanom, RTAB, in Thailand. They were used in conjunction with 'Spooky' gunships on nocturnal patrols along the Ho Chi Minh Trial. Other O-2s were flown by CIA FAC pilots on clandestine missions over Laos.

Crew
O-2 FAC aircraft were flown both solo and with an observer/artillery spotter, depending on the mission. Visibility was relatively poor compared to the O-1 which had a narrow fuselage and tandem seating. A cut-out window on the starboard door slightly improved the view for a solo pilot who flew from the left seat.

Weapons
The primary offensive weapon (and target-marking device) was the 2.75-in Folding Fin Aircraft Rocket (FFAR). Up to 28 could be carried in four LAU-32 or LAU-59 launcher tubes. A pair of SUU-11A 0.3-in (7.62-mm) gun pods with 1,500 rounds per gun could also be fitted to the wing pylons. A pair of M16 rifles could be strapped to the cabin sides for use by the crew in the event of a forced landing.

Engines
The O-2A was fitted with two 210-hp (157-kW) Continental IO-360-D horizontally-opposed flat-six air-cooled piston engines. The McCauley variable-pitch propellers rotated in the same direction with respect to the engine but, because of their 'push-me-pull-you' layout, they cancelled out each other's torque. The absence of propeller spinners was a common feature of the O-2, compared to the commercial Model 337.

Hardpoints
The O-2 had four MAU-3A bomb racks under the wing, each with a capacity of 350 lb (159 kg). Flares were a common store, with up to 16 available in four-shot launchers.

Communications
Pilots referred to the O-2 as a 'flying radio set', equipped as it was with a transceiver for communication with USAF and USN attack aircraft and friendly ground forces. This equipment included VHF (FM-662 and Wilcox 807) radio sets. An AN/APX-64 IFF was fitted, as was TACAN and ADF for navigation.

South Vietnamese Dragons

The Vietnamese Air Force (VNAF) existed for just 24 years, from the summer of 1951 when the French began training Vietnamese air crews, until the summer of 1975, when Saigon fell. During this time, the young Vietnamese pilots participated in some of the most savage battles of the Vietnam War and earned the title of flying 'Dragons'.

Top: With loudspeakers mounted on the left-hand side, these VNAF de Havilland Canada U-6As are seen engaged on a psychological warfare sortie over the Mekong Delta.

Above: Used as a communications and liaison aircraft, the Cessna U-17 was a military version of the Model 185. Later, the U-17 was used for FAC duties; for this role, the Cessna carried additional radio equipment and marker rockets under the wings.

The first positive step toward the creation of the Vietnamese Air Force was taken on 9 June 1951 when the organisation of an Air Training Centre at Nha Trang was authorised. Staffed by French personnel and equipped with Morane-Saulnier M.S.500 Criquets, the Nha Trang Air Training Centre began by training Vietnamese instructors selected from personnel previously trained at French flying schools. From July 1951, two operational squadrons were established in Vietnam. Although the squadrons had a limited combat capability, the French government later supplied Dassault M.D.312 Flamants equipped with underwing bomb racks. Later, a third squadron was established which conducted observation missions prior to bombing attack.

France quits

Following the end of the Indochina War and in preparation for the final withdrawal of its forces from the country, France, with the concurrence of the United States, undertook to provide additional aircraft to the VNAF by transferring a number of US-supplied aircraft. Among the types to be adopted by the VNAF were 20 Cessna L-19s; the Flamants were replaced in the liaison and transport roles by 10 Beech C-45s, 16 Douglas C-47s and a single Republic Seabee amphibian. At the same time, the VNAF took over control of the air bases at Bien Hoa, Da Nang, Nha Trang, Pleiku and Tan Son Nhut. In addition, France provided 28 Grumman F8F-1 Bearcats and started a pilot training programme at Vung Tau Airfield in preparation for the activation of the VNAF's 1st Fighter Squadron at Bien Hoa in June 1956.

Changing the guard

With French combat forces out of Vietnam, American officials fully expected the North Vietnamese to invade South Vietnam at any moment. The decision was therefore taken to supervise the armed forces of South Vietnam under the MAAG (Military Assistance Advisory Group). As far as the VNAF was concerned, this took the form of 16 additional Douglas C-47s and 10 ex-French H-19Bs, the latter providing Vietnam's first helicopter squadron. The absence of an effective command structure within the VNAF and the lack of experienced maintenance and flying personnel took its toll and, by 1961, the VNAF had only 70 serviceable aircraft on strength. Although some aircraft were lost in combat, many were lost through accidents and others were abandoned due to the inexperience of the crews.

Large numbers of Skyraiders were transferred as the war progressed, and these fought until the very last day of the conflict. This trio is carrying anti-personnel bombs and napalm, a devastating combination for troop concentrations.

A Cessna A-37B Dragonfly of the 518th Fighter Squadron operating out of Da Nang AB heads off on a bombing mission. In addition to its tip tanks, the aircraft carries two external wing tanks and four 500-lb (226-kg) Mk 82 bombs.

Fearing that the war would be lost, American air crews soon found themselves despatched to the war zone. Arriving in 1962 were 30 pilots to serve as co-pilots on VNAF C-47s. Known as the 'Dirty Thirty', these USAF pilots left South Vietnam on 3 December 1963, having clocked up more than 20,000 hours in C-47s. Other USAF crews were soon to follow, although American politicians were quick to point out that their role was strictly advisory.

Piston power

Following the VNAF's request for jets early on in the war, the transfer of two Lockheed T-33A jet trainers along with four RT-33A reconnaissance aircraft was suspended under the terms of the Geneva Convention. In their place, the VNAF received the well-armed (four 20-mm cannon and up to 8,000 lb/3692 kg of external stores) and well-protected ex-US Navy Douglas AD-6 (later redesignated A-1H) piston-powered attack aircraft, known as the Skyraider. The first arrived in mid-September 1960 and was followed by an additional 25 aircraft in May 1961 – the aircraft were used to re-equip the 1st Fighter Squadron at Bien Hoa.

In addition to normal in-country missions, the VNAF began to take over responsibility from the USAF for aerial psychological operations, flying de Havilland Canada U-6As, along with clandestine missions deep into North Vietnam. For these

activities, specially trained C-47 crews from the 1st and 2nd Transport Squadrons were tasked to fly at night from Nha Trang in order to drop sabotage teams to blow up bridges and power plants. Undertaken under the command of Major Nguyen Cao Ky (who eventually rose to the rank of Air Vice Marshal and

became the nation's prime minister after the 18 June 1965 military coup), these forays continued until July 1962 and resulted in the loss of three C-47s.

Jets at last

The bravery of the VNAF throughout the early 1960s finally led the United States to consent to Nguyen Cao Ky's request for jet aircraft. Transferred from USAF stocks

The F-5 required more maintenance and logistical support than expected. These F-5A/C Freedom Fighters are from the VNAF 23rd Tactical Wing and are seen on a bombing mission over South Vietnam.

on 1 June 1967 were 17 Northrop F-5A single-seat and two F-5B two-seat fighters from the 4503rd Tactical Fighter Squadron (Skoshi Tiger). The new unit, known as the 552nd Fighter Squadron, was entirely manned by the Vietnamese and, upon receiving the F-5s, immediately began flying operational missions. The monthly F-5 sortie rate steadily increased from 388 in June 1967 to 527 in December of the same year, and to 683 in March 1968. In spite of this achievement, the VNAF was not allowed any more F-5 squadrons until 1972.

In 1968 it obtained Cessna A-37Bs as its next combat jet. Initial delivery of the A-37B was made in November of that year, with the 524th Fighter Squadron becoming operational on the type in March 1969 and being quickly followed by the 520th and 516th Fighter Squadrons. Although not as effective as the old Skyraiders that they served alongside, being armed with a single 7.62-mm Minigun instead of four 20-mm cannon, and carrying only half the bombload, the A-37Bs had the distinct advantage of being new aircraft for which parts were readily available. This, combined with the fact that they were easy to fly and provided a good weapons-firing platform, meant that there were more A-37s in the VNAF inventory than any other aircraft.

As the war went on and America gradually withdrew its forces, the process of 'Vietnamisation' saw the VNAF's inventory swell with US-supplied

aircraft. Among the types offered were 150 Bell U-1Hs, 20 Boeing-Vertol CH-47A Chinooks, 16 Douglas AC-47 'Spooky' gunships, 16 Fairchild AC-119G 'Stingers' and 48 Fairchild C-123K Providers. Despite the additional aircraft, combat losses for the VNAF increased from 89 to 334 over the period from 1968 to 1972. America attempted to replace the lost aircraft under the Enhance Plus programme which saw the introduction of 18 F-5E Tiger IIs and RF-5As. Despite the extensive equipment and training provided to the VNAF, however,

the end came swiftly for Vietnam's air force. On 30 April 1975, with the war in its final hours, a VNAF AC-119K with two A-1H Skyraiders flew the last combat sortie in an attempt to halt the Communist advance. Two of the aircraft fell to North Vietnamese SA-7s.

From its modest debut with 'hand-me-down' aircraft, the VNAF had grown into a well-rounded organisation which, in terms of the number of aircraft, ranked fourth among the world's air forces. But, even though it was at war for most of its existence, the VNAF never shot down an enemy aircraft as its operations were almost exclusively conducted in support of ground operations, within the borders of South Vietnam. The final gallant act of the air crews of the VNAF, in the last 24 hours of the war was to 'troll' for enemy fire so that aircraft operating on the evacuation airlift could have a chance to depart safely.

On 29 April 1975, Nguyen Cao Ky, the former South Vietnamese premier and head of the VNAF, was flown to the carrier USS Midway by an Air America Huey. Later in the day, 29 UH-1s, two CH-47s and a single O-1 sought sanctuary aboard US Navy carriers.

Alpha Strikes

From their low-key entry into the war in 1964 until the final evacuation, the US Navy's carrier force was at the sharp end of the aerial campaign against North Vietnam. While Crusaders and Phantoms tangled with MiGs, many carrier aircraft fought a less glamorous 'dirty war', with bombs and rockets, in support of the ground troops. Carriers also possessed the unique ability to provide a complete package of aircraft, an 'Alpha Strike', capable of attacking the vital and heavily defended targets in the North.

The striking power of US carrier aviation was tested against North Vietnam on 5 August 1964, when President Lyndon Johnson authorised the Gulf of Tonkin air strikes to retaliate following attacks on American destroyers. The US Navy quickly became heavily involved in the struggle in South-East Asia.

The carriers operating off Vietnam launched strikes against the enemy from one of two positions, 'Dixie' Station for targets in the South and 'Yankee' Station for strikes against the North. The early operations used Vought F-8 Crusaders, Douglas A-1 Skyraiders, Douglas A-3 Skywarriors, Douglas A-4 Skyhawks and Grumman E-1 Tracer AEW aircraft. Gradually these aircraft were phased out of service as new designs reached the war zone, the more modern types including the McDonnell Douglas F-4 Phantom II, Grumman A-6 Intruder and E-2 Hawkeye, North American

RA-5C Vigilante and Vought A-7 Corsair II. The older types continued to serve later in the war on the smaller carriers such as *Bon Homme Richard*, *Ranger*, *Hancock*, *Intrepid*, *Oriskany* and *Ticonderoga*, by which time the larger ships such as the *Constellation*, *Forrestal*, *John F. Kennedy*, *Kitty Hawk* and *Midway* had re-equipped with the newer and more powerful aircraft.

Attacks against the North were often flown as massive 'Alpha Strikes' employing up to 70 or 80 aircraft in one huge aerial

armada, in an effort to inflict the greatest possible damage on a target. Military planners tended to divide North Vietnam up into 'Air Force' and 'Navy' regions, so that the aircraft aboard the carriers were given their own piece of geography to fly against. There were usually two carriers on Yankee Station at any one time, but when the fighting was at its heaviest as many as four were off the enemy coast. Other combat missions included the single-ship 'lone-wolf' missions for which the A-6 Intruder became famous.

The idea of an 'Alpha Strike' should not conjure up images of a massive World War II-style formation thundering towards its target. To the contrary, different components of the mission proceeded at different times, altitudes and headings. Each aircraft was assigned a specific mission such as flak suppression, combat air patrol, or actual strike

A bomb-laden Grumman A-6 Intruder leaps into the air from the forward catapult of the USS Ranger. The A-6 was instrumental in improving the strike capabilities of the naval air wings, introducing greater range, load-carrying and adverse weather capability.

once in the target area. The use of relatively tight formations during the flight into and out of the target area meant that defences would in theory be saturated. Each aircrew relied on the mutual support of the deceptive and defensive electronic gear, chaff and anti-radiation missiles carried by the other aircraft in the strike. It was also a distinct advantage to have other aircrew on the look-out to help spot any incoming MiGs and SAMs.

Air power

Targets would be assigned the night before a planned attack and a lone Intruder or two would

Protecting the strike wings were Vought F-8 Crusaders armed with heat-seeking air-to-air Sidewinder missiles and four internal 20-mm cannon. This pair from VF-211 flew missions from the smaller aircraft-carrier USS Hancock.

Early in the war A-3 Skywarriors performed bombing missions, even on targets in the heavily defended Hanoi area. As more advanced attack aircraft entered service, A-3s were converted into tankers. These KA-3Bs provided inflight-refuelling for the returning strike aircraft. Other variants such as the EA-3B provided electronic intelligence.

sneak into the target area, to hound and harass. For the other naval aviators involved a fitful night would pass, while the unsung but hard-pressed electricians, mechanics and armourers prepared the aircraft for battle. Air crew members

moving' A-7E Corsairs and A-6A Intruders would come next (the A-6s frequently being employed as daylight bombers, despite their all-weather capability). A-4E Skyhawks remained especially effective in the Iron Hand (anti-SAM) role armed with AGM-45

while being subjected to heavy enemy gunfire.

Ideally, several flights of aircraft attacked with short intervals between them and from different directions. North Vietnam's growing network of SAMs forced carrier aircraft to attack at relatively low altitudes but, despite the very formidable North Vietnamese MiG, missile and AAA defences, aircraft losses remained at an acceptable level.

Despite the awesome destructive capability of the 'Alpha Strikes', the North Vietnamese managed to continue the fight against the South throughout these aerial bombardments. But one thing was clear, the tactical benefits offered by a well co-ordinated carrier wing operating in the 'Alpha Strike' role would remain an important part of military doctrine for the US Navy in any future war.

In addition to being a fine attack aircraft, the Douglas Skyraider proved highly adaptable to other missions. One of the many variants was the EA-1F ECM version. During early missions the EA-1F provided jamming of North Vietnamese defences.

usually did not learn their assignments until morning, when weather, survival, target and threat briefings were conducted.

At dawn an RF-8A or RF-8G Crusader, escorted by fighters, checked out the weather and flew pre-attack reconnaissance over target. The first wave of the 'Alpha Strike' then followed, consisting of fighters assigned to drop ordnance, then remain in the area on TARget Combat Air Patrol (TARCAP) to engage MiGs. With the F-4 Phantom pilots deterring the North Vietnamese MiG force, the 'mud-

Shrike missiles. Douglas KA-3B Skywarriors provided inflight-refuelling support. Later in the war the Grumman E-2A Hawkeye AEW aircraft added an extra dimension to the 'Alpha Strike' forces' capabilities. Post-attack reconnaissance was the job of the RF-8A/G Crusader or the North American RA-5C Vigilante.

Various helicopters were available for the combat rescue mission, most of them based on destroyers sailing alongside the aircraft-carriers in the Gulf of Tonkin. One of the most widely used helicopter types was the Kaman UH-2C Seasprite. One Seasprite pilot won the Medal of Honor when he ventured into Haiphong Harbour, hovered over a moored merchant vessel, and snatched a navy pilot from the shallow waters of the port

When it entered combat for the first time on 4 December 1967, the A-7 Corsair II could carry all the latest weapons in the US Navy inventory, including Zuni rockets, AGM-45 Shrike anti-radiation missiles, cluster bombs and Bullpup air-to-surface missiles. A-7s remained in the front-line attack role until the end of the war.

Combat rescue

In order to save aircrew downed in combat over Laos and North Vietnam, the USAF developed a sophisticated rescue team of dedicated helicopters and support aircraft. Flying directly into harm's way so 'that others may live', these units saved many lives.

Combat rescue in Southeast Asia began as a small affair but, as US combat aircraft losses over North Vietnam grew, the need arose for an armed team to extract the downed aircrew. The basic principle called for a helicopter to move in to pick up the survivors under the cover of attack aircraft. Initially, Kaman HH-43 Huskie helicopters were used for short-range missions, but rescues at longer ranges required bigger, more sophisticated helicopters. The USAF hit upon the ideal combination of the Sikorsky HH-3 rescue helicopter (later replaced with Sikorsky HH-

53s) with the venerable Douglas A-1 Skyraider attack aircraft.

Despite the capabilities of the 'fast-mover' jets such as the F-4 Phantom II and F-105 Thunderchief, the USAF had found itself short of a slow aircraft which could carry a heavy weapons load, could loiter for a long time and, above all, was accurate. The USAF's elderly Skyraiders were found to be excellent for the rescue role, as they would have no trouble keeping station with the helicopters. These rescue escort aircraft were given the callsign 'Sandy', a word which was to

become the most widely respected in the flying fraternity.

The 'Sandy' missions suffered from the highest loss ratios in Southeast Asia and were widely regarded as the most dangerous. Although tough, the A-1 was a slow, cumbersome machine which was fairly easy to hit. The North Vietnamese quickly learned that a downed aircraft would attract large numbers of relatively vulnerable rescue aircraft and quickly sent large-calibre guns to hamper rescue efforts. Also, the rescue missions were always flown in daylight.

From dawn till dusk

Some rescue efforts lasted for days, and some attempts cost many more aircraft and US lives than just the original downed crew. 'Sandys' were on station from dawn till dusk during these operations, being replaced by back-ups when fuel and armament got low. There was no let-up; these missions were terminated only when the crew had either been rescued or there was absolutely no hope of pulling anyone from the scene.

Not all 'Sandy' missions were flown with regular USAF rescue forces, and often the Skyraiders would work with Air America (the CIA 'airline' operating throughout Southeast Asia). The Air America pilots usually knew their area far better than the USAF crews and would know the best

The bravest of the brave. Once the downed airman was located, the hovering helicopter lowered a jungle penetrator to winch him to safety. If the airman was injured, the parajumper rode the metal spike down through the canopy to extract him.

For airmen recently downed over enemy territory, no sight was more welcome than the big 'Jolly Green' helicopter coming in to rescue them. The HH-3 was gradually replaced with the faster, longer-ranged HH-53.

approach routes to the survivor. Many small rescues were effected by this method, particularly in Laos, releasing the main 'Jolly' and 'Sandy' resources for the larger rescues.

Many brave Skyraider, FAC and 'Jolly' helicopter crews lost their lives in the attempts to keep their comrades out of the clutches of the enemy, but the high number of USAF aircrew successfully saved stands as the greatest testimony to this brand of men who continuously put themselves at risk 'so that others may live'.

Anatomy of a 'Sandy' rescue mission

Although no two rescue operations were alike, a typical rescue mission called for seven aircraft, two in reserve, plus miscellaneous support aircraft. If a strike aircraft went down, its companions (or a patrolling command post aircraft) signalled the alert, and the rescue force swung into action. Most rescue missions began with a brief by the pilot of 'Sandy 1'. He led the actual rescue, and called the shots from the briefing to the final evacuation. Present at the briefing were the forward air controller (FAC), two helicopter crews and six Skyraider pilots, who formed the 'Sandy' force at any given time. 'Sandy 1' would give details of timing, ingress and egress routes, loiter areas, armament requirements and the overall plan. The aircraft would be quickly armed and would depart for the rescue scene. Two Skyraiders remained on the ground as a reserve, their pilots sitting in the cockpits until they were either called into action or received news of a successful mission; the other aircraft formed into two formations, one helo and two A-1s in each.

1 'Sandy 3' and 'Sandy 4', together with 'Jolly 2', would remain at high altitude over safe territory as an immediate back-up should the first rescue force fail or lose an aircraft. 'Jolly 1', supported by 'Sandy 1' and 'Sandy 2', sped to the rescue area at low altitude and began the rescue attempt. 'Sandy 2' and the helo loitered away from the immediate area while 'Sandy 1' moved in.

2 The orbiting 'Jolly 2' back-up helicopter could be refuelled by a Hercules tanker. The Skyraider was not equipped with a refuelling probe and thus had to rely solely on the fuel it carried.

3 The first job was to locate the downed airmen. Working in conjunction with the FAC, who was on station with his Cessna O-1,

O-2 or North American OV-10 Bronco, 'Sandy 1' used direction-finding equipment which homed in on the survival radio of the downed pilot. 'Sandy 1' was in touch with the pilot and, flying along a line towards the radio, would ask him to call out when he flew directly overhead. Once over the downed man, the A-1 would continue in a straight line for several seconds before pulling up so as not to give away the position of the pilot to any waiting enemy troops. The next task of 'Sandy 1' was to find the enemy, and he began flying low and slow over the jungle, trolling for fire.

4 Once the enemy big guns opened up, it was the turn of 'Sandy 2' to get in on the action and, using the FAC as their eyes, the two Skyraiders would attack the guns, hoping to put them out of action. If all was safe, 'Sandy 1' called the helo in to pick up the survivor, putting down a 'Willie Pete' phosphorus rocket marker as an initial point for the helo to start his run in to the survivor. The two Skyraiders kept up a low orbit of the area, watching over the survivor and guiding the helo in.

5 When it was a short distance away, 'Sandy 1' asked the pilot to light his orange survival flare so that the helo could move straight in and pick him up. If he was not too badly injured, a jungle penetrator was lowered down. This was a heavy pointed weight on the end of the winch cable which would penetrate the thick jungle canopy and drop down to the survivor. The downed man then unfolded arms from it to make a simple seat and strapped himself on, whereupon the winch hauled him to safety: even if he was hit during the ascent, the strap and arms would hold him on the penetrator. If the survivor was injured, a parajumper would have to ride the winch down to collect the wounded man.

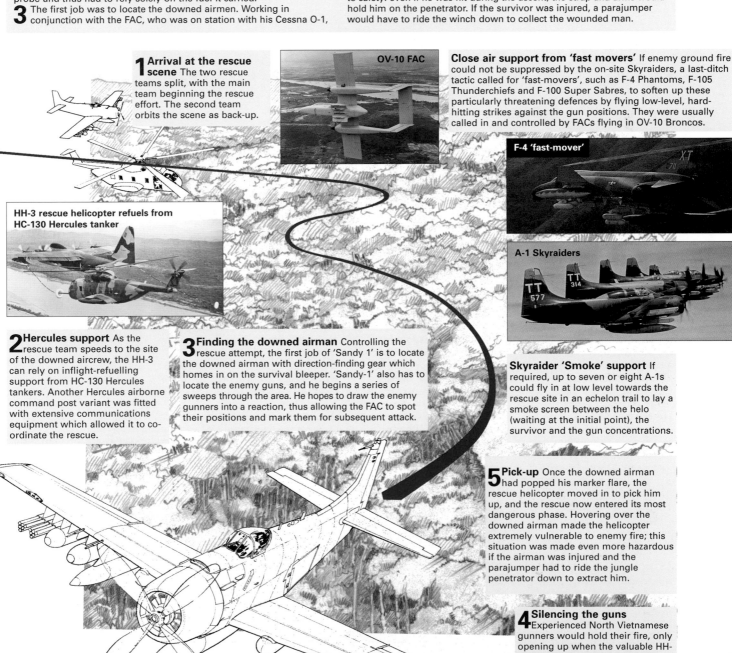

1 Arrival at the rescue scene The two rescue teams split, with the main team beginning the rescue effort. The second team orbits the scene as back-up.

OV-10 FAC

HH-3 rescue helicopter refuels from HC-130 Hercules tanker

2 Hercules support As the rescue team speeds to the site of the downed aircrew, the HH-3 can rely on inflight-refuelling support from HC-130 Hercules tankers. Another Hercules airborne command post variant was fitted with extensive communications equipment which allowed it to co-ordinate the rescue.

3 Finding the downed airman Controlling the rescue attempt, the first job of 'Sandy 1' is to locate the downed airman with direction-finding gear which homes in on the survival bleeper. 'Sandy-1' also has to locate the enemy guns, and he begins a series of sweeps through the area. He hopes to draw the enemy gunners into a reaction, thus allowing the FAC to spot their positions and mark them for subsequent attack.

Close air support from 'fast movers' If enemy ground fire could not be suppressed by the on-site Skyraiders, a last-ditch tactic called for 'fast-movers', such as F-4 Phantoms, F-105 Thunderchiefs and F-100 Super Sabres, to soften up these particularly threatening defences by flying low-level, hard-hitting strikes against the gun positions. They were usually called in and controlled by FACs flying in OV-10 Broncos.

F-4 'fast-mover'

A-1 Skyraiders

Skyraider 'Smoke' support If required, up to seven or eight A-1s could fly in at low level towards the rescue site in an echelon trail to lay a smoke screen between the helo (waiting at the initial point), the survivor and the gun concentrations.

5 Pick-up Once the downed airman had popped his marker flare, the rescue helicopter moved in to pick him up, and the rescue now entered its most dangerous phase. Hovering over the downed airman made the helicopter extremely vulnerable to enemy fire; this situation was made even more hazardous if the airman was injured and the parajumper had to ride the jungle penetrator down to extract him.

4 Silencing the guns Experienced North Vietnamese gunners would hold their fire, only opening up when the valuable HH-3 rescue helicopter came within their sights. Using the FAC as their eyes, the two A-1s would attack the guns, hoping to put them out of action.

The Linebacker campaigns

Plugged into a KC-135 Stratotanker, a B-52D refuels on its way to targets in North Vietnam, during the Linebacker II campaign. Designed for the delivery of nuclear weapons, the B-52 undertook conventional bombing missions during the war.

With no sign of a lasting peace settlement, the US unleashed a massive strategic bombing campaign against North Vietnam. The codename for these devastating raids was 'Linebacker'.

One of the most controversial aspects of the war in Vietnam was the degree to which the United States employed its strategic bomber force, the huge B-52 Stratofortress eight-jet heavy bombers. The aircraft itself stemmed from a 15-year old design and represented America's airborne nuclear deterrent and, when the B-52s commenced missions over Vietnam, they served to illustrate the USAF's frustration at the deteriorating situation of the war.

Having already sustained one aerial campaign against North Vietnam, the notorious Rolling Thunder campaign of 1965-68, without achieving any great success, those who planned the bombing of the North this time said that it was going to be different. Rolling Thunder had failed both to reduce the southward flow of supplies or to force Hanoi into making concessions during peace negotiations.

New tactics

'Linebacker' was the name given to the new air campaign. It was aimed at the entire North Vietnamese transportation system, and was a continuing effort involving USAF and US Navy tactical air power and naval gunfire

support. A new tactic to be employed was the use of 'smart' precision-guided (either by laser or electro-optically) munitions.

Linebacker I commenced with Operation Pocket Money, the mining of the North Vietnamese ports. The mines were sown by Navy A-6s on 9 May 1972. They were set for activation at 1800 hours on 11 May, giving the 16 Soviet-, five Communist Chinese-, two Cuban-, one East German-, two Polish-, five Somali-, and five British Hong Kong-registered ships time to pull out; only five did so. Since up to 85 per cent of all imports had arrived through the port of Haiphong during 1971, including oil, this was a devastatingly effective blockade.

Laser bombers

In addition, other vital supply lines were targeted, including the northeast and northwest rail lines, and eight other highways leading into China. With supply lines cut, USAF, Navy and Marine Corps aircraft set out to destroy the considerable stockpiles of weaponry within North Vietnam. They accomplished this to a degree that had been impossible during the Rolling Thunder campaign. Targets that were immune during early bombing campaigns either because of the fear of casualties among civilians, or because of operational difficulties, were successfully struck.

The Soviet-built Lang Chi hydroelectric plant, located northwest of Hanoi on the Red River, was attacked by F-4 Phantom IIs equipped with laser-guided bombs. They put 12 modified Mk 84 bombs through the roof of the building, destroying the plant's turbines and generators.

Linebacker I continued throughout the summer and autumn of 1972. In September,

Armed with LGBs (laser-guided bombs) for pinpoint bombing accuracy and equipped with LORAN (indicated by the 'towel rail' antenna on the spine of the centre aircraft) the F-4D offered a precision strike capability.

Operation Prime Choke attacked rail bridges in the buffer zone between North Vietnam and China. Laser-guided bombs allowed strikes in previously sensitive areas due in part to their increased accuracy. In fact, the laser bombers were so effective that Hanoi believed that it could not win the war militarily and sought a peaceful solution in Paris. Linebacker I was brought to an end while negotiations between America and the North Vietnamese commenced. The only bombing taking place was the interdiction of supplies in the southernmost part of North Vietnam.

Bombing resumes

Following the collapse of the peace talks in Paris due to the unreasonable demands of the

Vietnamese leaders and their constant refusal to sign an acceptable agreement, President Richard Nixon decided to hit North Vietnam hard. Rather than resume bombing with tactical aircraft alone, he decided to use B-52s.

Linebacker II

On 17 December, the Joint Chiefs of Staff sent a message to USAF units: *'You are directed to commence at approximately 1200Z, 18 December 1972, a three-day maximum effort, repeat, maximum effort, of B-52 tacair strikes in the Hanoi/Haiphong areas against the targets contained in the authorised target list. Object is maximum destruction of selected military targets in the vicinity of Hanoi/Haiphong. Be prepared to extend operations past three days, if directed.'*

The planners knew that the greatly increased aerial defences around Hanoi and Haiphong would make the missions dangerous, but the President was convinced of their necessity, seeing this as an opportunity finally end the war by the effective use of military power.

Six B-52s were shot down by SAMs (surface-to-air missiles) on 20 December 1972. This caused a reduction in the number of B-52 sorties while ECM (electronic countermeasures) tactics were refined to provide the Stratofortresses with better defences against SAMs. At the same time, reconnaissance aircraft searched for SAM storage and assembly areas, which were later attacked by LORAN (long-range aid to navigation)-equipped F-4 Phantom IIs. This helped to take some of the heat off the B-52s which had, in the past, been fired on by at least 220 SAMs in the course of a single desperate mission.

During the first three days of the campaign, a total of 11 B-52s were lost. The crews blamed many of the losses on tactics which often saw the bombers fly the same set bombing run day after day in small formations which, offered limited electronic jamming capability. Revised tactics prevented any further losses prior to the Christmas stand-down. For 24 hours on Christmas Day, no missions were flown. However, the next day, the most effective Stratofortress raid of the war took place, although two aircraft were shot down.

During the raid, a force of 120 B-52s devastated targets in the Hanoi and Haiphong areas as tight formations of bombers flew over North Vietnam, striking their targets during a 15-minute period from various altitudes and from different directions. They were supported by a variety of tactical aircraft including F-105G

Supporting the B-52s on their final run-in to Hanoi were F-105G Thunderchiefs, serving in the SAM suppression role, otherwise known as 'Wild Weasel'. The F-105s also carried out conventional bombing missions.

Thunderchiefs, EA-3A Skywarriors, F-4 Phantom IIs and support aircraft from the USAF, USN and USMC. More than 100 of the support aircraft were assigned to strikes on MiG bases and SAM sites.

On 27 December, 60 B-52s returned to Hanoi, 30 aircraft from Guam and 30 from U-Tapao, attacking SAM sites as well as strategic targets. A further two aircraft were lost. More SAMs were fired on that day than on any previous mission, but most were lacking in accuracy.

The B-52 returned to North Vietnam twice more before the Communists agreed to return to the Paris peace talks on 2 January 1973. North Vietnam was devastated. After many years of conflict, it had taken only 11 days of Linebacker II to prove what air power could do, if unleashed properly. For all practical purposes, North Vietnam had been taken out of the conflict by the bomber generals who had finally achieved what they wanted. Many commentators questioned why this could not have happened years earlier.

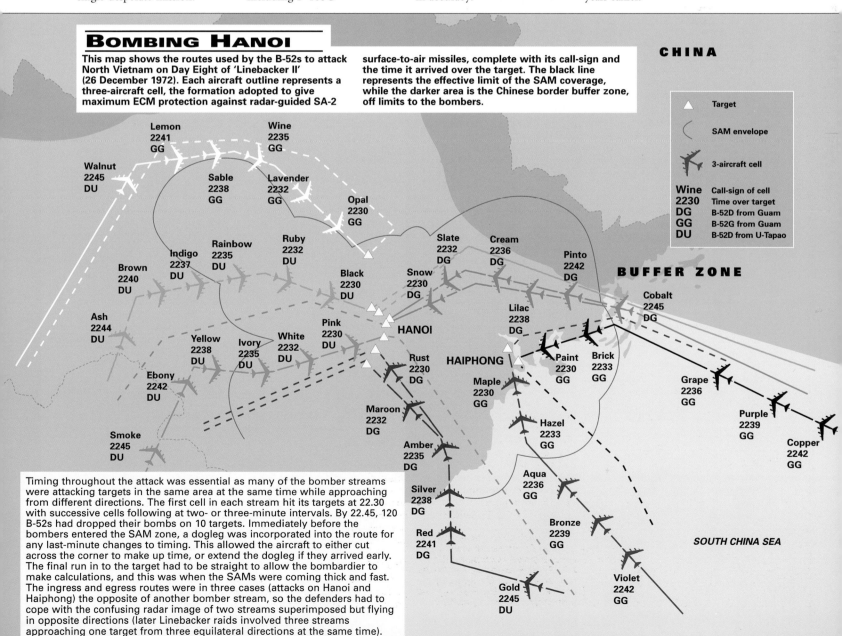

BOMBING HANOI

This map shows the routes used by the B-52s to attack North Vietnam on Day Eight of 'Linebacker II' (26 December 1972). Each aircraft outline represents a three-aircraft cell, the formation adopted to give maximum ECM protection against radar-guided SA-2 surface-to-air missiles, complete with its call-sign and the time it arrived over the target. The black line represents the effective limit of the SAM coverage, while the darker area is the Chinese border buffer zone, off limits to the bombers.

CHINA

△ Target

SAM envelope

✈ 3-aircraft cell

Wine	Call-sign of cell
2230	Time over target
DG	B-52D from Guam
GG	B-52G from Guam
DU	B-52D from U-Tapao

BUFFER ZONE

HANOI

HAIPHONG

SOUTH CHINA SEA

Timing throughout the attack was essential as many of the bomber streams were attacking targets in the same area at the same time while approaching from different directions. The first cell in each stream hit its targets at 22.30 with successive cells following at two- or three-minute intervals. By 22.45, 120 B-52s had dropped their bombs on 10 targets. Immediately before the bombers entered the SAM zone, a dogleg was incorporated into the route for any last-minute changes to timing. This allowed the aircraft to either cut across the corner to make up time, or extend the dogleg if they arrived early. The final run in to the target had to be straight to allow the bombardier to make calculations, and this was when the SAMs were coming thick and fast. The ingress and egress routes were in three cases (attacks on Hanoi and Haiphong) the opposite of another bomber stream, so the defenders had to cope with the confusing radar image of two streams superimposed but flying in opposite directions (later Linebacker raids involved three streams approaching one target from three equilateral directions at the same time).

Lemon 2241 GG
Wine 2235 GG
Walnut 2245 DU
Sable 2238 GG
Lavender 2232 GG
Opal 2230 GG
Indigo 2237 DU
Rainbow 2235 DU
Ruby 2232 DU
Slate 2232 DG
Cream 2236 DG
Pinto 2242 DG
Brown 2240 DU
Black 2230 DU
Snow 2230 DG
Cobalt 2245 DG
Ash 2244 DU
Pink 2230 DU
Lilac 2238 DG
Yellow 2238 DU
Ivory 2235 DU
White 2232 DU
Rust 2230 DG
Paint 2230 GG
Brick 2233 GG
Grape 2236 GG
Ebony 2242 DU
Maple 2230 GG
Purple 2239 GG
Copper 2242 GG
Maroon 2232 DG
Hazel 2233 GG
Smoke 2245 DU
Amber 2235 DG
Aqua 2236 GG
Silver 2238 DG
Bronze 2239 GG
Red 2241 DG
Gold 2245 DU
Violet 2242 GG

Boeing B-52 Stratofortress

Mainstay of the USA's strategic forces since its service entry in 1955, the B-52 Stratofortress, with its nuclear payload, was the symbol of American might throughout the Cold War. Even with the appearance of new aircraft like the B-1B and B-2, the B-52 is set to soldier on into the next century.

Boeing's 'Big Stick'

As the longest-serving warplane in history, the Boeing B-52 Stratofortress is held in affection by its crews and feared by its foes. Those who fly the B-52 speak not of its age or longevity, but of its capabilities: the B-52H model in service today can carry a greater variety of weapons and perform a broader range of missions than the B-1B Lancer, B-2 Spirit, or any other bomber in service.

In 1946, Boeing was revelling in its success in building the war-winning B-29 Superfortress, but did not yet know whether or not its post-war B-47 Stratojet would succeed. Approached by the Pentagon to build a new strategic bomber, Boeing began years of design work that ultimately led to the B-52.

Boeing began with its Model 462 and 464 designs, both straight-wing, turboprop

bombers of enormous size, capacity and range. Over time, the company considered no fewer than 30 combinations of engine, wing, and gross weight to achieve the Pentagon's speed and range requirements. Among drawing-board concepts that never made the grade was the Model 464-35, a swept-wing, four-engined turboprop aircraft similar to the Soviet Union's Tupolev Tu-95 'Bear'.

'Big Stick' shapes up

By 1950, Boeing's design efforts had yielded the Model 464-49, an eight-jet, swept-wing bomber, built for the USAF in the form of two prototypes, the XB-52 and YB-52. The prototypes had a braced tandem cockpit configuration, but otherwise were basically the same as the 744 production Stratofortresses that followed. Power was provided by the first

Above: B-52Hs still play an important part in the USAF's Air Combat Command, which is an amalgamation of Tactical Air Command and Strategic Air Command, around 84 aircraft remaining on active front-line duty. The Air Force Reserve, Air Force Test Center and NASA also operate a number of examples.

Top: Essentially a production version of the B-52A, the B-52B was outwardly indistinguishable from its predecessor, though it had uprated engines. On 18 January 1957, three B-52Bs completed a non-stop flight around the world in 45 hours, 19 minutes.

jet engine in aviation history to generate 10,000 lb (45 kN) of thrust, the Pratt & Whitney JT-3A, known to the military as the J57-P-3.

XB-52 and YB-52 prototypes were built under conditions of great secrecy and the YB-52 became the first to fly at Seattle, Washington, on 15 April 1952 with test pilot Tex Johnston at the helm.

To win a production order, Boeing had to show that its B-52 bomber was superior to the Convair YB-60, a kind of hybrid with a B-36 fuselage, new wings and tail, and jet engines. Boeing

had designed a bomber that was clearly superior in every respect, although the Convair team was held in high regard by Pentagon experts. In the end, however, it simply became obvious that the YB-60 was not a state-of-the-art aircraft.

By contrast, the B-52 had been built to the very latest design specifications. It resembled a B-47 Stratojet with its 35° swept wing, podded engines, 'bicycle' undercarriage and braced tandem canopy. From the B-52A model onward, the canopy was redesigned to provide side-by-side seating.

Although rolled out after the XB-52, the YB-52 was the first into the air by five months. During its maiden flight in 1952, it remained aloft for three hours and was well received by the test pilots (who were seated in tandem). The B-52 underwent the most rigorous testing of any aircraft of its time, and some three years elapsed before the aircraft entered regular USAF service.

Right: The XB-52 was first rolled out on the night of 29 November 1951, covered in tarpaulins for security reasons. The two B-52 prototypes differed from their successors by having tandem-pilot cockpits and no tail armament.

Below: The eighth production model of the B-52, the H is set to remain in service until at least 2030. The real strength of the B-52H today lies in its ability to carry a wider range of weaponry than any other US bomber.

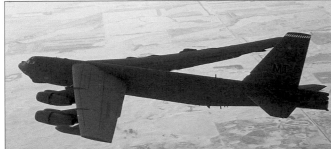

Changes in tailfin shape and powerplant came later.

Fuel capacity was greater than in any previous production aircraft at 38,865 US gal (147120 litres) with external tanks, as compared with 21,000 US gal (79493 litres) for the B-36. The eight engines were podded in pairs on four underwing pylons similar to the inboard pylons of the B-47. The gigantic fin, with only its trailing edge hinged to form a rudder, brought the bomber's height to 48 ft 3⅝ in (14.72 m) and could be folded to permit the bomber to enter standard hangars. The B-52 did not rotate on take-off but, rather, popped aloft, its wing set at

an incidence of 8° for a flyaway with the fuselage horizontal. On landing, the B-52 routinely employed a 44-ft (13.41-m) braking parachute, stowed in a compartment in the rear fuselage.

B-52 variants

Remarkably, the B-52 changed little from the beginning to the end of its 10-year production run. The initial Air Force production order was for three B-52As with J57-P-9W engines, followed soon by 23 B-52Bs with J57-P-19W, -29W, and -29WA powerplants.

RB-52B reconnaissance models were eventually modified to B-52C standard, in addition

to 35 new B-52Cs introduced from March 1956 with larger external tanks and increased fuel capacity.

The B-52D, first flown on 14 May 1956, was built in greater numbers (170 in total). These were followed by 100 B-52Es, with minor internal changes, and the manufacture of 89 B-52Fs, beginning in February 1959.

Boeing then went on to produce 193 B-52G aircraft. The B-52G introduced a shorter vertical tail, and a new integral-tank wing with fuel capacity increased to 46,576 US gal (176309 litres) and with underwing tanks reduced in volume to 700 US gal (2650 litres) each. Weight was increased to 488,000 lb (221357 kg). The B-52G was designed for the Douglas GAM-87A Skybolt missile, a two-stage, air-launched ballistic missile which underwent extensive Anglo-American design and development work before being cancelled as a failure. The B-52G's bomb bay

was also configured to carry four ADM-20A Quail decoy missiles; the aircraft also carried two North American GAM-77 (AGM-28) Hound Dog inertial-guidance cruise missiles.

On the B-52G, the gunner was relocated in the main crew compartment, operating his guns via the AN/ASG-15 fire control system. The armament of previous models, four .50-cal. (12.7-mm) machine-guns in the tail, was retained.

The USAF ordered 102 B-52H aircraft, taking delivery of the first on 9 May 1961. With the short vertical fin of the B-52G, the H model was powered by eight 17,000-lb (77-kN) thrust Pratt & Whitney TF33-P-1 or -3 turbofan engines. Tail armament of the B-52H was again remotely operated, but now comprised a single T-171 (later M61A1) 30-mm Vulcan cannon. The last B-52H was delivered to the USAF on 26 October 1962, bringing the final total of production Stratofortresses to 744.

Right: Range is one of the B-52's most outstanding features and it can be further increased with the aid of tankers such as this KC-135R. During the Gulf War seven B-52Gs flew from the USA to Saudi Arabia and back; the flight covered 14,000 miles (22530 km) and lasted 35 hours 20 minutes, making it the longest-ever combat mission.

Below: The B-52H was never intended as a 'bomb truck' and so has less lifting capability than some earlier variants. However, it can still carry up to 51 500-lb (227-kg) Mk 82A/82SE bombs.

Withdrawal:
One month to leave Saigon

In Saigon the end was near; the only escape from the Communist forces sweeping towards the city was by air. The US forces responded to the call magnificently, and initiated the largest aerial evacuation in history.

By 1 April 1975 it was clear to American leaders that the North Vietnamese offensive through South Vietnam would not be halted, and that Saigon would fall in a matter of weeks. A contingency plan, originally coded 'Talon Vice', and later known as 'Frequent Wind', had already been worked out for the evacuation of American personnel and South Vietnamese who had helped the USA during the long war years, together with their close families. On 1 April the Evacuation Control Centre (ECC) was set up to co-ordinate these operations, which started with a sealift from Saigon via Vung Tau. The ECC operated under the aegis of the Defense Attaché Office (DAO) which was originally conceived in October 1972 for administrative support of the South Vietnamese forces.

On the first three days of the evacuation, air transport was used mainly for Operation 'Babylift', the evacuation of Vietnamese orphans, handled by C-141 Starlifters and new C-5 Galaxies. Four days into 'Babylift' disaster struck, however; a C-5 flying 10 miles (16 km) out to sea encountered a massive structural failure in its rear cargo door which cut all the controls to the tail surfaces. With amazing airmanship, Captain Dennis Tatlor managed to nurse the aircraft towards Tan Son Nhut using only the ailerons and throttle control. He set up for an emergency landing but the C-5 struck a paddy field and bounced along the ground before breaking up into four segments.

Only minutes before the surrender, this O-1 Bird Dog was shot down and crashed in Saigon's thronged Cholon district. Many VNAF pilots and air crew continued to fight valiantly to the very end.

Fortunately, some 175 survivors managed to scramble clear and were rescued. Following this accident C-5 flights were suspended and operations were continued with C-141s and C-130 Hercules.

Rooftops around Saigon were picked out for helicopter landing

The USS Enterprise (CVAN-65) carries a full load of CH-53 helicopters on its bow to help in the final evacuation of Saigon. Also aboard are two squadrons of Grumman F-14 Tomcats, which were entering a combat zone for the first time.

Dramatic action as, unable to land on a crowded carrier deck, a VNAF pilot takes the desperate step of leaping into the sea from his low-flying helicopter.

pads so that personnel could be transported to Tan Son Nhut quicker as the roads around the city soon became cluttered with evacuees desperate to escape the advancing North Vietnamese.

At this time, the US Navy's Task Force 76 arrived off the coast of South Vietnam with three aircraft-carriers and around 50 ships in all to take part in and cover 'Frequent Wind'.

Despite the major effort involved in the airlift many aircraft were leaving Vietnam empty as a result of processing difficulties with the evacuees. Daily figures were low but many so-called 'Black Flights' were being undertaken, removing key intelligence personnel and documents from Saigon by covert methods. Predictably, these flights took place from the ramp of Air America, the CIA's airline. An 'underground railroad', complete with safe houses, was later in action, helping to remove Vietnamese CIA contacts who did not have

the necessary US sponsor to validate their extraction by the more usual routes.

On 21 April the airlift was stepped-up. There were now 21 C-141 flights by day, and a similar number by C-130s at night, together carrying enormous numbers of people. The orphan evacuation continued with 470 being airlifted out in two special flights in a Boeing 727.

The last efforts

On 29 April the DAO called in 60 aircraft for a final 10,000 passenger airlift. With all routes by both bus and helicopter from Saigon to Tan Son Nhut prepared, three C-130s arrived early in the morning and the first began loading. The second aircraft had just finished its landing run when the airfield

came under rocket attack. As the third aircraft came to a halt it was struck by enemy fire and exploded. A hail of enemy fire followed the departure of the first aircraft. In quick succession the second C-130 followed, so becoming the last US fixed-wing aircraft to leave Vietnam.

As the airfield was now clearly unusable helicopters became the only alternative. Anti-aircraft guns and SAMs were deployed around Saigon and fighters were launched to protect the helicopters entering the city. Grumman F-14 Tomcats flew top cover for all these missions in case NVAF MiGs attempted to halt proceedings, but in the event they were not needed.

At 03.00 on 30 April the final evacuation began from the American embassy, with CH-53s using the parking lot and CH-46s the roof, while Grumman A-6s kept watch over the proceedings. The helicopters flew a series of shuttle flights to the waiting aircraft-carriers, taking groundfire from both the North Vietnamese and disgruntled ARVN troops frustrated at not being able to get out.

Many VNAF helicopters also headed for the Task Force only

to end up being pushed over the sides of the ships when there was not enough room for others to land. One of the last helicopters to make the trip was a Bell UH-1 of Air America carrying Air Marshal Nguyen Cao Ky. At the very last came an armada of 29 UH-1s, two Boeing CH-47s and an O-1, heading for USS *Midway*; all made safe landings aboard the carrier.

Final cost

The evacuation of Saigon was over. In all 19,000 sorties were flown during April 1975 and only three aircraft were lost: an A-7, an AH-1J and a CH-46. Two crew were lost in the CH-46. This sortie total does not include the unknown figure for Air America which flew non-stop sorties throughout the month, equipped with a handful of UH-1s, and must have accomplished well over 1,000 flights.

It was perhaps an ironic but fitting conclusion to America's involvement in Vietnam that the helicopter, which brought so many American troops into the war, also carried the final American soldiers out of the country, battered and disillusioned after 10 years of fighting.

Right: The F-14 Tomcat's appearance was brief and involved no combat. The two squadrons assigned to fly top cover over the evacuation were VF-1 and VF-2. However, no enemy MiGs were encountered during their missions.

Below: The C-5A Galaxy was employed during the early days of the airlift before a crash halted its use. Airlift operations were flown from Tan Son Nhut.

Falklands invaded

When Argentina invaded the Falkland Islands, the response from the UK was one of belligerence. Britain immediately assembled forces to recapture the dependency and, spearheaded by two aircraft-carriers, the fleet headed southwards.

The Falklands have been a British possession since 1833, when the Royal Navy evicted newly-arrived Argentinian settlers and claimed the islands for Britain. The Falklands are bleak and inhospitable, but have served as a strategic naval base, as a useful centre for whaling, and have given Britain an internationally recognised 'share' of Antarctica. The islands' inhabitants regard

themselves as British, and fiercely oppose any transfer of sovereignty to Argentina, which has long claimed the islands as the Malvinas.

A military government was established in Argentina in 1976, and in 1977 a British naval task force was sent to the area after reports that an occupation of nearby South Georgia was likely. This move signalled that Britain would maintain sovereignty over

Above: This Fuerza Aérea Boeing 707 was the aircraft that discovered the British task force as it sailed south, under the codename Operation Corporate.

Top: A Lynx hovers over the deck of HMS Invincible, having dropped an underslung load of stores. The despatch of the task force was a triumph of logistics, and intensive use was made of helicopters during all phases of the operation.

Above: Argentinian ground crew load a Pucará with unguided rockets. Argentina deployed only lightweight attack aircraft to the Falklands, instead of laying a PSP (pierced-steel planking) runway from which Skyhawks could operate. This probably contributed to Argentina's failure to win the war.

Left: HMS Antrim's obsolescent Wessex HAS.Mk 3 was given the affectionate nickname of 'Humphrey'. It played a significant part in the war, recovering a Special Forces patrol from South Georgia (and the crews of the two Wessex HU.Mk 5s originally sent to perform the task) and later attacking and helping to beach the Argentinian submarine, Santa Fé.

Special Forces troops on Fortuna Glacier, South Georgia, approach the 845 Squadron Wessex HU.Mk 5, XT464, which had crashed in 'white-out' conditions a few minutes before while in the process of evacuating the troopers, luckily with no loss of life. A short time after, a further Wessex crashed, trying to evacuate the same personnel.

the islands, but doubt resurfaced when a new Conservative government came to power. It announced cuts in defence expenditure, including the planned withdrawal, without replacement, of the Antarctic survey vessel HMS *Endurance*, the area's *de facto* garrison ship.

To many, this was an indication that an Argentinian invasion of the Malvinas might not be opposed militarily. Argentinian scrap metal workers landed on South Georgia on 19 March

1982, and began dismantling the disused whaling station. Such an action was almost certainly intended to gauge how Britain might react to a full-scale invasion. Britain landed observation teams and Royal Marines from the *Endurance* on 23 and 31 March, while nuclear submarines headed south on 25 March. Had more publicity been given to these responses, the Argentinians might have reconsidered their decision to proceed with an invasion, taken

on 23 March. Two Argentinian task groups set sail on 28 March.

Argentinian assault

On 2 April, 2,800 Argentinians landed on the Falklands. The 80-strong British garrison surrendered after a brief fight, on the orders of the island's governor, Sir Rex Hunt. South Georgia was invaded the following day by a third Argentinian task group. The Royal Marine defenders put up fierce resistance, even downing an Argentinian Puma with a Carl Gustav anti-tank rocket, and a support Alouette was damaged by machine-gun fire before the Marines surrendered and followed their comrades into captivity. Argentina installed an AN/TPS-43F radar and established a control centre at Port Stanley, providing an integrated air defence network for the islands.

Having failed to deter the Argentinian invasion, Britain assembled a task force to retake the islands, under the codename Operation Corporate. The surface ships committed to the operation became TF.317, while the submarines already dispatched became TF.394. RAF air traffic control staff were sent to the US-run Wideawake Airfield on the British island of Ascension, to prepare it for its potential role as a staging post to the Falklands. Victor tankers and

Nimrod maritime patrol aircraft soon began flying operations.

The task force commander, Rear-Admiral John 'Sandy' Woodward, sailed from Gibraltar for Ascension on 2 April aboard HMS *Glamorgan*, accompanied by four destroyers, five frigates and three support vessels assembled for exercises in the Mediterranean. The carriers HMS *Hermes* and *Invincible*, with the assault ship HMS *Fearless*, four support ships, two frigates and four landing ships sailed from Portsmouth on 5 and 6 April. The hastily requisitioned liner *Canberra* set sail from Southampton on 9 April, with 2,000 troops drawn from 40 and 42 Commandos and from 3 Para. These caught up with Woodward as he paused at Ascension Island.

On 7 April Britain declared a 200-mile (322-km) Maritime Exclusion Zone around the Falklands, to become effective on 14 April, after which shipping in the area would be liable to attack without warning. From 21 April, a small element of the task force retook South Georgia. SAS and SBS soldiers were inserted and then recovered when the weather deteriorated, before Wessex, Lynx and Wasp helicopters attacked and beached the submarine *Santa Fé* on 23 October. Troops landed to take advantage of the surprise caused by this action, and the Argentinian garrison surrendered without a fight after a 235-shot naval bombardment.

⌐ Argentinian garrison

Argentina's invasion of the Falklands was primarily seaborne, although a small number of helicopters did participate. However, once the British garrison had surrendered, the Argentinians brought in Pucarás, T-34Cs and MB-339s for light attack duties, Short Skyvans for communications and patrol and a variety of helicopters from the army, air force and Prefectura.

Aermacchi MB-339A
The Argentinian navy deployed six Aermacchi MB-339As to Port Stanley from its main land base. They operated in the light ground-attack role with limited success.

Agusta A 109 Hirundo
Two A 109s were used by the Combat Aviation Battalion 601 of the Army Aviation Command in the Falklands. These were later captured by the British Forces and flown in Royal Marine markings. They still serve today as ZE411 and ZE412 with 7 Regiment (8 Flight) AAC in support of the SAS.

Lockheed C-130E Hercules
The C-130Es and C-130Hs of GTA.1 were augmented by Fokker F27s and F28s on the air bridge between their base at Comodoro Rivadavia and Port Stanley. One C-130 was shot down by a Sea Harrier.

During the 1968 Farnborough air show, the USMC was evaluating an early Harrier (right), seen here with one of the original T.Mk 2s. This test set in motion an order which would see 110 aircraft join the Corps, all of which were built by BAe at Kingston. The relationship with McDonnell Douglas was to prove crucial to the future of the Harrier programme.

Hawker Siddeley Harrier

V/STOL pioneer

Developed from the concept that numerous hidden dispersals were preferable to a vulnerable fixed base, the ground-breaking Harrier revolutionised aerial warfare and, with its VTOL capability, became one of the world's most instantly recognisable aircraft.

In the mid-1950s, when ideas were being formulated which, by painstaking developments, resulted in the Harrier, forward-thinking tacticians were looking with dismay at the fixed military installations upon which the security of NATO depended. On the principle that a moving target is more difficult to hit, there was an obvious need for a high-performance aircraft capable of operating away from vulnerable airfields. The answer to this problem was the combination of a French concept, American funding and assistance, and British industry. On 21 October 1960 the first Hawker P.1127 raised

itself a few inches from the ground, supported on the four columns of air from a Bristol-Siddeley Pegasus vectored-thrust turbofan engine.

Much more work was required before what came to be known as the Harrier entered service with the RAF. At first, the P.1127 was seen merely as a concept-proving demonstrator for the P.1154, which would have also joined the Fleet Air Arm. Nine developed P.1127s, known as Kestrels, were flown, but even as an evaluation unit was being formed, the P.1154 was dropped on grounds of economy and an extensively

Spain's sole Harrier squadron was Escuadrilla 8ª. Working-up commenced in 1976 in the US before this unit was installed at Rota in December of that year for operations from the **Dedalo**.

redesigned aircraft, known as the Harrier GR.Mk 1, was chosen by the RAF.

Introduction to service began on 1 January 1969 with the formation at Wittering of the Harrier Conversion Unit and, on 1 October of that year, No. 1

A trio of No. 3 Squadron's Harrier GR.Mk 3s is pictured in flight. No. 3 was the last RAF Germany Harrier squadron to form. The unit's badge is a cockatrice perched on a Stonehenge lintel.

Squadron was established as the world's first operational fixed-wing VTOL (vertical take-off and landing) unit. Pending arrival of the F-35, to date, only the Soviet Yakovlev Yak-38, with its outdated fixed lifting-engine concept, has joined the unique club founded by the Harrier.

The comparatively modest total of four RAF squadrons flew the early Harriers; these were assisted by an operational conversion unit (OCU) and two flights formed to meet demands

Below: The Harrier's baptism of fire came in the South Atlantic when Harriers of No. 1 Squadron (seen here on Ascension Island) were used to great effect in the ground-attack role during the re-taking of the Falkland Islands in 1982.

Both the surviving YAV-8B prototype, subsequently serialled 704, and this standard AV-8A, 718, were operated by NASA, wearing the blue and white NASA 'house colours'.

in Belize and the Falkland Islands. No. 1 Squadron was assigned to rapid intervention roles and as such was involved in the 1982 Falklands War.

Permanently in the potential front line were the Harriers of RAF Germany. Three units (Nos 3, 4 and 20 Squadrons) were installed at Wildenrath in 1970/71. When No. 20 disbanded, the remaining two units absorbed its aircraft and moved forward to Gütersloh. Off-airfield roles were taken seriously, with the result that, about three times every year, the Gütersloh wing took to the German countryside to practise flying from dispersed sites. Squadrons usually divided into three flights for this purpose, hiding in the woods when not in the air.

For the sake of simplicity, the aircraft has previously been described as having VTOL capability. This is true, but even in its subsequent GR.Mk 3 configuration, with a 21,500-lb (96.75-kN) thrust Pegasus Mk 103 giving 2,500 lb (11.25 kN) more power than the engine first installed in the GR.Mk 1, the Harrier could not lift a worthwhile warload without a short take-off run. Thus, training operations were typically flown from a 200-yard (183-m) strip of aluminium planking, from which the aircraft leapt into the air after gathering forward speed. In wartime, a stretch of road would have sufficed equally well. Landing could be accomplished vertically when weapons had been expended.

US Marines service

Ironically, it was the US Marine Corps – the only American armed service not to take part in the original Kestrel trials – which went on to be the largest operator of all, taking into account the second-generation Harrier II aircraft.

Well before the advent of the Sea Harrier, or the operation of 10 No. 1 Squadron aircraft from HMS Hermes during the Falklands War, the US Marine Corps was regularly operating its 102 AV-8As and eight TAV-8A trainers from assault carriers. Delivered between 1971 and 1976, these aircraft were exactly what the USMC sought for close support of amphibious landings.

Spain's naval air force, the Arma Aérea de la Armada, bought an initial six AV-8As and two TAV-8As through the US Navy in 1973, these having the local designation VA.1 and VAE.1 Matador respectively. Five more single-seat aircraft, loosely known by the designation AV-8s, followed directly from the UK during 1980. Spain later turned to the more advanced Harrier II to replace the AV-8As, which were sold to Thailand. In 2007 these remained the only first-generation Harriers in front-line use, although their actual 'deck time' is very limited.

Below: Up to 5,000 lb (2268 kg) of weaponry could be attached to the Harrier's seven strongpoints, three of them beneath the fuselage. Weapons included the Hunting BL755 CBU or a pod containing 19 68-mm (2.68-in) Matra SNEB air-to-surface rockets.

Above: Spain's seven surviving VA.1s and two VAE.1s were sold for operations with the Royal Thai Navy's Air Division. Delivered in September 1997, these are embarked on the carrier Chakri Naruebet.

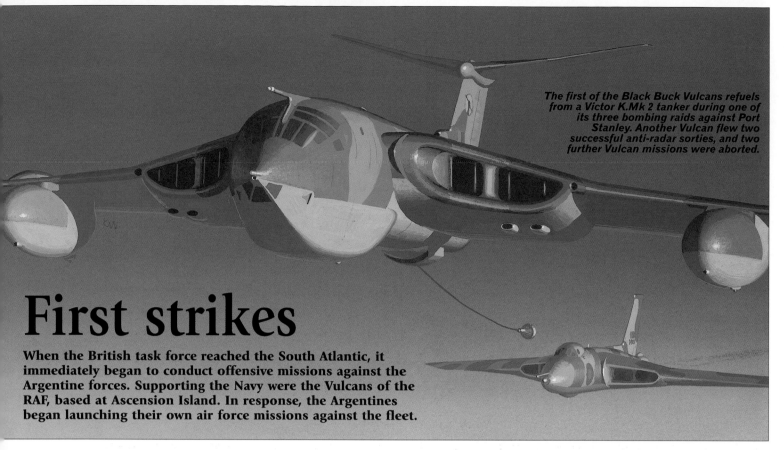

The first of the Black Buck Vulcans refuels from a Victor K.Mk 2 tanker during one of its three bombing raids against Port Stanley. Another Vulcan flew two successful anti-radar sorties, and two further Vulcan missions were aborted.

First strikes

When the British task force reached the South Atlantic, it immediately began to conduct offensive missions against the Argentine forces. Supporting the Navy were the Vulcans of the RAF, based at Ascension Island. In response, the Argentines began launching their own air force missions against the fleet.

As the British task force sailed south, it was reinforced by men and materiel (including the Harrier GR.Mk 3s of No. 1 Squadron, and aircraft from a third Sea Harrier squadron) flown to Ascension Island and then helicoptered or flown on to the waiting ships, while other elements of the British force manoeuvred into position. Canberra PR.Mk 9s and Nimrod R.Mk 1s almost certainly flew reconnaissance and Elint sorties from a still undisclosed location (probably from Chile), while maritime Nimrods and radar reconnaissance Victors operated from Ascension. In the UK, the MoD requisitioned the *Queen Elizabeth II* to carry 3,500 Welsh Guards, Scots Guards and Gurkhas to the Falklands.

On the Falkland Islands, the Argentine garrison prepared defensive positions and, by late April, had its own detachment of 24 Pucarás for close support, six naval MB.339As and four T-34Cs alongside a disparate group of army and air force helicopters. Port Stanley and Goose Green airfields were well defended by

Roland SAMs and 20-mm and 35-mm AAA.

The task force was located by an Argentine Boeing 707 on 21 April, whereupon the aircraft was escorted away by a Sea Harrier. On 30 April, with diplomatic moves to find a solution exhausted, Britain transformed its Maritime Exclusion Zone into a Total Exclusion Zone, while the USA formally endorsed Britain's position.

Long-range bombing

On 1 May a single Vulcan bombed Port Stanley, dropping a stick of bombs obliquely across the runway, sending a clear signal that no Argentine target could be deemed safe from potential air attack. Later that morning, the airfields at Port Stanley and Goose Green were attacked by Sea Harriers. From midday, warships began bombarding military positions around Port Stanley. The Fuerza Aerea Argentina (FAA) responded by launching attacks against the task force, damaging a handful of ships, but losing two Mirage IIIs, a Dagger and a Canberra to patrolling Sea Harriers.

Above: Royal Navy Sea Harriers and RAF Harrier GR.Mk 3s served together on the task force carriers, therefore reinforcing the Task Force's air power. The Sea Harrier became known as 'La Muerta Negra' (The Black Death) to the Argentines.

Left: Britain's operation to recapture the Falklands would have been impossible without its carriers, HMS Hermes (shown) and Invincible. These enabled the task force to travel south with its own air defence and close air support/ground-attack assets.

Intelligence-gathering in the Falklands

As in any conflict, the accumulation of information about enemy forces is crucial and, during the Falklands conflict, both sides utilised their air assets in this mission. It is believed that in addition to MR operations from Ascension, RAF Canberra PR.Mk 9s and Elint Nimrods flew sorties from a South American country, probably Chile, but this has never been confirmed.

Nimrod MR.Mk 2P
The programme to fit inflight-refuelling probes to the RAF's Nimrods was expedited as a result of the Falklands War, this modification allowing the aircraft to operate right into the Total Exclusion Zone. The Nimrods were augmented by Victors operating in the maritime reconnaissance role.

English Electric Canberra B.Mk 62
The Canberras of Grupo 2 flew 54 missions, including five surveillance, three tactical reconnaissance and four long-range anti-shipping sorties. These British-built aircraft also went on to fly 14 day- and 22 night-bomber sorties.

On 2 May the Argentine cruiser *Belgrano* was sunk by a British submarine (the HMS *Conqueror*), and Lynxes from HMS *Glasgow* and *Coventry* damaged a patrol craft as SAS parties were landed on the islands, while the night of 3/4 May saw the second Black Buck Vulcan raid against Port Stanley. There was also a second Sea Harrier airfield attack, one aircraft falling to a Tigercat SAM. Later on 4 May, two Super Etendards struck back by attacking RN ships on picket duty, fatally damaging HMS *Sheffield* (which sank while under tow six days later) and killing 26 of its crew. One Sea Harrier was shot down by AAA during an attack on Goose Green. Air attacks by both sides were mounted as the weather permitted, with Argentine losses mounting steadily due to the weather, Sea Harriers and ship-launched SAMs. On 9 May SBS soldiers, dropped from

Sea Kings, boarded the Argentine intelligence gatherer *Narwal* after it had been attacked by Sea Harriers. A raid by Skyhawks on 12 May against RN ships bombarding Port Stanley put the *Glasgow* out of action, though the bomb which hit the ship fortunately failed to explode. A planned third Vulcan raid was aborted due to high winds over the target on 13 May, but an SAS raid destroyed six Pucarás, a Skyvan and four Mentors at Pebble Island on 14 May. Task force helicopter losses continued to mount due to birdstrikes and accidents, while on 17 May a Sea King was burned by its crew at Agua Fresca, near Punta Arenas in Chile, after an

SAS insertion mission. The SAS and SBS teams had been inserted before the invasion force and spotted for naval guns.

While SAS and SBS units made diversionary attacks on Goose Green and Darwin, the full-scale British landings (Operation Sutton) began at San Carlos, under the cover of mist and darkness, before dawn on 21 May. The Argentines made a series of spirited attacks on the invasion fleet, damaging several ships for the loss of five Daggers, two Pucarás and five Skyhawks. The Argentine pilots won the respect of their adversaries, flying their attacks with reckless bravery and some degree of accuracy. One of

the Falklands-based MB.339s even entered the fray, making an accurate if relatively ineffective attack against the *Argonaut*, which suffered minor damage. Had Argentine bombs been better fused, or had their air forces been able to sustain a higher sortie rate, many ships might have been more severely damaged. Nevertheless, one of the damaged ships sank the following day. The British lost a Harrier GR.Mk 3 to a Blowpipe SAM, and two Gazelles to small arms fire. But at the end of the day, British forces were able to land, and consolidate their position the following day when bad weather prevented further attacks.

Above: Bomb racks and fuel tanks nearly empty, an A-4C Skyhawk refuels from the 'Chancha' (mother sow) as it heads home to Argentina after an anti-shipping strike over the Falklands. Refuelling gave the Skyhawk pilots greater flexibility when planning attacks.

Right: Argentina's five Super Etendards had an importance far beyond that suggested by their numbers. They were the launch aircraft for Argentina's five AM39 Exocet anti-ship missiles, which destroyed two task force vessels.

Above: An FAA Skyhawk receives damage during an attack on HMS Fearless. The FAA's Skyhawks were the most destructive aircraft fielded by Argentina, and proved a formidable foe, although they were very vulnerable to British fighters and SAMs.

Left: Army and Royal Marine Gazelles saw extensive service in the observation and reconnaissance, liaison, casevac and gunship roles, but were often casualties of small arms fire.

Final victory

As the British forces began to recapture the Falkland Islands, the conflict intensified and casualties mounted on both sides. Brave Argentine pilots flew low-level missions against British ships, causing much damage, although sustaining many losses on the way.

The Falklands War entered its third and final phase with the success of the British landings at San Carlos. Argentine air attacks had failed to prevent a beachhead from being established on 21 May 1982, and bad weather stopped the FAA from intervening on 22 May. At the same time, the British continued to land men and supplies, and established rudimentary air defences for the positions on shore and for the ships in San Carlos Water. By 23 May it was too late to prevent an eventual break-out from the beachhead which, in fact, took place on 27 May. Nevertheless, the FAA pressed home further attacks, losing an A-4 and a Dagger, but sinking the *Antelope*, which was lost while another unexploded bomb

was being made safe. Three more Daggers and an A-4 were lost the following day during attacks on shipping, and three A-4s were downed on 25 May, two of them by Sea Dart SAMs fired by the HMS *Coventry* on picket duty west of the Falklands. The ship was sunk by Skyhawks immediately after its successes.

Argentine response

On the same day the CANA (Comando Aviación Naval Argentina) fired the third and fourth of its five Exocet missiles, one of these accounting for the *Atlantic Conveyor* and its cargo of spares, and Wessex and Chinook helicopters, only one of the latter escaping the catastrophe.

On 27 May, an RAF Harrier was lost to groundfire while the

Argentines resisted the British advance, losing an A-4, an MB.339 and two Pucarás in the process. The next day, Pucarás made an unsuccessful attack using napalm, but fortunately this was the only occasion on which this weapon was used. The fourth Vulcan raid (intended as an anti-radar sortie using Shrike missiles) was aborted when one of the Victor tankers became unserviceable. Air activity continued unabated as the British infantry pushed eastwards towards Port Stanley, with both sides suffering losses. A further Sea Harrier fell victim to an accident on 29 May and another was shot down by a Roland SAM on 1 June. Sea Harriers shot down a C-130 Hercules on the same day. The Argentines lost a Dagger on 29 May, and two A-4s on 30 May, all to Rapier or Sea Dart SAMs. The A-4s were reportedly supporting the CANA's final Exocet attack, the fifth missile apparently having been successfully decoyed away from its target, the HMS *Exeter*. Poor weather limited air activity

until 8 June, one RAF Harrier being lost on 30 May after groundfire severed a fuel line. The pilot was forced to eject when he could not reach HMS *Hermes*.

The Harrier's reliance on the carriers (which had to stand off out of range of Argentine aircraft) was eased on 2 June, with the completion of 'Sid's strip', a temporary airfield at San Carlos where aircraft could be refuelled and re-armed. A Vulcan flew an unsuccessful fifth mission on 31 May, but followed this with a third anti-radar mission on 3 June, damaging a Skyguard radar in the process. Unfortunately, the aircraft was forced to divert to Rio de Janeiro after its refuelling probe broke on the journey home, and it was detained until the end of the war. During the poor weather, the FAA mounted a number of Canberra night-bombing raids, and a reconnaissance Learjet was downed by a Sea Dart SAM on 7 June.

When the weather cleared on 8 June, the Argentines were

A Sea King and a frigate come to the assistance of HMS Plymouth, burning off East Falkland after being hit by 30-mm cannon fire from FAA Daggers and five Mk 82 bombs, none of which exploded. However, a 30-mm round set off a depth charge.

Left: Based alongside the Vulcans at Ascension Island, Victor tankers (illustrated) were vital components of the Black Buck missions. Seven raids (Black Buck 1 to 7), were planned, but only five were flown. While the raids never caused any major damage, they did generate a real fear that the RAF could attack mainland targets, forcing the FAA to keep its best fighters in Argentina.

Below: Argentine pilots pressed home their attacks at very low level. One of Grupo 6's Daggers is visible behind the assault ship HMS Fearless, flying at bridge-top level.

On 13 June everything came right, and Harriers successfully bombed a company HQ at Tumbledown and a 105-mm gun at Moody Brook.

On 14 June two Harriers took off for an LGB attack against Sapper Hill, but were recalled because white flags were already flying in Port Stanley. An Argentine surrender was signed at one minute before midnight.

Britain had recovered the Falklands at minimal cost, with an apparently decisive victory which did much to enhance the reputation of its armed forces. The war also brought the government much-needed popularity (despite the fact that the war had been caused by its own defence cuts and inability to foresee their consequences), and an early election was called, bringing a victory which many ascribed to the 'Falklands Factor'. The disparity in losses hid the fact that the war had been closely contested at several points, while it was seldom recognised that Britain's continuing defence cuts would have made the operation impossible to carry out only a few months later. Useful lessons were learned from the conflict, and it also led to the rapid development and deployment of a number of key systems, perhaps the most important being the AEW Sea King, which was just too late to see front-line service in the war itself.

Argentina has not lost its ambitions to gain sovereignty over what it calls the Malvinas, even to the extent of offering cash to the Falkland islanders in return for their voting for Argentine rule. However, further military adventures have been prevented by a much enlarged British military presence on the Falklands, and by the construction of a full-size runway. The latter would allow rapid reinforcement by air, and houses a permanent detachment of four VC10-supported Tornado F.Mk 3s which form No. 1435 Flight.

faced with plum targets in the form of the assault ships *Fearless* and *Intrepid*, together with the landing ships *Sir Galahad* and *Sir Tristram*, which were busy moving troops from San Carlos to Fitzroy Cove in preparation for the final push on Port Stanley. The FAA mounted a raid by five A-4Bs and six Daggers (with four Mirages making a diversionary raid on San Carlos to draw off the Sea Harriers). *Sir Galahad* and *Sir Tristram* were badly damaged, and 43 Welsh Guardsmen and seven seamen were killed. Outbound, the Daggers crippled

HMS *Plymouth*, and all the FAA aircraft returned to base safely.

Events fared badly for that afternoon's second wave of Argentine aircraft. Three Skyhawks were shot down by Sea Harriers after the A-4s had sunk a landing craft.

Some of the heaviest fighting of the war took place on 12 and 13 June, as the Paras fought to take Mount Longdon and Wireless Ridge, being supported by SS11-firing Westland Scouts in the latter attack. *Glamorgan* was hit by a ground-launched Exocet that day (losing its Wessex helicopter) and, soon

afterwards, the Vulcan force launched its seventh and final mission, dropping airburst bombs on Port Stanley airfield. A final air attack came when a single Wessex HU.Mk 5 attacked Port Stanley Town Hall with AS12 missiles, aiming to hit a major conference taking place there. One missile hit the neighbouring police station, and the second missed altogether.

Argentine surrender

On 13 June, Argentine Skyhawks attacked the British Brigade HQ on Mount Kent, and a Canberra was shot down in the type's final appearance over the Falklands. Although LGB attacks had begun on 10 June, designation problems had rendered them unsuccessful.

Above: Wrecked Pucarás lie by the runway at Port Stanley after the war, as an RAF Hercules makes its final approach. In all, 29 aircraft were captured at Port Stanley alone, though few were flyable.

Right: Four of the 10 RAF Harrier GR.Mk 3s deployed to the Falklands were lost in action. Modifications included the addition of AIM-9s and Tracor AN/ALE-40 chaff/flare dispensers.

China and Taiwan

At their closest points, Nationalist and Communist China are within artillery range of each other. Clashes over ideology have ensured frosty relations between the two Chinas for over 50 years.

Top: The first F-104s to arrive on Taiwan were USAF fighters sent to bolster the Nationalists after the Quemoy confrontation in 1958. The CNAF took delivery of 67 ex-US examples in the 1970s, and became one of the last major users of the type.

Above: Along with its Starfighters, Taiwan also received F-86F Sabres to replace ageing F-47s and F-51s.

There were two main power bases in China at the end of World War II. The Soviet Union had liberated Manchuria, and equipped the forces of communist leader, Mao Zedong, which became the People's Liberation Army (PLA). Led by Chiang Kai-Shek, the Nationalists were armed and supported by the USA, and they brought about the surrender of the Japanese forces in the north and in key cities and ports. Talks between the rival Chinese forces collapsed as US forces departed in 1946, and the civil war which had been interrupted by Japan's invasion broke out again.

After early successes, by 1947 the Nationalists began to lose their advantage, and lost Peking and Tientsin in January 1949. The People's Republic was founded on 1 October 1949, and the Nationalist forces withdrew to the island of Formosa, establishing a rival Republic of China, now usually known as Taiwan. This has never declared its independence, and each of the rivals officially espouses an eventual reunification under its own leadership.

The outbreak of the Korean War in 1950 played an important part in the development of the Chinese People's Armed Forces Air Force (CPAFAF). In 1950 the CPAFAF had about 150 aircraft including F-51Ds, B-25Cs, C-46s, C-47s, La-11s and Yak-9s. In February the Soviets agreed to deliver the new MiG-15 fighter, and the first deliveries were made in March.

USA supports Taiwan

From 1951, the Nationalists received US support. They were seen as a bastion against the expansion of Communist 'Red' China. Taiwan also became a useful strategic base. By 1954 the Chinese Nationalist Air Force (CNAF) operated two wings of Republic F-84Gs, two wings of F-47Ds and one of F-51s; the bomber wings still flew the B-24 and B-25. The USA recognised and protected Nationalist China and in return used Taiwan; President Truman sent the US 7th Fleet to the Taiwan Straits at the start of the Korean War, and many secret missions into the mainland began in Taiwan.

Another, less formal, American involvement was with the airline, Civil Air Transport, or CAT. Founded by General Claire Chennault at the end of World War II, CAT was bought by the CIA in 1950. Used for covert intervention all over East and Southeast Asia, CAT was based on Formosa. CAT supplied the French in Indo-China and spawned further CIA covers including Air America, Southern Air Transport, Air Asia and the Asiatic Aeronautical Company. Agents were dropped, but not without risk: between 1951 and 1954, 106 US citizens were killed and 124 captured on covert missions. Many aircraft were lost, including several Boeing B-17s.

The Nationalists had retained forces on four offshore islands: Quemoy and Matsu, and the Tachen and Nanchi groups further north. Mainland pressure on the latter led to withdrawal in January 1954. The US 7th Fleet, covered by F-86Fs of the USAF's 18th FBW, evacuated 17,000 civilians and 25,000 troops. The PLA also turned its attention to Quemoy.

A massive artillery bombardment from the Communist naval base at Amoy began on 3 September 1954, and was countered by Nationalist shelling and air raids. Shelling continued intermittently, and in August 1958 CNAF RF-84Fs noted a build-up of MiG-17s on bases at Chenghai and Licricheng, followed by a new wave of shelling from 18 August.

On 29 August, Peking announced an impending invasion of Quemoy and the liberation of Taiwan. At least

Three-tone green MiG-17s line up on an airfield in Shenyang province. Entering service with the PLA in 1955 and licence-built as the J-5, the MiG-17 was China's main fighter in the early 1970s.

Eight RF-101A Voodoos were delivered to Taiwan after the 1958 Quemoy fighting. They were used on reconnaissance missions over the mainland, with Peking claiming to have shot down two of them in the 1960s.

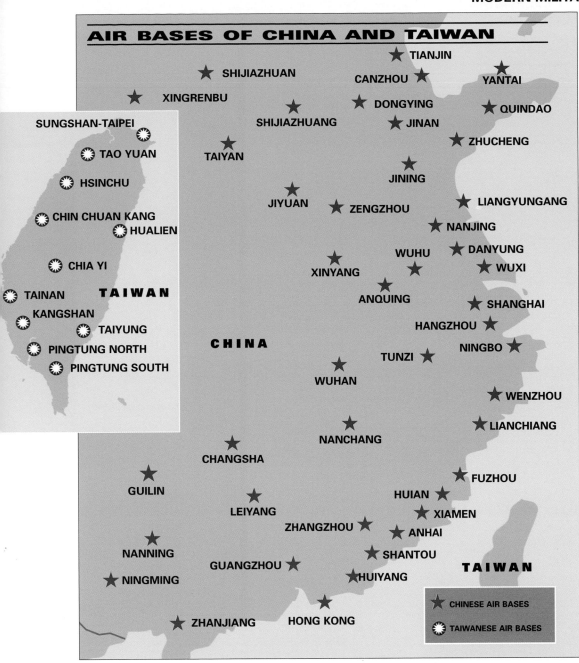

AIR BASES OF CHINA AND TAIWAN

TIANJIN
SHIJIAZHUAN
CANZHOU
YANTAI
XINGRENBU
DONGYING
QUINDAO
SHIJIAZHUANG
JINAN
ZHUCHENG
TAIYAN
JINING
JIYUAN
ZENGZHOU
LIANGYUNGANG
NANJING
WUHU
DANYUNG
XINYANG
WUXI
ANQUING
SHANGHAI
HANGZHOU
TUNZI
NINGBO
WUHAN
CHINA
WENZHOU
LIANCHIANG
NANCHANG
CHANGSHA
FUZHOU
HUIAN
GUILIN
XIAMEN
LEIYANG
ZHANGZHOU
ANHAI
NANNING
SHANTOU
GUANGZHOU
TAIWAN
NINGMING
HUIYANG
ZHANJIANG
HONG KONG

SUNGSHAN-TAIPEI
TAO YUAN
HSINCHU
CHIN CHUAN KANG
HUALIEN
CHIA YI
TAIWAN
TAINAN
KANGSHAN
TAIYUNG
PINGTUNG NORTH
PINGTUNG SOUTH

CHINESE AIR BASES
TAIWANESE AIR BASES

four air divisions had moved to bases around Foochow (Nantai, Kaochi, Swatow and Chulisein) and further afield at Chienou Tien-ho and Nan Hai.

The CNAF in 1958 comprised 350 aircraft, including three wings of F-84Gs, two wings of F-86Fs and one RF-84F squadron. In addition, the USAF rotated a wing of F-86F Sabres as part of defence commitments agreed in March 1955.

1958 Quemoy crisis

On patrols over the Taiwan Straits, Sidewinder-equipped

F-86s engaged increasing numbers of MiG-15s and MiG-17s. On 24 September, 10 MiGs were claimed to have been destroyed by a force of 14 Sabres of the 3rd Wing, including four by Sidewinders, the first time that air-to-air guided missiles had been used in combat. Prior to this, between 14 August and 24 September, some 31 MiGs had been claimed, for the loss of just two F-86s.

In October the USA increased its commitment to Taiwan, with two squadrons of F-100Ds, two of F-104As, one F-101C

squadron, one RF-101C squadron, two squadrons of C-130s and one squadron each of B-57s and KB-50s. In addition, the US 7th Fleet moved on station: its four aircraft-carriers carried 300 aircraft. In the event, there was no major confrontation, although shelling continued, and there was further air fighting when, on 5 July, 1959 five MiG-17s were destroyed in a 10-minute battle with CNAF Sabres.

A state of 'cold war' continued and the Nationalists claimed to have suffered from

399 mainland raids between 1963 and 1969. The F-104A had made a significant impression on both sides during the Quemoy crisis, but US dissatisfaction during its initial service was reflected by the release of 24 F-104As to Taiwan. These were augmented by further deliveries through MAP to help counter further aggressive Chinese tactics over the disputed Quemoy islands. In 1967, CNAF F-104Gs proved their combat prowess when they shot down two PLAAF MiG-19s from a formation of 12 over Quemoy.

The CNAF also operated U-2 spyplanes for the CIA. Many overflights of the mainland were made between 1959 and 1974, primarily to monitor the development of China's nuclear weapons programme at Lop Nor and Chiuchuan. Eight aircraft were lost over China.

As relations between Peking and Washington improved Taiwan felt the effect, with restrictions being imposed on delivery of the latest weapons. The thaw in Sino-American relations after the end of the Cultural Revolution became more permanent, and the position of the island republic became more tenuous. The US withdrew its forces from Taiwan in stages from 1974, and began scaling down its military assistance. In 1979, the USA broke off diplomatic relations with Taiwan.

This marked the low point in Taiwan's relations with the USA. Then the Tiananmen Square massacre focused attention on China's human rights record, and prompted improved relations with the USA, which most recently dispatched warships and aircraft-carriers when China seemed to be threatening invasion during Taiwan's 1996 presidential elections. Chinese relations with the West have ebbed and flowed since Tiananmen Square, with state visits being made by the governments of both East and West. The situation was not helped by the accidental bombing of the Chinese embassy in Belgrade during Operation Allied Force against Yugoslavia.

Based on the MiG-19 airframe, the Q-5 has been in series production since 1969, and is China's primary ground attack fighter. More than 900 have been delivered to the PLAAF.

Lockheed
F-104 Starfighter
Introduction

Designed in the 1950s, in the aftermath of the Korean War, as the ultimate clear-air dogfighter – lightweight, simple and with breathtaking performance – Lockheed's F-104 was eventually developed into a sophisticated all-weather interdictor. Today, the F-104 remains in limited front-line use, following upgrades that will see it survive until, perhaps, 2010.

Few aircraft have attracted such passionate feelings of love and hate, or excitement and fear, as the F-104 Starfighter. Setting out to create a brilliant world-beating air-combat fighter, its talented designers failed utterly. But the result turned out to be quite good at low-level attack and reconnaissance, and Lockheed sold an improved version to such good effect that it was, for more than 20 years, the leading tactical aircraft of the European NATO air forces and Japan, despite the fact that the US Air Force's only interest was to assist sales to others!

Lessons from Korea

It all began with a visit to Korea in 1952 by Clarence L. ('Kelly') Johnson, the chief engineer of Lockheed Aircraft. He found even the F-86 squadrons depressed, because they were unable to outclimb or outmanoeuvre the MiG-15 'Fagots'. They pressed Johnson for a fighter with the highest possible performance, even at the cost of reduced endurance and armament. Johnson returned determined to achieve superior performance at almost any price.

Lockheed made an unsolicited proposal of

High over San Francisco harbour, a pair of F-104As from the 337th Fighter Interceptor Squadron pass the Bay Bridge. The type proved less than ideal in the defence of the continental United States and enjoyed only a brief career with the USAF.

Despite the operation of the Tornado and the introduction of the AMX, the Italian air force still has front-line squadrons equipped with the F-104. For combat air patrol missions, the aircraft operate in conjunction with Tornado F.Mk 3s, which provide the Starfighters with extra radar information for interception work.

the Model 83 to the USAF in November 1952. On 11 March 1953, the USAF issued a letter contract for two XF-104s, numbered 53-7786/7. The first, powered by a J65 rated at 8,000 lb (35.6 kN), flew on 28 February 1954. The second, with an afterburning J65 rated at 11,500 lb (51.16 kN), followed on 5 October 1954. The J65 was envisaged only as an interim engine, pending availability of the more powerful General Electric J79 but, despite this, a speed of Mach 1.7 and height of 60,000 ft (18288 m) were soon reached. The bad news was that, predictably, the XF-104 was a real handful, requiring constant accurate flying. These demanding flight characteristics would soon reappear as the F-104 entered operational service, and many Starfighter pilots would lose their lives as a result.

In July 1954, a cautious USAF ordered 17 YF-104As; these were intended to be very close to production F-104As with a J79-GE-3 engine. The aircraft entered service in a test/development capacity with the 83rd Fighter Interceptor Squadron at Hamilton AFB near San Francisco. A total of 610 F-104As had been requested, but only 153 were actually built. They were phased out of USAF service in 1960, but were recalled by the Berlin and Cuban crises of 1961-62. Likewise, instead of the

planned 112 F-104B tandem-trainers, the USAF received only 26. At this point, Lockheed's Starfighter seemed to have been a failure, but Lockheed recognised that the USAF would not be a customer, except very peripherally. It therefore started to organise a powerful sales team to try to persuade foreign customers that, even if the USAF did not want the F-104, the improved Starfighter (now available) would be the greatest aircraft in the sky. The so-called Super Starfighter (F-104G) was equipped with an uprated powerplant, NASARR radar, strengthened fuselage and new mission equipment.

NATO allies were quick to adopt the F-104 Starfighter into service, with no fewer than nine NATO air forces operating the the F-104: Canada, West Germany, the Netherlands, Belgium, Italy, Turkey, Greece, Norway and Denmark. The aircraft was built under licence by consortia of Belgium, Dutch, Italian and German companies, and by Canadair.

Unjust reputation
Many air forces had problems operating the Starfighter, but in

West Germany, both in the Luftwaffe and Marineflieger, the F-104G losses reached crisis levels. By 1969, West Germany had lost more than 100 Starfighters in 10 years. This state of affairs needs to be looked at in context, however. West Germany was the world's major Starfighter operator, having taken delivery of 917 aircraft – the United States, by comparison, had 294 examples of the F-104G, Canada had 239 and Italy 149. When the German losses were viewed as a percentage of the number of aircraft operated, they were no greater than those of other F-104 operators.

Outside Europe, the major operator was Japan, which produced 200 F-104J single-seat and DJ two-seat Starfighters under licence, entering service with the JASDF in 1964. Ex-USAF Starfighters were supplied to Pakistan, Nationalist China and Jordan, while Spain received 21 F-104Gs and TF-104G trainers from the United States in 1965, in return for the American use of Spanish air bases.

The Starfighter did not see extensive combat during its service life, although Chinese Nationalist Air Force examples participated in

numerous combats with Chinese Communist fighters, scoring few victories. During the Indo-Pakistan War of 1965, the Pakistan air force's single Starfighter squadron scored several victories for the loss of at least one fighter in combat.

Stars in their eyes
Despite its unjust reputation the F-104 Starfighter remains in front-line service, although in a much modified form, with the Italian air force. Known as the F-104S, what the Starfighter initially lacked when it first entered service was solved in the 'S' variant. With extra fuselage missile pylons and an improved radar (with a 'look-down' capability enabling the aircraft to locate and shoot down at targets), the F-104S underwent a further upgrade programme during 1997 to emerge as the F-104S-ASA M.

With delivery of the Eurofighter delayed, Kelly Johnson's 'missile with a man in it' will be a constant sight in the skies over Europe well into the next century. By this time, Lockheed's Starfighter will have become the longest-serving operational fighter in history.

With its high speed, climb performance and high-altitude capability, the Starfighter was a natural choice for NASA's test fleet. Operating from Dryden's Flight Research facility at Edwards AFB, the Starfighter served until 1983, when it was replaced by the F/A-18 Hornet. This was an ironic move since the F-104 served as a chase aircraft during the Hornet's development.

Though not as capable in aerial conflict as the Sidewinder-armed Pakistani Sabres, the Indian Hunters proved adept at ground attack missions. A Hunter of No. 7 Squadron can be seen here bombing the airfield at Dhaka.

Below: The Chinese Shenyang F-6 formed the backbone of the PAF's fighter strength after 1965, 74 being taken on charge as Sabre replacements. These were later equipped with AIM-9 Sidewinders.

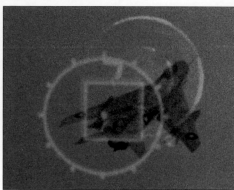

Indo-Pakistan air wars

Right: Pakistan claimed a kill:loss ratio of about 4:1 in the 1965 air war, crediting most victories to the F-86F Sabre (pictured), with a handful of credits for the then-new F-104 Starfighter.

As in so many places, the departure of the British colonial presence in India after the war brought with it much strife. The situation was worsened by the fact that the newly-formed Pakistan was split into two halves by the great mass of India. Fighting broke out almost immediately, and in 1965 a fierce, but largely inconclusive, clash was fought between the two countries.

Relations between India and Pakistan since partition in 1947 have always been uneasy. Apart from the fundamental religious differences between Moslem Pakistan and predominantly Hindu India, the Pakistanis have remained largely Western-orientated and retained military links with the USA from the days of the now-defunct CENTO (Central Treaty Organization) pact, while forging similar bonds with China. India, on the other hand, has been a leader of the neutralist 'third world', but has relied to a substantial extent on the USSR for its arms and military equipment.

Twice since partition, in 1965 and 1971, these differences erupted into brief but full-scale conflicts, between India and Pakistan. Inevitably, any conflict between the neighbouring countries on the Indian sub-continent is a David and Goliath situation, and the 14-day war of December 1971 ended in total military defeat for Pakistan, together with the loss of its entire eastern wing in Bengal. Comprising two components, separated by over 1,000 miles (1600 km) of Indian territory, East and West Pakistan – as

created by the 1947 partition agreement – were already in a different political and logistic situation, and when Indian forces began operating in West Bengal in support of Mukti Bahini rebels on 22 November 1971, the eastern wing became militarily unsupportable.

1965 war

As very much the smaller country (having, in 1971, only slightly more than a quarter of the population of India), from the military point of view Pakistan will never be able to compete in numbers with its massive neighbour. During the 1965 war, the PAF (Pakistan Air Force) could field only 12 combat squadrons by bringing into service all of its reserves, against 14 of the IAF, but by skilful tactics and deployment, managed to keep Indian air power from excessive interference with its army operations.

In May 1965 Pakistan armed and trained irregulars to infiltrate Kashmir, hoping to ferment a revolution which would then topple the state into Pakistan. The insurgents were backed by Pakistani artillery, and the Pakistani army then launched a major offensive against Indian forces in the Chhamb salient. The IAF lost four obsolete Vampires to PAF Sabres in the battle, on 1 September. This led to the immediate withdrawal of the Vampire and Ouregan from front-line service.

All-out war erupted between India and Pakistan, and during

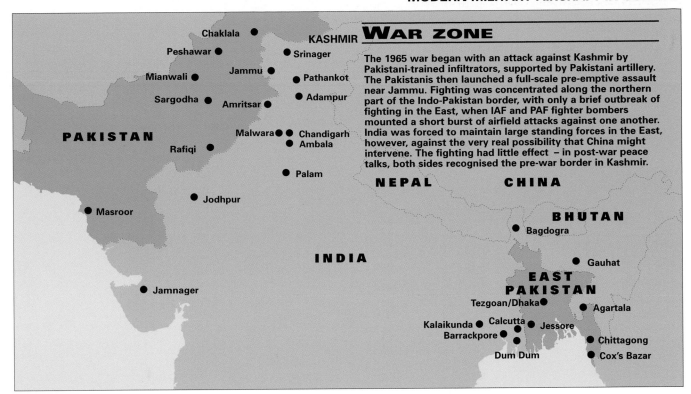

WAR ZONE

Chaklala
Peshawar
KASHMIR
Jammu
Srinager
Mianwali
Pathankot
Sargodha
Amritsar
Adampur

PAKISTAN
Malwara
Chandigarh
Rafiqi
Ambala

Palam

NEPAL
CHINA

Jodhpur

Masroor
BHUTAN
Bagdogra

INDIA
Gauhat

Jamnager
EAST
PAKISTAN
Tezgoan/Dhaka
Agartala
Kalaikunda
Calcutta
Barrackpore
Jessore
Chittagong
Dum Dum
Cox's Bazar

The 1965 war began with an attack against Kashmir by Pakistani-trained infiltrators, supported by Pakistani artillery. The Pakistanis then launched a full-scale pre-emptive assault near Jammu. Fighting was concentrated along the northern part of the Indo-Pakistan border, with only a brief outbreak of fighting in the East, when IAF and PAF fighter bombers mounted a short burst of airfield attacks against one another. India was forced to maintain large standing forces in the East, however, against the very real possibility that China might intervene. The fighting had little effect – in post-war peace talks, both sides recognised the pre-war border in Kashmir.

the vicious 17-day conflict, the PAF flew defensive CAPs over its own bases, offensive counter-air missions against Indian airfields, and close support and interdiction sorties, to which the Indians responded in kind. India retained much of its air force in the East, against the possibility of Chinese intervention, and as a result the air forces quite evenly balanced those in the West. The PAF's tactics kept the Indians at bay, but from 6 September, little attempt was made by either side

to stop fighter-bomber raids by the enemy. From this point on, the Indians flew more sorties, while the PAF tried to conserve its strength. However, the IAF never mounted missions in strength against its key targets, sending out its aircraft in small, often ineffectual, groups.

Indian ground forces launched a counter-offensive which drove the Pakistanis back across their own border in places, but generally the war became a bloody stalemate, and with 2,763 Indians and 6,917 Pakistanis dead

(and 375 and 350 tanks destroyed, respectively), a ceasefire was declared. The pre-war borders of Kashmir were confirmed by the subsequent peace talks.

The PAF lost some 25 aircraft (11 in air combat), while the Indians lost 60 (25 in air combat). This was an impressive result for the PAF, but it was simply not good enough. Pakistan ended the war having depleted 17 per cent of its front-line strength, while India's losses amounted to less than 10 per cent. Moreover, it has been

estimated that another three weeks' fighting would have seen Pakistani losses rising to 33 per cent and India's losses totalling 15 per cent. Air superiority was not achieved, and Pakistan was unable to prevent the IAF from flying daylight missions over Pakistan. Thus, 1965 was an expensive victory for the PAF, and one which was tainted by ridiculously exaggerated propaganda, which claimed a 4:1 or even 5:1 kill:loss ratio, when the reality was that it was less than half of this.

Early conflicts

The departure of the British from India and the subsequent formation of the independent Moslem Pakistan and predominantly Hindu India left a legacy of bitterness and rivalry. Both sides disputed certain key border areas including Jammu and Kashmir, the latter being predominantly Moslem, but ruled by a Hindu Maharajah. In 1947 Kashmir

was invaded by Pathan tribesman, and Azad 'Free Kashmiris' carried out an insurrection. This was put down by the Indian army, with air support from Spitfires and Tempests. Meanwhile, Pakistani Hawker Tempests (and later Furies) were kept busy policing the troubled North-West Frontier, where the tribes were in open revolt.

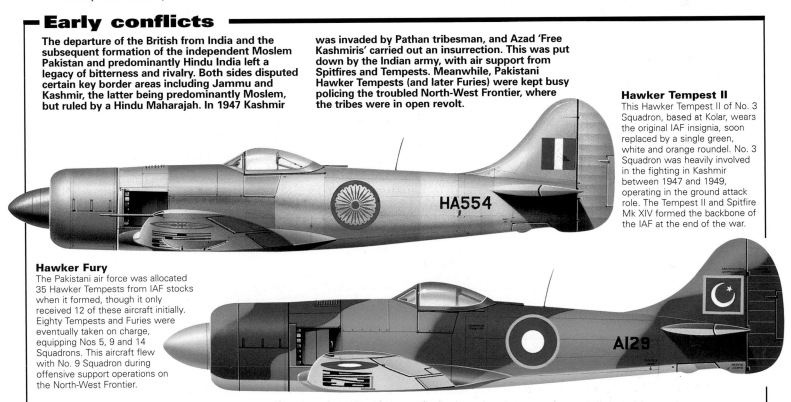

Hawker Tempest II
This Hawker Tempest II of No. 3 Squadron, based at Kolar, wears the original IAF insignia, soon replaced by a single green, white and orange roundel. No. 3 Squadron was heavily involved in the fighting in Kashmir between 1947 and 1949, operating in the ground attack role. The Tempest II and Spitfire Mk XIV formed the backbone of the IAF at the end of the war.

Hawker Fury
The Pakistani air force was allocated 35 Hawker Tempests from IAF stocks when it formed, though it only received 12 of these aircraft initially. Eighty Tempests and Furies were eventually taken on charge, equipping Nos 5, 9 and 14 Squadrons. This aircraft flew with No. 9 Squadron during offensive support operations on the North-West Frontier.

A pair of Indian Canberra B(I).Mk 68s makes a low-level attack on port facilities at Chittagong. The Indian Canberra pilots pressed home their attacks with great vigour, earning the respect of their adversaries.

Indo-Pakistan Air War, 1971

Six years after the initial conflict, India and Pakistan again went to war. The 1971 war was instigated by Pakistan, but lessons were learned by both sides, and India soon gained air superiority. Even today, there is a high level of animosity between the two nations.

India realised, before the 1965 war, that its air force had been something of a glorified flying club for its pilots, and that serious effort needed to be made to improve operational readiness and training, and to provide even the most basic essentials, like camouflage netting (and even camouflage paint for some of its front-line types!). By contrast, the PAF began to believe its own propaganda, that the kill/loss ratio had been about 4:1, rather than the actual 2:1 – still an impressive achievement, but simply not good enough in a war against India. Had the 1965 war lasted a little longer, the weight of Indian numbers alone might have defeated the PAF, even though India had retained more than half of its forces in the East, against the threat of Chinese intervention.

With Soviet aid, India established a modern early-warning radar system, including the recently introduced 'Fansong-E' low-level radar, linked with SA-2 'Guideline' surface-to-air missiles and a large number of AA guns. By December 1971 the IAF comprised a total of 36 combat squadrons (of which 10 were deployed in the Bengal sector), with some 650 combat aircraft.

Moreover, the 1965 war had resulted in the USA imposing a 10-year arms embargo on both sides. This had had no effect on India, which had always looked to Britain, France and even to Russia for arms, but was disastrous for Pakistan, which had been forced to acquire 90 obsolete, second-hand Sabres via Iran, a mere 28 Mirage IIIs from France, and 74 maintenance-intensive Shenyang F-6s. It was quite unable to replace losses among its (already weak) force of B-57s, or to acquire a modern interceptor in realistic numbers. Moreover, re-equipment and strengthening was not accorded a high priority, and the PAF was ill-prepared for war in 1971.

The 1971 war was rooted in the growing resentment in East Pakistan towards ruling from Islamabad, and during the subsequent civil war the popular Mukhti Babim independence movement received much aid from India. Pakistani forces were airlifted in when Bangladesh declared its independence and, when they started massacring the educated classes, India felt that it had to intervene, limited operations beginning in late October. In late November two PAF Sabres strafing Indian troops were downed by Ajeets, marking the first air combat between the two sides since 1965. On 3 December Pakistan launched what was intended to be a

Below: Indian navy Breguet Alizés attacked and sank this ferry near the Bangladeshi port of Khulna when it attempted to run the Indian navy's blockade. One INAS Alizé was shot down by an F-104 during the 1971 war, but overall the type performed well.

Below: A hastily camouflaged Su-7 lands at Pathankot on 11 December 1971, after a bombing attack over Pakistan. The 'Fitter' was handicapped by its limited payload/range capability, but proved fast at low level, and remarkably resilient.

decisive pre-emptive strike against Indian airfields, but managed only 28 sorties, spread thinly and with insufficient accuracy to cause serious damage. The IAF bit back with retaliatory strikes which proved more successful. At sea, the Indian navy sank a Pakistani submarine (a US Navy-leased vessel and the only Pakistani vessel with enough range to threaten India's fleet), leaving the Bay of Bengal clear for operations by India's sole aircraft-carrier, INS *Vikrant*. From then on, Pakistan was forced on the defensive by the numerically superior Indians.

No. 300 'White Tigers' Squadron with its Sea Hawks and No. 310 'Cobras' Squadron with Alizés, operated off the Vikrant, flying a variety of sorties, including maritime patrol, ASW, minelaying, attack and airfield denial.

The PAF's handful of Sabres at Tezgaon near Dacca in East Pakistan put up a useful resistance against all-out attacks by Indian fighters from 4 December. Between four and 11 of the attacking aircraft were claimed as shot down in air combat, with 17 more lost to ground fire. Five Sabres were also shot down. On 6 December, an IAF attack cratered the runways at both Tezgaon and Kurmitola, putting them out of action for the rest of the campaign. Apart from the IAF squadrons deployed in East Bengal, the *Vikrant* (with its Sea Hawk and Breguet Alizé) mounted attacks against the civil airport at Cox's Bazaar and Chittagong harbour. The embryo Bangladeshi air force, with three machine-gun-armed DHC Otters of the Mukhti Bahini Air Wing, made an appearance on 7 December. Indian airborne troops, in battalion strength, made an assault on Dacca on 11 December using An-12s and Fairchild C-119Gs. This was preceded on 7 December by a heliborne infantry assault by two companies, in nine Mil Mi-4s and Mi-8s, escorted by Alouettes.

Attacks on Pakistan

While India's grip on what had been East Pakistan tightened, the IAF continued to press home attacks against Pakistan itself. The campaign settled down to a series of daylight anti-airfield, anti-radar and close-support attacks by fighters, with night attacks against airfields and strategic targets by B-57s and C-130s (Pakistan), and Canberras and An-12s (India). The PAF's F-6s were employed mainly on defensive combat air patrols over their own bases, but without air superiority the PAF was unable to conduct effective offensive operations, and its attacks were largely ineffective. During the IAF's airfield attacks,

one US and one UN aircraft were damaged in Dacca, while a Canadian Air Force Caribou was destroyed at Islamabad, along with US military liaison chief Brigadier General Chuck Yeager's USAF Beech U-8 light twin.

Sporadic raids by the IAF continued against Pakistan's forward air bases in the West until the end of the war, and large-scale interdiction and close-support operations were maintained. The PAF played a more limited part in the operations, and was reinforced by F-104s from Jordan, Mirages from an unidentified Middle Eastern ally and by F-86s from Saudi Arabia. Their arrival helped to camouflage the extent of Pakistan's losses. Libyan F-5s were reportedly deployed to Sargodha, perhaps as a potential training unit to prepare Pakistani pilots for an influx of more F-5s from Saudi Arabia.

Hostilities officially ended at 14.30 GMT on 17 December, after the fall of Dacca on 15 December. India claimed large gains of territory in West Pakistan (although pre-war boundaries were recognised after the war), though the independence of Pakistan's east wing, as Bangladesh, was confirmed. India flew 1,978 sorties in the East and about 4,000 in the West, while the PAF flew about 30 and 2,840, respectively. About 65 IAF aircraft were lost (54 losses were admitted), perhaps as many as 27 of them in air combat. Pakistan lost about 72 aircraft (51 of them combat types), but admitted only 25 to enemy action. At least 16 of the Pakistani losses, and probably 24, fell in air combat (although only 10 air combat

losses were admitted, not including any F-6s, Mirage IIIs, or the six Jordanian F-104s which failed to return to their donors). But the imbalance in air losses was explained by the IAF's considerably higher sortie rate, and its emphasis on ground-attack missions. On the ground Pakistan suffered most, with 33,000 killed and wounded, compared to India's 15,000 dead and wounded. This represented a major defeat for Pakistan.

At war again

On 26 May 1999 India, in response to Islamic forces massing in the Kashmiri region, launched a series of air strikes. It has since emerged that these forces were trained and equipped by Pakistan, and Pakistani regular soldiers were also said to have made incursions into Indian territory. The original strikes were made with squadrons of MiG-21Ms, MiG-23BNs, MiG-27s and Mi-17s. The attacks were initially limited in scope but, as the conflict progressed, Mirage 2000Hs began to drop LGBs and MiG-29s flew top cover. However, there were no reported aerial clashes.

On 12 July, Pakistani and Islamic forces began to withdraw from the region and the air war ended. Indian troops dealt with any stragglers, while the air force counted the cost of the conflict. Three aircraft – a MiG-21M, MiG-27 and Mi-17 – were all lost, with five crew killed. Pakistan and Islamic forces suffered approximately 750 casualties, while the Indian army lost some 400 troops. The Pakistanis failed to gain any land, but an uneasy peace has hung over the two nations ever since.

Fighter-bomber adversaries

Both sides conducted extensive attack sorties throughout the war, although it was the Indians who put the most emphasis on this tactic. The IAF had several squadrons of supersonic fighter-bombers such as HAL Maruts and Su-7s, but these proved little more effective than existing Hunters and Canberras. The PAF still had small numbers of B-57s, but its lack of air cover meant that attack missions were few in number.

Martin B-57 Canberra
Pakistan received 25 B-57s from the US in 1959 and they played a major part in the 1965 conflict. By 1971, numbers of these aircraft were somewhat diminished, but they were still used in attacks on Indian airfields and military installations. The PAF finished the war with 11 aircraft.

Sukhoi Su-7BMK
The Su-7 was acquired due to delays in the Marut programme. The aircraft entered service in 1968, and six squadrons were operational by 1971. These operated in the low-level interdiction and tactical reconnaissance roles, one shooting down a PAF Su-7. Losses were heavy.

Above: Air Lt Dave 'Brick' Bryson unleashes a pair of 15-Imp gal (68-litre) 'Frantans' (frangible napalm tanks) from his Reims-Cessna 337 Lynx, during the RhAF's 'bush war'.

Left: Rhodesian Alouette IIIs, known as 'G-cars', usually carried 0.5-in (12.7-mm) door guns. This example is seen directing mortar fire on ZIPRA positions in Western Bulawayo during February 1981.

Rhodesia

For much of the period of African decolonisation, Rhodesia sought to resist the granting of independence on terms unacceptable to its minority white administration, headed by Ian Smith.

On 11 November 1965, after a period of resistance, Southern Rhodesia unilaterally declared itself independent from the United Kingdom. Despite efforts at mediation by the UK, international import and export sanctions were imposed by the United Nations on Rhodesia. On the home front, Rhodesian Provost T.Mk 52s were immediately posted to Wankie and Kariba to guard against guerrilla attack in the wake of the Unilateral Declaration of Independence (UDI). With Canadian help in the shape of four No. 437 Sqn, RCAF CC-130Es, the British decided to supplement neighbouring Zambia's oil stocks, airlifting supplies from Dar-es-Salaam and Leopoldville following the imposition of sanctions against Rhodesia.

In mid-November 1965, HMS *Eagle* arrived off Mozambique in order to prevent Royal Rhodesian Air Force (RRAF) disruption of the airlift. The predominantly white-staffed RRAF had a long and honourable tradition which stretched back to before World War II. No. 899 NAS Sea Vixen FAW.Mk 2s from *Eagle* were to provide air cover until relieved by No. 29 Sqn, RAF Javelin FAW.Mk 9Rs based at Ndola and Lusaka in Zambia from 3 December.

The oil lift began on 19 December, and ended on 31 October 1966, by which time Nos 99 and 511 Sqn Britannias had flown a total of 1,563 sorties.

Post-war strength

In the post-war years the RRAF had continued to maintain a small number of squadrons, equipped with British aircraft, and by the time of the UDI this force was spearheaded by No. 1 Sqn with Hunter FGA.Mk 9s, No. 2 Sqn with Vampire FB.Mk 9s and No. 5 Sqn with Canberra B.Mk 2s. Despite sympathies among members of the RAF, Rhodesia found itself without many allies and the UN sanctions were fairly effective in preventing a significant build-up of the RRAF. Meanwhile, relations between the UK and Portugal had deteriorated, and the FAP deployed F-84Gs of Esq 93 from Angola to Beira in February 1966, in order to counter any British intervention in Mozambique.

The RRAF's immediate task was support of the army, and consisted mainly of supply missions and limited patrol and reconnaissance duties. Ten Aermacchi AL.60-F5 Trojan transports were obtained covertly in 1967 and joined the Provosts of No. 4 Sqn.

The feeling of frustration in neighbouring black states at the failure of sanctions to bring down the administration under Ian Smith led to an escalation in the infiltration of 'Patriotic Front' terrorists into Rhodesian territory from bases in Botswana, Mozambique and Zambia. These were the guerrillas of Joshua N'komo's ZANU (Zimbabwe African National Union) and Robert Mugabe's ZAPU (Zimbabwe African People's Union) nationalist parties, both of which were outlawed by Rhodesia's white minority.

The first serious incursions from the north occurred in August 1967, when 90 ZAPU guerrillas were wiped out near the Victoria Falls. Operation

Below: A No. 4 Sqn Lynx carries a 'Mini-Golf' 'daisy-cutter' percussion bomb under its starboard wing, with a rocket pod and a 'Frantan' under the other. Note the 0.303-in (7.7-mm) machine-guns over the cabin.

This No. 5 Sqn, RhAF Canberra B.Mk 2 was based at New Sarum in 1970, and carries post-UDI insignia. Providing a long-range bomber-reconnaissance element during hostilities, the Canberras struck targets within the Rhodesian borders as well as in Zambia, Botswana, Mozambique and Angola. Two examples were lost over Mozambique.

Above: Pictured in 1966, this No. 38 Sqn RAF Shackleton MR.Mk 2 was one of those rotated into Majunga, Malagasy, in order to maintain a blockade of the port of Beira and prevent oil deliveries.

Right: No. 4 Sqn, RhAF Lynxes (based at Thornhill) were supplemented in the 'bush war' by dual-role trainer/light strike Genets (SIAI Marchetti SF.260W Warriors) of No. 6 Sqn (foreground), based at New Sarum.

Nickel saw RRAF Alouettes and Provosts play an important role. On 22 August, RRAF Hunters flew their first combat missions, strafing guerrillas. The second significant RRAF offensive operation saw a more determined attack on Karoi on 22 March 1968, led by Vampires.

With the 1969 proclamation of a republic, the 'Royal' prefix was dropped by the air force, which now amounted to seven squadrons of Hunters, Canberras, Vampires, Trojans, C-47s and other assorted transports.

By 1972 the role of the RhAF hardened to one of active counter-guerrilla operations, with hot-chase airborne landings by the Rhodesian Special Air Service and commando-style units in the outlying bush country, as well as rocket and bomb attacks by Hunters and Canberras on terrorist bases.

In 1976 18 Reims-Cessna FTB337Gs were obtained by covert means for counter-insurgency tasks, and around 35 Alouette III helicopters were supplied by South Africa to join No. 7 Sqn. In the transport role, aged C-47s were joined by a dozen ex-civil Britten-Norman Islanders for No. 3 Sqn, and in 1978 about 20 SIAI-Marchetti SF.260W Warriors were also obtained by clandestine means.

RhAF aircraft were frequently deployed on 'externals' over Mozambique, and to a smaller extent over Zambia and Botswana, the last posing the least threat. The first significant cross-border strike occurred on 28 February 1976, when Hunters attacked a Chinese-aided ZANLA (Zimbabwe African National Liberation Army) base at Pafuri, Mozambique. The only air opposition encountered by the RhAF came from a Botswana Defence Force Britten-Norman Defender, flown by a British pilot, which attacked ground troops during a raid near Francistown, but was itself shot down by a 'K-Car' helicopter (an Alouette III configured as a gunship with 20-mm cannon or quadruple 'fifties' for the escort role). Zambian MiGs were sometimes scrambled against the Rhodesian raiders, but usually arrived too late.

Fuel starvation

One of the potential dangers always faced by the RhAF was a possible drying-up of fuel supplies following imposition of oil sanctions. Alongside the Royal Navy, the RAF undertook a limited patrol task, with Shackletons based in Madagascar from March 1966 until February 1972, in order to keep watch for sanction-breaking tankers from the Middle East attempting to land their cargoes on the African coast.

Despite the presence of communist-supplied SAMs to neighbouring black states, the RhAF continued to operate highly effectively both over and beyond Rhodesian territory right up to the point at which an internal settlement of the country's future administration was reached in 1979. However, with the Marxist support of the ZANU and ZAPU which had, by 1979, reached substantial proportions, there is no doubt that the cost of military operations by the countering Rhodesian security forces was biting deep into the state's economy.

As the war progressed, the RhAF developed new weapons, particularly for the 337 Lynx, in order to counter guerrilla activity. Napalm bombs, for example, were found to be difficult to place accurately, and locally-built finned 'Frantans' were found to be more effective. Various anti-personnel bombs were tested, with the RhAF's Hunters carrying a 1,000-lb (454-kg) 'Golf' weapon with a 4-ft (1.20-m) proboscis, and the Lynx carrying the scaled-down 'Mini-Golf' version. The spherical 'Alpha' anti-personnel bomb, delivered from a carrier and detonated to explode 10 ft (3 m) above the ground, was carried by the Canberra and Hunter.

The RhAF lost a number of aircraft during its 'bush war' operations, notably an Alouette lost to a rocket-propelled grenade (RPG) over Mozambique in July 1978. Later that year, an Air Rhodesia Viscount was brought down by a ZIPRA (Zimbabwe People's Revolutionary Army) SA-7, Rhodesia's first SAM loss.

Yet, throughout the 14 years in which the country lay in the economic wilderness, the RhAF's adaptability and determination saw it survive as an efficient counter-insurgency force.

Fire Force

The loss over Mozambique of two AL.60s to SA-7 'Grails' made the RhAF highly SAM-conscious. Clandestinely-acquired Reims-Cessna 337s were fitted with IR-reducing exhaust shields, and comprehensive nav/com equipment, permitting their use as 'Telstar' airborne communications relay stations. This system was used extensively at night in support of external paradrops from DC-7s and INS-equipped AB 205s. Most Lynx sorties were in support of the Fire Force, for rapid-response 'anti-terrorist' operations. These missions usually saw a Lynx operating in concert with up to three 'K-Car' Alouette III gunships and as many 'G-Cars' and Cheetahs (troop-carrying AB 205s) as could be gathered. A C-47 'Para-Dak' with 16-20 paratroops and a 'Skyshout' psy-war Cessna 185 Kiwit or Islander equipped with a powerful loudspeaker system might also accompany the Fire Force. In the FAC role, the Lynx supported the fast jet force, with a 'jet effort' laid on targets too heavily defended for Fire Force action. Using a high dive profile, the Lynx would mark target areas with SNEB 1.46-in (37-mm) smoke or phosphorous rockets, or 'Frantans'. The Lynx pilot would then direct the jets, usually controlling a pair of Hunters, Vampires or Canberras (illustrated).

Spearheading the RhAF ground attack force were the Thornhill-based No. 1 Sqn Hunter FGA.Mk 9s, the most advanced aircraft available at UDI. In 1979, an example was lost over Mozambique.

During the early half of the 20th century, South American nations were traditionally equipped with aircraft that had long since been retired by the major world powers. However, by the 1980s, many Latin American countries were supplied with higher-performance aircraft, such as these Ecuadorian Kfirs.

South American air wars

Latin America

South America has remained free of major conflicts this century, but many small border conflicts, coups and revolutions have meant that this region remains constantly volatile.

Argentina

With the death of the much-loved Eva Perón on 26 July 1952, the right-wing dictatorship of Juan Domingo Perón lost popular support, and in 1955 there was a succession of uprisings. In June, the navy shelled Government House, and in September a naval uprising saw captured air force Meteor F.Mk 4 fighters being used against government troops – older aircraft such as navy PBY-5As, AT-11s, SNJ-4s and J2F-5s made strikes, with one J2F-5 being shot down by AAA. In response, loyalist air force Meteors attacked and damaged two destroyers. The revolt grew as more troops joined the rebellious navy. By the end of June 1956, Perón had been forced into exile and a military junta had assumed power.

In a two-day uprising in April 1963, naval aircraft supported rebels while the air force supported the government. Navy F4U-5s, F9F-2s, PBY-5As and SNJ-4s were used in attacks on army formations, in leaflet-dropping and reconnaissance, while air force Meteors, F-86Fs and Lincolns were used on bombing raids, destroying about 10 navy aircraft before the rebellion was finally crushed on 3 April.

In an air force revolt in 1975, Mirage IIIs flew a number of sorties and navy A-4Q Skyhawks attacked rebels in Buenos Aires.

Argentina's biggest conflict this century was the Falklands War against the United Kingdom, which is covered elsewhere in this publication.

Bolivia

Che Guevara instigated a revolt in 1965 against right-wing dictator General Barrientos, to which the government responded by using air force F-51Ds, T-28s and T-6s against guerrilla positions, with limited success. US-supplied HH-19B helicopters moved troops in the successful hunt for Guevara, who was killed in October 1967, supposedly by the CIA.

Barrientos died in a helicopter crash in 1969, and over the ensuing decade the air force took part in a number of coups, the most notorious being when F-51D Mustangs were used to strafe protesting students occupying the university quarter of the capital, La Paz.

British Guiana

In 1953, elections brought fear of a communist government and British troops were sent to the country. As resentment against British forces grew, Shackleton MR.Mk 2s, Wessexes, Whirlwind HC.Mk 10s, Auster AOP.Mk 9s and Canberra PR.Mk 7s were detached to crush riots, transport troops and carry out reconnaissance duties.

Chile

In September 1973 a military coup, led by General Augusto Pinochet Ugarte, overthrew the democratically elected Marxist president Salvador Allende. Hawker Hunter FGA.Mk 71s were used to bomb the presidential palace just before Allende's surrender and subsequent death.

Colombia

Between 1948 and 1958, a continuous civil war, known as La Violencia, ripped the country apart. The Colombian air force used its AT-6s and F-47Ds in COIN (counter-insurgency) operations.

During the 1970, 1980s and beyond, new missions for the air force lay in countering the drug trade and in undertaking operations against numerous left-wing guerrilla groups. Air force A-37s were used to strike at guerrilla strongpoints and rebel-held towns.

Ecuador against Peru

In 1981, a minor border conflict with Peru involved Ecuadorian Cessna T-37s, Mirage F1JAs and Jaguars which were opposing the armed reconnaissance sorties being flown by Peruvian Su-22s and Mirage 5Ps.

A more serious clash occurred in the Cordillera del Condor region in 1995, with Ecuadorian Mirage F1JAs claiming to have shot down two Peruvian Sukhoi Su-22 'Fitters' on 10 February. A Cessna A-37 was shot down by an Ecuadorian Kfir on the same day. Three Peruvian Mil Mi-8 'Hips' had been destroyed by ground fire on 30 January and 7 February, and hits were reported on two FAE Kfirs and an A-37B on 12 February.

Paraguay

Converted transports, captured from the government-loyal air

Argentina is one of the few nations to have used heavy bombers in anger in the post-World War II era. During an attempted coup by the navy in 1963, ageing air force Lincolns attacked rebel positions.

Below: During the Cold War, Soviet influence in the region increased, primarily in the supply of military equipment. Here, a Kalashnikov-armed Peruvian soldier fires from a Mil Mi-8 'Hip' helicopter during the 1981 border clash with Ecuador.

Above: British troops, helicopters and a flight of Royal Air Force Harrier GR.Mk 3s were deployed to Belize to deter Guatemala from invading the former British colony.

force, bombed Asunción in an unsuccessful 1947 army revolt. In 1960, air force T-6Gs and C-47s, equipped with bomb racks, stopped a rebellion aimed at overthrowing the fascist General Alfredo Stroessner.

Peru

Since the 1980s, a long-lasting COIN struggle has been conducted against numerous rebel groups, notably the Maoist movement known as Sendero Luminoso (Shining Path). Air strikes have also been made against guerrillas and Colombian cartel-backed drug traffickers, during which Mil Mi-8 and Mi-24 helicopters provided troops with an assault capability.

Venezuela

In 1958 the arrest of the army commander and his chief of staff, Colonel Leon, led to an uprising by the armed forces. Vampire FB.Mk 5s and F-86F Sabres were used to strafe the presidential palace and to bomb the National Security headquarters. However, the general populace did not support the rebellion and its leaders fled. Leon was released and went into exile in Colombia. In 1960, he led another rebellion, which was put down when government-loyal air force Canberra B.Mk 2s and B(I).Mk 8s bombed the rebels.

Canberras were used to bomb rebel troops in 1961, and again in 1962 when a Marine battalion unsuccessfully mutinied.

Reacting to violations of its air space by Colombian Mirage 5s, Venezuelan troops, supported by F-16s and Tucanos, were moved to the border region as a deterrent in 1987.

In 1992, a failed coup by paratroops was followed by a revolt by elements of the air force. Mirage 50EVs, OV-10A/E Broncos, T-2D Buckeyes, A-27 Tucanos and an NF-5B Freedom Fighter fought with loyal F-16 Fighting Falcons and NF-5As, managing to keep the rebels at bay until the intervention of ground troops. With the revolt quashed, a reported 1,000 officers and NCOs were arrested, severely damaging the credibility and effectiveness of the Venezuelan air force.

Central America

Some 100,000 people died in guerrilla activities in Guatemala while, at the same time, Guatemalan claims on Belize brought the country into confrontation with British troops and warplanes sent to defend the former colony. Honduras, which has fought a short war with El Salvador, and Costa Rica, which has abolished its army, have been continuously threatened by an

overspill of violence from their unsettled neighbours.

El Salvador

The Salvadorean army was victorious in the 10-day 'Football War' against Honduras in 1969, which erupted after the already hostile countries had played three bitterly contested matches in the build-up to the 1970 World Cup. Both nations had little in the way of modern fighter aircraft, with Corsairs equipping each side. The most notable aspect of the conflict was the downing, by an F4U-5, of the final Mustang to be lost in an air-to-air combat, on 17 July 1969.

After this conflict, El Salvador built up its armed forces, in particular its air force, though peace was made with Honduras in 1980. Internal strife later tore the country apart when military units – intent on upholding internal security – formed death squads that operated beyond the control of the country's leaders.

At this time, the Salvadorean air force consisted of a fighter squadron equipped with Dassault Ouragans and a light strike squadron of Fouga Magisters. US assistance from 1981 added at least 12 UH-1H helicopters, plus advisory help. After a number of rebel attacks, the USA delivered another 12 UH-1H Iroquois, eight Cessna A-37B Dragonflies, four Cessna O-2As and three Fairchild C-123 transports as replacements. The air force's principal tasks were flying strike missions against guerrilla units, transporting infantry units, and casualty evacuation. During the war, helicopters (due to their ability to land virtually anywhere) proved to be the government's most effective form of aircraft.

Government forces by then totalled 40,000. The rebels, who had united under Cuban and Nicaraguan auspices as the Frente Farabundo Marti de Liberación Naciónal (FFMLN), had about

one third of that strength, but controlled about 30 per cent of the country. The election of José Napoleon Duarte in 1984, the first freely-elected president in 50 years, signalled a change: despite continued skirmishes, talks began and, by 1992, the struggles finally came to an end.

Nicaragua

To the south, the left-wing Sandinista revolutionary government of Nicaragua had toppled the corrupt Somoza dictatorship in 1979. However, the Sandinistas were seen by US president Ronald Reagan as a threat to stability in the region, and determined American-backed efforts to overthrow them were made by CIA-trained groups of right-wing guerrillas. They included both emigré Nicaraguans and mercenaries, colloquially known as 'Contras', supported by their own helicopters and the Honduran air force.

Air power played little part in the conflict, despite rumours of a dozen Mikoyan-Gurevich MiG-21 'Fishbeds' delivered to Nicaragua from Cuba in 1981. As the Sandinistas had few serviceable fixed-wing aircraft, the burden of ground support fell on the helicopter arm; it played a major part in the conflict, giving Sandinista troops vital mobility against the 'Contra' rebels. Three Mil Mi-24 'Hind' gunships were delivered in 1984 to a growing fleet which included a dozen Mi-8 'Hips', two Aérospatiale Alouette IIIs and a ragtag collection of aging US types. The majority of the Mi-8s were acquired from 1983 and were equipped as gunships.

Although Sandinista president Daniel Ortega won a fair election in 1984, the civil war and US attempts to topple the government continued until 1990 when the Sandinistas were defeated in the polls and Violeta Chamorro came to power.

Helicopters played a major part in the civil war in Nicaragua. Soviet-built Mil Mi-8 and Mi-17 'Hip' transports, supported Mi-24 'Hind' gunships, proved vital in giving mobility to Sandinista troops fighting the American-backed 'Contra' guerrillas.

The only CH-46 lost in the Grenada campaign was this example which was shot down on 26 October during the rescue of American students from the Grand Arise campus of the Medical School.

US police actions 1983–95

On America's doorstep, the Caribbean/Central American region became an area of concern in the post-war period. During the 1980s and 1990s the US mounted a number of significant operations.

Operation Urgent Fury was successful in part because of the CH-53D Sea Stallion. Four of these were assigned to HMM-261, a unit involved in the Marines' landing on the island.

Having been under British rule since 1763, Grenada was granted full independence in February 1974, with a democratic government being formed. Five years later, a People's Revolutionary Government (PRG) was organised by Maurice Bishop.

The Cuban presence in Grenada quickly grew with the building of a new airport which had potential military applications in spite of its avowed commercial purpose, and became a concern for the US government over its potential use for Cuban military operations in Central America.

Then, in October 1983, with help from Cuban military advisors and a small number of Soviet Spetsnaz personnel, Prime Minister Bishop and several members of his cabinet were arrested and then executed by elements of the People's Revolutionary Army (PRA).

Chaos set in, and the lives of US and other foreign nationals were thought to be endangered. Still, there was no legal ground

for US intervention until 23 October, when six eastern Caribbean nations, together with Jamaica and Barbados, issued a formal request for assistance from the United States. Shortly thereafter, a letter from Governor General Sir Paul Scoon requested outside intervention and provided a legitimate cover for military action. Preparations for full military operations were initiated. Urgent Fury was under way.

To carry out the assignment, the US Navy's Commander-in-Chief, Atlantic was given operational control over air force, army and marine units in addition to his own forces. Transportation and paradrop of army troops was to be performed by USAF C-130 Hercules transports, heavylift support coming from C-141B StarLifters and C-5A Galaxies. The Marines were to be taken ashore by CH-46Es and CH-53Ds, escorted by AH-1T SeaCobra attack helicopters, based aboard the assault ship USS *Guam* (LPH-9), and by four landing ships of Amphibious Squadron Four.

Air support for Joint Task Force 120, as the combined service force was called, was to be provided by AC-130H gunships of the 1st Special Operations Wing and by three attack squadrons of Carrier Air Wing Six from the USS *Independence*.

After the go-ahead for the intervention was given by President Reagan during the evening of 23 October, Vice Admiral Joseph Metcalf III and his JTF-120 staff set the operation in motion. First into the fray was an AC-130H of the 16th Special Operations Squadron. It flew over the Point Salines Airport during the early hours of 25 October, using its advanced sensors to scan the area for anti-aircraft weapons and runway obstructions. Attracting much AAA fire, the gunship radioed back valuable information in time for field commanders to revise plans for the initial assault.

The Marines were first inserted by Sea Stallion helicopters near Pearls Airport at 0520 on 25 October, and 16 minutes later Rangers began jumping from USAF C-130s over Point Salines.

The principal navy fixed-wing

aircraft used during Urgent Fury were the A-7E Corsair IIs and A-6E Intruders of Air Wing Six. In general, the Corsair proved effective in providing air support for the ground forces.

As part of its reinforced complement, HMM-261 had four AH-1T SeaCobra attack helicopters aboard the *Guam*. These four machines saw much action, and two were shot down by the PRA during the fighting for Fort Frederick. The last two remained in the thick of the fight until the last Urgent Fury action.

CH-46E Sea Knights, the main Marine Corps transport helicopters, performed well from the assault against Pearls and Grenville in the early hours of 25 October until the last Marine operation, the taking of Carriacou Island on 1 November.

Another type making its combat debut during Urgent Fury, the UH-60A Black Hawk, earned praise on account of its reliability and its ability to be ferried over long overwater distances. However, three were shot down or damaged beyond repair, one heavily damaged, and two lightly damaged.

A Bell AH-1T SeaCobra of US Marine Corps squadron HMM-261 runs up its engines as deck crew on the USS Guam (LPH-9) top off its fuel tanks for an assault on Grenada's Pearls Airport.

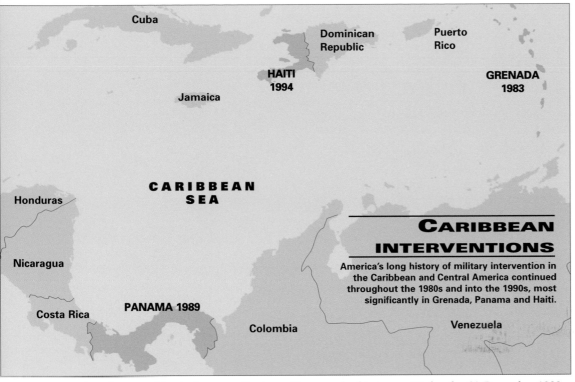

Cuba

Jamaica

Dominican Republic

Puerto Rico

HAITI 1994

GRENADA 1983

Honduras

CARIBBEAN SEA

Nicaragua

Costa Rica

PANAMA 1989

Colombia

Venezuela

CARIBBEAN INTERVENTIONS

America's long history of military intervention in the Caribbean and Central America continued throughout the 1980s and into the 1990s, most significantly in Grenada, Panama and Haiti.

American casualties during Urgent Fury included 19 dead and 116 wounded; Cuban casualties were 25 dead and 59 wounded, while Grenadian casualties, including civilians, were 45 dead and 350 wounded.

Panama

Panama's leader, General Manuel Noriega, had been indicted in an American court for drug offences and, after surviving a failed *coup d'état*, went so far as to 'declare war' on the US on 15 December 1989. Hints of impending action in Panama began on 16 December when a US Marine Corps lieutenant was murdered by Panamanian soldiers at a roadblock. US response was swift. Operation Just Cause began in the early hours of Wednesday 20 December 1989, when US Navy SEALS attacked Paitilla Airport, where Noriega kept a possible getaway Learjet. AC-130H Spectre gunships of the 16th Special Operations Squadron attacked key targets, including the Panama Defense Forces fortress known as the Comandancia, as well as the Puma Battalion barracks just outside Omar Torrijos Airport.

The initial assault made use of 7,000 of the 22,500 American troops eventually deployed for the operation, divided into five groups. The first wave of 77 C-141B StarLifters, 22 C-130 Hercules, and 12 C-5 Galaxies made a total of 84 air drops, followed by a second wave of 40 C-141Bs and 13 C-5s.

Task Force Red made a parachute assault on Torrijos Airport and the Puma barracks, spearheaded by an Army Ranger battalion and 82nd Airborne troopers. A second Ranger battalion parachuted into Rio Hato where some of Noriega's most loyal units were based. Task Force Pacific brought 20 C-141B loads of additional troops, which formed a second wave on parachuting into Torrijos Airport.

In retrospect, the most noteworthy event was the first combat use of the Lockheed F-117A Nighthawk. Flying non-stop from Nevada, with the aid of air refuelling, two F-117As from the 37th TFW dropped 2,000-lb (907-kg) LGBs in a field next to the barracks to frighten troops and to destroy an AA position.

After the first day, fighting was sporadic and scattered, though some PDF personnel continued to resist. Noriega took refuge in the Vatican ambassador's residence, before surrendering on 3 January.

Operation Just Cause's casualties included 23 American and 200 Panamanian combatants killed, as well as 202 Panamanian civilian fatalities. A number of Panamanian aircraft was destroyed or damaged. Numerous US aircraft were damaged, including 11 C-130s, and one OH-58, while three AH-6s were completely destroyed.

Haiti

In 1994 the military junta of General Raoul Cedras held on to power in Haiti in spite of elections won by Jean–Bertrand Aristide. A full-scale US invasion to restore democracy was averted when a last-minute agreement was brokered by former US President Jimmy Carter. General Cedras agreed to stand down with effect from 15 October 1994 and permit exiled President Aristide to assume power.

On 19 September, 2,000 US troops were airlifted ashore from the ships of Joint Task Force 190 located off the Haitian coast. US Army UH-60s ferried the troops to Haiti while AH-1 HueyCobras flew protective air cover. The helicopters operated from the aircraft-carrier USS *Eisenhower*. This was the first occasion in which the Adaptive Joint Force Package concept, involving the integration of various services, had been employed operationally. In excess of 50 US Army helicopters were embarked on the *Eisenhower* for the operation.

US Air Force aircraft played a supporting role, with the majority forward-deployed to the naval station at Roosevelt Roads, Puerto Rico. E-3 Sentries of the 552nd ACW monitored the skies above Haiti as well as the air space around Cuba.

Twenty-four F-15Cs of the 33rd FW from Eglin AFB, Florida were stationed at Roosevelt Roads along with nine KC-135s, as a precautionary measure to perform combat air patrols if needed. In the event, the Eagles were not required.

Other USAF types involved included three EC-130Es of the 42nd ACCS, 355th Wing from Davis-Monthan AFB, Arizona, which performed airborne battlefield management. AC-130H Spectre gunships were on hand to provide firepower if necessary, while RC-135 Rivet Joint aircraft monitored communications.

A Special Forces MH-53J lands on a football pitch next to the Vatican Embassy where General Noriega had taken refuge. In the foreground an American soldier keeps watch on the Embassy.

F-14 Tomcat

A VF-102 F-14B takes the wire during exercises. The F110 engine employed by the F-14B and F-14D allowed the aircraft to be launched in military power, increased combat radius by 62 per cent and gave the pilot the benefit of carefree engine-handling.

By 2006, when the last USN Tomcats were retired, the F-14 was almost four decades old. Its replacement is the multi-role F/A-18, especially in its E/F forms. Meanwhile, the Tomcat survives in service with Iran.

During the late 1970s the F-14 Tomcat was widely regarded as the most important aircraft in the US Navy, and was the dream billet for any ambitious trainee naval aviator.

Every US Navy aircraft-carrier (apart from the tiny *Coral Sea* and *Midway*) embarked a pair of F-14 squadrons, and these units were the oldest, most historic and proudest fighter squadrons in the Fleet. Only the Tomcat was felt to be capable of defending the Carrier Battle Group from long-range cruise missile carriers, with its unmatched potential to fire off a salvo of up to six ultra long-range Phoenix AAMs against high- or low-flying targets, and then to deal with any 'leakers' with Sidewinders or the internal 20-mm cannon. And nor was the Tomcat a lumbering bomber-destroyer. Agile and

Pictured here is a USN F-14A painted for aggressor training. As well as serving in the adversary role with the Naval Strike Air Warfare Center, F-14s performed various test duties.

with phenomenal acceleration, the F-14 was a better dogfighter than the F-4 and was superior in a close-in fight to the F-8.

Remarkably, even more than 30 years after it entered service, the F-14 retained a ragged

Right: Iran possesses a strong F-14 force, maintained mostly from local spares sources. The Hawk SAM has been integrated onto the aircraft as a medium-range AAM, and is known locally as the AIM-23C Sedjil.

glamour, and, up until its retirement, many regarded it as being the pivotal element within any carrier air wing. However, the credibility of the AIM-54 Phoenix was dented by a poor

showing in combat and trials, while the F-14 could not carry the AIM-120 AMRAAM. Plans to integrate the AIM-120 were cancelled, leaving the aircraft reliant on the ageing AIM-7

The Tomcat left US service in 2006, ousted by Boeing's Super Hornet, especially the two-seat version. The F-14 was active to the last, however, dropping a bomb over Iraq during its final sortie on 8 February 2006.

Sparrow and the AIM-54 in the BVR sector.

Although the weapon recorded numerous successes in Iranian hands, the only time six USN AIM-54s were ever fired together (against a close-packed formation of radar-signature augmented drones), just three missiles actually hit their targets. Impressive as an air-to-air dogfighter when it entered service, the F-14's agility was never on a par with that of the slightly newer teen-series fighters (F-15, F-16 and F/A-18), nor of aircraft like the Su-27. Against such aircraft, the Tomcat relies on its BVR capability, on superior tactics, and on the greater situational awareness that a well coordinated two-person crew can enjoy.

The original F-14A model was always severely constrained by the unreliability and limitations of its TF30 engines, which accounted for heavy losses of aircraft and aircrew. For many years, the Tomcat had little multi-role versatility, although it proved a remarkably useful tactical reconnaissance platform when equipped with the TARPS pod, and every Carrier Air Wing included two or three TARPS-capable F-14s. This recce capability was enhanced in later years by the addition of a digital TARPS reconnaissance pod and real-time datalink.

A shortage of F-14 airframes, coupled with the realisation that the F/A-18 Hornet was a more versatile aircraft, especially in the post-Cold War world, led to a dramatic reduction in the F-14 fleet. The composition of the Carrier Air Wing was revised, with only a single F-14 unit and

Open-air maintenance was standard practice at NAS Oceana. The base previously housed A-6s alongside its F-14s, but the A-6 apron was later turned over to the F/A-18.

three squadrons of F/A-18s (which could include a USMC Hornet unit) deployed aboard most carriers. Only two Air Wings (CVW-7 aboard the USS Dwight D. Eisenhower and CVW-8 aboard the USS Theodore Roosevelt) retained paired Tomcat squadrons – a result of a shortfall in F/A-18 numbers rather than a deliberate 'pro-Tomcat' choice.

By the mid-1990s, the Tomcat force was thus reduced from 28 squadrons (with separate Atlantic and Pacific Fleet training units) to just 12, with a single training unit. All of these (except VF-154) were based at NAS Oceana. The exception was based at Atsugi in Japan, where it supported CVW-5 aboard the USS Kitty Hawk.

This drawdown left three squadrons with the F-14D (VF-2, VF-11 and VF-31), four with the F-14B (VF-102,

VF-103, VF-143 and VF-211) and five with the F-14A (VF-14, VF-32, VF-41, VF-154 and VF-213). A shortage of F-14Ds led to the conversion of VF-11 to the F-14B in 1997, though VF-213 subsequently re-equipped with the F-14D version, VF-211 transitioned back to the F-14A, while VF-32 gained F-14Bs.

Persian 'cats

In Iran, the Tomcat also found a single export customer. A peek beneath the veil of security surrounding the aircraft reveals that as many as 44 Iranian F-14s remain operational early in 2007. These have been subject to local upgrade and are now armed with a range of indigenous weaponry, including Fatter IR-guided AAMs (similar in appearance to the AIM-9P Sidewinder) and a reverse-engineered version of the

AIM-54 Phoenix. Iran has also tested the F-14 in the air-to-ground role and integrated the Russian R-73 AAM.

The US F-14 force began assuming a limited clear-weather attack capability in 1992, and some began referring to the aircraft as the 'Bombcat'. Limited all-weather air-to-ground PGM capability was then provided through the integration of the LANTIRN (Low-Altitude Navigation and Targeting Infra-Red for Night) laser designator, and the aircraft could deliver a range of LGBs, dumb 'iron' bombs, Cluster Bomb Units and unguided rockets.

Work then moved on to integrating GPS-guided munitions, including JDAM (Joint Direct Attack Munition) though, even with all these capabilities, the only real advantage of the 'Bombcat' over the F/A-18C/D (let alone the far more capable F/A-18E/F) lay in its superior range and radius of action. Its disadvantages included very poor serviceability and huge operating costs.

The US Navy's F-14s remained in active service until 2006, seeing combat during Operation Iraqi Freedom. After 36 years of service, the Tomcat was officially retired by the USN during a ceremony held at NAS Oceana on 22 September 2006.

Desert Shield

Road to war

With its oil riches, Saudi Arabia was able to purchase the world's finest aircraft to defend its territories. Saudi Tornado ADVs, alongside F-15s, helped to patrol the airspace along the border with Kuwait.

Saddam Hussein's invasion of Kuwait resulted in one of the biggest military task forces ever assembled, being sent to the Persian Gulf in a bid to eject Iraq and safeguard the world's oil.

During the early hours of 2 August 1990, the Iraqi army, which had been massing for days, crossed the border and invaded Kuwait. The well-planned operation had been undertaken in the tightest security; foreign intelligence services only found out about Iraq's plans a few hours before the invasion. Even then, it was assumed that the Iraqis would merely capture disputed land along the border between the two countries and halt there. However, Iraq's forces failed to stop, and sped across the country, only meeting pockets of resistance from remaining Kuwaiti forces.

The United Nations Security Council quickly passed Resolution 660 which condemned the invasion and called for the immediate and unconditional withdrawal of Iraqi forces. However, over the following days, the Iraqi forces moved southwards until they reached the Saudi border and there they waited.

Defence in the desert

Four days later, Saudi Arabia's King Fahd invited foreign governments to send troops to his country to protect against a possible Iraqi invasion. President Bush immediately ordered the implementation of Operation Desert Shield, which would involve an immense transfer of military forces to the area. This was to be the largest military airlift the world had ever seen and it began with the movement of the 82nd Airborne Division and its equipment to Saudi Arabia. Over the next two days, 48 F-15C/D Eagles of the 1st Tactical Fighter Wing took off from Langley AFB, Virginia, and embarked on the longest operational fighter deployment in history, flying a route which took up to 17 hours and involved six or seven inflight refuellings from KC-135s and KC-10s. They were joined by E-3 AWACs and RC-135V Rivet Joint reconnaissance aircraft.

Over the following days, a number of countries around the world professed their intent to add to the forces protecting Saudi Arabia, in Operations Granby for the British, Daguet for the French, Locusta for the Italians and Friction for the Canadians. Arab forces also contributed, with Bahrain, Egypt, Abu Dhabi and the UAE joining Saudi Arabia, and escaped Kuwaiti forces added

McDonnell Douglas F-15Cs played a major part in the war. The first Western aircraft to arrive in the Gulf, they flew directly from the United States and joined up with their counterparts in the Saudi air force, the only other Coalition partner to fly the type.

to the defensive build-up.

The US Navy carrier USS *Dwight D. Eisenhower* and its battle group entered the Red Sea on 7 August and a unit of USAF B-52Gs deployed to the US base of Diego Garcia in the Indian Ocean. RAF Tornado F.Mk 3s, Nimrods and Jaguars arrived in the Gulf, as did F-15Es of the USAF's 4th Tactical Fighter Wing. The French sent the aircraft carrier *Clemenceau,* which was equipped with anti-tank helicopters, while Belgium and the Netherlands also agreed to send naval forces. On 21 August, the first of 22 F-117A 'Stealth Fighters' of the 415th TFS, 37th TFW arrived in Saudi Arabia under the full

US Navy aircraft were quickly deployed to the Gulf. The first carrier to enter the region was the USS** Independence **and it was joined by a further five carriers, dramatically boosting Coalition strength.

glare of media scrutiny. US Defense Secretary Dick Cheney also ordered the first in a series of Reserve and National Guard activations, beginning with three C-141B StarLifter and two C-5A Galaxy squadrons.

Iraqi response

During this time, President Saddam Hussein did not remain idle. His troops began to round up Western nationals and it was then announced that Iraq's occupation of Kuwait was 'irreversible'. He went on to announce that Kuwait was officially annexed and it was now the 19th province of Iraq. Saddam also called on Moslems all around the world to join in a 'Holy War' against the United States and Israel if any attempt was made to dislodge Iraqi forces from Kuwait. A few days later, Hussein launched his so-called 'peace initiative', in which he offered to end the Iraqi

occupation of Kuwait if Israel and Syria ended their occupation of Palestine and Lebanon, respectively. Although this offer was rejected by the West, it was repeated several more times in the following months. In a move to secure his eastern flank, Hussein ordered his troops to withdraw from all the Iranian territory captured during the 1980-1989 war, and Iranian prisoners remaining in Iraq were also released. Such a move made a mockery of the tens of thousands of people who died and the years of devastation in a war that Iraq had barely won.

In an effort to deter air attacks on his country, Saddam announced that Western nationals, including women and children, were to be placed at possible targets as 'human shields'. This act received worldwide condemnation and, although Hussein went on television to try to ingratiate himself with the West by attempting to make friends with an English child, his actions merely stiffened resolve.

Coalition forces continued to mass in the Gulf. By September, a mere month after the Iraqi invasion, there were more Coalition than Iraqi aircraft in the region. The majority were American, but British and Saudi forces also made a sizeable contribution. Ground troops and their support equipment were also pouring into the Persian Gulf. Tactical airlift aircraft such as the C-130 transported personnel and supplies around the region, Allied fighter aircraft carried out high-speed probing missions on the Iraqi border, and increasing numbers of naval forces were arriving, all adding to the massed firepower of the Coalition. In one operation, that would have been unthinkable even a year earlier, a Soviet navy warship requested and received assistance from an RAF Nimrod

Arguably the 'aircraft of the war', the Lockheed F-117A attracted enormous media attention as soon as it arrived in the Gulf. It was there to be used as a 'silver bullet', a euphemism for a weapon to be used against very high-value targets. This was the first official overseas deployment of the aircraft.

IRAQI FORCES ON THE EVE OF WAR

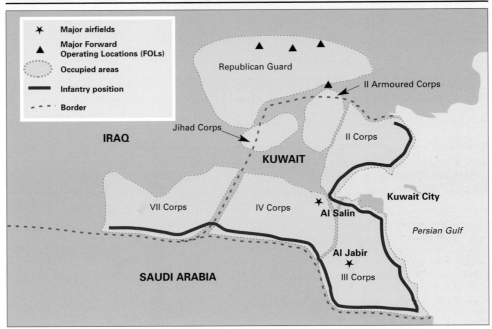

✱	Major airfields
▲	Major Forward Operating Locations (FOLs)
⬭	Occupied areas
▬	Infantry position
‒ ‒ ‒	Border

Republican Guard
II Armoured Corps
IRAQ
Jihad Corps
II Corps
KUWAIT
Kuwait City
VII Corps
IV Corps
Al Salin
Persian Gulf
Al Jabir
SAUDI ARABIA
III Corps

While the West built up its forces, Iraq responded in kind. Beginning in September with 14 divisions, the Iraqi army gradually increased its forces and, in November, it announced that it would send a further 250,000 troops into the theatre to counter Coalition aggression, bringing the number of personnel to approximately 680,000. In January 1991, the Defence Intelligence Agency estimated that Iraq had 42 or 43 divisions with 540,000 ground troops, more than 4,200 tanks, 2,800 armoured personnel carriers and 3,100 artillery pieces. In addition, there were more than 700 combat aircraft, a multi-layered air defence system, missile-firing patrol boats and Silkworm SAMs for coastal defence.

to intercept a suspected Iraqi blockade runner.

By December 1990, the US government announced that it now had the following forces in Saudi Arabia: 750 main battle tanks, 90 air superiority fighters such as F-14s and F-15Cs, 355 attack aircraft such as A-6s, AV-8Bs, A-10s, F-111Fs and F-117As, and 220 dual-purpose aircraft such as F-15Es, F-16s and

F/A-18s. Supporting these were F-4G Wild Weasel and EF-111A electronic support aircraft, large numbers of KC-10 and KC-135 tankers, plus several hundred helicopters and transport aircraft. By the time Desert Storm actually commenced, these figures had grown even larger, and the US forces were backed up by aircraft, troops and naval forces from over a dozen counties. The force now

present on Saddam's doorstep was of immense size and power. Although diplomats were still pursuing every possible channel in a bid to arrive at a peaceful settlement, it became clear that the 'mother of all wars' promised by Saddam would involve air power of an unprecedented nature, and all of Iraq's much-vaunted defences would be needed to stop attacking Coalition forces.

Strategic airlift

The transport units of the various Coalition forces made an invaluable contribution to the Western war effort. Within five days of President Bush declaring the beginning of Desert Shield, USAF C-5 and C-141B transporters had moved five fighter squadrons, an AWACs contingent and a brigade of the

82nd Airborne to Saudi Arabia. The aircraft were also responsible for delivering the Army's 11th Air Defence Brigade, equipped with the Patriots that generated so much interest in the war. The military aircraft were supplemented by activated elements of the Civil Reserve Air Fleet (aircraft owned by private companies, such as FedEx or Southern Air Transport, which can be called up by the American military in the event of war).

As part of Britain's Operation Granby, RAF Coltishall-based Jaguars, like this reconnaissance-configured GR.Mk 1A, were the first RAF aircraft to be sent to the Gulf, wearing their desert pink camouflage.

Disposition of Coalition forces

As the forces of the UN-sanctioned Coalition massed together in the Persian Gulf, an unprecedented amount of air power encircled Iraq, ensuring a swift and decisive start to the forthcoming war.

Straining at the leash, a USN F/A-18C prepares to take-off for a training exercise. Several USN and USMC Hornet squadrons took part in Desert Shield.

Slowly, yet consistently, the Coalition forces built up in the Persian Gulf. Soon it was evident that Iraq was being surrounded by Allied forces in neighbouring countries such as Turkey, Saudi Arabia, Bahrain, Qatar, Oman and the UAE. There were also six US aircraft-carriers in the Gulf and Red Sea, not to mention the significant presence of the other Coalition navies, all enforcing the will of the UN.

Airfields soon became full of aircraft from several differing forces. For example, Doha (Qatar) housed USAF F-16s, Canadian CF-188s, French Mirage F1s and Qatari F1EDAs – it was truly a multinational effort. America's most potent symbol of aircraft power, the B-52G, was, however, located at bases as far away as Diego Garcia in the Indian Ocean.

One of the most important aspects of this grouping together of forces was the cohesion it enforced between the various nations. Although many countries take part in the Red Flag training exercises in the US, this was the first time in decades, for some actually the first time, that they had fought together, and the implications of overseeing these vast assets was enormous.

The positioning of Coalition aircraft was also vitally important. Strike aircraft such as USAF F-111Fs and the RAF and RSAF Tornados were stationed at bases far away from Iraq such as Jeddah in Saudi Arabia or Al Dhafra in Oman, ensuring that they were unlikely to be hit by any unexpected Iraqi 'Scud' missiles or attacking aircraft. Fighter aircraft such as French Mirage 2000s were positioned at bases around the Iraqi border, enabling them to intercept any surprise attacks by Iraqi aircraft.

As Desert Shield progressed, Coalition aircraft flew constant training missions. Fighter aircraft would race towards the Iraqi border, only turning away at the last possible moment, and supporting electronic surveillance aircraft could then monitor any Iraqi radar transmissions. Attack aircraft would practise low level-missions, gaining vital knowledge of how to navigate in the featureless desert. Some RAF Tornados and Jaguars were used to give warships practice in dealing with air threats and often simulated anti-ship missiles.

Coalition problems

The months leading up to Desert Storm were not without problems, however. Politicians around the world were failing to agree on a effective solution to the Iraqi invasion. The US and UK were in favour of a military solution while France, a major exporter to Iraq's war machine, and Russia, who had supplied Iraq with equipment and training, were pushing for a diplomatic end to the crisis, sometimes openly disagreeing with the others' ideas.

There were also a number of non-combat Coalition losses in Operation Desert Shield. A C-5A Galaxy cargo aircraft carrying stores for Saudi Arabia crashed on take-off from Ramstein AFB, Germany, killing all on board. A USAF RF-4C Phantom, an F-111F, two USMC UH-1N Huey helicopters, an RAF Tornado GR.Mk 1, and a Jaguar GR.Mk 1A all crashed over a two-week period in the Gulf, killing all the crewmen. The result was a stringent review of air safety procedures, following which there was a marked decline in accidents.

On 9 January, US Secretary of State Baker met the Iraqi Foreign Minister, Tariq Aziz, in Geneva in a bid to arrive at a settlement acceptable to both sides. The talks, however, broke down after a few hours without agreement. The Security Council deadline for Iraqi withdrawal – 15 January – passed without military action; perhaps, as the Iraqi president told his people, the West had no stomach for a fight. The rest of the world held its breath and waited for the storm.

Maintaining a constant guard against the threat of incursion of Saudi airspace by Iraqi fighters, E-3 AWACs aircraft could usually rely on KC-135 or KC-10 refuellers to help lengthen missions.

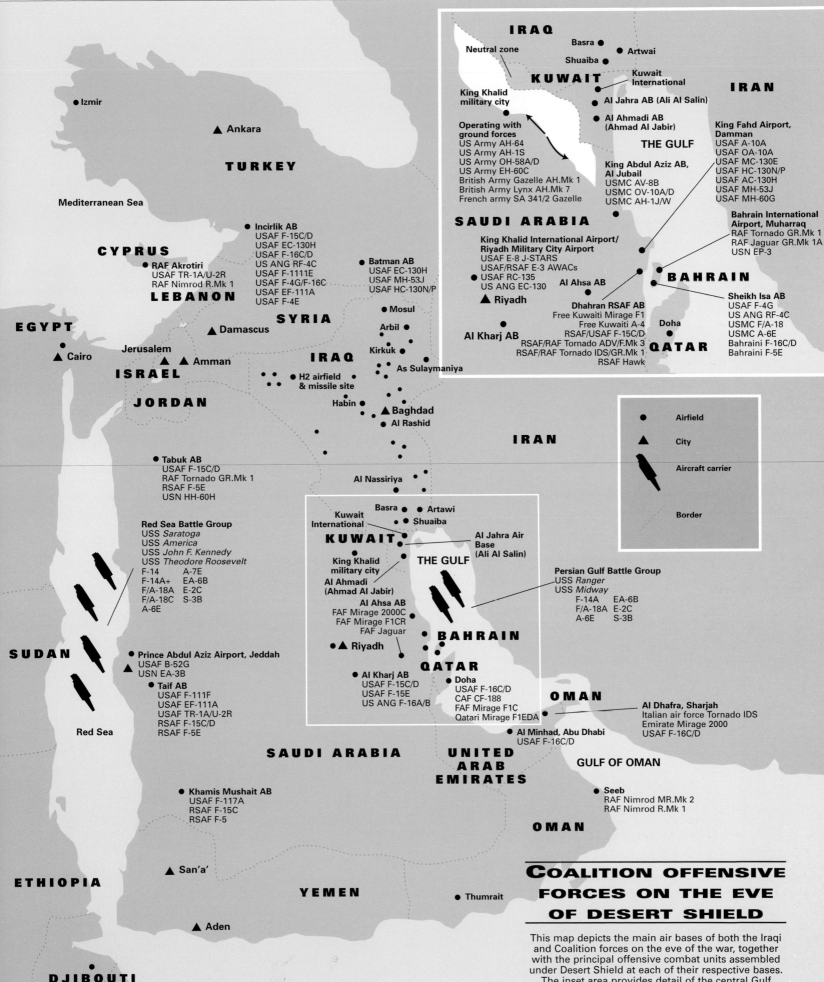

IRAQ

Neutral zone

Basra ● ● Artwai
Shuaiba ●

KUWAIT

Kuwait International

IRAN

King Khalid military city

● Al Jahra AB (Ali Al Salin)

● Al Ahmadi AB (Ahmad Al Jabir)

THE GULF

Operating with ground forces
US Army AH-64
US Army AH-1S
US Army OH-58A/D
US Army EH-60C
British Army Gazelle AH.Mk 1
British Army Lynx AH.Mk 7
French army SA 341/2 Gazelle

King Fahd Airport, Damman
USAF A-10A
USAF OA-10A
USAF MC-130E
USAF HC-130N/P
USAF AC-130H
USAF MH-53J
USAF MH-60G

King Abdul Aziz AB, Al Jubail
USMC AV-8B
USMC OV-10A/D
USMC AH-1J/W

SAUDI ARABIA

King Khalid International Airport/Riyadh Military City Airport
USAF E-8 J-STARS
USAF/RSAF E-3 AWACs
● USAF RC-135
US ANG EC-130
▲ Riyadh

● Al Ahsa AB

Dhahran RSAF AB
Free Kuwaiti Mirage F1
Free Kuwaiti A-4
RSAF/USAF F-15C/D
RSAF/RAF Tornado ADV/F.Mk 3
RSAF/RAF Tornado IDS/GR.Mk 1
RSAF Hawk

Bahrain International Airport, Muharraq
RAF Tornado GR.Mk 1
RAF Jaguar GR.Mk 1A
USN EP-3

BAHRAIN

Doha

Sheikh Isa AB
USAF F-4G
US ANG RF-4C
USMC F/A-18
USMC A-6E
Bahraini F-16C/D
Bahraini F-5E

● Al Kharj AB

QATAR

● Izmir

▲ Ankara

TURKEY

Mediterranean Sea

● Incirlik AB
USAF F-15C/D
USAF EC-130H
USAF F-16C/D
US ANG RF-4C
USAF F-111E
USAF F-4G/F-16C
USAF EF-111A
USAF F-4E

● Batman AB
USAF EC-130H
USAF MH-53J
USAF HC-130N/P

CYPRUS

● RAF Akrotiri
USAF TR-1A/U-2R
RAF Nimrod R.Mk 1

LEBANON

EGYPT

Jerusalem

▲ Damascus

SYRIA

● Mosul

Arbil ●

Kirkuk ●

As Sulaymaniya

▲ Cairo

▲ Amman

ISRAEL

JORDAN

IRAQ

● H2 airfield & missile site

Habin ●

▲ Baghdad

● Al Rashid

IRAN

● Tabuk AB
USAF F-15C/D
RAF Tornado GR.Mk 1
RSAF F-5E
USN HH-60H

● Al Nassiriya

Red Sea Battle Group
USS *Saratoga*
USS *America*
USS *John F. Kennedy*
USS *Theodore Roosevelt*

F-14	A-7E
F-14A+	EA-6B
F/A-18A	E-2C
F/A-18C	S-3B
A-6E	

Basra ● ● Artawi
Shuaiba ●

Kuwait International

KUWAIT

King Khalid military city

Al Ahmadi (Ahmad Al Jabir)

Al Jahra Air Base (Ali Al Salin)

THE GULF

Al Ahsa AB
FAF Mirage 2000C
FAF Mirage F1CR
FAF Jaguar

Persian Gulf Battle Group
USS *Ranger*
USS *Midway*

F-14A	EA-6B
F/A-18A	E-2C
A-6E	S-3B

SUDAN

● Prince Abdul Aziz Airport, Jeddah
▲ USAF B-52G
USN EA-3B

● Taif AB
USAF F-111F
USAF EF-111A
USAF TR-1A/U-2R
RSAF F-15C/D
RSAF F-5E

Red Sea

● ▲ Riyadh

BAHRAIN

QATAR

● Al Kharj AB
USAF F-15C/D
USAF F-15E
US ANG F-16A/B

● Doha
USAF F-16C/D
CAF CF-188
FAF Mirage F1C
Qatari Mirage F1EDA

OMAN

Al Dhafra, Sharjah
Italian air force Tornado IDS
Emirate Mirage 2000
USAF F-16C/D

● Al Minhad, Abu Dhabi
USAF F-16C/D

SAUDI ARABIA

UNITED ARAB EMIRATES

GULF OF OMAN

● Khamis Mushait AB
USAF F-117A
RSAF F-15C
RSAF F-5

● Seeb
RAF Nimrod MR.Mk 2
RAF Nimrod R.Mk 1

OMAN

Legend:
● Airfield
▲ City
Aircraft carrier
Border

ETHIOPIA

▲ San'a'

YEMEN

● Thumrait

▲ Aden

DJIBOUTI

SOMALIA

COALITION OFFENSIVE FORCES ON THE EVE OF DESERT SHIELD

This map depicts the main air bases of both the Iraqi and Coalition forces on the eve of the war, together with the principal offensive combat units assembled under Desert Shield at each of their respective bases. The inset area provides detail of the central Gulf region, where the majority of Allied air power was concentrated. Triangles denote the principal cities.

Desert Storm
Iraqi forces

Left: Iraq operated 40 An-12 'Cubs' from Iraqi Airways in the transport role. One unidentified Iraqi transport aircraft was destroyed by the Coalition and around 40 various types were evacuated to Iran, Mauretania or Tunis. Iran held on to all of the aircraft it received, claiming that they were being kept as 'payment' for damages received in the Iran-Iraq war.

Below: Much of the Iraqi air force was destroyed on the ground within hardened aircraft shelters (HAS). HASs offered some degree of protection to the aircraft within, but many were destroyed, with the damage caused to these 'Fitters' being typical.

Although initially thought of as being a powerful and dangerous adversary, in fact, the Iraqi air force found itself hopelessly outmanned, outgunned and outclassed by the Coalition forces.

When the 1991 Gulf War began, the Iraqi air force possessed some 550 fighters, bombers, attack and reconnaissance aircraft, thus making it the sixth largest air force in the world. However, there are few reliable figures on precise numbers. Many of these aircraft could have been decades old and so could not be compared to Western aircraft. Indeed, in the late 1980s, the Iraqi air force was still listing aged Hawker Hunter and Il-28s in its inventory.

The air force was supplemented by around 40,000 personnel and was commanded by Lieutenant General Hamid Sha'aben al Khazraji. Generally considered to be fairly efficient, the Iraqi air force was somewhat restricted by being tied to a central command and control system, as dictated by the Soviet model of an integrated air defence system which linked SAMs, fighter aircraft and AAA. Its front-line units were split between two major formations – the Air Defence Command and the Air Support Command.

The Air Defence Command was responsible for the defence of strategic sites and airfields, and controlled all fighter-interceptor units as well as air force personnel manning air surveillance radars and reporting systems. The Command was also responsible for those army units equipped with SAMs and AAA for the defence of strategic sites.

To supply airborne warning and control, the Iraqi air force possessed three Il-76 'Candid' transports modified to carry the French Thomson-CSF Tigre radar. However, these aircraft played no part in the war, so their effectiveness has never been satisfactorily judged.

Air Support Command

Air Support Command was responsible for supporting the army's land operations and the navy's sea operations. It controlled all fighter-bomber, bomber and dedicated

Iraqi fighters

At the beginning of the conflict, Iraq possessed a formidable array of fighters. The majority were Soviet-supplied, used in the war against Iran in the 1980s, and were now tasked with defending Iraqi airspace. Initially feared, they were to prove no match for their Western counterparts – during the first Gulf War, only one Iraqi fighter (a MiG-25) shot down a Coalition aircraft.

MiG-29 'Fulcrum-A'
Most capable of all Iraq's fighters, the MiG-29 'Fulcrum' was particularly feared due to its agility. Iraq started the war with approximately 13 'Fulcrums' including a two-seater MiG-29UB. At least five were destroyed during the conflict.

MiG-21MF 'Fishbed-J'
Most numerous of all Soviet exports, the IAF operated 80 MiG-21s in a number of variants and they conducted air defence, attack and training duties. However, they could not compete with Western F-15s, F-16s and F/A-18s.

A major weakness for the IAF was the calibre of its pilots. Saddam Hussein's constant fear of a military coup meant that he kept a tight rein on the armed forces, therefore stifling initiative and crushing morale, skills that are so vital to military air operations.

reconnaissance units within the air force, as well as air strikes on enemy shipping. Air Support Command's main weapon was the Su-24 'Fencer'; if a dedicated chemical weapons attack had been made against the Coalition or Israel by the Iraqis during the war, this aircraft would have been the one most likely to have succeeded.

For transport purposes, the Iraqi air force operated some 45 aircraft, most of them of Soviet origin. The aircraft of the government-owned Iraqi Airways could also be used – its fleet comprised Boeing 707s, 727s, 737s and 747s plus An-12 'Cubs', An-24s 'Cokes' and Il-76 'Candid' freighters.

Offensive forces

One of the greatest problems facing the Iraqi air force was the sheer diversity of the aircraft operated, with no fewer than 500 offensive aircraft. These consisted of 16 different fixed-wing types: the MiG-21 (and Chinese J7), -23, -25, -27, -29, Su-7, -20, -22, -24, -25, Tu-16

(and Chinese B-6), -22, Aero L-39 and Mirage F1. The aircraft were armed with a wide range of weapons including French Exocets, Soviet AA-6 and AA-7 air-to-air missiles and a host of other weapons picked up from Soviet and Western sources. There were also some 160 helicopters of numerous types including Aérospatiale Gazelles, Mil Mi-8s and Mi-24s and Bell 214STs.

The logistical problems involved in keeping all these different types continuously serviceable were enormous. Cases of aircraft being completely cannibalised to provide spares for others were not uncommon. The Iraqis seem to have bought aircraft where and when they were available and with whatever funds were handy at the time.

However, the infrastructure backing up this air force was by no means poor. Modern airfields with extensive protected shelters dotted Iraqi territory and they were often immense in size, in some cases approximately four

times bigger than Heathrow Airport, thus making them difficult to put out of service. Command, control and communications (C³) systems were superb, as was the layered air defence system, rail and road network, industrial base and energy programme. Nevertheless, this all collapsed when confronted with the might of the massed Coalition air forces.

Determined Coalition

From the earliest moments of Desert Storm, all of the hype, expectation and fear surrounding the Iraqi air force evaporated in the face of determined Coalition attack. Few Allied aircraft encountered Iraqi fighters on the opening night of the conflict. Nine Iraqi fighters were downed by American aircraft with no official retaliatory losses (although later it emerged that an F/A-18C was lost to a MiG-25). As the war progressed and as an increasing number of control sites and radar centres was destroyed, it became harder and harder for Iraqi aircraft to even

make it into the air without being detected and destroyed by Coalition forces. There was even a case where one MiG-29, in a moment of panic, shot down its wingman and then flew into the ground.

Eventually the Iraqis, in a decision harking back to the Iran-Iraq war (stemming from the idea that air forces are inferior to their army counterparts), decided to ground their aircraft. This belief was so strong that, shortly before the conflict, Saddam Hussein ironically uttered, "The United States relies on the air force and the air force has never been the decisive factor in the history of war." At the same time, Iraq's forces were still being destroyed on the ground and images of Coalition missiles flying through hangar doors saturated the media.

Iraq's next idea was to place its aircraft in residential areas or near to holy or archeologically important sites in an effort to stop attacks, but this too failed to stop further aircraft destruction. The unexpected step was then taken of evacuating the remaining aircraft from the country, and 130-150 aircraft were removed to Iran, with the possible (though ultimately unsuccessful) idea of bringing them back later in the conflict. A small number of transport aircraft also flew to Mauretania and Tunis.

With this withdrawal, the Iraqi air force seemed to be out of the war. Although their efforts look pitiful when compared to those of the West, it must be noted that, during the previous decade in which the Iraqis had been fighting the Iranians, they had not been faced with an opponent that was as technologically advanced or that had the same training and morale as the Coalition. In Desert Storm, therefore, the Iraqis simply had little choice but to be driven back. General Tony Peak, Chief of Staff for the USAF, spoke thus of the Iraqis: "I think they (the IAF) did rather well under the circumstances. They're a pretty good outfit. They happened to be the second-best air force in the fracas. Having the second-best air force is like having the second-best poker hand – it's often the best strategy to fold early. I think they folded early."

Captured Iraqi aircraft

Not all of the Iraqi aircraft that stayed in Kuwait were destroyed. This Bell Model 214 was captured by the US 1st Marine Division at Kuwait International Airport on 25 February 1991, with its crew being shot in the process. One of many Western aircraft operated by the Iraqis, it was later presented to the Commanding General of the 3rd Marine Aircraft Wing at MCAS El Toro, where it now resides in a museum.

McDonnell Douglas (Boeing) F-15 Eagle

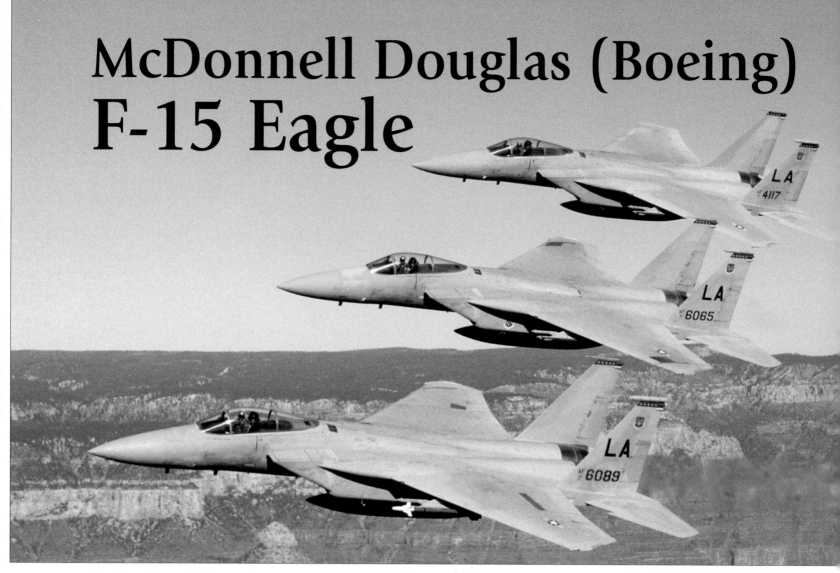

Developed as a fighter with a wide margin of performance and technological superiority over its rivals, the F-15 held the position of being the world's premier fighter for more than 20 years. It has also been developed into a successful strike platform.

Based at Luke AFB, Arizona, with access to large tracts of relatively empty airspace, the 58th Tactical Training Wing was the first recipient of the F-15. Renumbered as the 405th TTW in August 1979, the unit continued to train F-15A/B crews until 1988.

The history of the F-15 dates back to the late 1960s, when a far-reaching specification known as F-X was laid down by the US Air Force. This, in essence, required the basic F-4 weapons load (four Sparrows, four Sidewinders plus a 20-mm Vulcan cannon) to be repackaged into an aircraft optimised for air combat. The eventual result was the F-15 Eagle, which marked a major advance in virtually all areas.

Range and manoeuvrability were markedly improved, while the aircraft's AN/APG-63 radar ushered in a new era of look-down/shoot-down capability. The cockpit was designed to enable the single pilot to extract the maximum fighting capability from the impressive systems, utilising then-novel concepts such as a head-up display and HOTAS controls. The airframe was stressed for sustained high-g turning, while the F100

turbofans were fuel-efficient yet awesomely powerful. From the F-15C/D model onwards, the pilot could in theory also slam the throttles from idle to full without fear of compressor stall (although, in reality, the F100 proved very troublesome in the early days of the F-15). Similarly, the F-15 had a 'carefree' handling system which automatically limited control inputs from the pilot at the outer edges of the flight envelope to prevent departures.

Reaching service status in November 1974, the F-15A (and the equivalent F-15B two-seater) immediately demonstrated a dramatic improvement in combat power over the F-4E Phantom which was, at the time, the USAF's mainstream fighter. In January 1976 the 1st TFW became the first front-line unit to be declared operational. Other USAF units swiftly followed, both at home and overseas.

Multi-role fighter

In USAF service the F-15's repertoire was rapidly expanded to embrace all areas of the fighter role. Its rapid-reaction time, excellent radar and high speed/climb performance allowed it to perform the dedicated interceptor role with ease, and F-15s stood 'Zulu' ground alert in Korea and West Germany, as well as back home. Occupying most F-15s was, and is, the air superiority role, flying sweep, CAP and escort roles.

Israel became the first export customer for the F-15, receiving its first aircraft in December 1976. Israeli F-15A/Bs (locally named Baz) were soon in action against Syrian aircraft, achieving several successes. In 1982 Israeli Eagles scored around 40 kills for no loss during the hectic air fighting against Syrian MiGs over the Beka'a Valley.

Continuing development of the Eagle saw the introduction of

the F-15C/D in 1980, initial deliveries of which went to units in West Germany and Okinawa. The C/D introduced several new features, notably increased g capability, additional internal fuel and the ability to carry conformal fuel tanks along the fuselage sides.

Export eagles

In addition to the re-equipment of some USAF units, F-15C/Ds also went to Israel and Saudi Arabia, the latter country using the type to down two Iranian F-4 Phantom IIs at the height of the Iran-Iraq war in June 1984.

The F-15C/D was also the basis for the F-15J/DJ, the variant in service with the Japanese Air Self-Defence Force. Apart from the first few aircraft, F-15J/DJs were built by Mitsubishi and feature a significant percentage of Japanese equipment.

Left: Selected fighter units received F-15s from 1981 and used the type to effect numerous intercepts of Soviet prowlers. The busiest of these units was the Iceland-based 57th FIS, which patrolled the busy North Atlantic airlanes. Here the 'snooper' is a Tu-95RTs 'Bear-D'.

Like most Eagles worldwide, the JASDF's F-15s were initially armed primarily with AIM-9 and AIM-7 AAMs. This late-production F-15J carries a single Sidewinder on its port inner shoulder pylon.

With the baseline F-15C/D in service, development work turned to a Multi-Stage Improvement Program (MSIP). This primarily involved the adoption of AN/APG-70 radar in place of AN/APG-63 and added AIM-120 AMRAAM capability. The AN/APG-70 provided a vastly improved target detection capability and offered an all-important non-cooperative target recognition (NCTR) function, which allows the Eagle pilot to identify aircraft by type. The first MSIP aircraft were issued to the 33rd TFW, and it was these aircraft which bore the brunt of the air-to-air action in Desert Storm, during which the Eagle notched up 35 confirmed kills against Iraqi opposition. AMRAAMs were carried for the first time during this conflict, although none was fired in anger, the majority of Eagle kills being gained by the AIM-7 Sparrow in medium-range BVR combats.

During initial development it had been envisaged that the F-15 would have a secondary ground-attack role, and early test flights demonstrated the aircraft's ability to drop bombs accurately. However, the initial models were all optimised for air combat, and remain so to the present day.

One outcome of the early ground-attack work was the F-15 'Strike Eagle', a two-seat technology demonstrator developed by McDonnell Douglas and Hughes as a private venture. This aircraft was fitted with a developed AN/APG-63 radar (later AN/APG-70) with a ground mapping function and integrated weapon system. Bombs could be hung from fuselage racks and modified conformal fuel tanks. The aircraft became the basis for McDonnell Douglas's entry in the USAF's Enhanced Tactical Fighter competition which pitted the type against the cranked arrow-wing General Dynamics F-16XL.

In February 1984 the F-15E was announced the winner and production of an eventual 215 got under way, first deliveries being made in April 1988. Production aircraft had a strengthened airframe to allow for higher weights. The combination of its AN/APG-70 radar, LANTIRN targeting/navigation system, fully 'glass' cockpits and heavy weapon load,

the F-15E is arguably the world's finest strike/attack interdictor. Yet underneath the paraphernalia of the attack mission, the aircraft is still an Eagle – the world's best air-to-air fighter with a combat record unmatched by any current aircraft type.

The F-15E is optimised for the overland strike/attack role in all weathers, although it retains a potent air-to-air capability.

F-15E: The 'Mud Hen'

Turning the West's best air-to-air fighter into a nocturnal mud-mover was an idea opposed by many. However, today's F-15E is without doubt the most capable strike/attack platform in the world, while having lost little of its air combat prowess.

All F-15s were built with air-to-ground capability, and wired for the carriage of air-to-ground ordnance. They were originally intended as dual-role aircraft, but the ground attack role was abandoned in 1975, when it was decided not to incorporate the relevant software.

Trials of an air-to-ground F-15 began during 1982, when McDonnell Douglas modified the second TF-15A as the 'Strike Eagle', funding the project itself. The aircraft was conceived as an ETF (Enhanced Tactical Fighter) replacement for the General Dynamics F-111 and was chosen in preference to the 'cranked-wing' F-16XL Fighting Falcon. The 'Strike Eagle' demonstrator was joined by an F-15C and F-15D, which conducted trials with a variety of fuel and ordnance loads, usually with Conformal Fuel Tanks (CFTs) fitted. The resulting F-15E was given the go-ahead on 24 February 1984 and the first production aircraft made its maiden flight on 11 December 1986. McDonnell's 'Strike Eagle' name was not adopted, although some unofficial epithets such as 'Beagle' (Bomber Eagle) and 'Mud Hen' have been used on occasion.

In introducing new avionics and equipment for a 'mud-moving' role not assigned to earlier variants, the F-15E is very much a second-generation Eagle. The aircraft introduced redesigned controls, a wide field of vision HUD, and three CRTs providing multi-purpose displays of navigation, weapons delivery

Above: For many years an F-4E user, the 4th Wing at Seymour Johnson, North Carolina is now the premier F-15E operator, with four squadrons assigned. These examples are from the 335th FS 'Chiefs'. The squadron undertook strike missions over Iraq during Operation Desert Storm in 1991.

Right: The F-15 is potentially the most capable warrior over the battlefield. However, to use the F-15E and its systems to the full requires not only thorough instruction and practice, but also close co-ordination between the two cockpits.

and systems operation. The rear-cockpit WSO employs four multi-purpose CRT terminals for radar, weapons selection and the monitoring of enemy tracking systems. The WSO also operates an AN/APG-70 synthetic aperture radar and Martin-Marietta LANTIRN navigation (AN/AAQ-13) and targeting (AN/AAQ-14) pods. The navigation pod incorporates its own terrain-following radar,

which can be linked to the aircraft's flight control system to allow automatic coupled terrain-following flight. The targeting pod allows the aircraft to self-designate GBU-10 and GBU-24 laser-guided bombs. Basic flight controls are provided for the WSO and the crew sit on ACES II zero-zero ejection seats.

Power for the new variant was initially provided by F100-PW-220 turbofans, as used by the F-15C, with a digital engine control system. However, the powerplant was soon replaced under the Improved Performance Engine programme, whereby GE F110-GE-129 and P&W F100-PW-229 engines were both flown in F-15Es under competitive evaluation;

In Strike Eagle guise, McDonnell Douglas's two-seat F-15B demonstrator, 71-0291, was an awesome aircraft. It is illustrated with a full load of Mk 7 Rockeye CBUs on its wing and fuselage pylons. The aircraft wore both overall grey and two-tone schemes.

This Lakenheath-based F-15E from the 494th 'Panthers' was suitably decorated in tiger-stripe markings. This enabled it to participate in NATO's annual squadron meet of those units carrying a tiger as their emblem.

the Pratt & Whitney engine was eventually selected. Since August 1991 the new engine (from aircraft 90-0233) has been fitted on the production line, and other aircraft will be retrofitted. To adapt the F-15E to the rigours of the low-level role, the aircraft was structurally redesigned for a 16,000-hour life and loads of up to 9g. More use was made of superplastic forming and diffusion bonding in the rear

fuselage, engine bay and on some panels. The fuel tanks were filled with reticulated foam, reducing capacity to 2,019 US gal (7643 litres).

In 1988, the 405th Tactical Training Wing at Luke AFB, AZ, became Tactical Air Command's replacement training unit for the F-15E Eagle, a role since taken over by the 58th Fighter Wing in Air Education and Training

English Eagles

Since the 1960s, RAF Lakenheath has been a cornerstone of Western European defence. Equipped with F-84s, F-86s, F-100s and F-4s, the 48th TFW adopted the F-111F in 1977. It took the 'Earth Pig' into action against Libya and in a starring role in Desert Storm. Following the first Gulf War, the wing began winding down F-111F operations in preparation for the F-15E, the first example, (illustrated) arriving on

21 February 1992. The two F-15E squadrons, 492nd and 494th, have made regular deployments to Aviano to provide night attack cover for the UN ground forces in Bosnia. Another ongoing commitment has been to Operation Provide Comfort – policing the UN safe haven in Northern Iraq.

Command. The first operational F-15Es were delivered to the 4th TFW, Seymour Johnson AFB, NC, replacing the F-4E Phantom.

On 12 August 1990, as the US began Operation Desert Shield, F-15E Eagles from the 336th TFS, 4th TFW, deployed to Al Kharj air base, Saudi Arabia. F-15Es of that wing's 335th TFS followed. During Desert Storm, F-15Es were assigned strike missions against a variety of targets, including five/six-hour sorties in search of 'Scud' missile launch sites. Out of 2,200 sorties totalling 7,700 hours, just two F-15E Eagles were lost in combat.

In 1991, the Secretary of Defense overruled USAF leaders who wanted to keep the F-15E Eagle in production. Although the F-15E is an exceedingly potent warplane for the strike mission, critics point out that its

low wing-loading produces a rough ride, especially for the backseater, and that the aircraft's payload is less than that of the 30-year old F-111. However, this short-sighted decision was later reversed and another small batch of F-15Es was ordered.

In addition, long-standing F-15 operator Saudi Arabia, ordered 72 aircraft, designated F-15S, similar to the American aircraft but lacking certain ECM equipment. Responding to this potential threat from its near neighbour, Israel followed suit with a total order for 25 F-15Is. Known as the Ra'am (Thunder) within IDF/AF service, the aircraft were built almost to the full specification of USAF examples. A further customer emerged in 2002 in the form of South Korea, whose 40 General Electric F110-229 powered F-15K aircraft were delivered between 2005 and 2008.

F-15E Eagle

This aircraft represents that of the 48th FS wing commander, based at RAF Lakenheath, Suffolk, UK. The wing retired its four squadrons of F-111Fs in favour of two F-15E squadrons in 1992. Today, the aircraft fly alongside one squadron of F-15C/D 'fighter' Eagles.

Cockpit
The F-15E has a state-of-the-art cockpit, the pilot having a wide-angle HUD and three MFDs. The WSO has four MFDs. All vital flight and attack inputs are made via an upfront control and stick/throttle controls.

Powerplant
Late production F-15Es, like this one, are fitted with the F100-PW-229 IPE, each offering 29,100 lb (130.9 kN) of thrust with full afterburning.

CFTs
The conformal fuel tanks each hold 723 US gal (2737 litres) of fuel, and have a continuous pylon (with three attachment points) and three stub pylons for the carriage of weapons.

Radar
At the heart of the F-15E's capability is the APG-70 radar, a vastly-improved version of the F-15C's APG-63. As well as having improved air-to-air modes, the APG-70 offers a high-resolution synthetic aperture mapping mode. This allows highly accurate 'patch maps' to be taken of the target area which, in turn, allow the precise designation of the desired aimpoint.

LANTIRN pods
The LANTIRN system consists of the AAQ-13 navigation pod under the starboard intake and the AAQ-14 targeting pod under the port. The AAQ-13 consists of a wide-angle FLIR, which projects an image on the pilot's HUD, and a Texas Instruments terrain-following radar, which interfaces with the aircraft's autopilot system to provide safe low-level flight in all conditions.

Armament
This F-15E is loaded for a close air support/battlefield air interdiction mission with 14 SUU-30H cluster bombs. AIM-9s are carried for self-defence. Lakenheath F-15Es also carry AIM-120 AMRAAMs on the outer launch rail, with Sidewinders on the inner rail.

Chairman of the Joint Chiefs of Staff Powell and Commander of Coalition Forces in the Gulf Schwarzkopf confer at an air base in central Saudi Arabia on the eve of the war.

Planning the war

Desert Storm necessitated months of detailed planning by various coalition strategy-makers. By the time the conflict loomed, the coalition felt confident of achieving certain victory.

On 5 August 1990, three days after Iraq's invasion of Kuwait – which was also when the UN first isolated Iraq politically and economically – President George Bush outlined US aims in the region. They led to the following military objectives: (1) neutralisation of the Iraqi national command; (2) ejection of Iraqi forces from Kuwait and the destruction of Iraq's offensive threat; (3) destruction of known nuclear, biological and chemical weapons; and (4) assistance in the restoration of the Kuwaiti government. Less than three weeks later, General Schwarzkopf, the head of US CENTCOM (Central Command) and of all US forces in the Gulf, briefed General Colin Powell, chairman of the JCS (Joint Chiefs of Staff), on the outlines of a plan to force Iraq from Kuwait. There was no clear-cut plan for the ground forces role, yet the concept of the air campaign had already evolved.

USCINCCENT (Commander in Chief, US Central Command) declared that: "We will initially attack into the Iraqi homeland using air power to decapitate his leadership, command and control, and eliminate his ability to reinforce Iraqi ground forces in Kuwait and southern Iraq. We will then gain undisputed air superiority over Kuwait so that we can subsequently and selectively attack Iraqi ground forces with air power in order to reduce his combat power and destroy reinforcing units."

At this point, no precise 'air campaign plan' existed, although the Soviet threat and the nature of the area had long shaped the expected role of air power in the region. However, there was some concern that this was directed more at the logistics of moving vast forces to the theatre than their activities once they arrived. Generally, there were three phases. Initially, US forces would attempt to discourage an aggressor who was already acting in a hostile manner. Air forces would arrive first with tactical fighter squadrons, heavy airlift aircraft, aerial tankers and airborne command and control aircraft. These would be supported by carrier task groups and Marine Corps and brigade-size Army aviation assets.

Next would come a defensive phase: the United States would gain air superiority against the attacking enemy, protect military bases and attack enemy lines of supply and communication. If needed, air power would also be used for close air support.

Once sufficient forces had arrived and the enemy's combat power had been reduced, counter-offensive operations would begin. The specifics of this last phase received almost no consideration, other than a reference to the tasks of defeating enemy forces and regaining control of key facilities.

This general plan went by the name of Internal Look 90 and, while it was far smaller than the final Desert Strike plan, it offered valuable insights into a Persian Gulf war.

Instant Thunder

Plans for the actual war began to be formulated in greater detail as time passed, though emphasis was still on air power due to the speed with which aviation assets could deploy compared to their ground counterparts. Colonel John A. Warden III and his Checkmate planning team developed Instant Thunder, which called for an intense six-day air campaign with the aim of decapitating Iraqi leadership and destroying its key military capabilities. Warden's campaign revolved around 'centres of gravity' – key elements of the state and the military – the destruction of which would aid in the effort to bring the enemy to its knees. Because Saddam Hussein's ability to lead was all-important, there were to be strikes against telecommunication buildings and command centres. A psychological warfare campaign against the Ba'ath party was also to be carried out. Strikes against electrical power, oil and military production sites and railroads were necessary. The aim of all these strikes was not to maximise civilian casualties but, rather, to demonstrate to the people of Iraq that the United States was attacking Saddam Hussein. Therefore, the reasoning went, by removing him, the war would stop. The plan was enhanced as elements of the Marine Corps and Navy were included.

On 25 August 1990 General Schwarzkopf briefed General Powell on the plan, now code-named Desert Storm. The first phase – the strategic air campaign – was essentially the Instant Thunder plan with an added aim of preventing further Iraqi forces from reaching Kuwait. The second phase was to achieve air superiority over Kuwait. The third phase consisted of air operations to reduce Iraqi ground forces' capability before the ground attack.

The fourth phase, which still required much work, was a ground attack into Kuwait.

This four-phase planning concept was identical to the one executed the following January and February. Schwarzkopf estimated that he could execute the first three phases by October,

Left: According to some military officials, Saddam himself had to be a legitimate military target. His removal would hopefully inspire the Iraqi people to rise up and wrest control from his allies and the all-powerful Ba'ath party.

Below: General Michael Dugan was the outspoken USAF officer who dared to say what others thought and, in doing so, lost his job. Ultimately, USAF planners did target Hussein, as was demonstrated in the Winnebago hunt.

but could not conduct the ground phase until December.

As the planning effort grew, representatives from other coalition forces, including the RAF and RSAF, joined the effort.

The plan was growing in scale. The original Instant Thunder had called for approximately 150 attack aircraft; the plan offered to the president in October by the Black Hole planning team – comprised of 'Jedi Knight' officers, a top secret group formed by Brigadier General Buster C. Glossom – would utilise more than 400 attack aircraft with another 300, including helicopters, for defensive duties. The list of targets was also growing rapidly, nearly tripling in size between August and December.

The importance of the Republican Guard grew as the planning progressed. They were considered important enough by CENTCOM to be included in the first phase of the campaign, identified as a key 'centre of gravity' and a priority target for the air campaign. They constituted a strategic reserve for the Iraqi army, plus they gave essential support to Saddam Hussein's regime. The Black Hole group felt that if the Guard were broken, they could not help Hussein rebuild or retain order in the country. The command went out to block the roads and rail lines south of Basra to prevent the withdrawal of Republican Guard units.

As the amount of forces grew in the region, a tremendous co-ordination and support effort had to be formulated. Air forces from several nations would all be performing different duties. From American F-16s to French Mirage 2000s and all manner of supporting fighters, interceptors, transports and intelligence platforms, the air would be full of aircraft. Every day an ATO (Air Tasking Order) would be issued; the size of a telephone directory, this document would co-ordinate the attacks of all air assets including coalition forces, special operations, naval and marine air

missions, Army ATACMS (Army Tactical Missile System) and helicopter units.

AWACS (Airborne Warning and Control System) would have the major responsibility for control of these forces, and for avoiding mid-air collisions and 'blue on blues', i.e., friendly forces engaging each other. One AWACS crewman later recalled, "It was like running a combination of Chicago, Atlanta, Washington, Denver, New York and Los Angeles air traffic control, and doing so in the middle of a war."

Outspoken Dugan

The planning for the war was not without problems. In September 1990, General Michael Dugan, the USAF chief of staff, revealed America's targeting plans to the media, an act which he claimed was authorised by the Joint Chiefs. This list was far more comprehensive than people had been expecting if the sole aim was to merely liberate Kuwait. For this, Dugan lost his job. He had advocated a massive bombing campaign against Baghdad and, in particular, Saddam Hussein. This, he believed, would be the only way to force Iraq from Kuwait. Dugan thought that the military should have been given a relatively free hand on the choice of targets and that political considerations should be ignored. "Going for Saddam, his family, his personal guard and his mistress," as General Dugan put it, "might make military sense, especially as Iraq's fortunes rely solely on his directives." Politically, though, such aims could never be given official approval. The majority of America's coalition partners and other UN members would have voted against any Washington stand against Saddam if they thought his death and the destruction of Iraq's military capability were being planned. However, as the war progressed, many of Dugan's predictions seemed to be validated.

In December 1990, the designers of the air campaign came together when the plans for the subsequent phases and a combined coalition air force operation emerged. The plan was highly secret, so secret in fact that most non-US aircraft would not be included in the initial attack. The size of the coalition air forces had grown, allowing flexibility in assets for various parts of the campaign. By 15 January, these forces consisted of more than 1,000 fixed-wing attack aircraft and another 800 air defence fighters and electronic combat aircraft.

Two days later, when the air campaign began, planners and commanders were confident that the war could be won. They expected only low casualties, perhaps 100 or so losses, and they thought that the objectives set out in the initial plan could be met. There were

concerns that the Iraqis might strike first, but the coalition defences seemed strong enough to repulse them. The threat of chemical warfare was also lurking, but it would be more of a danger to ground forces than the air forces.

Planners had little doubt that within a month the Iraqi army would flee Kuwait or, more likely, lie shattered in place; that Iraqi military industry and the Iraqi air force would be destroyed; and that Saddam Hussein's grip on Iraq would be, if not removed, then weakened beyond repair. General Powell claimed that "air power is the decisive arm so far, and I expect it will be the decisive arm until the end of the campaign, even if ground forces and amphibious forces are added to the equation. If anything, I expect air power to be even more decisive in the days and weeks ahead."

'Scud' missile launchers

One group of targets that came to be more closely studied later in the planning was the 'Scud' missile launchers, some of which were expected to escape detection and fire their weapons. Although early plans had intended to attack fixed 'Scud' sites, they had no strategy for a search-and-destroy scheme for dealing with the mobile launchers. The Black Hole regarded 'Scuds' as a nuisance weapon, with little strategic or operational ability due to their poor accuracy, but of great political use. If they were fired at Israel and the Israelis responded, the coalition could potentially fall apart. The coalition relied on Arab unity against Iraq and Hussein, but if the Israelis entered the conflict the Arabs would pull out, leaving the coalition in tatters and providing Hussein with an embarrassing victory. The strategists responded by making provisions for attacking fixed sites, support bases and production facilities, but left the mobile launchers alone.

Air war chronology

An F/A-18C Hornet patrols the skies above Kuwait while, in the background, two of the oil wells lit by the Iraqis belches smoke and adds to the terrible pollution in the region.

The war in the Gulf was conducted at lightning speed by the most high-tech force ever assembled. From the start of the campaign, the Iraqi war machine was devastated by the superior Coalition air forces.

16 July to 1 August 1990

Iraq accused Kuwait and the UAE of aggression and claimed that Kuwait was part of Iraqi territory. Iraqi troops massed on the Kuwait border. Urgent negotiations between Gulf states were ultimately fruitless.

2 August 1990 to 16 January 1991

At 2.00 a.m on 2 August, Iraqi troops crossed the border and rapidly seized Kuwait. The UN urged immediate action. George Bush ordered implementation of Desert Shield, and USAF aircraft moved quickly to the region. The UK also announced its intention to send troops. Over the next six months, forces of several nations massed in Saudi Arabia and the surrounding areas, in the largest mobilisation of armed forces since World War II.

17 January to 25 January 1991

With the UN deadline over, US Army AH-64 Apaches destroyed a radar site in Iraq, thereby creating a corridor which allowed waves of Coalition aircraft to proceed to their targets undetected. F-117 'Stealth' fighters from sites in Saudi Arabia proceeded to destroy air defence installations west of Baghdad. With attendant fighters such as F-15Cs providing cover, attack aircraft such as Tornado IDS, F-15Es and F-111s attacked runways, communications and other high-value targets. A number of air-to-air kills were made while the Coalition also suffered several losses.

The Iraqis responded by firing a 'Scud' missile at Dhahran, but this was intercepted by a Patriot missile and destroyed – the first ever operational shoot-down of a ballistic missile. By the end of

17 January, the Coalition had flown over 2,000 sorties.

Over the next few days, more 'Scud' missiles were fired unsuccessfully at targets in Israel and Saudi Arabia. Airfields and air-related targets continued to be destroyed, while B-52s and A-10s attacked targets in Kuwait. 'The Great 'Scud Hunt' also began, with F-15Es hunting for the mobile launchers. Iraq's air force continued to take heavy losses. The US Marine Corps began to use its AH-1W Cobra helicopters to attack ground targets in Kuwait. More 'Scud' missiles were launched at Coalition sites, but most were downed by Patriot missiles. The Coalition also began to attack hardened aircraft shelters at Iraqi airfields. Allied naval forces captured the small island of Qaruh off Kuwait. In response, Iraqi forces began to pump oil into the sea, causing a massive oil slick off the coast, intended to hamper Allied naval operations in the Gulf.

26 January to 10 February 1991

Coalition attention was now partly directed at hitting targets in southern Iraq and Kuwait in preparation for the ground offensive. Iraq's high command began to evacuate its aircraft to Iran in the vain belief that this would save its remaining air forces; many aircraft were shot down en-route.

To halt the flow of oil into the Persian Gulf, three F-111Fs of the 48th TFW delivered a precision attack with GBU-15s on the two pumping stations involved.

With their powerful GAU-8 Avenger cannon, A-10 Thunderbolts devastated Iraqi armour, destroying hundreds of tanks. Two A-10s even managed to down Iraqi helicopters.

By the end of January, more than 100 Iraqi aircraft had fled to Iran and several more had been downed. More Iraqi naval vessels were destroyed by Allied naval helicopters, RAF Tornados continued to attack Iraqi airfields and F-111Fs began a sustained campaign against bridges that formed part of the Iraqi supply route. On 30 January, Iraqi forces began to make short thrusts into Saudi Arabia, but they were repulsed by AH-1 Cobras and AV-8Bs. Eventually, one force managed to reach the abandoned town of Khafji. In an attack to re-take the town, the USMC lost its first troops of the conflict. A-10s and AH-1s were called in to destroy Iraqi tanks.

Allied forces continued to attack Iraqi ground forces and by the 30 January, it was announced that the Coalition had achieved total air superiority over the Iraqi air force.

Attacks were now beginning to concentrate on the Republican Guard and, by 5 February, it was claimed that a third of its tanks had been destroyed. The Iraqis now made no attempt to mount defensive air missions against the Allies. B-52s, operating out of RAF Fairford, Gloucestershire, began to make attacks on Iraqi positions.

11 February to 23 February 1991

By now, the systematic attack of Iraqi forward positions was at an advanced stage and Allied

planners turned once more to targeting Iraqi air fields.

RAF Tornados began to use the TIALD (Thermal Imaging and Laser Designation) pod, while USAF F-15Es destroyed four mobile 'Scud' launchers.

In an unfortunate accident on 13 February, F-117s dropped two laser-guided bombs on a bunker thought to be a command facility but which was, in fact, housing civilians; the attack killed and injured some 300 people.

On one tank-busting mission, 46 GBU-12-armed F-111Fs destroyed 132 tanks, representing a 71 per cent hit rate under operational conditions.

On 15 February, the Iraqis released a press statement claiming that they were to pull out of Kuwait, but when their conditions for withdrawal became apparent, the deal fell through. Special Operations MC-130s also began to drop BLU-82 'Big Blue' weapons to destroy minefields.

President Hussein delivered a speech promising terrible losses for the Coalition if it dared to launch a ground offensive. The following day, President Bush declared that if Iraq had not pulled out of Kuwait by 20.00 on 23 February, they would be removed by force. The Iraqis failed to withdraw, but continued to set fire to oil wells in the desert. A-10s equipped with Maverick missiles were tasked with destroying the valves on the pipes to halt the flow of oil.

24 February to 28 February 1991

US, British and French armoured divisions were now poised to launch a series of thrusts aimed at outflanking the Iraqi lines. The huge force had managed to manoeuvre into position completely undetected due to Iraq's failure to put any reconnaissance aircraft in the air.

On 24 February at 04:00, Coalition troops with strong air and artillery support attacked Iraqi units in Kuwait and southern Iraq. In the largest helicopter assault operation ever launched, 2,000 men of the US 101st Airborne Division, transported by 100 UH-60 Blackhawks and CH-47 Chinooks and escorted by attack helicopters seized a position 50 miles (80 km) into Iraq.

The following day, in response to Allied attacks, Republican Guard units mounted a counterattack but this was blunted by A-10 Thunderbolts. Allied helicopters continued to harass Iraqi ground units while the Iraqis continued to light oil wells. The Iraqis also fired a 'Scud' at Dhahran, but it missed and hit a building at nearby Khobar which was billeting US troops – 28 died and 89 were wounded.

On 26 February, Saddam Hussein announced that his forces were pulling out of Kuwait and that it was no longer a part of Iraq. However, Allied ground forces continued to engage enemy forces. During the morning, Iraqi forces pulled out of Kuwait city; the great stream of Iraqi forces departing the area caught the eye of a J-STARS, and USMC aircraft were called in to smash them. By the end of the day, 21 divisions had been destroyed.

The following day, the Iraqi ambassador stated that Iraq was ready to agree with all the UN's resolutions. However, President Bush demanded assurances of surrender from Hussein himself.

In the last attack on Baghdad of the war, two F-111Fs of the 48th TFW each dropped a single GBU-28 'bunker-buster' bomb on the important underground command centre at Al Taji airfield, north of Baghdad.

At midnight on 28 February, President Bush declared a ceasefire. On hearing this, the Iraqis claimed victory, but decided to abide by the ceasefire.

The war was over and for the first time in history, air power had lived up to all of its expectations, it had smashed Iraq's defences and devastated its economy. It had been one of the most one-sided conflicts ever.

COALITION COMBAT LOSSES		
DATE	AIRCRAFT	MEANS OF DESTRUCTION
17 Jan 1991	F-15E	AAA
17 Jan 1991	Tornado GR.Mk 1	AAA
17 Jan 1991	A-4KU (KAF)	SAM
17 Jan 1991	F/A-18C	MiG-25
17 Jan 1991	Tornado GR.Mk.1	SAM
17 Jan 1991	A-6E	SAM
18 Jan 1991	IDS (ItAF)	?
18 Jan 1991	OV-10A	SAM
19 Jan 1991	Tornado GR.Mk 1	SAM
19 Jan 1991	Tornado GR.Mk 1	SAM
19 Jan 1991	F-15E	SAM
19 Jan 1991	Tornado GR.Mk 1	AAA
19 Jan 1991	F-16C	AAA
19 Jan 1991	F-4G	AAA
20 Jan 1991	Tornado GR.Mk 1	SAM
21 Jan 1991	F-14A+	SA-2
22 Jan 1991	Tornado GR.Mk 1	?
22 Jan 1991	AV-8B	Pilot error
23 Jan 1991	F-16	Mechanical failure
24 Jan 1991	Tornado GR.Mk 1	Mechanical failure
24 Jan 1991	F/A-18	Mechanical failure
28 Jan 1991	AV-8B	AAA
31 Jan 1991	AC-130H	SAM
02 Feb 1991	A-10	SAM
02 Feb 1991	A-6E	Pilot error
02 Feb 1991	B-52G	AAA
03 Feb 1991	A-7E	Mechanical failure
05 Feb 1991	F/A-18A	?
07 Feb 1991	A-7E	Mechanical failure
07 Feb 1991	A-6E	Mechanical failure
07 Feb 1991	Tornado GR.Mk 1	SAM
09 Feb 1991	AV-8B	SAM
13 Feb 1991	F-5E (RSAF)	?
13 Feb 1991	F-15	?
14 Feb 1991	EF-111A	Pilot error
14 Feb 1991	A-10A	SAM
14 Feb 1991	A-10A	SAM
14 Feb 1991	Tornado GR.Mk 1	SA-2
15 Feb 1991	F-16C	?
17 Feb 1991	F-16C	Engine malfunction
19 Feb 1991	OA-10A	SAM
22 Feb 1991	A-10	SAM
22 Feb 1991	AV-8B	SAM
27 Feb 1991	OA-10	SAM
27 Feb 1991	AV-8B	AAA
27 Feb 1991	F-16C	?
27 Feb 1991	F-16C	AAA
27 Feb 1991	F-16C	SA-16
27 Feb 1991	UH-60	?
27 Feb 1991	AV-8B	?
27 Feb 1991	OA-10A	Crashed, landing in bad weather

Most air forces also suffered non-combat losses, before, during and after the conflict and these numbered approximately 43 in total. The losses were attributed to various causes, including mechanical problems and pilot error.

AERIAL VICTORIES			
DATE	IAF AIRCRAFT DESTROYED	ALLIED AIRCRAFT/ UNIT	KILL BY
17 Jan 91	Mirage F1	EF-111A/43 ECS	GRND
17 Jan 91	MiG-29	F-15C/58 TFS	AIM-7
17 Jan 91	Mirage F1	F-15C/58 TFS	AIM-7
17 Jan 91	Mirage F1	F-15C/58 TFS	GRND
17 Jan 91	Mirage F1	F-15C/71 TFS	AIM-7
17 Jan 91	MiG-29	F-15C/58 TFS	AIM-7
17 Jan 91	MiG-29	F-15C/59 TFS	AIM-7
17 Jan 91	F-7 (MiG-21)	F/A-18C/VFA-81	AIM-9
17 Jan 91	F-7 (MiG-21)	F/A-18C/VFA-81	AIM-9
19 Jan 91	MiG-25	F-15C/58 TFS	AIM-7
19 Jan 91	MiG-25	F-15C/58 TFS	AIM-7
19 Jan 91	MiG-29	F-15C/58 TFS	GRND
19 Jan 91	MiG-29	F-15C/58 TFS	AIM-7
19 Jan 91	Mirage F1	F-15C/525 TFS	AIM-7
19 Jan 91	Mirage F1	F-15C/525 TFS	AIM-7
24 Jan 91	Mirage F1	F-15C/No. 13	AIM-7
24 Jan 91	Mirage F1	F-15C/No. 13	AIM-7
26 Jan 91	MiG-23	F-15C/59 TFS	AIM-7
26 Jan 91	MiG-23	F-15C/58 TFS	AIM-7
27 Jan 91	MiG-23	F-15C/58 TFS	AIM-7
27 Jan 91	MiG-23	F-15C/53 TFS	AIM-9
27 Jan 91	MiG-23	F-15C/53 TFS	AIM-9
27 Jan 91	MiG-23	F-15C/53 TFS	AIM-7
27 Jan 91	Mirage F1	F-15C/53 TFS	AIM-7
29 Jan 91	MiG-23	F-15C/32 TFS	AIM-7
29 Jan 91	MiG-23	F-15C/58 TFS	AIM-7
02 Feb 91	IL-76	F-15C/525 TFS	AIM-7
06 Feb 91	MiG-21	F-15C/53 TFS	AIM-9
06 Feb 91	MiG-21	F-15C/53 TFS	AIM-9
06 Feb 91	Su-25	F-15C/53 TFS	AIM-9
06 Feb 91	Su-25	F-15C/53 TFS	AIM-9
06 Feb 91	BO-105	A-10A/706 TFS	30-mm
06 Feb 91	Mi-8	F-14A/VF-1	AIM-9M
07 Feb 91	Su-7 or -17	F-15C/58 TFS	AIM-7
07 Feb 91	Su-7 or -17	F-15C/58 TFS	AIM-7
07 Feb 91	Su-7 or -17	F-15C/33 TFS	AIM-7
07 Feb 91	Helicopter	F-15C/22 TFS	AIM-7
11 Feb 91	Helicopter (Puma)	2 x F-15C/525 TFS	AIM-7
15 Feb 91	Mi-8	A-10A/511 TFS	30-mm
20 Mar 91	Su-22	F-15C/22 TFS	AIM-9
22 Mar 91	Su-22	F-15C/53 TFS	AIM-9
22 Mar 91	PC-9	F-15C/53 TFS	GRND

GRND = Aircraft flew into the ground
30-mm = GAU-8 30-mm Avenger cannon

In a press meeting on day two of the war, Lt General Chuck Horner shows video tape from gunsight cameras aboard US aircraft during air raids on Iraqi positions. The press were kept informed of most military activities during the war, images being broadcast all over the world.

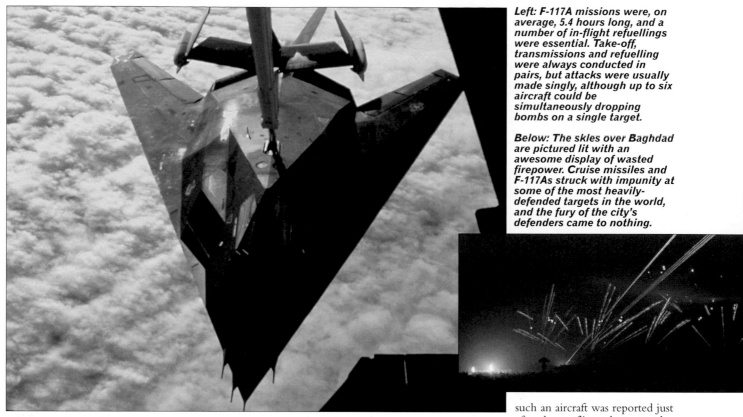

Left: F-117A missions were, on average, 5.4 hours long, and a number of in-flight refuellings were essential. Take-off, transmissions and refuelling were always conducted in pairs, but attacks were usually made singly, although up to six aircraft could be simultaneously dropping bombs on a single target.

Below: The skies over Baghdad are pictured lit with an awesome display of wasted firepower. Cruise missiles and F-117As struck with impunity at some of the most heavily-defended targets in the world, and the fury of the city's defenders came to nothing.

High technology in the Gulf

The 1991 Gulf War will always be remembered for being a conflict in which television played a large part. Cameras captured nearly every aspect of the Coalition effort, both in the air and on the ground, revealing to the world the awesome results of decades of Cold War expenditure.

The real nature of Desert Storm was brought home to many by the sight of missiles plunging through the windows of buildings or of F-117s preparing to strike another Iraqi target as they peeled away from a refuelling aircraft. Television companies such as CNN showed footage of B-52 or ship-launched Tomahawk cruise missiles as they followed roads through Baghdad, and of Patriot missile blasting Iraqi 'Scuds' out of the sky. The first Gulf War was a technological battle like no other before it, in which the West's finest equipment was displayed in all its devastating glory.

Desert ghost

Undoubtedly, the aircraft that attracted the most attention during the war was the F-117A Nighthawk. Although the 'stealth' fighter made a brief appearance over the skies of Panama during that conflict, Desert Storm was the F-117's first official overseas deployment.

The 'stealth' fighter, with its faceted fuselage and low radar cross-section, was immediately tasked with the most demanding missions of the war – striking at strategic targets in heavily-defended areas of Iraq. Accurate INS navigation took the F-117A to the target area. The pilot then used FLIR to locate and positively identify the target, followed by tracking, bomb release and laser designation using the downward-looking infra-red/laser turret. Such were the characteristics of many of the F-117A's targets that it had to operate to the full extent of its abilities as it orbited a target while the pilot ascertained the exact aim-point (often small and well concealed). Conventional aircraft would not have been survivable enough to pinpoint the required targets in the majority of these cases.

No information has been released so far as to whether Iraqi forces were able to track the Nighthawk, but the fact that none of the aircraft was damaged seems to signify that they did not have this capability. While some infra-red sensors may have picked up heat signatures, the F-117A's unique ceramic-tile 'platypus' exhausts reduced any IR trace, thus making the aircraft difficult to identify.

One aircraft rumoured to be operating in the Gulf was the TR-3A, although this is still unconfirmed and the types existence has not been confirmed. Supposed evidence of such an aircraft was reported just after the conflict, when several were believed to be in USAF service alongside F-117A units. These aircraft were claimed to be reconnaissance platforms and came to light when examples of target designation film were discovered. The images were supposedly captured through an F-117A's FLIR but, on closer inspection, seemed to have come from another aircraft.

Reconnaissance assets

One of the aircraft to make its combat debut in Desert Storm was the E-8 J-STARS (Joint Surveillance and Attack Radar System). Two E-8s, which were still in the development stage, were rushed to the Gulf only hours before the conflict. Every night thereafter, one of the two aircraft flew wide-area surveillance and targeting missions over Iraq.

UAVs launched from battleships circled prospective targets and provided valuable targeting data for gunners, enabling them to accurately hit targets and often take them by complete surprise.

Before AH-64 Apache pilots set off, a UAV would sometimes be launched to fly the proposed mission route order to gain vital intelligence on enemy defences and terrain.

enhanced aiming capability and were able to enter buildings through windows or ventilation shafts; BLU-82 (15,000-lb; 6804-kg) 'Daisy Cutter' bombs were used to set off minefields; GBU-28 'Deep Throats' were introduced late in the war to penetrate Iraqi bunkers, with one success; Tomahawk cruise missiles picked out targets from hundreds of miles away, while the latest generation of Sparrows destroyed the remnants of Iraq's air force.

The first Gulf War demonstrated America's military prowess in matters technological, even in this era of downsized forces. Before the conflict, Iraq's war machine had been made to appear unstoppable and numerous 'pundits' had appeared in the media claiming that the Coalition would suffer horrific losses. Instead, Iraq wilted under the might of Coalition air power and could offer little resistance to the high-tech wave that engulfed it.

However, this modern war of high-speed action and television cameras was not without its faults. When the world was confronted with images of massacred Iraqi troops on the road to Basra, it was horrified; the impersonality of modern technological warfare – with TV and computer screens – had distorted people's perceptions of the true nature of war.

It is worth noting that, while the conflict did utilise the latest military equipment, there was also a place for technology that was sometimes decades old. 1950s-vintage B-52s carpet-bombed the battlefield; Vietnam-era F-4G Phantom 'Wild Weasel' aircraft, Buccaneer bombers and C-130 Hercules transports were often flown by pilots younger than the airframes in which they sat. It was this combination of proven systems and high-technology, together with superbly trained and highly disciplined troops, that enabled the Coalition to enjoy the success it achieved.

J-STARS was intended to achieve for the land war what the E-3 Sentry does for the air war, namely to provide a complete picture of vehicles in a given area. A giant Norden side-looking radar is mounted underneath a Boeing 707 airframe, with operator stations inside the cabin. In SAR (Synthetic Aperture Radar) mode, it can detect and locate stationary objects such as parked armour. By alternating the SAR mode with a Doppler moving target mode, the radar can accurately plot slow-moving objects and display an overall tactical picture on screen.

During the first Gulf War, its systems beamed back real-time data on everything from the movement of 'Scud' missile launchers to the location of concertina-wire barriers and traffic on previously undetected military roads. On one occasion,

Laser-guided bombs accounted for the destruction of 37 highway and nine railway bridges during the conflict, denying Iraqi forces access to vital supplies and reinforcements.

J-STARS detected an Iraqi convoy carrying 'Frog' surface-to-surface missiles fitted with chemical munitions. US officers immediately targeted the convoy and it was destroyed by F-16s. So successful was the J-STARS that, after the conflict, several military leaders claimed that the US would never fight another battle without such an aircraft.

Drones and UAVs

Though by no means a new invention, the use of drones and other remotely-piloted vehicles (RPVs) in the Gulf proved highly successful. UAV (Unmanned Aerial Vehicle) units were attached to army, navy and marine units, flying some 300 missions and being used for a number of tasks. Perhaps the most devastating UAVs were those attached to the USS *Wisconsin* and USS *Missouri*. These 14-ft (4.26-m) long Pioneer vehicles, driven by two 26-hp (19.4-kW) two-stroke engines, were tasked with reconnaissance and intelligence-gathering as well as searching for targets for each battleship's 16-in guns. Equipped with high-quality video sensors, the UAVs could operate under adverse conditions, often in areas where other aircraft could not survive. On one occasion, a Pioneer from USS *Wisconsin* spotted an Iraqi supply vehicle and followed it to an unknown bunker complex. After waiting for the forces inside to emerge, the *Wisconsin* fired its 2,000-lb

(907-kg) shells at the unwary troopers. On another occasion Iraqi troops, who had been subjected to a devastating barrage from the *Missouri*, surrendered to a UAV.

The UAV's companion, the drone, was also used extensively in the conflict. Launched from attacking aircraft, these decoys would be fired ahead of advancing forces towards defending SAMs. The SAMs would be fired at the drones and then the attacking 'Wild Weasel' aircraft, such as F-4Gs, would destroy the SAMs with Anti-Radiation Missiles (ARMs).

Of all the weapons used in the conflict, the HARM (High-Speed Anti-Radiation Missile) and ALARM (Air-Launched Anti-Radiation Missile) systems played possibly the most important role. It was these weapons that destroyed Iraq's ground-based defence system of radar-laid AAA and SAMs. The missiles would home in on the radar emissions and destroy the emitter. As the war progressed, Iraqi radar operators, recognising the lethal nature of these systems, would either shut the weapons off completely (therefore rendering them useless), or would quickly flick them on and off in order to gain an impression of the enemy's location, but this was still often enough to attract attention from ARMs.

Other weapons in the Gulf proved equally devastating: laser-guided bombs, though not a new development, had a further

Right: The 1991 Gulf War was the first conflict in which the BVR (Beyond Visual Range) missile achieved a significant number of kills. Pictured here is a French Super R530D, carried by the Mirage 2000s shown in the background.

Reconnaissance and surveillance

RC-135s put in long hours during Desert Storm, with 14-hour missions being the norm. Despite this, the mission-capable rate remained at 90 per cent throughout the conflict.

The gathering of intelligence on enemy movements is vital in any war and, during Desert Storm, the Coalition utilised several types of intelligence-gathering platforms, with mixed results.

Two E-8 J-STARS aircraft took part in Desert Storm and were constantly in demand from air and ground commanders who utilised their data to vector friendly forces onto or, indeed, away from enemy ground units.

Reconnaissance assets in Desert Storm could be roughly divided into three categories: space systems, strategic platforms and tactical aircraft. The spacecraft included six meteorological satellites, three Defence Support Program satellites that scanned for the signature heat bloom of launching 'Scuds', and two civil satellites, the US LANDSAT and the French SPOT.

Strategic reconnaissance platforms were dominated in numbers, like so many other areas of this conflict, by US forces. A total of nine RC-135 Rivet Joints in the U, V and W variants was used to gather electronic emissions and they operated in the south and north of the region. The ageing aircraft, "all old enough to vote", studied enemy communications, undertook electronic warfare missions and monitored Iraqi air-defence radars. Particular Rivet Joint radar collection targets were the lower-frequency Iraqi early warning radars that may have had the potential to detect F-117A 'stealth' aircraft. It was also Rivet Joint aircraft that produced the information which demonstrated that Iraqi air-defence radars would shut down as soon as they detected the action of F-4G 'Wild Weasel' aircraft switching on their fire-control radars, therefore demonstrating the effectiveness of the 'Weasel'. Moreover, the Elint gathered by RC-135s was increased further by the ability of the Rivet Joint to provide its information to ground commanders on a real-time basis.

Five U-2s/TR-1s took part in Desert Storm, using their

The 1704th Reconnaissance Squadron (Provisional) was established at Taif, Saudi Arabia, with U-2Rs and TR-1As. Dozens of missions were flown throughout the conflict, gathering vital Comint and Elint.

Two RAF Jaguar GR.Mk 1As were based at Bahrain and assisted in the Coalition hunt for 'Scuds' from 11 February 1991. One aircraft would carry the standard BAe pod (illustrated), while the other would carry the LOROP pod, both on centreline mounts.

ASARS-2 nose-mounted radar to peer deep into Kuwait and Iraq, gathering information on truck and armoured vehicle movements. These aircraft were also used in their more traditional photo-reconnaissance role, but this mission was often hampered by poor weather or by the palls of smoke that hung over the battlefields after the Iraqis torched the oil wells.

Performing similar roles, but for air operations and land operations, respectively, were the E-3 AWACS and the E-8 J-STARS. AWACS aircraft kept up a steady patrol above Saudi airspace, They kept an ever-watchful eye out for attacking Iraqi fighters, detailing F-15s, Tornado F.Mk 3s and Mirage 2000s to protect vulnerable transport, attack and intelligence aircraft. The E-8 J-STARS monitored the movements of Iraqi ground forces, therefore enabling allied commanders to ambush advancing armoured columns with air strikes miles before they were able to engage Coalition forces.

A number of other forces contributed to the strategic effort; the US Navy provided EP-3Es and EA-3Bs, the US Army RC-12s, RV-1Ds and EH-60s,

while the Marines had at least one Senior Warrior C-130 in action. The RAF provided the Nimrod R.Mk 1 and MR.Mk 2s, although the presence of the R.Mk 1 in the region has never been officially confirmed, despite the presence of battle honours. France deployed one EC.160 Gabriel and two Elint-modified SA 330 Pumas. It is also believed that there was a number of other Elint platforms, both US and allied, whose secret work is likely to remain classified for many years.

Shortfall

Despite this collection of extravagant intelligence-gathering platforms, the planners of the war still faced the problem that none of these aircraft was capable of operating over enemy airspace with impunity. Even the high-flying U-2s were subject to regular shadowing from MiG-25s. This shortfall of real-time enemy surveillance caused many problems and on one occasion, due to the lack of up-to-date satellite coverage, General Schwarzkopf is said to have growled, "Get me some SR-71 coverage". Indeed, it was partly this shortfall that later prompted

the USAF to temporarily reintroduce a pair of Blackbirds.

The number of dedicated tactical reconnaissance aircraft in the Gulf proved to be woefully deficient. At the beginning of the conflict, the USAF could only muster six ageing RF-4Cs and, even by its end, merely 24 such aircraft had been used. Indeed, out of these 24, 12 did not arrive until the very beginning of the air war and six were based in Turkey. The RF-4Cs carried out daytime (only) tactical surveillance, taking part in the 'Great 'Scud' Hunt'. Tac-recon aircraft were awarded a low priority by the USAF, with further RF-4Cs being denied due to 'lack of ramp space'. The USAF had been scaling down its tac-recon force for some years, as had other US forces; the US Marines retired its own version of the reconnaissance Phantom, the RF-4B, only months before the war and prior to an operational replacement being available.

Other allied forces were able to muster a number of dedicated tactical reconnaissance aircraft. Six GR.Mk 1A Tornados, with their filmless Tornado Infra-Red Reconnaissance System (TIRRS), performed sterling work searching for 'Scuds' in the Iraqi desert. The Armée de l'Air operated the Mirage F1CR, although it was initially grounded due to fears of confusion with Iraqi Mirage aircraft. Saudi Arabia also flew 10 RF-5E Tigereyes.

To help bridge the reconnaissance gap, a number of fighter aircraft flew missions equipped with camera or surveillance pods. Examples included RAF Jaguars with

LOROP (LOng-Range, Oblique Photography) pods and US Navy F-14s with TARPS (Tactical Air Reconnaissance Pod Systems).

The US Army, Navy and, in particular, the US Marines also flew Pioneer unmanned aerial vehicles (UAVs); in all, these flew some 300 sorties in a variety of night or day missions. However, these remotely-piloted vehicles had neither the range nor the capability for large-scale reconnaissance.

Conclusions

Desert Storm highlighted a number of serious shortcomings in the reconnaissance and intelligence-gathering capabilities of the US military. While satellites and aircraft like the U-2 could provide images of fixed sites and cities, they were of little use to troops in the field. At his post-war testimony to Congress, General Schwarzkopf claimed that "the intelligence-gathering community as a whole did a great job....but as a theatre commander he was not well served". Intelligence that was being gathered was often not being analysed correctly and there were wild discrepancies about the sizes of enemy forces, performance of weapons or the numbers of vehicles being destroyed.

Ultimately, the problems were that there were inadequate numbers of aircraft to penetrate enemy airspace to gather reconnaissance of enemy targets, and the satellites that were so heavily relied upon were hampered by poor weather conditions, smoke and time-delays. Unless it is ever proven that the unconfirmed TR-3A, the near mythical Aurora or some other exotic intelligence-gathering aircraft was used to collect data during Desert Storm, it seems that reconnaissance and surveillance were one of the few aspects of the Coalition effort that were seriously lacking in capability.

Above: AWACS was invaluable in assisting commanders to maintain real-time control of the air battle and in maintaining the integrity of allied airspace. If Iraqi fighters had been able to penetrate allied defences unseen and destroy high-value targets, the course of the war could have been significantly altered.

Right: The French Aviation Légère de l'Armée de Terre operated a single surveillance Puma which carried a simplified version of the experimental Orchidée system. It flew 24 sorties between 3 and 27 February, including some in support of US Army AH-64s.

The most successful fighter of the war was the F-15C Eagle. This example belongs to the highest scoring unit, the USAF's 58th TFS and carries a full load of Sidewinder and Sparrow missiles.

Stopping Iraq's air force

The assault on Iraq's air force was two-part in nature. The Coalition had to nullify the Iraqi airborne threat to safeguard its attack and support aircraft and its ground forces. Then Iraqi air bases and aircraft shelters had to be destroyed, preventing future large-scale operations.

When Saudi Arabia and the UN called for the world's help in stopping any further Iraqi aggression, the US, UK and after some persuasion, France responded by sending interceptors to curtail Iraqi air operations.

During Desert Shield USAF F-15Cs, RAF Tornado F.Mk 3s, Armeé de l'Air Mirage 2000Cs, US Navy F-14s plus RSAF F-15Cs and Tornado ADVs were all employed in air defence sorties along the Saudi border. Their mission was never to actually enter Iraqi airspace, but to gather information on Iraqi responses, radar and tactics. Vital lessons were also gained about operating over the hostile and featureless terrain of the region. To ensure combat skills were kept to a finely honed edge, practice missions were also flown against other nation's aircraft. From the first deployments in August 1990 until January 1991,

long, arduous CAPs and practice missions continued, so that by the time the war began, the crews were at peak readiness.

Desert Storm began on 17 January when Apaches destroyed an Iraqi radar site, creating a corridor along which Coalition aircraft could pass undetected. On the first night of the war, the majority of sorties were flown by US aircraft. The planning up to this point had been so secret that the only aircraft from other nations to be involved were RAF Jaguars and RAF and RSAF Tornados.

Escorting all the strike and support aircraft, bar the radar-evading F-117s, were F-14s, F-15s and Tornado ADVs and it was during the early hours of 17 January, that the first air-to-air kill was claimed. Captain Tate of the USAF's 71st TFS, was escorting a mixed strike package en route to Baghdad when an Iraqi Mirage F1 threatened the

This F-15C is one of the few fighters to have scored two kills during Desert Storm. Kill markings are traditionally worn by the victorious aircraft for the duration of its service and Capt. Williams himself did not score kills in the first Gulf War.

strike force – Tate dispatched it with an AIM-7 Sparrow.

The F-15C dominated air-to-air combat, being the USAF's most capable air-to-air combat fighter. As such it was usually F-15Cs that were vectored into possible engagements by AWACs aircraft. By the end of the war, out of the 42 air-to-air kills claimed, 37 were credited to F-15s, and all but two of these were to USAF Eagles, the other two; both Mirage F1EQs, fell to Captain Ayehid Saleh al-

Shamrani of No. 13 Squadron, RSAF on 24 January. One US Navy F-14 and two F/A-18s, plus two USAF A-10s also claimed kills, however the forces of other Coalition nations were not so fortunate and there were complaints (particularly from the US Navy) about the partisan nature of the AWACS crews when vectoring fighters to bogies. However, F-14 pilots have also claimed that their lack of air-to-air kills was due to the fact that Iraqi aircraft would flee when they picked up the tell-tale emissions of the Tomcat's AN/AWG-9 radar.

Anti-air base action

As well as destroying Iraqi aircraft in the air, it was

RAF Tornados such as these F.Mk 3s of No. 5 Squadron, had little difficulty deploying to the Gulf. Since the Saudis fly the same type of aircraft, a complete support and maintenance infrastructure was already well established.

Left: Auxiliary fuel tanks were part of the standard F-15C 'fit' and allowed the Eagles to remain airborne on CAPs for up to three hours. However, inflight refuelling was still required on longer sorties.

Below: The Grumman F-14 Tomcat's war was something of a non-event. Its sole kill, a Mil Mi-8 helicopter, came almost as an embarrassment when compared to the USAFs multitude of victories and the fact that bomb-laden F/A-18s and even A-10s achieved more kills.

Above: The Canadian CF-188 force numbered 24 aircraft by the start of the conflict and the 'Desert Cats' maintained a 24-hour watch over about a fifth of the Coalition fleet.

important to destroy the locations they flew from to prevent further operations. For the first few days of the war, this dangerous mission fell to RAF Tornados with their JP233 airfield denial dispensers. An assault on an airfield would usually be led by radar jammers such as the EF-111A and EA-6B, and SEAD aircraft such as the F-4G 'Wild Weasel' and ALARM-carrying Tornados. F-15Cs and/or Tornado ADVs flew top cover. Once enemy defences had been softened, the JP233-toting Tornados would dash in at low level (200 ft/ 61 m) dispensing submunitions

and theoretically rendering runways unusuable while also making their repair difficult. This mission was extremely dangerous and two Tornados were lost on the first day of the war alone. During the opening three days of the conflict, over 40 JP233 sorties a day were launched but as casualties rose and the Iraqi air force disintegrated, Tornados were moved onto safer medium-altitude bombing missions.

After this initial phase, air base attacks began concentrating on hitting Iraqi hardened aircraft shelters (HASs) and the aircraft hiding inside. RAF

Tornados dropping LGBs on targets designated by Pave Spike-equipped Buccaneers or TIALD equipped Tornados, and USAF F-111Fs, dominated this role. By 17 February, 350 of Iraq's 594 HASs had been destroyed, along with a sizeable percentage of its air force. Attacks were then directed back at runways and taxiways in case

Iraq planned to launch a last-ditch chemical-bombing raid on advancing Coalition troops.

By the end of the war, the aircraft of Iraq's much vaunted air force had either been destroyed, usually on the ground, or had fled to neighbouring countries and, in truth, they had never truly threatened the Coalition.

Right: Not content with merely bombing Iraq's airfields, Tornado GR.Mk 1 ZA447/EA earned the sobriquet MiG Eater, having fortuitously dropped a bomb on an Iraqi MiG-29 'Fulcrum'.

Above: Armourers fit JP233s to an RAF Tornado during the early days of Desert Storm. Carried only by Tornado GR.Mk 1s, these weapons eject runway-cratering bomblets and anti-personnel mines.

Right: For all the Iraqis' Western and Eastern European help during the 1980s-90s, their air bases soon fell victim to allied bombing. Even hardened aircraft shelters were no protection from precision-guided bombs.

Transport & tanking

C-130s were invaluable throughout the conflict, as Military Airlift Command's chief, Colonel Johnson, explained: "These crews saved the day after the ground war began. The worst weather in 15 years turned much of the desert into a swamp. When the Army's truck convoys were bogged down, our C-130s airdropped tonnes of ammunition and supplies to our forces deep in enemy territory. Without them, there would have been no 100-hour victory."

Often overshadowed by their more glamourous counterparts, the Coalition's transport and tanking fleets enabled the multinational force to move massive volumes of supplies quickly to the region. Without the Coalition's extensive tanker fleet, it seems certain that the air offensive which presaged the ground war would have lasted very much longer and would have been greatly limited in scale.

Above: One of the three types of RAF aerial refuellers in the Gulf, Handley Page Victor K.Mk 2s from No. 55 Squadron were used to refuel RAF Tornados and Jaguars (as above) and carrier-based aircraft of the US Navy.

Desert Shield saw the greatest airlift in history bring hundreds of thousands of troops and millions of tons of supplies to the Gulf in the race to build up a force able to depose Saddam Hussein from Kuwait. On the basis of millions of ton-miles (MTM) per day – the product of aircraft cargo weight in tons and the distance flown – Desert Shield/Desert Storm activity far surpassed earlier airlifts. The peak period of the conflict saw the Coalition transport effort reach 17 MTM per day, compared with Operation Nickel Grass to Israel in 1971 which reached 4.4 MTM per day, and the

Berlin Airlift of 1948/49 which reached 1.7 MTM per day.

Dominating the strategic and intra-theatre airlift were USAF C-5 Galaxies, C-141B StarLifters, and commercial cargo and passenger aircraft mobilised for military service as part of the Civil Reserve Air Fleet (CRAF). Materiel Air Command created an airbridge that took crews on exhausting 38-hour missions from a US base to a European one, followed by the hop down to Saudi Arabia. The C-141Bs flew the majority of the missions (52 per cent), the C-5s carried most of the cargo (42 per cent), and the CRAF aircraft carried the most passengers (64 per cent).

Above: While several RAF Chinooks and Pumas went to the Gulf by sea, some were airlifted to the region on board USAF Lockheed C-5 Galaxies. Here, a Puma is loaded at RAF Brize Norton.

Left: Activated for the first time, the Civil Reserve Air Fleet (CRAF) played a valuable part in the airlift, with 16 airlines carrying more passengers than any other transport medium. This Boeing 747-200 was flown by US supplemental carrier, Tower Air.

Left: Once supplies arrived in-theatre from strategic airlifters they were distributed by a 'spoke' network of C-130s. These aircraft flew regular routes to all regional bases and supported large ground unit transfers within the theatre.

Below: Virtually all the KC-135A, E, Q and R (shown below) aircraft in the SAC, Air Force Reserve and Air National Guard inventory – more than 630 – were either stationed in the Middle East or provided direct support to the operation.

Left: In the forefront of any land or amphibious operations, the US Marine Corps is heavily reliant on rotary wing mobility. For rapid deployment of troops or underslung loads, the Sikorsky CH-53 is a vital asset (illustrated is a CH-53D).

Aerial refuellers such as KC-10s and KC-135s (assigned to Strategic Air Command) also took part in the airlift, bringing in supplies and personnel from their own, and other, units.

Once in-theatre, transport was handled by smaller aircraft such as C-130E/H Hercules and C-21A Learjets, which fanned out like the spokes of a wheel from hubs at Dhahran and Riyadh. At this level, non-USAF aircraft could also become involved. As well as the multinational C-130 force, TriStars, VC10s, C.160s, C-2As, C-22s and even a Fokker F28 were all employed. On the smallest level, helicopters such as UH-1s, CH-47s, UH-60s, CH-46s, CH-53Es, Pumas, Chinooks and Sea Kings transported troops and supplies to units and forward operating areas.

Aerial refuelling

One of the least publicised, yet one of the most important aspects of the air war was the part played by inflight refuelling. As the largest force in the Gulf, it was only natural that the USAF should have the largest tanker force with no fewer than 256 KC-135 Stratotankers and 46 KC-10A Extenders. SAC was heavily committed to the refuelling mission, but such was the scale of the operation that it had to be supplemented by aircraft and crews from the Air Force Reserve and Air National Guard. Additional US tanker resources included USMC KC-130s, while the USN supplied KA-6Ds and 'buddy' refuelling packs on aircraft like the F/A-18 and A-7E. The RAF dispatched virtually its entire refuelling fleet to the region, with nine VC10s at King Khalid Airport, Kuwait and seven Victors at Bahrain. Later, supported by a pair of TriStars, the RAF fleet was able to refuel RAF Jaguars, Tornados, Buccaneers, CF-188s, Mirage 2000s and a variety of USN and USMC aircraft. Canada, France and Italy also helped in the refuelling effort by supplying CC-137s, C-135FRs and 'buddy'-configured Tornados, respectively.

Above: Operating alongside their American counterparts, Royal Saudi S-70A-1s transported people and light supplies across the region. A pair of French Pumas in the background awaits a mission.

Left: As part of the multi-national war effort, Egypt supplied Lockheed C-130Hs to aid intra-theatre transport. The size of the theatre and the number of bases made extensive intra-theatre airlift essential, ranking second only to interdiction in the total number of sorties flown during the war.

Right: At the peak of Desert Shield, there was little let-up in the intensity of airlift operations. It quickly became a round-the-clock mission, with C-5s and C-141Bs landing at Dhahran every seven minutes on average, backed up by SAC tankers and elements of the CRAF.

The carrier war

Although the role of the carrier was somewhat diminished in the face of increased air force performance, the naval aviation assets of the US, Britain and France played a valuable part in the conflict. Aircraft were used in a variety of roles that incorporated air strikes, combat air patrol and anti-shipping operations.

As soon as the United Nations called for action to be taken against the Iraqi invasion of Kuwait, the United States Navy began to prepare itself for war. On 8 August 1990, the aircraft-carrier USS *Dwight D. Eisenhower* and its battle group arrived in the Red Sea; a further five USN carriers were to play some kind of role in the conflict that followed.

Since World War II, carriers have played an integral part in any US action, their mere presence in a conflict zone usually being enough to deter any opposition. In recent times, however, the global reach of the USAF has meant that USN aviation has been somewhat overshadowed. Nevertheless, the carriers still have a contribution to make, as was the case during the first Gulf War.

Desert Shield

As soon as the carriers arrived in the Persian Gulf, they were put to work in support of Operation Desert Shield. Their duties included patrolling the borders of Iraqi airspace so as to to gain electronic information, and carrying out reconnaissance

missions, troop transport, training and anti-shipping duties. The latter mission was particularly important due to the UN-ordered blockade of seaborne trade. Here, the US Navy worked in co-operation with the forces of several other nations – RAF Nimrods patrolled the skies, while CF-188s offered strike capability. RN Lynxes which, with their Sea Skua missiles, were the most powerful helicopters of their class in the region, took part in the anti-shipping mission and they would go on to claim 15 ships destroyed out of Iraq's small navy. Regular patrols of Saudi waters were conducted by Saudi AS 565 Panthers and AS 532 Cougars. French and Free-Kuwaiti Pumas were also involved in the transport effort. The Royal Navy's conventional aircraft-carriers, HMS *Ark Royal*, *Illustrious* and *Invincible*, were involved in other duties at the time.

Desert Storm

US Navy aircraft were involved from day one of the campaign. F-14s flew top cover or escort for attack units such as A-6s while A-7s, in their last-ever

Above: The US Navy had its own tankers, but also utilised USAF KC-135 Stratotankers. VA-72 A-7E Corsair IIs are seen here as they prepare to receive fuel from a KA-6D and a KC-135.

Right: Although Britain did not send any of its conventional carriers to the Gulf, the various Royal Navy and Royal Fleet Auxiliary ships that were involved were capable of operating helicopters. These were used for troop transport (pictured is a Sea King HC.Mk 4) or naval warfare missions.

USS Theodore Roosevelt *and* **USS** America *are pictured in the Persian Gulf on 28 February. The six US Navy carriers deployed to the Middle East made a huge contribution to the air power available to the Coalition.*

Left: AA401 (the Hornet in the foreground) was the aircraft in which LCdr Fox scored his historic kill. While on a bombing mission, Fox and his wingman were intercepted by a pair of Chengdu F-7s. Instead of dropping their bombs and then engaging the fighters, they simply changed radar modes, shot down the F-7s and continued on their bombing mission.

Below: While in the vicinity of Cyprus, the Kennedy's two Tomcat squadrons took time out to engage RAF Phantoms in mock air battles as they sought to refine their skills in anticipation of combat. Here, an F-14 of VF-32 flies next to a No. 19 Squadron Phantom after one such session.

war, and F/A-18s, carried HARM missiles in the SEAD role. EA-6B Prowlers provided electronic jamming support and KA-6D Intruders offered a refuelling capability. For the most part, the opening night of the war proved successful for the US Navy, although there were casualties – in the only shoot-down of a Coalition aircraft by an Iraqi aircraft, an F/A-18C of VFA-81 was downed by a MiG-25, with the Hornet pilot being lost. A pair of A-6Es were

also destroyed that night. Later in the war, further A-6s and an F/A-18 were also shot down. And, on 21 January 1991, an F-14A+ was shot down by an SA-2 SAM. In a dramatic rescue, the pilot was picked up by a USAF Special Operations MH-53J, supported by A-10s. His wingman, however, was not so lucky, being caught by the Iraqis and remaining a PoW until the end of the war.

To secure freedom of action in the northern Persian Gulf,

Coalition aircraft attacked numerous Iraqi naval targets. These included Iraqi ports and associated facilities, operating locations, oil terminals, 'Silkworm' missile sites and fleets of patrol boats, missile-firing boats (which posed a significant threat to Coalition battle groups and amphibious forces in spite of the small size of the Iraqi navy) and mine-sweepers. Engagements during the war resulted in 143 out of 178 Iraqi naval vessels being destroyed, including 12 of the 13 missile boats (the other fled to Iran).

The attacks against the 'Silkworm' sites, however, were less successful. These surface-to-surface missiles, which were used for coastal defence, proved to be as elusive a target as the mainland 'Scuds' and just two of the seven known 'Silkworm' sites were believed to be destroyed by the beginning of the ground war.

Only two launches of 'Silkworm' missiles were recorded during the war, from a site south of Kuwait city on 25 February. The missiles were probably fired just before capture of the site; one of the missiles apparently crashed into the sea immediately, and the other was shot down by a missile fired from HMS *Gloucester*.

Minesweeping was a role dominated by the US Navy – two MH-53E squadrons were deployed to Dhahran to conduct mine clearance of the northern Persian Gulf to enable warships to transit this area safely. HM-14 helicopters were deployed on LPH-10/USS *Tripoli* until the ship was damaged by a mine on 18 February. The helicopters temporarily operated from the LPH-11/USS *La Salle* while the *Tripoli* underwent repairs. USMC RH-53Ds and RN Sea King HAS.Mk 5s assisted in the minesweeping role.

Above: During the war, every US Navy carrier participating in the conflict was assigned one EA-6B Prowler squadron. The aircraft provided ECM coverage for most Coalition operations, usually involving one to three HARM shoots per aircraft.

Above: SA 330 Pumas of the 5ième Regiment d'Hélicoptères de Combat land aboard the carrier Clemenceau after exercising ashore in Djibouti. The Pumas were deployed as part of Operation Salamandre, the initial French military response to the Iraqi invasion of Kuwait.

Right: This F/A-18C Hornet (the type was the dominant US Navy aircraft of the conflict) of VFA-81, armed with bombs and Sidewinders, prepares for refuelling en route to a target.

Lockheed Martin F-16 Fighting Falcon

The Netherlands is a major European F-16 operator and, with a host of other NATO Allies, looks set to employ its upgraded F-16s well into the 21st century.

The 'Viper'

Conceived and still marketed as the ultimate air combat machine unequalled in a dogfight, the General Dynamics/Lockheed Martin F-16 Fighting Falcon has more often been used in the fighter-bomber role.

At its conception, the F-16 was radically different from other aircraft. It was a cheap, simple, unsophisticated, single-engine, single-seat fighter design at a time when fashion dictated expensive, all-purpose, two-seat twin-engined warplanes. But when it left the drawing boards and metal was cut, the F-16 went from being a lightweight fighter to being a robust, multi-role warplane.

There were many reasons for the change – a bantam fighter was never the right solution for a nation which often deploys its forces halfway around the world – but most importantly, the US Air Force felt, initially at least, that its F-15 Eagle was too expensive and important for close air support, battlefield interdiction, and ground-attack duties. Supporters of the F-15 resisted altering their aircraft with the cry 'not a pound for air-to-ground', and the F-16 was made bigger and heavier and given the bulk of the air-to-ground portfolio.

The F-16 is easily recognised by its low-slung engine air intake and by the 'blended' approach that merges the wing with the fuselage. Its external appearance was thought odd when it first appeared, but with more than 4,000 F-16s built, it is now taken for granted. Another innovation of the F-16 – more commonly known to its pilots as the 'Viper' – was the fact that it was one of the first warplanes to introduce a 'fly by wire' flight control system, in which a computer operates the flight controls.

Expanding roles

Many continue to use the F-16 Fighting Falcon as a dogfighter. It has an impressive thrust-to-weight ratio and is extremely manoeuvrable at close quarters. With the incredible visibility afforded by its canopy and the pilot's high-up posture, and with its stability as a gun platform, the F-16 can take on almost any fighter in the world today and win. However, its fly-by-wire control system imposes finite hard limits, preventing the kind of post-stall 'ragged corner of the envelope' manoeuvring which can be performed by the latest Russian superfighters, or by the thrust-vectoring F-22 Raptor. The earliest F-16 models also lack an IRST (infra-red search and track) capability

Fast, agile and able to deliver a respectable weapon load, the F-16, once envisaged as a pure dogfighter, has developed a number of specialised roles. European air arms – an aircraft of the Danish air force is illustrated – were consequently quick to adopt the type.

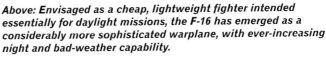

Above: Envisaged as a cheap, lightweight fighter intended essentially for daylight missions, the F-16 has emerged as a considerably more sophisticated warplane, with ever-increasing night and bad-weather capability.

Seen over a desert practice range delivering two 'dumb' bombs from its inboard wing pylons, the F-16 ushered in a new era, able to undertake air-to-air and ground attack roles in a single mission.

and helmet-mounted sight, and still rely on the aged Sidewinder missile and a cannon with arguably too small a calibre. However, later variants and upgrades add both the AIM-120 AMRAAM for BVR engagements and the Joint Helmet Mounted Cueing System (JHMCS) for off-boresight targeting.

As a fighter-bomber, the F-16 excels. Cheap enough to deploy in large numbers and supportable enough to sustain an intensive sortie rate, the F-16 carries a remarkable warload (for an aircraft of its size) and, moreover, has been integrated with a huge variety of offensive weapons, sensors and systems, enabling it to perform a wide range of air-to-surface tasks over land and sea.

An ideal tactical fighter aircraft for contingency operations, capable of performing almost any mission, the Fighting Falcon has matured into a 'jack of all trades' – much more useful than being a master of only one.

Bird of Peace

Recent world events have seen the F-16 become an airborne peace negotiator for the West, with units being deployed to both the Afghan and Gulf theatres. Having proved its offensive capabilities here through the attacking of ground targets, the F-16s remain on guard, ensuring that future resolutions and agreements are rigidly enforced.

Despite its small size and often muted lack of range, the F-16 remains a potent combat aircraft. Its sheer worldwide sales and the various mid-life update packages currently being offered to improve earlier models will enable the F-16 to undertake any combat mission in an increasingly hostile air combat environment.

Pakistani F-16s have seen action on the border with Afghanistan, claiming Afghan and Soviet air force warplanes during border scuffles. In one instance, a Soviet Su-25 'Frogfoot' was shot down.

In 1982, it was announced that the USAF's Thunderbirds flight demonstration team would trade in its T-38 Talons for F-16 Fighting Falcons. Only slight modifications were made to the aircraft, one of which was the removal of the internal gun.

Back to Iraq

After the end of Desert Storm, Coalition forces remained active in the area surrounding Iraq. Saddam's forces often failed to abide by the resolutions set by the UN and their treatment of the Kurds led to an international effort to provide help.

Above: A Ramstein-based F-16C approaches a KC-135 tanker during Provide Comfort. Armed with cluster bombs, the F-16 would have provided close air support/defence suppression if Iraq had tried to intervene.

Still wearing its camouflage from Desert Storm, an RAF Special Forces Chinook lifts a twin load from Silopi to the mountain safe havens. The Chinooks' long-range fuel tanks allowed them to deploy further east than other helicopters, going as far as Hakkari and Yuksekova, near the Iranian border.

The end of Desert Storm brought with it a plethora of problems in and around the war zone. While the rebuilding of Kuwait was of paramount importance, the question of what to do about the considerable refugee problem was to occupy the military for the following months. In Turkey, in particular, Kurdish refugees were living in squalor, and they were resented by the Turks, who had their own problems and who were encouraging the newly-arrived Kurds to return to Iraq. The Kurds, meanwhile, were frustrated by Western indifference after the initial encouragement they had received from Western agencies to rise up against Saddam Hussein. They were also understandably anxious about returning to an Iraq where they would be persecuted.

Provide Comfort

On 5 April 1991 President George H.W. Bush launched a relief effort named Operation Provide Comfort which had the twin goals of preventing starvation and disease in the Kurdish camps and repatriating the refugees in Iraq. This necessitated military involvement and 13 nations would eventually join in the effort.

Air operations began almost immediately, with C-130s, French C.160 Transalls and Italian G222s air-dropping food, while A-10As operated in the close air support and target spotting roles. F-15s and F-16s provided top cover in the unlikely event of the Iraqi air force attempting a counter-strike. However, bad weather prevented food drops reaching all of their intended targets and so a large fleet of helicopters augmented, and then replaced, the fixed-wing fleet. CH-53s from the US Navy, USMC and Luftwaffe joined Chinooks from Spain, the UK and the US

Right: Where the US Marines go, their own air support goes with them. For Provide Comfort, four AH-1Ws armed with TOW AGMs, AIM-9s and rockets, flew escort missions from Silopi.

Below: A HARM-equipped F/A-18C comes in to land on USS Kitty Hawk in the Persian Gulf. A total of 35 aircraft, including eight Hornets, was involved in the 1993 strikes, hitting targets across south-east Iraq.

Left: At least 36 UH-60As from the US Army were dispatched to northern Iraq as part of Provide Comfort. They were used to fly supplies directly to the mountaintop refugee camps.

Below: 846 Naval Air Squadron Commando HC.Mk 4s played a pivotal part in the capturing of the safe havens for the returning Kurds. Troops and supplies were ferried to forward operating locations, one of which – Sirsenk – was within a few miles of Saddam Hussein's summer palace.

Above: A pair of US Navy CH-53Es (two of the four aircraft deployed from HC-4 at Sigonella) is seen at Diyarbikir in support of the 24th MEU. These aircraft were the first to arrive at the safe havens and were able to fly non-stop from Incirlik to Silopi. Conditions for the crews were very primitive, with tented accommodation as standard, and the flying was extremely challenging, with high temperatures and mountainous terrain posing particular problems.

Below: As they had done in Desert Storm, the Italians played an important part in relief operations. This Lockheed C-130H was detached to Turkey from 46ª Brigata.

Army, while a host of other helicopters from different nations joined the effort.

During late 1992 and early 1993, the last days of Bush's administration, Iraq mounted a series of challenges to the UN policies regarding 'No-Fly-Zones'. SAM sites were moved into, or close to, the 'Zones' and Iraqi fighters would penetrate the banned areas. On 27 December 1992, F-15Es of the 335th FS tangled with MiG-25s and, on the same day, an F-16D of the 33rd FS downed another MiG-25 with an AMRAAM, the first kill for both an American F-16 and an AMRAAM.

On 13 January 1993, a large strike force comprising aircraft from the USAF, USN, RAF and Armée de l'Air struck 17 targets including AAA, SAM and air defence command and control sites. Poor weather hampered the mission and results were mixed. The attacks did little to curb Iraqi

aggression, and continuing infringements of UN airspace by the Iraqis led to further shootdowns and Tomahawk cruise missile strikes on selected targets.

Coalition presence

Operation Southern Watch, the name of the Coalition's mission to cover the airspace of southern Iraq below the 32° parallel, continued until the 2003 invasion, with clashes between Iraqi and Coalition forces occuring on a near-daily basis at some periods. The climax to these flashpoints came with the initiation of Operation Desert Fox in December 1998, which saw concerted large-scale attacks across Iraq.

Between June 2002 and the invasion in March 2003, Operation Southern Focus intensified the bombing of Iraqi installations and stepped up intelligence gathering, in what is now evident were preparations for the imminent invasion.

Above: This chartered Metro Cargo Ilyushin Il-76 flew humanitarian supplies into Turkey. Metro Cargo was a Swiss-owned, Luxembourg-based carrier which used mainly leased Soviet aircraft. The Soviet Union itself played no part in the operation.

Left: USAF MH-53Js from the 21st SOS (Special Operations Squadron) at RAF Woodbridge in the UK ferried Special Forces troops from more than one nation into northern Iraq to police the safe havens for the returning Kurds. The MH-53Js performed this basic transport role, but were also on standby (alongside HC-130N/P tankers of the 39th SOW) for the combat rescue mission if needed.

A Tornado GR.Mk 1A launches from Ali al Salem, carrying a pair of GBU-24 Paveway IIIs. This aircraft displays evidence of a variety of camouflage schemes: grey/green fuselage camouflage, medium-grey for the Sky Shadow pod, air defence grey for the port fuel tank and 'desert pink' for the starboard tank. The lack of uniform desert camouflage was not an issue due to the fact that targets were attacked solely at night.

Desert Fox
Western retribution

Continuing difficulties over access to UN weapons inspectors brought the West to the brink of war with Iraq in November 1998, but the strikes were aborted at the last minute. However, further provocation could not be ignored and Desert Fox was launched in response.

Operation Desert Fox was launched on 16 December 1998, coinciding with a coup attempt against Saddam Hussein from within the Iraqi army. The air attacks by American and British warplanes and cruise missiles were briefly in the world's spotlight, while the internal situation within Iraq remained in shadow. Within months, the four-day Desert Fox effort had been eclipsed by Operation Allied Force, the larger air campaign against Yugoslavia – but, while it lasted, Desert Fox introduced new weapons and tactics, and returned to action an array of familiar combat aircraft.

Supposedly aimed at Iraq's ability to produce WMD (weapons of mass destruction), which Iraq refused to let the UN inspect, Desert Fox in fact had an entirely different purpose – the decapitation of Iraq's leadership. It would have disappointed no-one in the allied chain of command if the attacks had struck at Saddam himself.

In the US, the timing of the strikes drew criticism. Combat sorties began at 17.00. Washington time (midnight in

Baghdad) on 16 December. Not only was this the opening day of the Muslim holy month of Ramadan, but the strikes commenced a few hours before the House of Representatives was scheduled to debate and vote on a committee recommendation to impeach President Bill Clinton. Secretary of Defense William Cohen insisted that the timing of strikes against Iraq was dictated solely by military considerations.

The military campaign capped off a period of frustration for members of the US armed forces. In October, US bombers had deployed overseas for action in Kosovo that came to the brink, but never took place (although it was to occur months later). In November, US warplanes were actually in the air en route to Iraqi targets – as part of Operation Desert Viper, a vastly more ambitious undertaking than the subsequent Desert Fox – when a stand-down was ordered at the last minute.

Carrier war

From the standpoint of the Royal Air Force and the US Air

Force, there was no action in the first 24 hours of Desert Fox. The campaign – by naval forces – began with hundreds of attacks in Baghdad, Basra and against Republican Guard installations by BGM-109 Tomahawk cruise missiles. F-14B Tomcat fighters from squadron VF-32 'Swordsmen' struck air defence installations around the fringes of hostile territory, using laser-guided GBU-12 and GBU-24 bombs. *Enterprise*'s F/A-18 Hornets also carried GBU-24s, with their 2,000-lb (907-kg) warheads, to targets in Iraq. On the third day, USS *Vinson* arrived to join the fray, bringing F-14D 'Bombcats' and more Hornets.

As usual, the US Navy's fleet of EA-6B Prowlers was kept busy, having to accompany the

majority of the strike packages most of the way to their targets. Unpowered ADM-141 TALDs (Tactical Air-Launched Decoys) were dropped by USN and USMC F/A-18C Hornets and S-3B Vikings to confuse and confound Iraqi defences – and to prompt Baghdad to claim, inaccurately, that it had shot down over 100 cruise missiles.

Mixed force

Eventual participants included RAF Tornado GR.Mk 1s and USAF B-52H Stratofortresses with AGM-86C Block 1 CALCMs (conventional air-launched cruise missiles). A-10 'Warthog' attack aircraft dropped leaflets telling some Iraqi troops that they were not being targeted and that they should

One of several important 'firsts' for Desert Fox was the participation of female aircrew in combat. Lt Carol Watts from VFA-37 'Raging Bulls' discusses her first mission on 17 December.

Desert Fox marked the delayed baptism of fire for the B-1B. Two aircraft flew a long dumb bombing mission against a Special Republican Guard barracks. Here, two aircraft from the 28th Bomb Wing are seen at their temporary base in Oman.

USMC Hornets of VMFA-312 were at the heart of Desert Fox operations, flying from Enterprise. Here, a HARM-armed F/A-18C launches the second wave of attacks, on 18 December.

stay still. The B-1B Lancer made its combat debut on the second day when two B-1Bs, flying from Oman, bombed a target near Baghdad. The B-1Bs dropped 500-lb (227-kg) Mk 82 general-purpose gravity bombs on the SRG (Special Republican Guard) Al Kut barracks north-west of Baghdad. The USAF quietly pointed out that, thanks to surveillance by E-8C Joint STARS (Surveillance & Target Attack Radar System), B-1Bs in

the theatre were provided with real-time, moving target information.

After the shooting started, one key allied target was a batch of Czech Aero L-29 Delfin trainers at Al-Sahra, north of Baghdad, which US officials claimed had been modified into drone anthrax carriers.

Defense Secretary William Cohen and Joint Chiefs' Chairman General Henry 'Hugh' Shelton announced an end to

The F-16CJ Block 50 has played an important part in ongoing operations against Iraq. This HARM-carrying 'Viper' from the 23rd FS, 52nd FW is seen in January 1999 while on Northern Watch patrol.

Desert Fox, hours into the celebration of Ramadan. Desert Fox involved 656 sorties, used more than 200 cruise missiles, and struck about 100 targets associated with Iraq's development of missiles and chemical, biological, and nuclear weapons. Saddam Hussein announced 'victory' when the action ended after four days, even though his forces had made almost no attempt to mount a defence.

An analysis of target sets compels the conclusion that the real purpose of Desert Fox was to attack the Iraqi leadership. Among early targets were Saddam Hussein's sleeping quarters on the outskirts of Baghdad, in the Radwaniyah complex adjacent to the now-vacant Saddam International Airport. Other targets, including buildings that house secret units of the SSO (Special Security Organisation) and the SRG (Special Republican Guard), were locations where Iraqi leaders were expected to be.

There is also grounds for belief that American and British intelligence supported an unsuccessful attempt to topple Saddam Hussein, while bombing him. On 18 December, while Iraqi troops mopped up what was

clearly a coup attempt, the vice chairman of Iraq's ruling Revolution Command Council, General Izzat Ibrahim, reportedly sent a letter to Saddam Hussein noting that 'we have instructed the armed forces to restrict their mission to the protection of the borders of the homeland'. The letter, broadcast on Iraqi radio, noted that all internal security had been arranged for using 'other armed bodies'. In other words, the coup was over and Iraq was, at least internally, secure.

Between Desert Fox and the 2003 invasion there were sporadic encounters between US/UK and Iraqi forces. On 28 December 1998 F-16CJs and F-15Es attacked air defence targets in the 'No-Fly Zone'. In early January 1999 an F-16CJ attacked a mobile 'Bar Lock' early warning radar and another F-16CJ attacked an AAA and SA-6 battery.

On 5 January 1999 USAF fighters attacked Iraqi MiG-25s, scoring no kills for four missiles (three AMRAAMs and a Sparrow). Some 15 minutes later, two F-14D Tomcats fired two AIM-54C Phoenix missiles at a second group of MiG-25s, again without success. The air-to-air altercation was the first in Iraq since 27 December 1992, when a US F-16 shot down an Iraqi MiG-25 'Foxbat'.

Having brought an end to weapons inspections within Iraq, Desert Fox seemed also to have opened up a new era of frequent, persistent skirmishes against Iraqi air defences and other forces. As late as November 1999, the RAF reported that a pair of Tornado GR.Mk 1s had suffered a near miss from Iraqi AAA fire. However, the endgame for Saddam was about to begin.

AL SAHRA AIRFIELD, IRAQ

An important target set for Desert Fox was Iraq's WMD facilities. Al-Sahra airfield was suspected of housing aircraft modified for the aerial spraying of chemical/biological warfare agents, and received appropriate attention. Parked around the airfield are agricultural aircraft, mainly PZL Dromaders, which may have been capable of CW/BW delivery.

Allied Force

Hitting Yugoslavia

B-2s flew non-stop missions from Whiteman AFB, Missouri, to use JDAM weapons against infrastructure targets, some within Belgrade city limits.

Above: The F-15E formed the backbone of the precision strike force assembled for Allied Force, 26 aircraft from the 48th FW being assigned to the 31st AEW at Aviano.

NATO's strategic air campaign against Yugoslavia began on the evening of 24 March 1999 with cruise missile strikes against key air defence targets throughout Serbia.

In early March 1999, diplomatic negotiations were held in Paris to try to resolve the Kosovo crisis. However, with these talks seemingly deadlocked, the US government and its NATO allies decided to begin air strikes in an attempt to force the Yugoslav regime of Slobodan Milosevic to compromise and offer autonomy to the predominately ethnic Albanian province of Kosovo.

Cruise missile strikes

NATO's 5th Allied Tactical Air Force, based in Italy, was given the task of leading the air offensive, which would also draw on more than 200 allied aircraft based in Italy and located on aircraft-carriers in the Adriatic Sea. The aircraft would be supported by ship- and submarine-launched US Navy and British Tomahawk Land Attack Missiles (TLAMs), and by USAF strategic bombers, operating both from the UK and from home bases in the continental US.

With a wave of several dozen cruise missiles launched from ships, submarines and aircraft, Operation Allied Force commenced. Some 23 air defence sites around the Yugoslav capital of Belgrade, Kosovo and Montenegro were attacked at 20.00 on 24 March. Three follow-up waves – which continued until early the next morning – of manned strike aircraft then hit command and control, army bases and support facilities. Yugoslav air defence forces fired scores of surface-to-air missiles (SAMs) and launched MiG-29 and MiG-21 fighters to resist the intruders. NATO F-15C Eagle and F-16A/C Fighting Falcon fighters escorting allied strike packages were on hand to intercept the Yugoslav MiGs, shooting down at least three of them. Allied suppression of enemy air defences (SEAD) aircraft, principally USAF F-16CJs, USN and USMC EA-6B Prowlers and Luftwaffe Tornado ECRs, were also flying close protection for the strikes, and fired scores of AGM-88 High Speed Anti-Radiation (HARM) missiles at any hostile radars that came up to guide Serb SAMs.

This pattern of strikes continued for the first two to three weeks, as the allies worked to grind down the Serb air defences by systematically hitting known SAM batteries, radar sites, communications centres, air defence force logistic sites and home bases, air bases and fighter dispersal sites. This effort was by no means one-sided – Serb air defence commanders scored their biggest coup of the war on 27 March when they were able to shoot down a USAF F-117 Nighthawk 'stealth' fighter near Belgrade.

Striking Belgrade

In response to the allied air strikes, Serb army, police and paramilitary forces stepped up their campaign of ethnic

French Mirage 2000C fighters joined the Allied air defence effort. Only US F-15s and US and Dutch F-16s enjoyed air-to-air success, however.

Above: Luftwaffe Tornados played a significant part in operations over Bosnia, based at Piacenza, and flew combat missions again during Allied Force.

Right: Large pieces of the F-117 downed near Belgrade remained relatively intact, including the rear fuselage and parts of the tail section.

In order for the NATO attack forces to operate safely over Yugoslavia, it was a prerequisite to neutralise the considerable SAM force. Crucial to this effort was the EA-6B Prowler fleet.

Below: The ubiquitous Hornet flew not only from US carrier decks (F/A-18C), but also from land bases with the US Marine Corps (F/A-18D), Spain (EF-18+) and Canada (CF-188).

cleansing against the Albanian population of Kosovo, sending more than 800,000 refugees into neighbouring countries. Outraged at reports of Serb atrocities, allied leaders ordered the air campaign to be intensified and the NATO target list was expanded to include strategic targets throughout Yugoslavia, including a number of prestige targets in downtown Belgrade.

At first, the brunt of these strikes was borne by air- and sea-launched cruise missiles, the F-117s and B-2 Spirit 'stealth' bombers flying from the US to deliver GPS-guided Joint Direct Attack Munition (JDAM) bombs. As the air defence threat lessened, other allied aircraft were drafted into the strategic effort, including B-52Hs and B-1B Lancers which dropped scores of unguided 'dumb' bombs at a time on huge-area targets such as airfield runways and barrack complexes. Strike aircraft employed some 8,000 highly accurate precision-guided munitions, including GBU-10/12/24/27/28 Paveway series laser-guided bombs, AGM-130 powered television-guided stand-off weapons, AGM-142 Have Nap stand-off missiles and GPS-guided Joint Stand-Off Weapons (JSOWs).

Over the final two months of the 79-day long air campaign, allied bombers took advantage of NATO's air superiority to strike around the clock at a huge range of targets. At the direction of NATO's Supreme Allied Commander Europe, US Army General Wes Clark, allied missiles and aircraft were directed against targets that would bring home to the Yugoslav population the fact that allied pressure would continue until Milosevic pulled his troops out of Kosovo.

Systematic destruction

By the time Operation Allied Force ended on 9 June, some 35 per cent of Yugoslavia was without electric power after almost every powerplant in Serbia had been hit. All of the country's petroleum refining production capability had been destroyed, along with 50 per cent of its explosive production capability, 65 per cent of its ammunition production capability, and 40 per cent of its armoured vehicle production capability; 70 per cent of its aviation assembly and repair facilities had also been damaged by allied bombs. Serb command and control facilities were heavily hit, with 30 per cent of its microwave relay system and 45 per cent of the television broadcast system sustaining damage. The transport infrastructure of the country was badly disrupted, with 70 per cent of road bridges over the Danube river destroyed and all rail lines to ports in Montenegro put out of action.

On top of NATO's systematic attempts to destroy key Serbian infrastructure, a number of attacks were made against high-profile targets associated with the Milosevic regime. These included his party headquarters in downtown Belgrade, one of his residences, and businesses owned by his key political associates. The Yugoslav regime did not take these attacks lying down and mounted a huge propaganda effort to convince the world's media that NATO was deliberately targeting civilians. However, NATO only admitted to 20 weapons going astray and hitting civilians, out of around 23,000 weapons employed during some 10,000 strike sorties.

Left: A yellow star MiG-29 kill marking was added to the HARM launch marks of this USAF 78th EFS F-16CJ after its victory on 4 May 1999.

Above: This F-15C wears kill marks for both a MiG-29 shot down over Kosovo and an Su-22 'Fitter' downed in the aftermath of Desert Storm.

DATE	TYPE	UNIT	LOCATION	NATO TYPE/UNIT	SERIAL	WEAPON
NATO AIR-TO-AIR KILLS OF KOSOVO WAR, 24/3/99 TO 9/6/99						
24/3/99	MiG-29	127 Sqn	near Belgrade	F-16A 322 Sqn, RNLAF	J-063	AMRAAM
24/3/99	MiG-29	127 Sqn	near Belgrade	F-15C 493 FS, USAF		AMRAAM
24/3/99	MiG-29	127 Sqn	near Belgrade	F-15C 493 FS, USAF		AMRAAM
26/4/99	MiG-29	127 Sqn	eastern Bosnia	F-15C 493 FS, USAF		AMRAAM
26/4/99	MiG-29	127 Sqn	eastern Bosnia	F-15C 493 FS, USAF		AMRAAM
4/5/99	MiG-29	127 Sqn	near Belgrade	F-16CJ 78 EFS, USAF	AF 91-353	AMRAAM x 2

Attacking the Serb army

The A-10As mainly employed Mk 82 bombs, AGM-65 Mavericks and target-marking rockets. The force worked daily, alongside RAF Harriers and USAF F-16CGs.

Below: The RAF's Harrier GR.Mk 7s flew from Gioia del Colle, one of the closest Italian bases to Kosovo, maintaining a very high sortie rate.

NATO mounted a powerful interdiction campaign against the Yugoslav army and special police units operating in the wartorn province of Kosovo.

As Allied strike aircraft and cruise missiles continued to pound strategic targets deep in Yugoslavia, Allied air commanders were ordered to increase attacks on Serb army and special police units which were conducting a reign of terror against ethnic Albanians inside Kosovo.

NATO's 5th Allied Tactical Air Force in Italy was initially ill-placed to conduct close air support and interdiction strikes against Yugoslav forces dispersed around the mountainous and forested province. Within days, reinforcements were on their way to the Balkans to boost NATO's firepower and surveillance capabilities. Additional squadrons of USAF A-10A 'Warthogs', B-1B Lancers, F-16 Fighting Falcons, F-15E Eagles, USMC F/A-18D Hornets and air refuelling tankers were mobilised to help NATO. The US Navy ordered the nuclear carrier USS *Theodore Roosevelt* across the Atlantic at top speed. Britain sent extra Harrier GR.Mk 7s and Tornado GR.Mk 1/4s, France provided more Jaguars, Mirage 2000s and Mirage F1s. Belgium, Denmark the Netherlands, Norway, Portugal and Turkey all despatched extra F-16s.

To fill the gap in NATO's intelligence-gathering capability, the USAF sent two of its E-8C Joint STARS ground radar

surveillance aircraft to Europe, supported by USAF RQ-1A Predator and US Army Hunter unmanned aerial vehicles (UAVs). Britain, France, Germany and Italy sent additional UAVs, and France also ordered its Puma-mounted Horizon radar surveillance system to Macedonia to look for Serb targets in Kosovo.

Engagement zones

On the back of an improved intelligence flow, NATO attack aircraft started to roam over Kosovo, hitting tanks, armoured vehicles, artillery pieces, troop concentrations, command posts and supply dumps. Serb forces tried to protect themselves from Allied air attack by basing themselves in Albanian villages and towns, which greatly complicated the job of NATO's pilots.

Tight rules of engagement (ROE) were introduced to prevent Allied pilots from accidentally hitting civilians and these gave a key role to NATO airborne forward air controllers (AFACs) and UAVs. Two 'eyes' were required to identify tactical and mobile targets inside Kosovo, before pilots could attack them. Usually, the UAVs would first find targets and an A-10A, F-16CG, F/A-18D or F-14 AFAC would confirm the target. It was then the job of the AFAC to guide in waves of attack aircraft against the target.

While the ROE kept civilian casualties and collateral damage to an absolute minimum, it posed major command and control challenges to Allied pilots and significantly slowed the tank kill rate to less than five a day. The low kill rate was further complicated by terrible weather and the 15,000-ft (4572-m) hard deck imposed by NATO governments to protect Allied aircraft from Serb air defences. In spite of these measures, 10 Allied aircraft received battle damage during the war, with two aircraft, an F-117 and an F-16CG, being shot down. Both pilots were successfully rescued by CSAR forces.

A-10s and B-52s

By May 1999 the Allied reinforcements were in place at air bases in France, Italy, Hungary and Turkey, which boosted NATO's daily attack sortie rate to 250 compared to 150 a day in April. Some 323

US and 212 Allied strike aircraft were now filling the skies over Kosovo around the clock.

The AFACs had a constant stream of attack aircraft to direct at Serb targets and an offensive by the Kosovo Liberation Army (KLA) from

Right: Seen approaching a tanker, two USAF F-16Cs show off their LANTIRN pods, which provide the aircraft with its day/night-attack capability.

NATO AIR BASES

NATO aircraft flew Allied Force-related missions from all of the bases shown. Bases closest to the action, in particular Aviano, became so crowded that ramp space simply became unavailable. This situation led to RAF Tornados flying strikes directly from Bruggen in Germany. Aviano housed Portuguese F-16ADFs, RAF Sentries, Spanish EF-18+ aircraft and most of the US 31st Air Expeditionary Wing. In addition, USAF B-52s and B-1Bs flew missions from Fairford in the UK, while B-2As flew direct from the US. In addition, both the US and French navies provided aircraft-carriers.

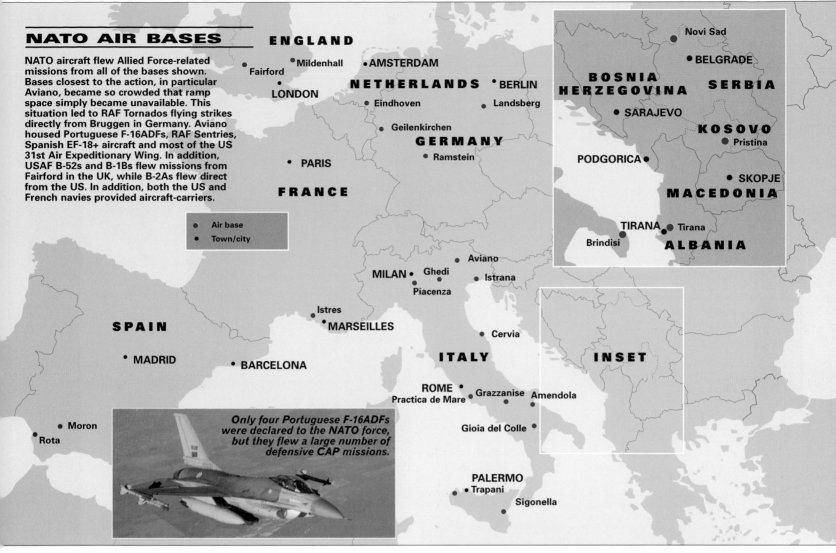

- Air base
- Town/city

Only four Portuguese F-16ADFs were declared to the NATO force, but they flew a large number of defensive CAP missions.

Albania finally forced the Yugoslav army to break cover.

In a series of spectacular strikes along the border with Albania, the A-10s and B-52s unloaded thousands of unguided 'dumb' bombs on Serb troop concentrations on a daily basis. Working on information provided by KLA fighters to senior US commanders as well as tactical intelligence from US Army artillery-locating radars inside Albania, 'Warthogs' and 'Buffs' were given real-time targeting. Media crews filmed these strikes from Albania and the results were broadcast live around the world. In one of these attacks the Pentagon claimed that a B-52 strike had caught a Serb infantry regiment in an assembly area and inflicted hundreds of casualties.

Ending the war

In early June, Slobodan Milosevic at last agreed to NATO's terms to end the war and Serb troops started to withdraw from Kosovo. Allied air strikes were called off on the afternoon of 10 June and NATO peacekeeping troops started moving into the province. J-STARS surveillance aircraft and UAVs monitored the progress of the withdrawal, while NATO attack aircraft flew CAPs above advancing Allied ground troops to ensure that the Serbs were not tempted to renege on their promises of good behaviour. US Army AH-64A Apaches, rapidly moved from Albania into Macedonia, at last were given their chance to fly into Kosovo, escorting Allied helicopters carrying peacekeepers. The US government had held the Apaches back from action because of fears that they lacked effective defensive aids and night vision systems.

By 20 June the last Serb soldiers had left Kosovo and Operation Allied Force officially came to an end.

Above: Special Hercules variants included the EC-130H for communications jamming, and EC-130E Rivet Riders (illustrated) for psychological warfare broadcasts.

Seen on 9 June, the day before the NATO air campaign officially ended, this F-16 demonstrates its flares to the cameraman. The aircraft had been dropping leaflets over Kosovo.

A-10A/OA-10A
Service history

The 'Warthog' is best known for its service in Europe, where it equipped the USAF's largest wing. However, it also served as far afield as Alaska, Korea and locations in the United States.

Naturally, the first USAF unit to get its hands on the A-10 was the 6510th Test Wing at the Air Force Flight Test Center, Edwards AFB. This unit was responsible for the pre-service tests and trials, using prototype and pre-production aircraft. Another early recipient was the 3246th Test Wing at Eglin AFB, which performed armament trials.

The next step in the introduction to service was the establishment of a training unit, the 355th Tactical Fighter Wing at Davis-Monthan AFB, Arizona, which began trading in Vought A-7s for A-10s in March 1976. The initial squadron was the 333rd Tactical Fighter Training Squadron ('Lancers'), joined soon after by the 358th TFTS 'Lobos'.

It was the 354th Tactical Fighter Wing at Myrtle Beach, South Carolina, that was the first operational unit to trade in A-7s for A-10s, a process which began in late 1976. The wing stood up three squadrons (353rd, 355th and 356th TFS) and these were instrumental in pioneering operations with the new aircraft. This task was taken over by the 57th Tactical Training Wing, at Nellis AFB, Nevada, which began its operational evaluation work with the 'Warthog' in October 1977. At about that time the critical JAWS (Joint Attack Weapons System) trials took place, which set down the way A-10s would work with artillery and battlefield helicopters.

Central Europe
With training, trials and a US-based organisation in place, it was time to begin equipment of

Top: Slow when compared to other battlefield types, the A-10 relies on its excellent low-level agility to survive. The traditional anti-armour role has been expanded to include FAC missions.

Above: The 354th TFW was the first operational A-10 unit, this pair demonstrating the initial paint scheme to be adopted: MASK-10A. The Wing's aircraft were soon busy on overseas deployments.

what was arguably the most important wing to receive A-10s: the 81st Tactical Fighter Wing in England. Central Europe was where the A-10 was expected to fight and a large proportion of the front-line force was earmarked for the 81st TFW. From the first aircraft arriving on 26 January 1979, the 81st built up to a six-squadron wing (78th, 91st, 92nd, 509th, 510th and 511th TFS) accommodated at the twin bases of RAF Bentwaters and Woodbridge. From here, the A-10s could deploy to six

Forward Operating Locations (FOLs) in West Germany, each squadron being assigned a specific FOL. The FOLs were spread across both 2 ATAF and 4 ATAF areas, and regular deployments allowed squadron pilots to familiarise themselves with the terrain in the areas they would be expected to defend in time of war. A-10 operations were naturally aimed primarily at the anti-armour role, and the pilots used their peacetime detachments to identify natural tank-killing grounds and potential vehicle choke points.

In the reserves
Following the establishment of the European unit, attentions turned to swelling the ranks of US-based operators who could

The 355th TFW was the nominated A-10 training unit, although it later added an operational role. The clear skies and extensive ranges of Arizona offered excellent training conditions.

Right: Initially envisaged for the war in Southeast Asia, the A-10 was eventually tailored to the Central European theatre. Six squadrons were based in England throughout the 1980s, poised to rush into pre-prepared forward bases in Germany to blunt a WarPac armoured thrust.

Below: For operations in snow, the A-10 has been painted with temporary white camouflage. This example is seen during a 1982 exercise in Alaska.

be called upon to reinforce the 81st in a European war. Five Air National Guard squadrons (103rd TFS/CT, 104th TFS/MA, 128th TFS/WI, 174th TFS/NY and 175th TFS/MD) were equipped with the type, beginning with the 103rd in May 1979. This was significant as it represented the first time that an ANG unit had received new aircraft directly from the manufacturer, as opposed to having used equipment 'cascaded' from active-duty units. In 1990-91 two more ANG units began flying the OA/A-10 (110th TFS/MI and 111th TFS/PA).

Air Force Reserve units also began to receive A-10s in the same time-frame, beginning with the 917th TFW in October 1980. Others were the 442nd TFW, 926th TFW and 930th TFW.

More active-duty units were also formed in the early 1980s, consisting of the 23rd TFW at England AFB, Louisiana as a second Stateside unit, plus the 51st and 343rd Composite Wings. Both of the latter were based in the Pacific region, the 51st in Korea and the 343rd in Alaska. Both received A-10s in the winter of 1981/82 to complete the initial deployment of the A-10 force.

1980s changes

The A-10 force disposition remained little changed for a decade, although two squadrons of the 81st split off to form the 10th TFW in RAF Alconbury in 1988 – their operational task remained unchanged, however. In October 1987 the 602nd Air Control Wing at Davis-Monthan AFB began its adoption of the 'Warthog' in the Forward Air

Control (FAC) role as the OA-10A, introducing a new arrow to the A-10's quiver.

A-10s went to war in a variety of roles during Desert Storm, aircraft coming from a number of units in the US and Europe to fly with the 23rd and 354th TFW (Provisional), but returned home to face uncertainty. Once slated for complete retirement, the A-10 convinced planners in the Gulf War that it still had much to offer, especially in the FAC role and for combat search and rescue support. In areas of low-density defences, the A-10 could still operate in its traditional close support roles.

Nevertheless, the end of the Cold War caused dramatic changes in the A-10 community,

not least of which was the dismantling of the vast USAFE force, leaving just one squadron based with the 52nd FW at Spangdahlem AB in Germany. This unit has since seen considerable action. Elsewhere, the CONUS force was reduced to just one active-duty unit (355th Wing) and several ANG/AFRes units, while a squadron remains in Korea. Today, each 'Warthog' squadron operates a mix of A-10As and OA-10As, illustrating a mixed attack/FAC tasking. In reality, there is no difference between the two variants and both have seen extensive combat in recent operations over the Balkans, Afghanistan and Iraq.

Above: CONUS-based A-10As were a key part of the rapid-reaction forces, being able to fly at very short notice to troublespots. Here, an A-10 taxis in past EAF F-4 Phantoms at an Egyptian base during Exercise Bright Star 1982.

Left: Alaska has been an important base for the A-10 since the first example arrived with the 18th TFS in late 1981. As well as deterring any land aggression from across the Bering Strait, the A-10s were also on alert for rapid deployment to the Korean peninsula to bolster US forces there.

War on the Taliban
Afghanistan post 9/11

On 9 September, 2001, hijacked airliners flown by al-Qaeda-trained terrorists smashed into the twin towers of the World Trade Center, New York, and the Pentagon, causing massive devastation and terrible loss of life. The President of the United States, George W. Bush, immediately ordered massive retaliation against known and suspected al-Qaeda and Taliban fundamentalist bases in Afghanistan. The stated purpose of the mission was to capture the al-Qaeda leader, Osama bin Laden, destroy al-Qaeda, and remove the Taliban regime, which had provided a safe haven for the terrorist organisation.

Below: US Air Force Reserve (USAFR) Maintenance personnel at Bagram Air Base, Afghanistan, inspect an A-10 Thunderbolt II aircraft assigned to the 23rd Wing on the flight line after a mission in support of Operation Enduring Freedom.

The military operation, code-named Enduring Freedom, was to have been short and swift and was intended to achieve an overwhelming victory. Instead, it precipitated a guerrilla war that still rages today.

Operation Enduring Freedom began on 7 October, 2001, less than a month after the attacks on the United States, with a series of air strikes by land-based B-1, B-2 and B-52 bombers, carrier-based F-14 and F/A-18s, and Tomahawk cruise missiles launched from US and British ships and submarines. These operations were controlled from a command centre at Prince Sultan Air Base, Riyadh, Saudi Arabia, nearly 1,600 km (1,000 miles) from the operational area.

Initial attacks

The first series of attacks was carried out by some fifty Tomahawk cruise missiles, twenty-five aircraft from the carriers USS *Enterprise* (CVN-65) and *Carl Vinson* (CVN-70), on station in the Arabian Sea, and fifteen US bombers, the majority B-52s operating from Diego Garcia in the Indian Ocean.

The Northrop Grumman B-2 'stealth' bomber was also involved in this initial phase, flying six sorties in the first three days of the operation. The B-2s flew to their targets directly from Whiteman AFB in the United States, landing at Diego Garcia after their attacks and changing crews for the flight back to Whiteman. Each sortie took 70 hours to complete. The US Navy's F-14s and F/A-18s were flight-refuelled by Lockheed S-3 Viking aircraft, the aircraft using an air corridor over Pakistan to reach the Afghan border.

The first Coalition troops on the ground in Afghanistan were US Special Forces, their task being to engage in unconventional warfare tactics alongside anti-Taliban groups, the latter joining up to form an armed force known as the Northern Alliance. The first city to be liberated from the Taliban, on 9 November, was Mazar-e-sharif, followed by Talogan, Herat and Shindand in succeeding days. The Taliban were driven out of the Afghan capital, Kabul, on 13 November, and Jalalabad on the following day. The capture of Kabul was preceded by twenty days of air strikes, which destroyed the Taliban's air defences and other assets; it took the Northern Alliance only twenty-four hours to

Above: Two US Navy F/A-18 Hornets on patrol over Afghanistan. The aircraft are carrying external fuel tanks and are armed with Paveway II laser guided GBU-16 454-kg (1,000-lb) bombs and AIM-9 Sidewinder missiles.

take the capital after this softening-up.

With these objectives secured, the US Marines of Task Force 58 were deployed to the combat zone. On 25 November they seized 'Objective Rhino', a desert airstrip south of Kandahar, where a Forward Operating Base (FOB) was established. Before the end of November the last remaining Taliban stronghold in the north, Konduz, had fallen to Coalition forces, and Bagram airfield near Kabul became a Forward Operating Base.

Meanwhile, between 9 October and 7 November 2001, a steady stream of US transport aircraft had been flying a regular flow of supplies into Afghanistan, making regular air drops to the civilian population as well as to Coalition forces. The transport aircraft employed were 78 C-17s

and five C-130s, supported by 128 KC-135 tankers, which refuelled the transports over the Black Sea. Some of the tankers were deployed to Bezmer Air Base in Bulgaria, from where they were able to refuel warplanes operating over Afghanistan. The route took the transports over Romania, Turkey and Turkmenistan.

Huge firepower

By 23 October 2001, more than 10,000 bombs and missiles had been expended in Afghanistan, of which some 60 per cent were precision-guided munitions. Most of the 4,700 tons of munitions was dropped by the eight B-1s and ten B-52s of the 28th Air Expeditionary Wing, operating out of Diego Garcia. On average, the B-1s flew four sorties a day and the B-52s five. Each sortie might last from twelve to fifteen hours and involve a round trip of 8,849km (5,500 miles), as loiter time over potential targets in Afghanistan was often involved.

By the end of November 2001, the US Air Force had

flown more than 15 per cent of the combat missions in support of Operation Enduring Freedom. Aircraft employed included the B-1, B-2, B-52, F-15E, F-16 and AC-130H/U. These aircraft had dropped about 10,000 tons of munitions, amounting to more than 75 per cent of the Operation Enduring Freedom total. During the same period a total of 600 cluster bombs wasdropped, consisting of 450 BLU-103 and 150 BLU-87 munitions. By the end of November 2001 Air Force support aircraft - UAVs, RC-135, U-2, E-3, and EC-130E/H - had flown more than 325 missions. Also heavily involved was the USAF's

AWACS fleet, whose aircraft were constantly airborne over Afghanistan, gathering vital intelligence and directing strike aircraft. At the end of February, 2002, Coalition forces launched Operation Anaconda, its aim to destroy the remaining enemy forces in south-eastern Afghanistan. The operation marked the virtual end of the campaign. The war was only just beginning.

Above: US Air Force munitions specialists from the 28th Air Expeditionary Wing downloading a Joint Direct Attack Munitions (JDAM) weapon from a B-52 bomber. The JDAM is based on the Mk.84 907-kg (2,000-lb) bomb.

Above: A USAF B1-B Lancer bomber flight refuelling from a KC-10 Extender over the Indian Ocean prior to a bombing sortie into Afghanistan. Both aircraft are from the 28th Air Expeditionary Wing.

Operation Iraqi Freedom

On 20 March, 2003, US-led Coalition forces launched a second invasion of Iraq in an operation called Iraqi Freedom. The main pretext for this invasion was that Iraq, under the leadership of President Saddam Hussein, was continuing the development of weapons of mass destruction (WMD), in defiance of an agreement signed under the auspices of the United Nations after the Gulf War of 1991, and was close to deploying such weapons; and that the Iraqi leadership had links with the terrorist organisation al-Qaeda.

It was later established that no such weapons of mass destruction existed in Iraq, and no links between the Iraqi government and al-Qaeda were ever proven.

The air campaign that preceded the land invasion of Iraq in 2003 was greatly different from the massive air onslaught that was launched in January 1991, heralding Operation Desert Storm. Then, the initial objective had been to destroy Iraq's military infrastructure by means of massive air strikes directed against strategic target sets that included command and control facilities, nuclear, biological and chemical (NBC) facilities, aircraft, airfields and the integrated air defence system. Once this objective had been achieved, the full weight of Coalition air power was used in support of Allied land forces. In 2003, the principal objective was the elimination of Saddam Hussein and his military staff, so the Iraqi leader's many presidential palaces and other places frequented by the military executive were high on the target list.

The air attack began at 0543 local time on 20 March, 2003, when two Lockheed Martin F-117A 'stealth' aircraft of the 8th Fighter Squadron, USAF, supported by Northrop Grumman EA-6B Prowler electronic warfare aircraft, bombed three targets on the outskirts of Baghdad. This was followed by precision strikes by some 40 Tomahawk cruise missiles, launched by the warships USS *Cowpens*, *Bunker Hill*, *Donald Cook*, *Milius* and *Bunker Hill*, and the submarines USS *Cheyenne* and *Montpelier*.

Navy squadrons

The venerable Northrop Grumman F-14A Tomcat, which had played an important part in the 1991 Gulf War, was heavily involved in this second conflict. F-14 squadrons were deployed on five carriers: VF-2 'Bounty Hunters' on USS *Constellation*, VF-31 'Tomcatters' on the USS *Abraham Lincoln*, and VF-154 'Black Knights' on USS *Kitty Hawk*, all in the Persian Gulf, and VF-32 'Swordsmen' (USS *Harry S. Truman*) and VF-213 'Black Lions' (USS *Theodore Roosevelt*) in the Mediterranean. The Tomcat squadrons operated continuously during the three weeks of the land campaign, supporting ground forces with Joint Direct Attack Munitions

A USAF B-52H Stratofortress bomber of the 93rd Bomb Squadron (BS), Barksdale Air Force Base (AFB), Louisiana (LA), returns home after a successful combat sortie to Iraq, staging via Diego Garcia in the Indian Ocean.

Right: An aerial view of the Al Salam Presidential Palace in Baghdad damaged during Operation Iraqi Freedom. Saddam Hussein's many palaces were high-priority targets, as they were used as covert command centres.

(JDAM) and laser-guided bombs, and one F-14 detachment was based permanently ashore.

Also operating from carriers in the Mediterranean was the McDonnell Douglas F/A-18 Hornet, deployed alongside the Tomcats on the USS *Harry S. Truman* and *Theodore Roosevelt*, which formed Carrier Task Force 60 (CTF 60). It had been originally planned that both aircraft carriers and their air wings were to support an invasion of northern Iraq from Turkey by 65,000 Coalition troops (including the entire 4th Infantry Division), supported by 225 combat aircraft and 25 helicopters, but the Turkish government voted against Coalition forces being based on its soil, so the tactical air strength was switched to supporting special forces' teams engaged in diversionary operations while the main coalition thrust approached Baghdad. Six Hornet squadrons bore the brunt of CTF 60's operations in northern Iraq.

Operation Iraqi Freedom also saw the combat debut of the F/A-18F Super Hornet, which arrived in the Persian Gulf in March on the USS *Nimitz* (CVN 68). *Nimitz*'s two Super Hornet squadrons were VFA-14, with F/A-18Es, and VFA-41 with F/A-18Fs.

The Americans were not the only Hornet operators in Iraqi Freedom. In February 2003, fourteen F/A-18As of No 75 Squadron, Royal Australian Air Force, deployed from their home base at RAAF Tindal in the Northern Territory to Diego Garcia in the Indian Ocean, refuelling seven times from USAF KC-10s, and then proceeded to Al Udeid air base in Qatar, from where they flew numerous air strike and counter-air missions from day one of the offensive.

Strikes by the USAF during the campaign were conducted by B-1B Lancers, B-2s, B-52s, F-117As, F-15E Strike Eagles and F-16 Falcons, while the US Marine Corps deployed its AV-8B Harriers. The United Kingdom's contribution to the campaign, Operation Telic, included detachments of Tornado GR.4s and Harrier GR.7s, with Nimrods providing maritime surveillance and the Royal Navy furnishing helicopter support.

No Iraqi air opposition was encountered during the campaign, for the Iraqi Air Force had ceased to exist as a fighting force. Iraqi aircraft were captured on the ground, all in a very poor condition, and only a few helicopters were seen in the air.

The invasion phase of Operation Iraqi Freedom lasted 26 days and was a truly multi-national enterprise. For example, Poland commanded a multi-national division comprising troops from Ukraine, Bulgaria, Hungary, Latvia, Lithuania, Slovak Republic, Romania, Thailand and the Philippines. But although Saddam Hussein was toppled and eventually captured, Operation Iraqi Freedom did not bring freedom to Iraq, as subsequent events showed.

Below: A Lockheed Martin F-117 from the 8th Expeditionary Fighter Squadron leads out a trio of F-15 Eagles as they prepare to launch from a forward air base in support of Operation Iraqi Freedom.

Fighting the Insurgents

Above: A line-up of CH-47 Chinook helicopters on the flight line of Bagram Airfield in Afghanistan. The Chinook has proved indispensable in operations in mountainous and desert terrain.

Left: A Tornado F3 of No 43 Squadron, Royal Air Force, waits for takeoff clearance on a mission in support of Operation Iraqi Freedom at an air base in Qatar. The Tornado F3's role was air defence.

The 'shock and awe' tactics used against the Taliban in Afghanistan in 2001 and Saddam Hussein's military regime in Iraq two years later produced relatively swift victories. Allied intelligence, however, had failed to predict the speed with which insurgent movements would develop in both countries, launching an ongoing guerrilla war made more deadly and protracted by the infiltration of well-trained fighters from countries hostile to the United States.

In both Iraq and Afghanistan, the need for real-time intelligence on the movements of insurgent forces has seen the use of surveillance aircraft of all types, and perhaps the most dramatic development has been the deployment of Unmanned Aerial Vehicles (UAV), which have also been employed increasingly in an offensive role. The principal surveillance UAV is the MQ-1 (originally RQ-1) Predator. Although not designed as a strike platform, the Predator, armed with Hellfire missiles, has proved

very effective in the war on terror, and has been used to target individual al-Qaeda leaders. On 17 June, 2004, a pro-Taliban tribal leader, Nek Mohammed, and five of his companions were killed in Waziristan by a missile that was almost certainly launched by a CIA-controlled Predator.

The spearhead of the offensive against the insurgents is provided by special operations forces. Such forces rely heavily on air support, provided in the main by the AC-130H Spectre and AC-130U Spook Hercules

gunships operated by Air Force Special Operations Command (AFSOC), which operates eight of the former and fourteen of the latter. The AC-130H is armed with one 105mm M102 howitzer and one 40mm L-60 Bofors cannon which can fire 100 rounds per minute. The AC-130U is armed with the 105mm howitzer and two Mk 44 30mm cannon. The 20mm L61A1 cannon formerly carried by the Hercules gunship is no longer used, as missions are flown at an altitude that exceeds the slant range of the shoulder-launched missiles known to be in the hands of the insurgents. In both Iraq and Afghanistan, insurgent forces are in possession of the Russian-built Kolomna Stela-2 (Arrow-2), known to NATO as SA-7 Grail, and its Chinese reverse-engineered variant, the Hong Nu-5 (Red Cherry), as well as the more modern Strela-3 (SA-14 Gremlin).

Air operations over Iraq and Afghanistan are conducted by several Coalition nations, with

the United States and its principal ally, Great Britain, at the forefront. Operations over both countries are coordinated by the Combined Air Operations Center (CAOC), which is based in Qatar and replaces an earlier one that was located at Prince Sultan Air Base, Saudi Arabia. The British contribution comprises squadron-sized detachments of Tornado GR.4s at Al Udeid, Qatar, and Harrier GR.7s at Kandahar in Afghanistan, with VC-10 tankers at Bahrain and Akrotiri, Cyprus. RAF in-theatre transport forces are provide by C-130 Hercules and C-17s, with TriStars flying the long-distance routes. Other detachments include Nimrod MR.2s at Basra and Seeb, with Merlin, Puma and Chinook helicopters at various locations in Iraq.

The hub of all USAF and US Army air operations in Afghanistan is Bagram Air Base, to the north-east of Kabul. F-16 detachments from Belgium, Denmark, the Netherlands, Norway and Portugal operate

A U.S. Navy F/A-18C Hornet aircraft assigned to the 'Knighthawks' of US Navy Strike Fighter Squadron VF-136 takes on fuel from a USAF KC-135 Stratotanker over Iraq during a close air support mission. VFA-136 is assigned to Carrier Air Wing One, aboard nuclear-powered aircraft carrier USS Enterprise (CVN 65).

missions are not new to the RAF, which used the tactic very successfully in the Aden Protectorate in the 1960s.

The story of counter-insurgency operations in Iraq and Afghanistan is one of multinational cooperation, even though US commanders are sometimes prevented from sharing vital information with their allies until it has been subjected to a stringent filtering process, with consequent delays. In the front line, however, despite occasional tragic 'friendly fire' incidents that capture the headlines, cooperation is excellent. What the headlines do not say, but which the front-line forces know, is that the war on terror – albeit slowly and ponderously – is being won.

from Kabul International Airport as part of the European Expeditionary Air Wing. These military deployments, usually involving four aircraft with tanker support, are routed via Turkey, Georgia, Azerbaijan and Turkmenistan. France is also a noteworthy participant in Afghan air operations, fielding Mirage 2000 and F-1 fighter-bombers and Super Etendards, the latter operating from aircraft carriers.

Helicopter assets

In both theatres, the helicopter remains a key asset in counter-insurgency operations, in particular the formidable AH-64A Apache, which is used by both the US Army and the British Army Air Corps. The principal support helicopters are the UH-60 Black Hawk and CH-47D Chinook.

While air strikes continue to be a feature of operations in Afghanistan, much of the air

effort in Iraq continues to be devoted to surveillance, with combat types such as the Tornado GR.4 being used to monitor pipelines and transmission lines, on the lookout for possible sabotage. These sorties are known as terrain denial missions, intended to make a show of force and to deny terrorists the use of areas from which they might launch mortars or rockets. Such

Right: An MQ-1 Predator surveillance drone aircraft prepares for landing at Balad Air Base, Iraq, after a combat mission. The Predator is also used in an offensive role, armed with Hellfire missiles.

Below: A C-17 Globemaster III aircraft waiting to be loaded at an air base in Afghanistan. The C-17, with its huge load-carrying capacity, has proved an enormous asset in supporting anti-terrorist operations conducted far from the continental United States.

Trailing the rival YF-23 by a month and two days due to delays associated with the General Electric YF120 engines, the first YF-22 took to the air in September 1990, with Dave Ferguson at the controls. The aircraft's distinctive planform and widely-spaced tail surfaces are clearly evident.

Lockheed Martin
F/A-22 Raptor
America's cutting edge

F-15 Eagles may have ruled the skies for decades, but today the aircraft is ready for replacement, especially if it is to face competition from Russian types. The USAF's next-generation air dominance fighter will be the Lockheed Martin F-22 Raptor.

In late April 1991 the USAF chose Lockheed/Boeing/ General Dynamics to develop its proposal of the Advanced Tactical Fighter (ATF) over rival Northrop/ McDonnell Douglas's YF-23. As a replacement for the Eagle, the ATF represents the single biggest advance in fighter performance since the first jets. It combines 'stealth' with a huge increase in supersonic endurance and manoeuvrability, and it is the first military jet to reflect the revolution in computer technology in its basic design and on-board electronics. Lockheed Martin encountered numerous design problems in its development of the YF-22, leading to significant visible changes from the original artist's impression of the aircraft. It was 29 August 1990, some three years after construction had begun on the earliest prototype, that the first aircraft (N22YF) was unveiled at Lockheed's Palmdale facility in California.

This first prototype flew for the first time on 29 September, while a second aircraft (N22XF) followed it into the air on 30 October. Each prototype received a different powerplant, both of which were still under evaluation by the USAF. Pratt & Whitney's YF119 turbofan proved to be more reliable than General Electric's similar YF120.

Following an extended flight-testing period, to allow for final engineering adjustments, the

Above: The ATF programme was conceived in 1981. By 1985, Lockheed had produced a fanciful and misleading artist's impression of what would eventually become the F-22.

An F-22A over the extensive test ranges in the Nevada desert. The Raptor has been painted in at least three different experimental camouflage patterns, including the one seen here.

Above: Restrained by heavy chains, the Pratt & Whitney YF119-powered YF-22 is seen here undergoing afterburner tests during one of the many static tests conducted during the programme.

Above: In general, no external weapons are carried on the Raptor in an effort to retain the aircraft's 'stealth' characteristics. Instead, four weapons bays (two in the engine intake sides and two under the fuselage) house AAMs and/or bombs.

USAF announced on 23 April 1991 that the YF119/YF-22 combination had been selected and issued a contract for 11 (since reduced to nine) Engineering and Manufacturing Development (EMD) flying prototypes on 2 August (including two tandem-seat F-22Bs which will now be completed as F-22A single-seat aircraft), plus one static and one fatigue test airframe.

Combat reassessment

As construction commenced on the first two F-22A Raptors, an expansion of the aircraft's role was proposed – this will see the addition of air-to-ground attack missions, the aircraft being armed with precision-guided munitions (PGMs) and having been redesignated F/A-22.

The first production aircraft (91-4001) made its maiden flight on 7 September 1997. The F-22A incorporated noticeable design changes, among the most prominent being the broader undernose fairing and repositioned intakes. A second Raptor took to the air on 29 July 1998, with 18 development and pre-production F/A-22A aircraft flying by late 2003.

On 12 December 2007, the USAF officially declared the F-22 fully operational, three years after the first F-22 Raptor arrived at Langley. The current number of F-22s on order from Lockheed Martin is 183.

YF-22 PAV No. 1

N22YF was the first YF-22 Prototype Air Vehicle (PAV) and was powered by the General Electric YF120 engine. After the exhaustive development and test programme was completed, the rival Pratt & Whitney YF119 was selected for production F-22 Raptors.

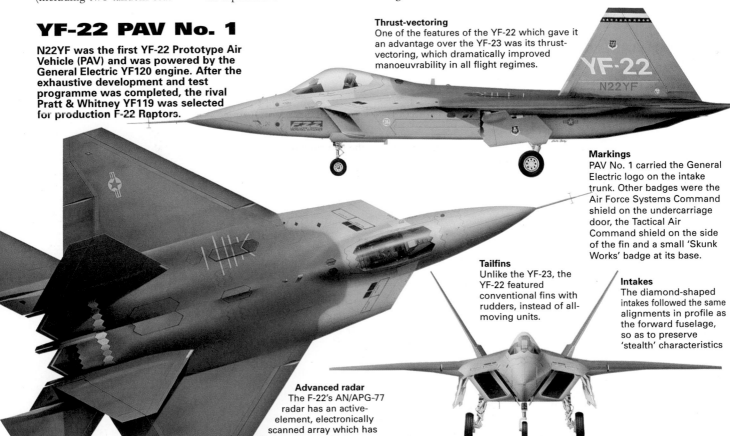

Thrust-vectoring
One of the features of the YF-22 which gave it an advantage over the YF-23 was its thrust-vectoring, which dramatically improved manoeuvrability in all flight regimes.

Markings
PAV No. 1 carried the General Electric logo on the intake trunk. Other badges were the Air Force Systems Command shield on the undercarriage door, the Tactical Air Command shield on the side of the fin and a small 'Skunk Works' badge at its base.

Tailfins
Unlike the YF-23, the YF-22 featured conventional fins with rudders, instead of all-moving units.

Intakes
The diamond-shaped intakes followed the same alignments in profile as the forward fuselage, so as to preserve 'stealth' characteristics

Advanced radar
The F-22's AN/APG-77 radar has an active-element, electronically scanned array which has long range and high resolution for the early detection of opposing fighters. It can provide detailed information about multiple threats, allowing the pilot to rapidly assimilate targets. The radar also has a low passive-detection signature.

Missile bays
The F-22 was designed to carry AAMs in bays underneath and to the sides of the engine intake ducts. The latter can hold four AIM-120 AMRAAM missiles, which fall away from the aircraft on launch before their motors ignite. The shorter side bays can carry AIM-7s or AIM-9 Sidewinders in pairs, the missiles being ejected sideways on launch.

Index